Educational Administration, Policy, and Reform: Research and Measurement

A Volume in

Research and Theory in Educational Administration

Educational Administration, Policy, and Reform: Research and Measurement

Edited by

Wayne K. Hoy
The Ohio State University

and

Cecil G. Miskel
The University of Michigan

INFORMATION AGE
PUBLISHING

80 Mason Street • Greenwich, Connecticut 06830 • www.infoagepub.com

Library of Congress Cataloging-in-Publication Data

Educational administration, policy, and reform : research and
measurement / edited by Wayne Hoy and Cecil Miskel.
    p. cm. – (Research and theory in educational administration)
  Includes bibliographical references.
  ISBN 1-59311-134-7 (pbk.) – ISBN 1-59311-135-5 (hardcover)
  1. School management and organization–United States. 2. Educational
change–United States. I. Hoy, Wayne K. II. Miskel, Cecil G. III.
Series.
  LB2805.E334 2004
  371.2–dc22

                                                         2004008233

Printed in the United States of America

CONTENTS

EDITORS' COMMENTS

Wayne K. Hoy and Cecil G. Miskel

This book is the third in a series on research and theory dedicated to advancing our understanding of schools through empirical study and theoretical analysis. Scholars, both young and established, are invited to publish original analyses, but we especially encourage young scholars to contribute to this series. The current volume is similar to its two predecessors in that it provides a mix of beginning and established scholars and a broad range of theoretical perspectives; in all 23 authors contributed to 12 separate but related analyses, which were selected for publication this year.

The book begins with three chapters on *school reform*. The first chapter, by Jane Coggshall, views standards-based reform through the three theoretical lenses of organizational learning, neoinstitutional theory, and practical drift. Each perspective offers an important but different vantage point for understanding. Organizational learning highlights the importance of professional development and helping organizational members to learn, improvise, interact, and explore in their practice so that the collective can benefit. The institutional perspective highlights the hidden barriers and forces in the institutional environment whereas practical drift theory cuts across all levels of analysis—individual, community, organization, and environment—to illuminate how situated local action can unintentionally undermine reform efforts. Next, John Sipple's chapter builds on the

Educational Administration, Policy, and Reform: Research and Measurement
A Volume in: Research and Theory In Educational Administration, pages vii–x.
Copyright © 2004 by Information Age Publishing, Inc.
All rights of reproduction in any form reserved.
ISBN: 1-59311-000-0 (hardcover), 1-59311-000-0 (paperback)

impact of institutional theory as well as structuration theory in reform efforts. Sipple examines and contrasts the factors behind both quick, superficial institutional responses to state-led school reform and more substantive change. In the third chapter, Meredith Honig examines partnerships between school districts and communities using resource dependency and the new institutionalism theories. Her analysis underscores three predominant forms of district-community partnerships—contractual, collaborative, and control. The results of her analysis point to the importance of using multiple perspectives to understand the nuances of partnerships for school improvement, and the significance of both resource dependency and the new institutionalism are illustrated in this research.

The next set of papers focuses on *school improvement* through the efforts of teachers, departments, principals, and professional development. In Chapter 4, Susan Printy and Helen Marks elaborate the notion of a community of practice as a vehicle for professional learning. Their research shows that when there is full participation and rich interaction of teachers in their communities of practice, their learning to improve instruction, their sense of competence, and their use of standard-based pedagogy are increased, but such improvement is not without substantial resistance. These sources of resistance as well as improvement are presented and analyzed. In chapter 5, Sang-Jin Kang, Brian Rowan, and Steven Raudenbush examine a neglected area of study in schools, the impact of academic departments on educational processes in schools. Using a relatively new statistical technique, "crossed multi-level modeling," the researchers examine the effects of individuals, disciplines, schools, and academic departments on perceptions of organic management in high schools. Academic departments had a significant influence on the leadership of the principal, on staff cooperation, and on teacher control, but the researchers hypothesize that academic departments could have an even greater effect on organizational structure and climate. In Chapter 6, Richard Halverson, Carolyn Kelly, and Steven Kimball see the implementation of teacher evaluation systems as an important way to shape instructional practice. Although the purpose of such evaluation systems is to improve student learning, few principals and teachers in the study linked the process to student achievement, accountability, or even improving teaching quality. The researchers discuss this rather surprising finding and suggest some strategies to link evaluation with teacher and student improvement and make the connection clear to teachers. The section of papers on school improvement concludes with Chapter 7 by Ellen Goldring and Nancy Vye as they explore the implementation and impact of case-based professional development for practicing school leaders, which specifically uses technology to link learning to leading. The results of the study support the use of multimedia, case-based leadership training programs in the professional development of leaders and the development of expertise.

The focus in the third set of chapters is on the *measurement* of four important concepts that show promise in influencing student achievement and development—advocacy coalitions, social capital, trust, and mindfulness. In chapter 8, Thomas Shepley is concerned with developing a reliable method for understanding how policy making takes place. Within the Advocacy Coalition Framework, he develops and successfully demonstrates a new approach to identify advocacy coalitions. The results of his research are encouraging and provide researchers with a useful technique to test more fully the Advocacy Coalition Framework. Social capital has emerged as an important explanatory construct in education. In chapter nine, Patrick Forsyth and Curt Adams critique the literature on social capital by examining the conceptual and operational adequacy of the term in the educational literature. They argue for a definition and measure of social capital that has two important dimensions–cognitive and structural–each with multiple characteristics, and find that most extant measures of social capital are flawed. They then use the concept of trust to demonstrate their procedures to operationalize social capital in a more refined manner, and then in their study relate social capital and school performance. In chapter 10, Allen Shoho and Page Smith also underscore the importance of trust. They review the theoretical underpinnings of the construct, and use factor analytic techniques to develop a trust scale to be used to study relations in higher education. In particular, three reliable measures of trust are proposed and tested—faculty trust in students, in colleagues, and in the dean. Their analysis concludes with a discussion of the research and practical implications of their work. In chapter 11, the notion of mindfulness, which has its early scientific roots in social psychology, is addressed. Wayne Hoy, Quint Gage, and John Tarter review the literature on individual mindfulness and organizational mindfulness before turning to the development of a conceptual framework and operational measure of school mindfulness. Using factor analytic techniques in a series of empirical studies, they develop a short, stable, reliable, and valid measure of school mindfulness. They conclude by presenting the measure and sketching a research agenda to demonstrate the heuristic nature of the construct.

This volume ends with Chapter 12 by Khaula Murtadha and Colleen Larson, which is a socially *critical theory* of leadership. The inquiry examines how African-American women make sense of their roles as leaders within poor and marginalized school communities. Four dominant themes of the leadership of African-American women are articulated: critical institutionalism, rational resistance, an ethic of risk and urgency, and deep spirituality. The authors argue that these four themes exemplify and illuminate the "outsider-within" standpoint of African-American women leaders.

This book series on *Theory and Research in Educational Administration* is about understanding schools. We welcome articles and analyses that explain school organizations and administration. We are interested in the "why" questions about schools. To that end, case analyses, surveys, large data base analyses, experimental studies, and theoretical analyses are all welcome. We provide the space for authors to do comprehensive analyses where that is appropriate and useful. We believe that the *Theory and Research in Educational Administration Series* has the potential to make an important contribution to our field, but we will be successful only if our colleagues continue to join us in this mission.

Wayne K.Hoy
The Ohio State University

Cecil G. Miskel
The University of Michigan

CHAPTER 1

REFORM REFRACTIONS
Organizational Perspectives on Standards-Based Reform

Jane G. Coggshall

Theories of the organization provide multiple lenses through which to view the adoption and impact of standards-based education reform policy. In this review, the author draws from several disciplines and examines three such theories—organizational learning, neoinstitutional, and practical drift. Each variously faceted theory predicts the trajectory of standards-based reform and has significant implications for its designers, implementers, end users, and students.

INTRODUCTION

Standards-based education reform, if it should live up to its promise, is a killer app. Given the current policy cacophony surrounding public education in America, it is a daring idea, proposing not only to change the way teachers teach and administrators administer, but also to change the very operating system of schooling itself. As conceived, standards-based reform

Educational Administration, Policy, and Reform: Research and Measurement
A Volume in: Research and Theory In Educational Administration, pages 1–23.
ISBN: 1-59311-000-0 (hardcover), 1-59311-000-0 (paperback)

1

(SBR) is a gargantuan and coherent system of challenging academic standards, aligned criterion-referenced assessments, professional development, and accountability measures (including choice and privatization) that promises to alter significantly the way local school organizations function. But will SBR topple the institutions that shape the way we practice education? Will its implementers stay true to its design? Or will the killer app be just another blip on the screen of the status quo?

In this paper, I examine these questions using multiple theoretical lenses—organizational learning theory, neoinstitutional theory, and practical drift. I begin by defining SBR as an ideal type, and then make the case that depending on which theoretical lens we use this definition acquires a different sheen. Each of these definitional variants in turn has different implications for the adoption and likely impact of SBR.

STANDARDS-BASED REFORM

Statewide systems of standards, assessments, professional development, and accountability are relatively new phenomena in America's tortured history of educational reform. Massell (2001) traces their origin to the "educational excellence" movement spurred by the oft-cited1983 report, *A Nation at Risk*. The movement has focused on intensifying course requirements in the core academic subjects and establishing stronger criteria for promotion and college entry. States began to impose more tests in more subject areas and grade levels and increased high school graduation requirements. Although some gains were apparently made, critics of the movement charged that many of the new tests were merely minimum competency tests and that coursework (even in advanced placement classes) was far from rigorous, emphasizing factual knowledge and rote memorization. When students' scores on the National Assessment of Educational Progress failed to improve, some reformers argued for a more systemic approach toward reform.

As articulated by Smith and O'Day (1991), the grand vision of systemic reform consists of curriculum frameworks, aligned instructional material and curricula, both in-service and pre-service professional development, student assessments, accountability, school site restructuring and local autonomy, and supportive services from districts and states. All these policy instruments are to be designed around state educational curriculum frameworks that would be:

> [D]eveloped through a collaborative process involving master teachers, subject matter specialists, and other key members of the state community and would be updated on a regular basis to reflect our changing understanding of the teaching and learning process. (p. 261)

Then, built on these frameworks, the state would establish "challenging achievement goals," or standards, on which teachers and local education professionals would base their pedagogical strategies. Smith and O'Day also maintain that standards would constitute the basis for professional development—even going so far as to suggest that the state withhold teaching licenses if teachers fail to "show command of the material and the ability to teach it" (p. 261). Further, the state would use these frameworks as templates to design assessments in order to hold local schools and districts accountable for student achievement (or lack thereof).

This systemic approach slowly began to be incorporated in federal legislation such as Goals 2000 (P.L. 103-227), the Improving America's School Act of 1994 (P.L. 103-382), and the Individuals with Disabilities in Education Act of 1997 (P.L. 105-17). It was variously taken up by the states—some states took several years to draft standards, while others had mature accountability systems in place by the late 1990s. By now, however, with the implementation of the No Child Left Behind Act of 2001 (P.L. 107-110), all 50 states have at least nominally committed to the SBR strategy (Olson, 2003). Thus, although we have had over a decade of experience with the ideas of SBR, it remains a relatively new innovation and its effects are yet to be wholly felt. For these ideas to have any real impact on instruction requires multiple people at multiple levels of the organization to absorb new learning, requires improving (and in some places creating) the technical capacity to track student performance, requires the transfer of best practices within and across organizations, and requires globally coordinated, task-based action in a notoriously uncertain technical environment.

Notwithstanding the numerous practical challenges to SBR, Smith and O'Day's (1991) original formulation can be viewed in several different lights. Table 1 outlines some of the different ways that the prisms of organizational learning, neoinstitutional, and practical drift theories refract this important policy innovation. In the remainder of this paper, I discuss each of these theoretical refractions of SBR reform in turn. With judicious use of these theories, speculation, and my own observations of its implementation so far, I discuss the likely adoption, diffusion, and impact of SBR. Finally, I conclude by attempting a preliminary integration of these theories that I hope will help us understand this phenomenon better.

ORGANIZATIONAL LEARNING THEORY

Among policymakers, a major rationale for the need for SBR is that educational practitioners are either not doing enough (exploiting received knowledge) or do not have the knowledge or skills necessary to effect adequate student achievement. A major assumption for the appropriateness of SBR is that the state (as a compendium of higher education institutions as

TABLE 1
Refractions of Standards-Based Reform

Theoretical lens	SBR can be seen as ...	Relevant authors
Organizational learning theory	An attempt to foster the conditions for organizational learning in schools	Leithwood & Louis (1998)
	Exploitation of knowledge to produce effective organizational routines and structures	March (1991); Zollo & Winter (2000); Crossan, Lane, & White (1999)
	An attempt to integrate learning and innovation in communities of practice	Brown & Duguid (1991); Wenger (1998)
	The generation and maintenance of knowledgeability in distributed operations	Orlikowski (2002)
Institutional theory	Strengthening the technical environment while simultaneously weakening the institutional environment	Rowan & Miskel (1999), Hoy & Miskel (2001)
	A rationalized institutional myth	Meyer & Rowan (1977)
	An attempt to tighten coupling between organizational units	Weick (1979); Orton & Weick (1990)
	A design to mediate between innovations and institutions	Hargadon & Douglas (2001)
	An innovation with interpretive flexibility	Pinch & Bijker (1987); Orlikowski (1992)
Practical drift	Global procedure decoupled from situated logics of action	Snook (2000); Vaughn (1998)

well as government agencies) *does* have the requisite knowledge—it knows "what works." Therefore, reform is simply a matter of transferring that knowledge to teachers and administrators through professional development activities, thereby helping local school organizations learn "what works" (build capacity) so that the state need not re-distribute the knowledge every time a new teacher enters the field. Finally, all the state then needs do is hold the school organizations accountable for the learning.

Thus, both individual and organizational learning is crucial to the successful implementation of SBR. The literature on organizational learning in the disciplines of business and management is enervatingly vast. In the educational literature, on the other hand, the number of studies and reviews of organizational learning theories are relatively few, but growing. Much of this growth is exhibited in the form of unpublished doctoral dissertations and conference presentations (e.g., Collinson, Cook, & Conley, 2001, not reviewed here; Mitchell, 1995; Sackney, Walker, & Hajnal, 1995). Notable exceptions include the book edited by Leithwood and Louis (1998) and other work by those authors (e.g., Leithwood, Leonard, & Sharratt, 1998), as well as work from a research group in Australia (Silins, Mulford, & Zarins, 2002).

Although many of these works conflate *organizational learning* with *learning organizations*, it is important to distinguish between these two constructs. The classical definition of organizational learning as advanced by Cyert and March (1963) is adaptive behavior over time. That is, organizations (as an aggregate of their individual members) adapt their goals, how they attend to their environment, and the rules they follow to search for problems—all as a function of experience. This definition has since been sculpted and stretched to include the construction and modification of theories-in-use (Argyris & Schon, 1978); the development of insights, knowledge, and associations between past actions, the effectiveness of those actions, and future actions (Fiol & Lyles, 1985); the codification of inferences from history into organizational routines that guide behavior (Levitt & March, 1988); the establishment of a balance between knowledge exploitation and exploration (March, 1991); the changed capacity to do something new (Watkins & Marsick, 1993); and the means toward strategic renewal (Crossan, Lane, & White, 1999). Thus, organizational learning is a body of thought that attempts to describe processes of collective learning. The term *learning organizations*, on the other hand, is more prescriptive and is used more often in practitioner literature to describe what organizations *should* look like. Hoy and Miskel (2001) invoke Senge's (1990) definition of learning organizations as places where:

> participants continually expand their capacities to create and achieve, where novel patterns of thinking are encouraged, where collective aspirations are nurtured, where participants learn how to learn together, and where the organization expands its capacity for innovation and problem solving (p. 32).

Nevertheless, both ways of thinking about learning in school organizations are useful.

Much of the more recent work on organizational learning grapples with the relationship between individual and collective learning (see, e.g., Crossan, Lane, & White, 1999), calling into question the appropriateness of using cognitive explanations of individual learning to represent the processes of learning at the group or organizational level (e.g., Leithwood, Leonard, & Sharratt, 1998). For example, the literature is rife with such terms as "organizational memory," "organizational cognition," and "collective mind." Such metaphors are inadequate, Leithwood et al. (1998) argue, because the science of cognition at the individual level is under development and often contested and, more fundamentally, because individuals and organizations are two entirely different entities and operate in very disparate ways.

Organizational theorists will also attest that organizational learning is not simply the sum of the learning of the organization's members. However, because "all learning necessarily takes place in human heads," Simon (1991) contends "organizations learn in two ways: (a) by the learning of its members, or (b) by ingesting new members who have knowledge the organization didn't previously have" (p. 125). Nevertheless, what an individual has learned or can learn is related to what others within the organization have learned. The diversity and breadth of the stores of knowledge among its members as well as how much sharing of knowledge takes place in an organization are crucial to the ability of the organization to learn on a collective level (Cohen & Levinthal, 1990). In turn, what its members know has "great bearing on how the organization operates" (Simon, 1991, p. 125).

Organizational knowledge, once "learned," is embodied in routines—"forms, rules, procedures, conventions, strategies, and technologies around which organizations are constructed and through which they operate [as well as] the structure of beliefs, frameworks, paradigms, codes, cultures, and knowledge that buttress, elaborate, and contradict the formal routines" (Levitt & March, 1988, p. 320; Zollo & Winter, 1992, p. 32). Thus, the ability to turn either new or existing knowledge into effective organizational routines that are efficient and adaptable is the essence of positive organizational learning (Zollo & Winter, 2000).

Organizations learn through direct experience via two mechanisms: trial-and-error experimentation and organizational search or scanning (Levitt & March, 1988). In their review of the organizational learning literature, Fiol and Lyles (1985) write, "Learning enables organizations to build on organizational understanding and interpretation of their environment and to begin to assess viable strategies" (p. 804). These authors, among others, draw a distinction between unreflective organizational adaptation and learning. Moreover, they distinguish between lower- and higher-level learning (fairly synonymously with Argyris and Schon's single- and double-loop learning). Lower-level organizational learning consists of "focused learning that may be mere repetition of past behaviors—usually short term, surface, temporary, but with associations being formed" (Fiol & Lyles, 1985, p. 810). Higher-level learning is "the development of complex rules and associations regarding new actions," where central norms, frames of reference, and assumptions are changed. Higher-level learning affects the entire organization (p. 810). Cohen and Levinthal (1990) contend, however, "the ability to evaluate and utilize outside knowledge is largely a function of the level of prior related knowledge" that an organization holds (p. 128).

Crossan et al. (1999) argue further that organizational learning is the principal means of attaining the successful renewal of an enterprise (something that policymakers hope to achieve in schools through SBR). Successful renewal necessitates that organizations maintain an appropriate balance between exploration of new knowledge and exploitation of received knowledge (March, 1991). Exploration involves experimentation, risk taking, flexibility, discovery, innovation, and even play. Exploitation includes such processes as selection, refinement, implementation, and execution. As March states:

> Adaptive systems that engage in exploration to the exclusion of exploitation are likely to find that they suffer the costs of experimentation without gaining many of its benefits. Conversely, systems that engage in exploitation to the exclusion of exploration are likely to find themselves trapped in suboptimal stable equilibria. (p. 71)

Unfortunately, exploration and exploitation processes compete for scarce resources, and therefore accomplishing both is a challenge.

Much of the organizational learning research in education attempts to illuminate the constitutive elements of schools that would facilitate such learning (in other words, this research attends more to the question of how to make schools into learning organizations). For example, Silins et al. (2002) have identified seven constructs from their review of the non-educational literature and define learning organizations as schools that:

a. [E]mployed processes of environmental scanning,
b. developed shared goals,
c. established collaborative teaching and learning environments,
d. encouraged initiatives and risk taking,
e. regularly reviewed all aspects related to and influencing the work of the school,
f. recognized and reinforced good work, and
g. provided opportunities for continuing professional development. (p. 617)

Based on these constructs, the authors have developed a questionnaire that they piloted, revised, and then administered to teachers and principals. Employing exploratory factor analysis, the authors in turn developed a four-factor nested model of organizational learning:

Factor 1. *A trusting and collaborative climate,* or the "extent to which collaboration is the norm and discussions among colleagues are open and candid" (p. 617).

Factor 2. *Taking initiatives and risks,* or "the extent to which staff feel empowered to make decisions and feel free to experiment and take risks; the school structures support teacher initiatives; and the administrators promote inquiry and dialog and are open to change" (p. 618).

Factor 3. *A shared and monitored mission,* or "the extent to which the school culture encourages critical examination of current practices and continuous learning for improvement, staff keep abreast of external events that may affect their school; curriculum is aligned with the school's vision and goals" (p. 618).

Factor 4. *Professional development,* or "the extent to which staff engage in ongoing professional development; professional reading is a source of learning, and so are other schools; developing skills to work and learn in teams is seen as important; external advice is sought as appropriate, and school leaders provide all the support they can to promote professional development" (p. 618).

Based on this model, Silins et al. (2002) found that organizational learning had no direct effects on students' social engagement or academic participation in school (they did not measure achievement); it did, however, affect teachers' work (as reported by students). Not surprisingly, they also found that leadership (as exhibited by both administrators and distributed among staff) had significant direct effects on organizational learning as they defined it.

Unfortunately, Silins et al. (2002) neither attempt to describe the process by which schools might learn as organizations nor offer an explanation of just how an improved capacity for organizational learning might, as their implicit hypotheses suggest, translate to improved student outcomes (increased organizational effectiveness). Another limitation (although it is arguably outside the scope of their paper) is that they do not attempt to measure the schools' actual learning. In other words, did the organization actually change its routines or patterns of search, improve its knowledge, or adapt its goals simply by virtue of the presence of the conditions for learning? This question is not trivial because it has enormous implications for the adoption and impact of SBR.

Through the lens of organizational learning theory (as I describe it above), there are several ways of looking at SBR. First, SBR can be seen to improve some of the conditions for organizational learning. That is, using Silins et al.'s (2002) four factors as a framework, SBR promises to facilitate a school's shared and monitored vision (Factor 3) by aligning the curriculum with the school's goals (which presumably include improving test scores to ensure survival) and impressing on teachers that the policy environment ought to concern them. SBR should also facilitate professional development (Factor 4). The No Child Left Behind Act, as an embodiment of SBR, provides some funding for professional development activities, as well as pre-service education. Unfortunately, SBR does little to foster Silins et al.'s first two factors. It may undercut trust (Factor 1), as teachers' professional commitment is implicitly viewed as lacking, and risk taking (Factor 2) may be discouraged if improved student achievement is not felt in a short timeframe. As Weick (2001) reminds us, "Norms of compassion encourage the vulnerability that is a precondition for learning; yet, organizations are often unsafe and devoid of compassion" (p. 219). This was echoed in an account of successful reform in Texas school districts, where "positive support" of teachers was seen as a "key ingredient" of successful transformation (Skrla, Scheurich, & Johnson, 2000). A climate of accountability may hinder organizational learning if teachers do not feel safe to try new practices and open themselves to new experiences and new learning.

Second, from an organizational learning standpoint, SBR can be seen as the redistribution of the stores of knowledge of best practices through the reification of shared understandings. That is, if the education system is taken as a whole, state actors develop standards based on what they know about pedagogy, child development, and subject matter content. That knowledge becomes reified into standards, which school-level practitioners receive as organizational artifacts. Some teachers enact that knowledge in their work, while others may fail to learn it or use it. Professional development is intended to promote the enactment of received knowledge. However, one likely consequence of the SBR movement is that schools will favor the exploitation of state knowledge (in the form of standards) and eschew risk taking and initiative, thereby trapping schools in states of "suboptimal stable equilibria."

Third, the feedback provided by students' test scores may help increase the rate of learning for school organizations. Because organizations learn from experience incrementally in response to feedback about outcomes (as observed by Levitt & March, 1988), the increase in the sheer volume of information provided by a strengthened state accountability system may provide the experience necessary for higher-level learning. However, this depends almost entirely on how the information is distributed and used, whether it reaches the teachers, and whether teachers know what to do with the information. A more likely scenario is that SBR, in terms of improving feedback about outcomes, will merely facilitate lower-level learning. That is, schools will learn how to administer and prepare their students for days of rigorous assessments, but they will not change the guiding assumptions and central norms that shape the practice of instruction.

Finally, as Senge (1990) noted, we almost "never directly experience the consequences of many of our most important decisions" (p. 23). Thus, while we may experience a raising or lowering of student academic achievement as a result of the implementation of SBR within a relatively short time span, we will not know whether American schools are succeeding in any of their other professed aims, such as whether they are preparing good citizens or informed consumers or healthy adults, until long after the students have left the classroom.

Organizational Learning Theory: The Next Generation?

In his book, *Community of Practice*, Wenger (1998) argues that the proper unit of analysis in a study of learning is neither individuals nor organizations but communities of practice. Organizations are "communities of communities" and it is within these informal communities of practice that organizations "do what they do, know what they know, and learn what they learn" (p. 241). Organizations assemble a set of practices in which their members mutually engage, around which they build shared histories, and through which they learn, for, he argues, participation in practice is itself a process of learning.

This concept of organizational learning differs from more conventional organizational learning theories because it does not view acquisition of knowledge as the important factor of learning, but rather views learning as taking place in the enactment and modification of knowing. In other words, as Brown and Duguid (1991) state, "much conventional learning theory, including that implicit in most training courses, tends to endorse the valuation of abstract knowledge over actual practice and as a result to separate learning from working and, more significantly, learners from workers" (p. 41). This separation is false, for as Orlikowski (2002) argues, "knowing is an ongoing social accomplishment" (p. 252). Learning happens when people modify their practice through improvisation and interaction with other members of their community, who are involved in other communities of practice. Thus, "learners are acquiring not explicit, formal 'expert knowledge,' but the embodied ability to behave as community members" (Brown & Duguid, 1991, p. 48) to perform a task, such as teaching.

This concept of knowing-in-practice complicates the picture of SBR. If one of the aims of SBR is to improve the technical core of teaching and learning by increasing teachers' knowledge ability, policymakers then cannot view knowledge as a "separate entity, static property, or stable disposition embedded in practice" (Orlikowski, 2002, p. 250), but rather as something that teachers enact every day and over time. Further, the generation of competence in teachers is not simply a matter of distributing a set of best practices to school organizations. As Orlikowski contends:

> A view of knowing as enacted in practice does not view competence as something to be "transferred," and suggests that the very notion of "best practices" is problematic. When practices are defined as the situated recurrent activities

of human agents, they cannot simply be spread around as if they were fixed and static objects. Rather, competence generation may be seen to be a process of developing people's capacity to enact what we may term "useful practices"—with usefulness seen to be a necessarily contextual and provisional aspect of situated organizational activity (p. 253).

Wenger (1998) also places situated activity at the center of his argument, and suggests that competence is an organizational quality that develops by virtue of the practicing of its communities of practice. In his words, "Communities of practice are thus key to an organization's competence and to the evolution of that competence" (p. 241).

This view of organizational learning then has implications for the successful design of SBR policy instruments. Teachers' interpretations and understandings of standards, for example, will depend on the functioning of the communities in which they practice, as well as their interactions with other communities. Professional development would also have to be reconceived as other than training, knowledge sharing, or the distribution of best practices, but rather as encouraging teachers' productive interactions within and among communities of practice and allowing for improvisation; thereby enhancing their knowledge ability. Thus, this perspective predicts that SBR will fail if it is conceived as a global cure-all, because:

> [N]o practice is itself global. Even when it deals with global issues, a practice remains local in terms of engagement. From this standpoint, design will create relations, not between the global and the local, but among localities in their constitution of the global. No practice has the full picture. No practice subsumes another (Wenger, 1998, p. 234).

Thus, Wenger (1998) identifies the challenge of large-scale, multicommunity change. He calls it the paradox of design: "No community can fully design the learning of another. And at the same time, no community can fully design its own learning" (p. 234). SBR, as conceived by Smith and O'Day (1991), attempts to bridge these two constraints. They envision:

> A well-designed professional development system, based on networks of teacher cadre and teacher-practitioners [that] can foster both the knowledge base and the leadership experience necessary to help empower the teaching force, thus further liberating the initiative and creativity of "bottom-up" reform (p. 251).

They acknowledge, however, that "the state cannot simply establish such a system." Perhaps they would agree with Wenger's proposition that:

> Communities of practice are already involved in the design of their own learning because ultimately they will decide what they need to learn, what it takes to be a full participant, and how newcomers should be introduced into the community (no matter what training these newcomers receive else-

where). Whenever a process, course, or system is being designed, it is thus
essential to involve the affected communities of practice (p. 234).

Current developers of standards and assessments have necessarily limited
the participation of every community of practice within each state in the
design of standards and assessments. This will perhaps speed its downfall.

Moreover, there is preliminary evidence that even when the practitioners of SBR physically participate in the design of its instruments, this participation is detrimentally limited. State teaching standards, for example,
are assumed to reflect professional consensus, yet, as Moss and Schutz
(2001) demonstrate, this assumption is inherently problematic. The
researchers show how the standards used in the creation of assessments, far
from reflecting pure consensus, actually "under represent, misrepresent,
or exclude groups of voices within the community" (p. 65). Whereas most
developers of standards consider the standards to be "works-in-progress" as
educational knowledge and research evolves, the standards they create are
often used by test developers as established, professionally agreed-upon
frameworks when they write assessments (often away from the public and
professional eye).

On a more positive note, in her analysis of a large, geographically dis-
persed software company she calls Kappa, Orlikowski (2002) offers hope.
She found that this company was able to perform complex, innovative
work while spread over 15 countries on five continents in an uncertain
technical environment. Using a repertoire of practices and activities that
comprise those practices to produce types of knowing, Kappa was able to
accomplish its organizational goals—successful global product development despite distributed operations. For example, organizational actors
enacted the practice of "aligning effort," which included the activities of
"using common models, methods, and metrics; and contracting for expertise annually," and the knowing that was embodied in the practice of aligning effort was "knowing how to coordinate across time and space." This
practice was joined by other practices, such as "sharing identity, interacting
face to face, learning by doing, and supporting participation" (p. 257).
Competence, she concludes, "is both collective and distributed, grounded
in the everyday practice of organizational members" (p. 249).

With a touch of imagination, it is not difficult to see the manufacture of
student achievement through SBR as "global product development."
Although education practitioners are not attempting to produce the same
product across time and space, they are attempting to produce students
who are capable of knowing and capable of doing everything that state
standards say they need to do. State education standards, even if they are
flawed reifications of practitioner knowledge, may "generate the common
ground on which distributed product development work is structured,
[and provide for organization members] the means of local and global
identification within their daily activities" (Orlikowski, 2002, p. 257).

Although organizational learning theories provide a great deal of insight into how organizations may or may not improve through the learning of their members, the theories fail to address the institutional constraints on change. It is to this problem that I now turn.

NEOINSTITUTIONAL THEORY

Schools are institutions in almost every sense of the word. They are large, stable organizations that are usually influential in a community. They care for and socialize children (and sometimes even "challenged" individuals as in the image evoked by the term "state institutions"). Most importantly, they contain rules, norms, and procedures that constrain behavior and guide social thought and action (Meyer & Rowan, 1977). It is in the latter sense that I talk about institutions. Moreover, in this perspective, institutions have legitimacy. Suchman (1995) encapsulates several theorists' definitions of legitimacy into one that I find useful:

> Legitimacy is a generalized perception or assumption that the actions of an entity are desirable, proper, or appropriate within some socially constructed system of norms, values, beliefs, and definitions (p. 574).

Scott (2001) categorizes the sources of organizational legitimacy based on a typology of three "pillars" of institutions. These pillars—the regulative, normative, and cultural—cognitive pillars—both comprise and support institutions. Mawhinney (2002) contends that these pillars are more properly "dimensions" of institutions in that they are interdependent and mutually reinforcing. Analytically, however, it is more useful to regard them as separate because what is taken as evidence of legitimacy varies depending on which pillar is privileged in an analysis of legitimacy (Scott, 2001).

The regulative pillar comprises the formal and informal rules that constrain and regularize behavior. DiMaggio and Powell (1983) identify coercion in the form of formal and informal rules as the mechanism of control in this pillar and emphasize that sanctions are necessary aspects. Legitimacy resides in conforming to those rules.

The normative pillar is based on "normative rules that introduce a prescriptive, evaluative, and obligatory dimension into social life" (Scott, 2001, p. 54). Normative rules specify how things ought to be done to pursue valued ends. Thus, this pillar privileges what is valued, preferred, or desirable. The main source of legitimacy in this pillar is normative, taking on an almost moral tone—organizations must do what is "appropriate" (DiMaggio & Powell, 1983). Evidence of legitimacy is the extent of normative compliance and stems primarily from professionalization through accreditation and certification processes.

The cultural–cognitive pillar is composed of the "shared conceptions that constitute the nature of social reality and the frames through which meaning is made" (Scott, 2001, p. 57). The source of cultural–cognitive legitimacy is mimetic isomorphism—actors must adopt a common frame of interpretation consistent with the one that prevails in the sociocultural system. Scott (2001) invokes Berger and Luckmann (1967) who wrote, "Legitimation 'explains' the institutional order by ascribing cognitive validity to its objectivated meanings" (pp. 92–93). Thus, actors' understandings of social reality begin as subjective meanings, but once legitimated, they become objective fact, or an institutional rule. Nevertheless, as Scott (2001) points out, "Legitimate structures may, at the same time, be contested structures" (p. 60).

Organizations strive for legitimacy in order to extract resources from their environment and to increase their prospects for survival (Meyer & Rowan, 1977). Schools inhabit highly institutionalized environments. Therefore, to acquire and maintain their legitimacy, not only must schools conform to a hodgepodge regulative framework of federal and state laws, but they must also conform to the normative and cultural–cognitive demands of a public that has been willing to ignore technical efficiency in favor of some notion of what's good about a school (or what good schools should merely *look* like).

Educational organizations have, in response, become loosely coupled (Weick, 1976) or even de-coupled (Meyer & Rowan, 1977). In a loosely coupled situation, elements of the organization affect each other "suddenly (rather than continuously), occasionally (rather than constantly), negligibly (rather than significantly), indirectly (rather than directly), and eventually (rather than immediately)" (Weick, 2001, p. 383). Thus, teachers have astutely learned to close their classroom doors to buffer themselves from the resulting policy cacophony, and school leaders have expended enormous energy in "face work" rather than working to actually improve teachers' practice. Rationalized myths of teacher expertise, for example, serve as substitutes for direct supervision (Meyer & Rowan, 1977).

Thus, schools have existed in highly institutionalized environments with weak (though nevertheless present) technical environments (Rowan & Miskel, 1999). This accounts in part for why schools look very similar and yet have vastly different educational outcomes. SBR can be seen as an effort to change this state of affairs by strengthening the technical environment while simultaneously weakening the institutional environment. It will do this by undermining the public's logic of confidence in schools and teacher expertise by widely disseminating student test scores. Moreover, under the accountability measures provided within the No Child Left Behind Act, schools' very organizational survival will depend on whether teachers change their practice. Thus, it is not unreasonable to predict that coordination and control will become tighter and more centralized within district offices and teachers and administrators will be given less discretion to buffer their work from environmental demands. That is the reformers' hope, at any rate.

In their 1999 chapter, Rowan and Miskel speak directly to the question of what institutional theory predicts about SBR. The authors argue that SBR will place additional technical demands on schools; however, they do not see a concomitant decrease in institutional demands for conformity. Organizations with both strong institutional and technical environments, such as hospitals, experience high levels of conflict (according to theorists Parsons and Scott & Meyer, as cited in Rowan & Miskel, 1999). Rowan and Miskel thus conclude: "Although institutional theory seems to predict the current state of conflict in American education, it says little about the likely outcomes of such a conflict" (p. 365). I believe—although it is ultimately an empirical question—that the public (with the help of the conservative press and a new ability to inspect organizational outcomes) will be more willing to accept new forms of schooling and no longer be lulled by the myths of expertise. SBR, if its design is enacted correctly, will be the engine of this change.

Nevertheless, it is an open question whether state standards and assessments have themselves become rationalized institutional myths (see Coggshall, Athan, DeYoung, & Miskel, 2003). If that becomes the case, then practitioners will continue to employ all sorts of Enron-like ruses to appear to conform to the demands of SBR (including outright cheating, obfuscating, and aggressive face work) while, again, not actually improving the work of the technical core.

Moreover, as Scott (2001) cautions, "to attend too rigidly to the distinction between levels of analysis is to ignore the ways in which social phenomena operate as nested, interdependent systems, one level affecting the others" (p. 126). That is, school organizations can affect their environments and politics can play a central role in negotiating institutional change, insofar as change is possible (Clemens & Cook, 1999). School-level resistance to output controls may percolate to parents, the media, and policymakers, which may challenge the legitimacy of SBR. Furthermore, standards and assessments will encounter resistance from professional organizations and higher education institutions that are also struggling for legitimacy in a changing institutional landscape. Traditionally, these organizations have exerted normative control over teacher certification and school accreditation. SBR may undermine these sources of legitimacy. The ability of the state to implement SBR will be a direct test of state organizations' regulative legitimacy.

Nevertheless, if policymakers follow the lessons provided by Hargadon and Douglas's (2001) analysis of Thomas Edison and his design of the electric light, SBR, as an educational innovation (composed of policy tools, new ideas, and new artifacts and thus may be thought of as a technology), has the potential to replace existing institutions or at least to "throw the otherwise static institutional background into stark relief" (p. 476). The authors argue, "to be accepted, entrepreneurs must locate their ideas within the set of existing understandings and actions that constitute the institutional environment yet set their innovations apart from what already exists" (p. 476). According to Hargadon and Douglas, it is in the concrete details of an innovation's design that developers can walk this tightrope. Thus, if the "particular arrangement of concrete details" of SBR is such that it mediates between Smith and O'Day's revolutionary vision and the institutional environment of schools that resists such a revolution, it has the potential to be accepted and fully adopted over time.

The process of designing these concrete details can be both intended and emergent (Hargadon & Douglas, 2001). In the case of SBR, the design is largely emergent, as state committees develop standards, test developers develop assessments, and policymakers write sanctions for accountability and implement mechanisms for its enforcement. All these people, in addition to parents and students and other stakeholders, make sense of SBR in terms of what they already know or have experienced about schools. The No Child Left Behind Act, as one concrete arrangement of SBR elements, will evoke different understandings among different people, and therein lies its possibilities. As the innovation of the No Child Left Behind Act confronts school institutions, the possibility exists that new understandings and actions may emerge. However, its design must be what Hargadon and Douglas call "robust." Its designers must take into account the "interdependent relationship between the technical and the social" (p. 492) in order to mediate between the innovative vision of SBR and the institutions of schooling.

Orlikowski (1992) also discusses this interdependent relationship between technology and social institutions. Borrowing from the work of Pinch and Bijker (1987), Orlikowski suggests that different technologies (and by extension different policies) have different degrees of interpretive flexibility. That is, users' interpretation of designers' technologies can vary widely; however, interpretation is nonetheless "constrained by the material characteristics of that technology [and] by the institutional contexts (structures of signification, legitimation, and domination) and different levels of knowledge and power affecting actors during the technology's design and use" (p. 409).

Orlikowski (1992) describes how interpretive flexibility works:

> The interpretive flexibility of technology operates in two modes of interaction. In the design mode, human agents build into technology certain interpretive schemes (rules reflecting knowledge of the work being automated), certain facilities (resources to accomplish that work), and certain norms (rules that define the organizationally sanctioned way of executing that work). In the use mode, human agents appropriate technology by assigning shared meanings to it, which influence their appropriation of the interpre-

tive schemes, facilities, and norms designed into the technology, thus allowing those elements to influence their task execution (p. 410).

Thus, the concrete details of SBR policy reflect the designers' knowledge, abilities, resources, and norms. In turn, the "users" of the SBR policy instruments will interpret those details and assign their own meanings to them. Orlikowski proposes that the more users participate in the design, the less interpretive flexibility the technology will have or, in other words, the more rigid the artifact. Although Orlikowski does not describe the specific mechanisms that would cause this, we could imagine, in the education context, that such an overlap would produce more realistic policy and more consistency in its implementation. As Rowan and Miskel (1999) write, only "clarity and consistency in institutional rule-making can produce real effects on work activities within the technical core of schools" (p. 373).

Institutional theorists, then, might have some of the same recommendations as the new generation of organizational learning theorists. For example, both illuminate the advantages of involving the implementers in the design of policy intended to change human organizations. Moreover, although institutional theory provides some guidance for what might happen when technical innovations meet institutional environments, it has less to say about what happens when these designs meet real people. I consider this problem in the next and penultimate section of this paper.

PRACTICAL DRIFT

In his analysis of the organizational failure that led to the accidental shoot down of two friendly U.S. Black Hawk helicopters during peacetime in northern Iraq in 1994, Snook (2000) found that a process of "practical drift" had occurred. Practical drift is the "slow, steady uncoupling of local practice from written procedure" in organizations (p. 220). To illustrate this process, Snook developed a three-dimensional matrix. On the axes are situational coupling (from tight to loose) and logics of action (from rule-based to task-based). The resulting four quadrants describe states of any given organization at different points in time—the third dimension. Snook argues that organizations shift stochastically between loose and tight coupling, basing this contention on Weick's (1976) notion that organizational functioning depends on the patterning of loose and tight coupling over time (rather than simply the degree of coupling among certain elements of the organization at any given point in time). As for organizational shifts along the other axis, Snook maintains, "organizational members shift back and forth between rule- and task-based logics of action depending on the context and these shifts have a predictable impact on the functioning of an organization" (p. 188). These shifts in logic are behaviorally determined rather than probabilistically determined.

Snook (2000) argues that these shifts follow a general, circular pattern. Tightly coupled organizations that operate via rule-based logics of action (the first quadrant of Snook's matrix) exist only in the minds of planners. Thus, he calls this organizational state, the "designed" state. Because "planners live in an unusually isolated rational world where many of the assumptions underlying an economic model of behavior fit relatively well" (p. 191), they tend to over design organizational structures and assume tight couplings among organizational elements.

However, as the design moves to implementation, situational couplings loosen, while rule-based logics of action still apply. As a result of uncertainty and sanctions, organizational members tend to follow the rules as designed by the planners. This state is called "engineered" (and occupies the second quadrant of Snook's matrix). The engineered state is inherently unstable, as the accumulated experience of daily practice teaches members of the organizations that the rules as designed are rarely appropriate for the situation. Over time, the organization is driven to an "applied" state (quadrant 3), where members' logics of action shift from being rule-based to being task-based. That is, the organization experiences "practical drift."

Snook (2000) defines practical drift as the almost inexorable uncoupling of local practice from global procedure—the net effect of which is the "general loosening of globally defined rationality" (p. 197). Many organizations experience this drift because, as Snook argues:

> As each uneventful day passes in a loosely coupled world, it becomes increasingly difficult to demonstrate the integrative benefits of global standardization over the practical benefits of local adaptation. Hence, the behavioral balance tips in the direction of local adaptation at the expense of global synchronization (p. 196).

Depending on one's perspective, practical drift can "appear either rational and effective or random and dangerous" (p. 228).

The "applied" state of organizations is fairly stable because the logic of action "matches" the loosely coupled situation. Organizational members engage in practical action, or "behavior that is locally efficient, acquired through practice, anchored in the logic of the task, and legitimized through unremarkable repetition" (Snook, 2000, p. 182). One may argue that American educational organizations have existed in this "applied" state for many years. The "ever-present demands of minute-to-minute practice" (p. 194) cause incremental drift, and these new repertoires of task-based actions become institutionalized over time within each subunit (i.e., district or school). Eventually, practitioners begin to see global rules as irrelevant, even irrational.

Unfortunately, either by "design or happenstance," the situation can become tightly coupled very quickly, leading to a "failed" state of the organization (the fourth quadrant of Snook's matrix). This occurs when drifting subunits are "wrenched back together" in a "stochastically induced fit of tight coupling" (p. 200). The resulting interdependence heightens the risk of failure, when members (who are themselves operating with situated, task-based logics of action) assume that other subunits are operating under globally synchronized rule-based logics of action that are no longer valid. Such a "failed" state, Snook argues, led to the deaths of 26 peacekeepers by friendly fire on a crisp and clear April day almost a decade ago.

The organization itself (the U.S. military), however, survived. Snook (2000) theorizes that organizations react to a failed state by shifting back into the first quadrant—into a heady state of "redesign," wherein the "typically bureaucratic overkill response" is to write even more rules and procedures. Snook is not optimistic:

> Left unchecked, such organizational knee jerks provide the system with the necessary energy to kick off subsequent cycles of disaster. Tighter design criteria increase the likelihood that such rules will be perceived as overly controlling, wholly inappropriate in a primarily loosely coupled world, and clearly unsustainable in the long run (p. 201).

I argue that educational organizations undergo this process in fits and starts, in an endless loop (although with arguably less immediately horrific results). While most of the time schools remain comfortably in an applied state of affairs, occasionally, as when test scores are published in the local paper, instruction and outcomes become tightly coupled and the school slips into a "failed" state. Enter SBR, direct instruction, externally developed whole school reforms (but I digress).

The process of practical drift has much in common with Vaughn's (1996) normalization of deviance theory. In her analysis of another disaster, the *Challenger* explosion in 1986, she found that in the years preceding the decision to launch the shuttle, NASA "engineers and managers together developed a definition of the situation that allowed them to carry on as if nothing were wrong when they continually faced evidence that something was wrong" (Vaughn, 1998, p. 36). However, in the case that Snook (2000) analyzes, each subunit of the organization constructed a separate definition of the situation. That is, the F-15 Air Force pilots knew one thing and practiced their own logic, the air traffic controllers made sense of the situation differently because they were on a separate trajectory of practical drift, and the Army pilots of the Black Hawk helicopters practiced yet another set of situated logics of action. When the different units suddenly became completely interdependent (tightly coupled), a total failure of coordination, a fiery crash, was the result.

The friendly fire example harshly illuminates the potential problems of local adaptation in light of the global disconnects it might cause. Insofar as a solution to this organizational problem exists, it must lie in the balance between the local and the global. Policymakers must design for "deviance," taking care to allow for practical action, meanwhile attempting to direct the drift.

CONCLUSIONS

Organizational learning theory, institutional theory, and practical drift all illuminate different problems and potentialities of standards-based education reform in the United States. The perspective provided by organizational learning theorists highlights the importance of professional development, of the cultivation of knowledge and of knowing, and of allowing organizational members to improvise, interact, and explore in their practice so that the collective can benefit. The institutional perspective allows us to see the hidden barriers and sly forces of a tenacious institutional environment, yet also shows us the way toward appropriating them in order to engineer their abdication through robust policy design. Finally, practical drift theory cuts across all levels of analysis—individual, community, organization, and environment—to illuminate how situated, local action can inadvertently undermine global design.

Even though this article is an analysis of policy, I have purposefully not employed theories of policy creation or implementation processes. I believe that theories of organizations provide more useful insight into the soul of the question that motivates this inquiry: How can we design policy that would help human beings engage in purposeful and positive collective action, while still accounting for all of the micro politics and micro processes that make life interesting? Is there even such a thing as a killer app in human affairs? Although all the theories I have reviewed here provide some insight into these questions, none provides wholly satisfying answers.

All three selected theories imply that the design of the policy is important to its effectiveness, but not sufficient. They all imply that action is important, but do not tell us what action by whom and when is best. They all imply that the individual is inseparable from the collective. They all imply that the Achilles' heel of standards-based education reform is that it is too-rational a mechanism to change an irrational system. Some harbor more hope than others.

There are some 88,000 public K–12 schools in some 15,000 school districts in some 50 sundry states in America. Standards-based education reform is a bold and, upon reflection, amazing attempt at getting them all to start petting the same dog—or, rather, the same, different dog than they were petting before. Whether this dog will bark or not is an empirical question—for theory, as this paper may demonstrate too clearly, only gets us so far.

REFERENCES

Argyris, C., & Schon, D. A. (1978). *Organisational learning: A theory of action perspective.* Reading, MA: Addison-Wesley.

Berger, P. L., & Luckman, T. (1967). *The social construction of reality.* New York: Doubleday.

Brown, J. S., & Duguid, P. (1991). Organizational learning and communities-of-practice: Toward a unified view of working, learning, and innovation. *Organization Science, 2*(1), 40–57.

Clemens, E. S., & Cook, J. M. (1999). Politics and institutionalism: Explaining durability and change. *Annual Review of Sociology, 25,* 441–466.

Coggshall, J. G., Athan, R. G., DeYoung, D. A., & Miskel, C. G. (2003). *Constructing legitimacy: Policy actors' perceptions of statewide standards and assessments.* Paper presented at the Annual Meeting of the American Educational Research Association, Chicago, IL.

Cohen, W. M., & Levinthal, D. A. (1990). Absorptive capacity: A new perspective on learning and innovation. *Administrative Science Quarterly, 35,* 128–152.

Collinson, V., Cook, T. F., & Conley, S. (2001). *Organizational learning: Theory and applications for schools and school systems.* Paper presented at the Association for Teacher Education in Europe, Stockholm, Sweden.

Crossan, M. M., Lane, H. W., & White, R. E. (1999). An organizational learning framework: From intuition to institution. *Academy of Management Review, 24*(3), 522–537.

Cyert, R. M., & March, J. G. (1963). *A behavioral theory of the firm.* Englewood Cliffs, NJ: Prentice-Hall.

DiMaggio, P. J., & Powell, W. W. (1983). The iron cage revisited: Institutional isomorphism and collective rationality in organizational fields. *American Sociological Review, 48,* 147–160.

Fiol, C. M., & Lyles, M. A. (1985). Organizational learning. *Academy of Management Review, 10*(4), 803–813.

Hargadon, A. B., & Douglas, Y. (2001). When innovations meet institutions: Edison and the design of the electric light. *Administrative Science Quarterly, 46,* 476–501.

Hoy, W. K., & Miskel, C. G. (2001). *Educational administration: Theory, research, and practice* (6th Ed.). New York: McGraw-Hill.

Leithwood, K., Leonard, L., & Sharratt, L. (1998). Conditions fostering organizational learning in schools. *Educational Administration Quarterly, 34*(2), 243-276.

Leithwood, K., & Louis, K. S. (Eds.). (1998). *Organizational learning in schools.* Lisse, The Netherlands: Swets & Zeitlinger.

Levitt, B., & March, J. G. (1988). Organizational learning. *Annual Review of Sociology, 14,* 319–340.

March, J. G. (1991). Exploration and exploitation in organizational learning. *Organization Science, 2*(1), 71-87.

Massell, D. (2001). Standards-based reform in the states: Progress and challenges. In R. H. Hall (Ed.), *Education reform for the 21st century* (pp. 135–168). Chicago: University of Illinois Press.

Mawhinney, H. B. (2002). *School principals' agency in the implementation ecology of high-stakes educational accountability.* Presentation at the annual meeting of the American Educational Research Association, New Orleans, LA: April 2002.

Meyer, J. W., & Rowan, B. (1977). Institutionalized organizations: Formal structure as myth and ceremony. *American Journal of Sociology, 83,* 440–463.

Mitchell, C. (1995). *Teachers learning together: Organisational learning in an elementary school.* Unpublished doctoral thesis, University of Saskatchewan, Saskatoon.

Moss, P. A., & Schutz, A. (2001). Educational standards, assessment, and the search for consensus. *American Educational Research Journal, 38*(1), 37-70.

Olson, L. (2003). All 50 states submit accountability plans. *Education Week, 22,* 28.

Orlikowski, W. J. (1992). The duality of technology: Rethinking the concept of technology in organizations. *Organization Science, 3*(3), 398–427.

Orlikowski, W. J. (2002). Knowing in practice: Enacting a collective capability in distributed organizing. *Organization Science, 13*(3), 249–273.

Pinch, T. J., & Bijker, W. E. (1987). The social construction of facts and artifacts. In W. E. Bijker, T. P. Hughes, & T. J. Pinch (Eds.), *The social construction of technological systems* (pp. 17–50). Cambridge, MA: MIT Press.

Rowan, B., & Miskel, C. G. (1999). Institutional theory and the study of educational organizations. In J. Murphey & K. S. Louis (Eds.), *Handbook of educational administration* (2nd Ed.). San Francisco: Jossey-Bass.

Sackney, L., Walker, K., & Hajnal, V. (1995). *Organisational learning, leadership, and selected factors related to the institutionalization of school improvement initiatives.* Paper presented at the American Educational Research Association, San Francisco.

Scott, W. R. (2001). *Institutions and organizations* (2nd ed.). Thousand Oaks, CA: Sage.

Senge, P. (1990). *The fifth discipline: The art and practice of organizational learning.* New York: Doubleday.

Silins, H. C., Mulford, W. R., & Zarins, S. (2002). Organizational learning and school change. *Educational Administration Quarterly, 38*(5), 613–642.

Simon, H. A. (1991). Bounded rationality and organizational learning. *Organization Science, 2*(1), 125–134.

Skrla, L., Scheurich, J. J., Johnson, Jr., J. F. (2000). Equity-driven, achievement-focused school districts: A report on systemic school success in four Texas school districts serving diverse student populations. Austin, TX: The Charles A. Dana Center.

Smith, M. S., & O'Day, J. (1991). Systemic school reform. *Politics of Education Association Yearbook,* 233–267.

Snook, S. A. (2000). *Friendly fire: The accidental shootdown of US Black Hawks over Northern Iraq.* Princeton, NJ: Princeton University Press.

Suchman, M. C. (1995). Managing legitimacy: Strategic and institutional approaches. *Academy of Management Review, 20*(3), 571–610.

Vaughan, D. (1996). *The* Challenger *launch decision: Risky technology, culture, and deviance at NASA.* Chicago: University of Chicago Press.

Vaughan, D. (1998). Rational choice, situated action, and the social control of organizations. *Law & Society Review, 32*(1), 23–61.

Watkins, K., & Marsick, V. (1993). *Sculpting the learning organization.* San Francisco: Jossey-Bass.

Weick, K. E. (1976). Educational organizations as loosely-coupled systems. *Administrative Science Quarterly, 21*(1), 1–19.

Weick, K. E. (2001). *Making sense of the organization.* Malden, MA: Blackwell.

Wenger, E. (1998). *Communities of practice: Learning, meaning, and identity.* Cambridge, U.K.: Cambridge University Press.

Zollo M. and S. G. Winter (2000). *From organizational routines to dynamic capabilities.* Working paper. Philadelphia, PA: Reginald H. Jones Center, Wharton School, University of Pennsylvania.

CHAPTER 2

LOCAL ANCHORS VERSUS STATE LEVERS IN STATE-LED SCHOOL REFORM
Identifying the Community Around Public Schools

John W. Sipple

This study aims to shed light on the range of community influences on school district decision-making in response to significant changes in New York State education policy and examine how such external involvement varies by local contextual factors. Following Arum's (2000) review of schools and their communities, I contrast the traditional ecological definition of community with a broader institutional definition of an organizational field (DiMaggio & Powell, 1991) and ground this study in institutional and structuration theories. Through case studies of three school districts and a statewide survey, I find evidence that the change in state policy has quickly motivated superficial and institutional responses (e.g., simply renaming positions) but also more substantive change as the state-imposed constraints are resulting in new opportunities for teachers and students.

Educational Administration, Policy, and Reform: Research and Measurement
A Volume in: Research and Theory In Educational Administration, pages 25–57.
ISBN: 1-59311-000-0 (hardcover), 1-59311-000-0 (paperback)

INTRODUCTION AND BACKGROUND

American public education has long been guided, funded, and critiqued at the level of the local community. In fact, the historical development of public schools cannot be separated from the debates, conflicts and needs found within local communities (Kaestle, 1983; Rury, 2002).[1] In contrast, contemporary American Education is guided as much by state interests and influence as local. On average, the funding of American schools is split between local and state dollars and with the recent surge of state curriculum frameworks and assessments, the state is playing a major role in *what* is being taught in local schools. The earliest schools had little state or federal influence and relied on interested local citizens to set priorities and gather resources for their local schoolhouse. More often than not this instruction was focused on basic literacy, numeracy, religious doctrine, and morality all under the umbrella of strict discipline and order. Whether viewed as "educational wastelands" (Bestor, Karier, & McMurray, 1985) or as "pillars of the new republic" (Kaestle, 1983), what was certain was that early schools were rich in local influence. While great debate and rancor exist today as to whether the shift to increased state control leaves schools more equitable and/or excellent (Orfield & Kornhaber, 2001), a question remains of who is really shaping contemporary educational decisions in America's public schools?

With the steady development and rationalization of a system of public schools, a variety of agents external to the local schools have emerged. Among them are school district central offices, state governments and departments of education, intermediary units serving as agents in between state government and local school districts, professional associations including teachers unions and councils of teachers of mathematics or English, business associations, and other local community groups including a recent trend in local foundations to aid in the financing of school programs (Brent, 2002; Spring, 1993).

Concurrent with the rise of the complex environment in which schools operate, school governance has changed dramatically over this last century and is encapsulated in two broad trends: Loss of local community control to local education professionals (teachers, administrators, unions); Loss of local control (whether it be parents or teachers) to state and federal government officials.[2] As historians have discussed (Callahan, 1962; Tyack & Hansot, 1982), the growth of the administrative layer of schools and the creation of school districts had a profound impact on the structure, procedures, location, and size of schools (see e.g., Callahan, 1962; Meyer, Scott, Strang, & Creighton, 1988). It was argued that this professionalization of schools served to separate school governance from political whims and corruption of local municipalities and created distance between individual parent interests and the education their child would receive in school (Kaestle, 1983; Ravitch, 1974, 2000).

Currently, states are establishing curriculum frameworks, mandating assessments and generating interest in and attention on outcome measures for schools, teachers, and students. In doing so, many states are also dictating requirements for high school diplomas, increasing academic course requirements, and calling for additional professional development opportunities (Fuhrman, 2001). The federal government, albeit not without debate and controversy, is now mandating testing in grades three thru eight, requiring the reporting of academic gains by student subgroups (e.g., race, poverty) and providing a definition for a qualified teacher in the No Child Left Behind Act of 2001.

It is logical and plausible that these developments in both local school administration and state policy will further complicate the environment of public schools (see, e.g., Boyd & Miretzky, 2003). In doing so, these trends may further usurp local community influence as well as the influence and autonomy of local educators. Given the growth of local, state, and federal education bureaucracy and influence, the current policy environment raises questions as to what influence remains for local communities? What role do local boards of education, parent, business, and citizen groups play in this day and age of complex professional and political school governance?

This study aims to shed light on these questions, documenting the range of influences on decision making in schools, and examine how such influence varies by local contextual factors (e.g., geography, wealth). Following Arum's (2000) review of schools and their communities, I analyze the dimensions of the communities (or community) in which schools operate. Arum contrasts traditional ecological definitions of communities as neighborhoods with a broader concept of organizational field (DiMaggio & Powell, 1991) that guide school organization and practice rendering local neighborhood effects overstated. Confronting these two conceptualizations of community begs a final question: Do local interests compete with (or conversely mirror) those of professional educators in the schools and the broader interests of the state?

To guide this study and answer these questions, I ground this study in institutional and structuration theories. I do so because of institutional theory's collective emphasis on identification of agents who influence organizations, organizational continuation and survival resulting from adherence to socially prescribed and symbolic patterns of organization, and finally with its concern for the multiple layers of the legal, professional, and cultural systems in shaping and scripting organizational practice (Rowan & Miskel, 1999; Scott, 2000). Structuration theory is relevant because of its emphasis on the dualities of constraint and opportunity, and structure and agency (Giddens, 1979, 1984). Local communities and state government, no doubt, place constraints on school districts' practice. These constraints, however, may also provide opportunities for local action unavailable without the imposed constraints. Similarly, as the structure and bureaucracy of the educational system grows more complex and integrated (from local classroom to the state and federal levels), the socially structured agency of local educators and community members is impacted. Together, institutional and structuration analyses offer "complementary" insight into the "interplay between actions and institutions" and assists in addressing "the practical problem of how to study institutional maintenance and change in organizations" (Barley & Tolbert, 1997, p. 112).

While the empirical and theoretical analyses in this study are of interest to scholars, policymakers, and practitioners, this paper is grounded in current policy activity and school district response in New York State (NYS). Specifically, this study is part of a larger research program in which we examine district responses to a new set of Learning and Graduation Standards in New York State. In institutional terms, I suggest most school districts in the state are experiencing what Greenwood and Hinings (1996) term 'radical organizational change." Throughout the past century, students, parents, and educators had the option of adhering to locally determined graduation standards (resulting in local diplomas) or state-determined college-preparatory graduation standards (resulting in Regents diplomas). However, beginning in 2000 (and fully phased in by 2005) the only option for a high school diploma available to students and schools is the state-endorsed Regents diploma. In real terms, this policy adjustment demands a shift in courses and exams offered by schools such that all students have the opportunity to pass the requisite courses and exams lest they do not graduate. I view this as requiring radical organizational change on the part of most school districts because as recently as 1999, only 45% of all graduating seniors earned a Regents diploma. Given current state policy, this number will soon need to be 100%; this represents approximately 125,000 students per grade level that need to be moved into college preparatory courses. The policy changes in NYS are not restricted solely to high school graduation requirements. The recent reforms call for grade K–4 and 5–8 examinations in multiple subject areas, increased staff development, additional course requirements in high school, and the provision of additional hours of academic instruction for underachieving students. This final provision is termed Academic Intervention Services (AIS) and while it provision is mandated, the details of scheduling, instruction, and content are only vaguely suggested leaving room for local interpretation in its implementation.[3]

To successfully implement these policy changes in New York State, schools and districts must alter class schedules, teacher assignments, teacher professional development, and provide the requisite and supplementary academic and non-academic services for under-performing students. What makes these organizational responses interesting and important is that they necessarily take place within the context of preexisting regulations, normative professional practice, and culturally embedded taken-for-granted scripts that have shaped and constrained educator decision making for decades, if not centuries (Rowan & Miskel, 1999). Given this context, I argue that the current decisions and practices to comply with the new state policy are made in light of state policy levers and community anchors. Prior to the new state policy imposition in 2000, local school districts offered academic programs and opportunities that reflected local interests and needs. In other words, if the local community desired that most of their children attend college, the high school academic program would be organized to allow sufficient opportunity for college preparation (typically a set of courses leading to a Regents Diploma). Conversely, districts serving communities with less interest in seeing many children attend college would offer alternatives to a college preparatory program resulting in many fewer students participating in a college-preparatory high school curriculum. It is in these sets of decisions related to how districts alter their own program, staffing, and instructional practices—once confronted with dramatic changes in graduation standards—that signal the mediation of the potentially competing forces of state policy and local community interests.

To examine these issues and practices, I offer the following questions to guide this investigation. *Given recent and uniform state policy requirements that must be implemented in varied local school contexts...*

1. What is the range of priorities and responses by school districts to the new state policy?
2. How similar are the district responses by local context?
3. How do the responses mediate between state policy and local community interests?
4. How do state-imposed constraints create new opportunities for local educators?

I seek to answer these questions by drawing on illustrative case studies (Yin, 1994) of three school districts as well as survey and archival data from a representative sample of school districts in New York State. Specifically, I seek to situate district responses within the context of local community interests and state policy changes. I pay special attention to the tensions between the interests of the local community, educators, and the state. Despite concerns suggesting that local communities have lost much of their control over their own schools, the evidence presented here suggests the contrary. While school districts do comply with federal and state policy, the interests and influence of the local communities remain central in how the districts respond to this policy shift. The findings also suggest important contextual factors associated with relative levels of local participation in key decisions.

This work is important because it focuses attention on the triad of local educators, local communities, and state policy implementation. Examining the strategies and relative levels of community involvement is an important piece in our quest to better understand the complexities of state policy implementation and the early stages of what may be the institutionalization of new school practice.

THEORETICAL DEVELOPMENT

Defining the community in which schools operate is not a simple task. The research on local community effects on schools and students is mixed though the contradictions may be related to the explicit definition of the community. A key research question is whether the community is defined as the local neighborhood in which the school is situated, or the broader array of regulations, norms, and cultural elements that collectively shape and define the broader environment in which the schools operate (Arum, 2000). In the former definition, the ecological dimension of wealth, size, racial makeup, and involvement of local actors are important dimensions and determinants of school organization, practice, and student performance. Within these ecological dimensions, Coleman (1966) and Jencks (1972) attribute significant community effects on students performance, so much so that many others have suggested schools themselves have little effect on student learning. More recent work, for example, Entwisle and Alexander (1992, 1994) have begun to tease out the impact of ecological versus school factors in estimating school versus community effects on summer and school year learning.

The latter definition, however, highlights institutional dimensions of communities representing a broader set of constraints and scripts that shape local school organization and behavior. This work, predominantly found among neo-institutional sociologists, focuses on the homogeneity of structure and purpose and the symbolic value to the organization of mirroring the socially determined and accepted patterns of organization and practice found in the environment. DiMaggio and Powell (1991) refer to these clusters of organizations, regulations, and cultural elements as *organizational fields* while Scott and Meyer (1991) term them *organizational sectors*. Whatever the name, the emphasis on the institutional dimensions of schools and their communities and how they shape organizational behavior has, some argue, rendered the impact of local neighborhood communities as "inconsequential" (Arum, 2000, p. 397; Bowles & Gintis, 1976; Parsons, 1959)

Institutional Theory

In reaction to the emphases on rational actors (both individual and collective) and the quest for rational organizational practice leading to improved efficiency and performance, institutional theory emphasizes the symbolic value of organizational structure and practice. The theory purports that by adhering to socially prescribed norms in the environment, organizations can increase external support and hence increase their chance of survival (DiMaggio & Powell, 1991; Meyer & Rowan, 1977). Institutional theorists have often examined public schools because they are agencies that have rarely enjoyed laudatory descriptions or evaluations though only on rare occasions do they go out of business (Meyer & Rowan, 1978). Many scholars have applied institutional theory to assess the value of certain organizational practices such as health care provision (Rowan, 1982), site-based management (Ogawa, 1994), and tracking (Pallas, Entwisle, Alexander, & Stluka, 1994). Recently, Ogawa and his colleagues (Ogawa, Sandholtz, Martines-Flores, & Scribner, 2003) examined a school district as it implemented a state-mandated standards-based curriculum. They describe school district leaders enacting "a myth of rationality" in adopting a standards-based strategy (p. 172). In doing so, Ogawa et al. make a distinction between the level of the environment in which district leaders operate (institutional level) and that in which the teachers operate (technical level) and how these two levels of the environment encourage different action by being constrained by different institutions.

Barley and Tolbert (1997) target the concepts of *institutions* and *actions* and argue that institutional theory alone does little to explain the process of institutionalization. They argue that in order for institutional theory to "fulfill its promise for organizational studies" (p. 94), researchers must develop a more dynamic model of institutions and devise methods for the investigation of how institutions and actions are "recursively related" (p. 94). In defining an institution as the "shared rules and typifications that identify categories of social actors and their appropriate activities or relationships" (p. 96), they stress the definition holds for any level of analysis. The explicit mechanisms by which the actions of agents at different layers of the system are constrained and perpetuated are ill-defined by institutional theory. Barley and Tolbert (1997) suggest a fusion of institutional theory with structuration theory to achieve a more powerful analytic lens with which to understand the relationship between institution and action.

Structuration Theory

Whereas institutional theory emphasizes macro influences on organizational and individual behavior, though acknowledging the agency of individuals (DiMaggio, 1988), structuration theory offers insight into the mechanisms by which individuals interacting with institutions recursively perpetuate behavior. Moreover, structuration theory offers a model for how new institutions can be formed though the interaction between macro-level constraint and individual-level action (Giddens, 1979, 1984). The duality of structure and opportunity is that structure (institution) is both a product of, and constraint on, individual action. Day-to-day activities and decisions are constant interactions between individual behaviors and societal institutions. Barley and Tolbert (1997) add to Giddens' structuration theory in suggesting the use of scripts as representing "behavioral regularities." These behaviors are observable recurrent activities of individuals and "local variants of more general principles" (Barley & Tolbert, 1997, p. 98). Hence, observing individual (or organizational) patterns of activity can be viewed as the product of pre-existing institutions but also as an active constraint on future action. These ongoing (moment to moment) actions are not static, and not fixed, allowing for change over time in individual, organizational, and institutional change.

DATA AND METHODS

This study includes two sets of analyses. The first analysis is a set of qualitative case studies of three school districts. The second analysis estimates the relative involvement of various agents in key decisions, specifically investigating how the involvement varies across urbanicity, community wealth, and position in the district.

Case Studies

The data for the case studies of individual school districts came from extensive interviews with district personal and community leaders and analysis of district documents. The districts were purposively selected in 2000 based on independent evidence of either successful efforts to expand student participation in NYS's exam program or failure to move additional students into the Regents academic track. We referred to these districts, respectively, as Movers and Stayers. We also categorized districts by their gains in student performance over time. Some districts showed great increases in student performance (in terms of passing rates on the HS English exam) while others showed dramatic decreases or no change in passing rates. We refer to these districts, respectively, as Hot and Cold. We then selected five districts that could be categorized as Hot-Stayers, Hot-Movers, Cold-Stayers, or Cold-Movers.[4]

Teams of four to seven researchers made daylong visits to each of five districts during the winter and spring of 2001. We interviewed administrators, teachers and community leaders and collected relevant documents. Interviews ranged in length from 20 to 120 minutes, with the average length being approximately 40 minutes. In total, we conducted 95 interviews with 133 individuals from five school districts. All participants signed an informed consent statement indicating that their participation was voluntary and their identity (and that of the district) would be kept anonymous. All interviews were tape recorded, transcribed, and coded using a common set of indicators using N-Vivo software. While a complete profile of each district's demographics and performance levels and the respondents' perceptions and beliefs and their organizational and programmatic response to the new learning standards are presented elsewhere (Monk, Sipple, & Killeen, 2001), this study focuses more narrowly on the issues of interaction between the local communities, their school district personnel, and the other non-local agents. Among the topics discussed herein are the major issues facing each district, the degree to which local educators and community leaders believe that all children can learn at high levels, and the variety of pressures felt by educators. We also investigated and report on the explicit strategies put in place by districts to address the issues of academic intervention services (AIS), professional development, dropout management and its' relation to GED participation, and the allocation of resources including staffing teacher reassignment. I selected three of our five completed cases to report here as they represent a rural, suburban, and urban district with three different models of community involvement in their schools.

Survey

The primary unit of analysis for this portion of the study was the school district. However, in order to identify personnel within the district for the survey, a three-stage sampling framework was designed. One hundred and twenty-one districts were selected from a total possible pool of 643 districts with high schools (18.8% of the population of non-NYC districts).[5] To ensure a representative sample of urban and rural, wealthy and poor districts, we stratified the sample based on the New York State defined Need/Resource Capacity Categories and randomly selected from each of five needs categories. The need categories result from an assessment of educational need (school district student poverty) in relation to the fiscal capacity of the school district to place districts into six distinctly different categories: New York City (1), Other Large Cities: 'Big Four districts' (2), High Need Urban and Suburban (3), High Need Rural (4), Average Need (5), and Low Need (6). Each district in a category faces similar challenges, and is able to draw on comparable resources (see http://www.emsc.nysed.gov/repcrd399/simliar.html). Given the small number (4) of Large City Districts, all were included in the study. In the remaining strata 15% or 20 districts were selected, whichever was greater.

Letters were mailed to the superintendents of selected districts in early January 2002, asking them to individually participate in the study and to allow permission for their district to be included in the study. Calls were made to superintendents in each stratum until the quota for each stratum was met. All surveys were conducted by telephone using a CATI (computer-assisted telephone interviewing) system and conducted by individuals employed by the Survey Research Institute (SRI) at Cornell University.[6] A total of 121 superintendent surveys were completed. Similar methods were used to identify and survey principals (n = 114) within the districts selected and teachers within the high schools[7] selected (n = 503). This resulted in a total of 738 participants within 121 districts.

The purpose of the survey was to document how districts are responding to the new State policy requirements. Questions focused on such strategies and responses as academic intervention services, professional development, dropout prevention, GED, and student grouping. The surveys for the superintendents, principals, and teachers were nearly identical. The only difference between them was the context the interviewee was asked to consider when answering the questions. Superintendents were asked to reflect on their district, the principal on their school, and the teacher on their department. Questions were closed-ended and interviews averaged 23 minutes.

FINDINGS

I now present findings from two sets of data. First, I describe the district response of three school districts as they each, in their own way, set out to adhere to the new state expectations and regulations. Of interest in these case descriptions are the variety of agents with whom the educators in the districts interact and feel pressure. As the reader will see, the three districts not only respond in different ways, but report a different set of constraints, opportunities, and priorities that shape their responses. Following the cases, I present findings from a broader, representative sample of school districts in NYS (n = 121). These data provide evidence of the variability of which agents (or agents' messages) are involved when key decisions are made, and how such variation is keyed to the location of the district and the wealth of the local community. Taken together, these two sets of findings offer valuable insight into the complex environments in which school reform takes place. Specifically, they show the tugs between the local neighborhood community, the school district, the state, and other intervening agents in the system.

In reviewing these cases, I remind the reader of the four questions that guide this study. These questions offer guidance in reading the three cases and each question will be answered in the discussion section below:

1. *What is the range of priorities and responses by school districts to the new state policy?* In other words, to what and whom are the educators in the districts paying attention;

2. *How (dis)similar are the district responses by local context?* What is the relationship (causal or not) between local ecological factors and the district and school response.

3. *How do the responses mediate between state policy and local community interests?* In what ways does the district face and meet competing pressures and expectations from local and non-local agents?

4. *How do state-imposed constraints create opportunities for local educators?* What constraints enable responses by educators otherwise unavailable?

Case Analyses[8]

District K[9]

District K is a small rural school district tucked away in a wealthy suburban county outside a major metrolitan area in New York State. Two elementary schools and one combined middle/high school serve the district's 1200 students, of whom more than 95% are white. The state's measure of local community wealth (Combined Wealth Ratio: CWR; a combined index of propoerty wealth and income wealth in each school district with a state mean of 1.0 and median of .8) is almost 2.0, though, according to several educators, the figure is skewed in this district due to a very small number of "billionaires" mixed in with the modal blue collar family. Suspension and drop-out rates are significantly lower than the state average at less than 1%. Free and reduced price lunch (FRPL) rates have remained stable at around 10% over the past five years. New York State classifies this district a low need suburban district. Academically, District K's Regents English passing rates have approached 100% for the past two exam administrations. Regents math scores indicate that 60% of District K's pupils succeeding on the test. Moreover, 62% of graduating seniors earned Regents diplomas for the 1999–2000 school year (state average was 43% in 1999), roughly unchanged since the spring of 1998.

Since this is a small district, teachers and administrators generally recognized the difference each child can make with regard to the test scores. One student's success or failure can add or subtract 1.5%–2% points form the district average. This serves as a strong motivator for the educators to pay attention to each and every student. Interviewees reported on the pressure they felt from community and parents to produce high test scores. All but two participants in District K reported feeling a tangible sense of pressure related to the new standards. Teachers identified the state, administrators, and themselves as sources of pressure; however, the parents and community members (including the local newspaper), were by far the most reported sources of pressure by teachers. Several administrators corroborated teachers' emphasis on the community as a source of pressure and on parents' strong influence in the district.

Repeated by several respondents was the recounting of the day after the scores were released the previous year and printed in the newspaper, signs appeared in front lawns around town congratulating the students and teachers for their success. Several teachers remarked that they were pleased with such a positive response, but were concerned about what would happen if scores ever dropped.[10] Another manifestation of the parental involvement was a reported increase in parental requests for student placement with a particular teacher. Interestingly, these requests did not seem to be based on test scores. Rather, three teachers indicated the quality of teacher bulletin boards as viewed during open houses at the elementary level and years of experience (ideal were teachers with between five and 15 years of experience) were the key determining factors for what teachers were more or less desirable.

A consistent sentiment among educators at all levels was the pressure felt to alter instruction in order to achieve the new standards. Several teachers applauded the effects of pressure on their instruction. Among their comments were praises for the "reduced uncertainty" and the new "structure for mastery." Two teachers that identified learning standards and tests as major issues both describe the exams as a "driving force" toward curricular changes. They describe classroom content and practices changing to better prepare students for the Regents' exams required for graduation. The pressure also led to increased networking among teachers and to seeking out new resources to support instruction, according to one teacher.

Most other teachers were less complementary about the effects of standards and testing on their practice. They described a loss of "spontaneity" or creative license in the classroom as they aligned their instruction with the standards. The reported costs of these changes included the reduction of "fun, beneficial tasks" and "in-depth exploration" for students. One remarked, "Test accountability takes a lot of the joy out of teaching."

Several educators remarked that students are also feeling the pressure to perform. For one this was a welcome result of the heightened pressure on the system as students are feeling pressure to work harder in and out of school. All but one teacher referred to efforts made with all students to ensure their successful performance on exams. Each of these discussions included some remark about the support provided outside of the classroom by the Resource Room, not as part of a standard pull-out program, but as additional academic time with the basic skills teachers. One teacher describes how much easier it is to recommend students to the Resource Room since the district has been held accountable for student performance on the state tests. The hiring of these full-time, certified "Basic

Skills," "AIS," and "Resource Room" teachers and the general use of their services (in contrast to restrictions of service to Title 1 and special education students) at both the elementary and secondary levels suggests a broader commitment to all students in the district, not just classified students.

The building level administrators and central office administrators made similar references to the support services provided to increasing numbers of students with the addition of basic skills/AIS/Resource Room teachers. Though two administrators explicitly expressed doubt that all students could pass the state exams, all refer to efforts to include increasing numbers of previously classified special education students in inclusive classes. Though it is unclear how many of these students are taking state exams with modifications to their testing environment. One administrator did state: "We're losing some of the options that we truly need for kids" with the loss of a "strong vocational diploma track."

In addition to high test scores, central office administrators discussed the pressure to keep tax increases to a minimum. A community member and a central office official emphasized the fiscal concerns related to the tension between increasing the school budget and maintaining only modest increases in property taxes. Prior to any major tax or spending initiatives (e.g. capital construction projects) are brought to the table, public hearings are held for local community members to voice their concerns. The superintendent also identified the state as a source of pressure. Though consequences for under-performance are not clear, consequences for non-compliance or poor performance are strongly implied or assumed. When asked what would happen if the superintendent did not make the deadline for completion of a state mandated report on district wide efforts at staff development, the superintendent snapped, "We'd be dead." When asked to clarify how this would impact him or the district, he paused, sat back, chuckled briefly, and said, "I don't know."

In general, AIS services appear to be an extension of special education services to serve unclassified students. These services are offered through a resource room setting. In most interviews, distinctions between AIS, remediation, and resource room services were difficult to distinguish. At the secondary level, several teachers and administrators describe referrals to the Resource Room for students who score below competency levels on the state exams. These students use study hall time to work with subject area AIS teachers who help to coordinate class work and provide other, unidentified academic support. Both a teacher and an administrator emphasize that AIS is focused on skills, not homework management. The teachers comment that resource room assistance provides the extra time and attention for students that the classroom teacher cannot afford. They also note that the AIS regulations allow teachers to more easily identify a student who requires assistance without the time and expense of classifying a new special education student.

Two new Basic Skills teachers (two certified FTE positions) have been hired at the elementary school to work with the existing Resource Room teacher. At the secondary level, the part-time remedial mathematics and ELA positions have been converted to full-time AIS positions in those areas, again as certified FTE positions, and a part-time AIS position in social studies was created. A request for a part-time AIS teacher in science is anticipated.

Administrators also report efforts within the district to practice inclusion and to classify fewer students as special education students. The high school, for example, eliminated the self-contained special education classroom three years ago, and the special education teacher co-teaches classes in which special education students are placed. Honors and AP level classes are offered at the high school as well. Student grouping at the elementary and intermediate level is less clear, as various teachers describe some "pullout" practices, enrichment for "more mature" students, and the elimination of the honors track at the intermediate level.

District L[11]

District L is a suburban, middle class school district in central New York State serving nearly 6000 predominantly white (98%) middle class students. Community elementary schools provide primary level instruction with students then attending two intermediate schools. One high school services the entire community. Drop-out rates for secondary students have declined from 2.2 percent in 1998 to .8% in 2000. Free and reduced lunch rates have similarly declined two percentage points to a low of 10.2% in 1999–2000. Suspension rates, however, have jumped nearly two percentage points to approximately 6.2% for the same time period. The most recent CWR for District L is .8 with 1 being the State average. Overall, District L is considered to be an average need suburban district by the State Education Department.Academically, the percent of Regents diplomas in District L, which has remain virtually unchanged between June of 1998 and 2000, is 67%. Correspondingly, 90% of students passed the Regents English and mathematics courses duriung the 2000 administrations.

With few exceptions, the majority of interviewees reported gearing up for the new standards as the districts most immediate and pressing task. One building administrator stated "we are most concerned about getting all of our students at or above what the state has set as acceptable levels." District L's instructional staff is also feeling the pressure from the state and the district to get improved results on the new assessments. Consequently, most teachers reported a number of initiatives targeted toward the instruction and grading for the new assessments. In addition, there was a concern expressed for balancing increasing curricular and staff needs with continued fiscal responsibility. Finally, a small number of interviewees mentioned insufficient staff development opportunities and a lack of technology as other important issues facing the district.

A concern raised by the local business leaders was the issue of students loitering on Main Street after school. They argued this was bad for business and the kids should have productive activities after school. In conjunction with the local chamber of commerce, the schools began offering more after school activities in addition to the regular athletics. These programs ranged from ice cream making classes to a community wide character education campaign. While not academic in nature, the after school activities and the character education were both direct responses to community demand.

When respondents reported feeling a sense of pressure related to the new standards, many expressed the perception community members would have of the school should students fail to perform on state assessments. One building administrator shared her belief of how the "community perceives how well [students] do on the tests with how the district is performing." Most of the teacher respondents reported being strongly concerned with the stigma attached to poor test results. The source of this, according to one central office official, can be attributed to "the media blowing up the significance of the school report card." Teachers also reported feeling significant pressure. Practically every teacher expressed, whether they liked it or not, that the bottom line was to improve test performance. Several teachers reported a district-wide practice of linking performance evaluations with student test results. One teacher alleged a junior colleague's failure to receive tenure was based "solely on his student's poor test results." Another reported being so frustrated with her results that "she cried." Central office officials confirmed the use of test scores as part of the information reviewed in making tenure decisions. Finally, most teachers voiced frustration at having to compromise their subject curriculum in an effort to get as many students through the assessments as possible. Many felt this approach came at the expense of what some teachers considered real or significant learning.

Programmatically, District L has taken a limited approach in its effort to address the delivery of Academic Intervention Services and serve low performing students. At the secondary level, the equivalent of two full time Teachers—one full time global studies teacher, one half-time math, and half-time English Teacher—were hired to work with students demonstrating need in those areas. At the elementary level, the district began using early intervention and identification techniques to identify students at risk for failure. Despite these proactive measures, the actual framework of the district's plan seems to rely heavily upon the voluntary use of existing remedial programming. Math, reading, and writing labs are open to students by referral or on a walk-in basis. Teachers are scheduled to cover these labs in lieu of other scheduled duties such as cafeteria or bus duty. Extra Study Period (ESP) is a voluntary option for students desiring extra help on homework assignments or test preparation. AIS and other support services are scheduled to fit within a student's normal school day, though many teachers reported staying after school to offer extra help. Students are free to walk into math, reading or science labs during lunch periods, study halls other free periods. Teachers may refer students to the resource room or a support lab during regular instructional periods in an effort to support and reinforce key teaching concepts. Finally, supplemental AIS classes (i.e., formal courses in addition to regular academic classes) are scheduled during the regular school day for students demonstrating profound deficiencies in targeted academic areas. Alternative Regents Classes (ARC) are available to students desiring to take Regents courses at a slower, more deliberate pace. According to one teacher, emphasis in these classes is on "in-class work" with very few homework assignments. Administrators emphasize that AIS services focus on skills based support for students rather than homework management, which seems to fit with the minimal homework policy adopted by the ARC teachers. Several respondents also cited efforts to actively engage students with learning disabilities in all levels of learning. Resource room support is available to students with requisite I.E.P.'s. The district has an active inclusion program with consultant teachers "pushing in" to provide services at both the primary and secondary levels. It should be noted, however, that a few teachers voiced frustration at having to over simplify curriculum in an effort to better engage students new to Regents classes. Teachers further noted many instances where high achieving students were left bored and unchallenged with class expectations in courses where inclusion was the rule.

District M[12]

District M is an urban district in economic decline with many of the district's demographic indicators reflecting the changing face of a once-thriving ethnic city. During the past decade, this community has lost its major employer resulting in the loss of 5000 jobs and about 20% of the student population. Where once many children of executives and service officers attended the school, there is now a growing number of poor and transient children. In 2000, the district enrollment was 6000 students, though enrollment drops of 3–400 students per year have been common since the closure with the district losing 350 students in the fall 2000 semester alone. The district is 90% white, with African American and Hispanic students make up the remaining 10% of the student population. The drop-out data reflect a steady rate of nearly 3.5%. Suspension rates have been consistent with the 1999–2000 figure being 9.4%. In June of 2000, the percent of students earning a Regents diploma was 55%. Probably the most telling demographic statistics is the escalating free and reduced lunch figure. For 1999–2000, District M reported a 44% free and reduced lunch rate, which has more than doubled in the last decade. This district has been labeled as a high need urban district by the New York Sate Education Department. Academically, District M has shown relatively stable Regents English and diploma rates (~50%). On the other hand, Regents math scores passing rates have recently dropped from 84% in 1997–98 to 62% in 1999–2000.

The closure of the city's major economic engine continues to have a profound impact on this community and its school system. Almost all of those interviewed in the district mentioned the dramatic impact the loss had on the community's economic outlook and the demographics of the student body. The demographic shifts have resulted in an upward pressure on the local property tax rate. As property values dropped (including the loss of $170 million dollars from the tax base), the press for increases in the tax rate to maintain programs became quite real. This has gotten to the point where the educators and community leaders question whether the community can afford the cost of the new standards on top of basic school operation and other community services (e.g., fire, police). A central office official summed up the districts fiscal picture: "The financial issues are clearly driving a lot of what we do. We clearly do not have the money to do what needs to be done. We can settle our teachers' contract, but each year the budget becomes pulling rabbits out of the hat, trying to pull some financial maneuvers."

Coupled with the bleak fiscal picture in the community, the new state standards are also a major issue facing the district. We found that educators and community leaders are consciously and actively working toward the new learning and graduation standards. As identified by the educators and community leaders, the inter-related effects of a reduced tax base and a shifting student population places the district in a bind as to how they will ensure that all students will reach the new graduation standards. The common sentiment is that the new children will require additional resources at the very time they have fewer resources on which to draw. Tied in directly are issues of staffing and cost intensive special education services for a growing special education population. But among other issues mentioned, school facilities was by far the most prevalent. The district is building a new high school, though the other buildings were noted to be in need of renovation. Issues of school violence were mentioned only twice as a major issue.

We identified two main sources of pressure in the district and a board member summarizes them: "We are at the crossroads where there are two conflicting forces. One is to improve education and the other is to lower taxes, and it's a battle." The pressure to improve education seems to originate with the State (e.g., Board of Regents and the State Education Department) and then "trickles down" through the administration and ultimately to the teachers. When a central office leader was asked to identify the source of this pressure, the response was revealing:

Well it feels like God some days. You know the State Ed Department tells us [to improve] so we tell [teachers] to. Because certainly, if our 8th grade scores don't get better this year, I'll feel it, the superintendent will feel it, the board will feel it. We're going to share that wealth. The teachers are going to feel it.

Administrators were much more likely than teachers to report pressure coming from the board, local community, or the State. This felt pressure may come from high levels of interaction with the community. In particular, two central office staff members have spent a tremendous amount of time interacting with the community. Last year they had 23 town meetings and have formal relations with the mayor, the county executive, and the Rotary. The leadership philosophy has been to always inform and get buy in from the community before moving forward on a major district initiative. There is some concern on the part of building administrators that if they do not get their scores up they may become a School under Registration Review: Signaling greater state oversight and involvement in the operation of the district.

To varying degrees, teachers identified the administration—both building and central office—as a source of their pressure. Few teachers reported pressure from the community. According to some teachers, this may be because parents are not concerned about their children's education. Virtually all teachers and building administrators reported that the central administration and the Board wanted improved performance as measured by the test scores, though this was more tangible for the administration. A junior high school teacher remarked:

I have a responsibility to the district, basically the building administration, but [with regard to] curriculum to the district. And I think the district is feeling pressure from the state and it's basically a trickle down effect.

After several years of staff and parents believing that these state-led reforms were going to "go away," teachers have voiced a heightened sense of pressure from the continued implementation of the standards-based reforms. We found that district M only began to substantively reform their efforts to gear up for the new standards and graduation requirements in the previous year. A teachers' description offers insight into why the district may have been so late in responding to the state policy changes. He described a principal who had tried to push a data-driven reform strategy in 1998 by sharing bar graphs of teacher and student performance and attempting to begin a conversation about how the teachers needed to focus on student performance and academic improvement for all children:

> I guess I kind of took it as a joke. I didn't really take it seriously when he did that...I think he did it to try to intimidate some of the teachers to get them motivated to do *something* (emphasis added).

This *something* may represent the difficulty in motivating local implementation of new standards and assessment by the state. It may be difficult for some teachers and administrators who fail to adequately understand or who have not bought into the push for standards-based reform efforts to be motivated to make changes in their practice. As one teacher put it, "the pressure that I'm feeling as a teacher is that we have to get the kids to do well on the test. And I'm not really seeing the background connection on why it's so important to know certain things...what's the purpose of this test?"

During the time of our interviews no one doubted the seriousness of the reform, only the district's ability to successfully implement reform policies given the transient student population and an uncertain fiscal environment. Nevertheless, some teachers and administrators reported a positive in all this pressure to perform. Nearly everyone we spoke with described recent changes geared toward the standards. A building principal stated:

> I think the pressure is making us better. I feel we're up to date on everything. The courses we're offering and why. What we're doing to increase assessments, developing plans, the whole bit is opening our eyes and light, I think because of that we're more aware, because we taught ourselves of what it is all about so I think staring at the barrel [of a gun] is actually a good thing.

The second main source of pressure, centered on the property tax rate, comes directly from the local community. The local newspaper is very active and has "really taken the finances of the district and brought them out to the open." This has included building construction and renovation in addition to the regular budget issues. Everyone in the district is aware of local community interest to keep tax rate increases at a minimum.

The AIS programs developed in District M are, for the most part, more formalized versions of remediation programs that previously existed at both the elementary and secondary schools. While the exact nature of the AIS programs are still under development and just beginning to be phased in, the general framework for district M's AIS programming is starting to take shape. Qualification for services is now more specified, as is the amount of time allotted for AIS help. More formally specified responsibilities are given to the ELA and mathematics AIS teachers (formerly named remedial reading and math teachers). The district is in the process of adding social studies and science AIS staff.

For ninth grade teachers and students, the identification is a particular problem. The scores on the 8th grade exams were not released to the districts until well into the fall.[13] This makes planning for 9th grade AIS services difficult and causes much disruption when students need to be placed into AIS in mid-semester (and removed from other courses they had two months invested in). Once students are identified, typically through a mix of teacher recommendations and those who score a 1 or 2 on the 4th or 8th grade state exams, AIS students are offered an extra class meeting per cycle. Since the district is on a four-day cycle, identified students will be offered an extra class period every four days. In science they will receive two lab periods per cycle instead of the typical one for most students. AIS teachers are fully certified and teach these extra course sections. The former resource rooms will continue to exist, but instead of a pull-out model, AIS will involve both pulling students out of regular classes and some push-in where the resource (AIS) teachers will provide services in the regular class.

Above and beyond the additional instructional time during the regular school day, district M is offering an extended day option during which students can receive extra help before and after school. Assisting with the process of extending the school day is a new clause in the recently negotiated teacher contract. The clause states that within the next two years, the district can seek teacher volunteers to assume either an "elementary" or secondary" work schedule. This means some teachers will start at 7:30am and finish at 2:30 while others will work from 9:00am to 4pm. While this change will not increase "true time" worked by teachers, the effect will be to lengthen the school day for students at all buildings in the district, particularly for those in need of additional AIS instruction before or after school.

At the junior high schools, two teacher volunteers provide food, tutoring, and homework assistance Monday through Thursday in the four main subject areas. In addition to the teachers' time, the other expense associated with this is the after-school bus run. Without the recently initiated after-school bus, it would not be possible for many students to stay after school for additional academic support. All 8th graders are now beginning *Math A* (typically the required math course for 9th graders), though different classes will have varying numbers of semesters to complete the course (e.g., three to six semesters).

Summer school has begun to play a major role in helping children succeed with the new learning standards. Funded primarily with Title 1 monies, central office leaders estimate that up to 20% of 7th graders are kept on track for high school through the summer school program. Among administrators, we found near universal commitment to the issue of staff development. One building administrator noted that the district "is pretty good at letting staff development happen." The open nature of staff development seems to provide a wide range of opportunities not constrained to state standards. Making use of the local BOCES services, a local teachers' center, and the districts own resources, district M is able to offer a wide array of professional development opportunities for its teachers.

Involvement on School and District Decision Making

Following our first year visiting with the participating districts and in response to a request from the State to identify the prevalence to the programs and strategies we identified in our cases, we surveyed more than 700 teachers, principals, superintendents in 121 school districts representing 18% of the school districts with high schools in the state. While a more complete treatment of these findings are discussed elsewhere (Killeen & Sipple, 2002), here I narrowly target the range of agents reported to be involved in key decisions. I do this because these data provide insight into the "community" surrounding local public schools, whether the ecological neighborhood community or the institutional community reflecting the heightened rationalization and centralization of the educational system (Arum, 2000).

We asked participants to rate the involvement of a variety of agents (State Education Department/Board of Regents, BOCES, central office administration, principal, teachers, professional organizations, and local community) in decisions related to staff assignments, AIS programming, student grouping arrangements, and GED offerings. We intended to determine which types of decisions involved different internal and external agents. In examining the descriptive statistics, factor analyses, and reliabilities, I found the variation among responses was more pronounced between agents (e.g., state vs. community) rather than between decisions (e.g., staffing vs. academic programming). In short, it mattered less what actual decision was being made than what agent was involved. The reliabilities for these factors of agents are modest, with the highest for professional associations (alpha = .76), principals (.74) and local communities (.74), and the lowest reliabilities for Central office administration (.59), state education department/Board of Regents (.62) and teachers (.64).

Figures 1 and 2 summarize the variation in the relative levels of involvement of agents in making key decisions in their local districts by district location and community wealth. The center horizontal line represents the standardized mean response (mean = 0, standard deviation = 1) for all respondents. Any bar above or below the mean line represents a standardized unit above or below the mean involvement reported by all respondents. The agents represent different aspects of the local horizontal community including the local school board, parents, and media in addition to the vertical set of agents including the superintendent, teachers union, BOCES (i.e., intermediate school districts), and the state (including the State Education Department and the State Board of Regents). In effect, the null-hypothesis for these analyses is no difference in involvement among various levels of contextual factors (locality, wealth, level of position in district) and the involvement of agents. This is not to suggest equal involvement of the various agents, but rather to suggest the involvement of the various agents is consistent across district location and community wealth. A rejection of the null hypothesis would support the conceptualization of community that it varies by district context and that there is not a single overarching institutional community in which all public schools in the state of NY are operating.

Involvement by Geography

I first measure the level of involvement of agents in key decisions across different school district locations, as reported by superintendents, principals, and teachers (See Figure 1). This analysis offers evidence as to whether the geography of the district (e.g., degree of urbanicity) appears to distinguish the environment of school districts. I find the reported involvement by the State is above average in the urban districts in comparison to the suburban and rural districts. This may be a reflection of the comparatively low achievement in New York State's largest urban districts and hence are under the most pressure from the state to improve their test scores. BOCES have above average involvement in rural school districts when compared with suburban or urban districts, and represent a significant external influence on local decision making in rural districts. The noticeable lack of BOCES involvement in urban districts is to be expected, as BOCES have no responsibility for the five largest urban school districts. Professional Associations (namely teachers' unions) have above average involvement in local decision-making in urban and rural districts when compared with suburban districts. This may signify a greater need for union protection and hence contract language that shapes the staffing and student arrangements in urban and rural areas than in suburban districts. Finally, the local community (parents and school boards) plays a greater role in suburban school districts than elsewhere. Exactly what type of involvement this entails is unclear, though there is extensive literature documenting greater parent involvement among high than low socioeconomic parents (see e.g., Lareau, 1987; Lareau & Horvat, 1999).

Involvement by Wealth

Relative levels of community wealth (family income and property values) also play a role in differentiating the levels of involvement of various agents. School administrators and the state have above average involvement in poorer communities in contrast to wealthier communities, again possibly reflecting the priorities of the state for their policy implementation and attention (See Figure 2). The wealth quartiles also serve to clarify in which districts BOCES are more involved, with local educators in the second quartile reporting above average involvement of these intermediary school districts. Involvement of local communities (including parents, school boards, and the media) is below average in the lowest two quartiles in direct contrast to the above average involvement in the upper quartiles.

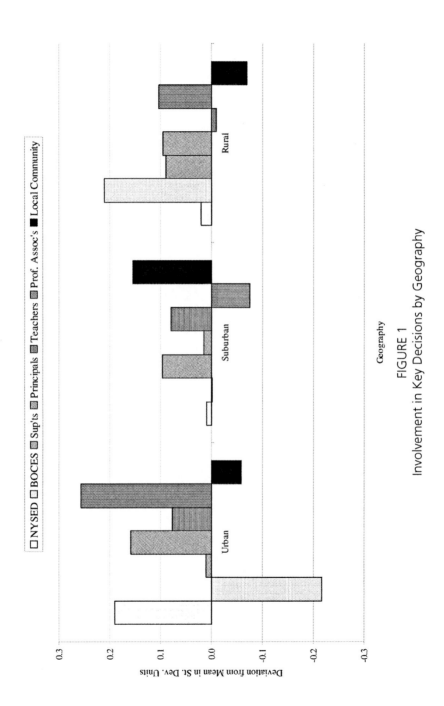

Geography

FIGURE 1

Involvement in Key Decisions by Geography

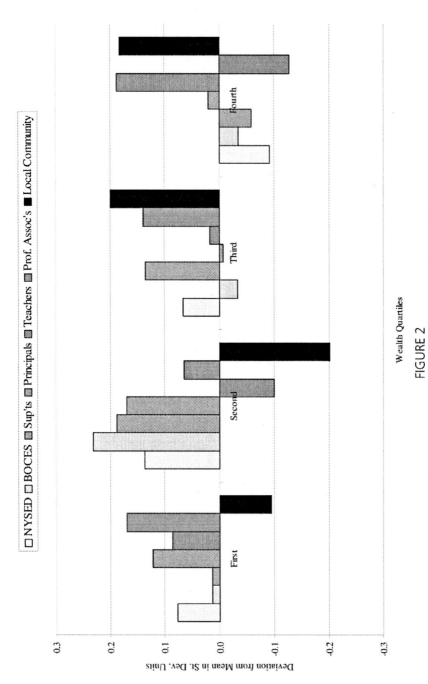

Wealth Quartiles

FIGURE 2

Involvement in Key Decisions by Community Wealth

The involvement of Teachers Unions is reduced for districts in the wealthiest communities, while they have above average influence in the first thru third quartiles.

Taken together, the findings on community, union, and teacher involvement in these key decisions suggests what may be called a "professional" model of decision making in the wealthiest quartile of communities: Teachers and local communities are more strongly involved in local decision making along with a reduced involvement of unions. Conversely, in poorer communities, the involvement of teachers and the local community is reduced while the involvement of teacher professional associations and the state increases.

DISCUSSION AND CONCLUSIONS

In this study, I set out to analyze the composition and involvement of the communities surrounding local school districts and the early changes in local school district practice and governance in light of major education policy changes in New York State. In doing so, I hoped to contribute to the literature exploring how community involvement in schools differs by the local ecological dimensions of neighborhood communities or how a broader, more coherent, institutional community (e.g., organizational field) exists and shapes local decision making and practice (Arum, 2000; Rowan & Miskel, 1999). I also aimed to contribute to the literature on the mechanisms for institutional change in examining local responses to dramatic changes in learning and graduation standards. In bringing together structuration and institutional theories (Barley & Tolbert, 1997), the conceptual interpretation of local school district response to state-led school reform is enriched. State-imposed constraints offered opportunities for new local practice and focused attention on the recursive activity of individuals acting under the constraints of institutions—the result of which is to allow for institutional and organizational change.

The illustrative case studies offer a close-to-the-ground look at the implementation of the state education policy changes. The state regulations clearly establish a target and timeline for how many (all) and when (within five years) students need to participate in the Regents college-preparatory program. Districts K, L, and M had regents diploma rates of 62%, 68%, and 55% respectively, and hence all had a third to a half of their students needing to be moved into the Regents program. Two districts (K & L) have stable local tax bases and economies, while District M was in a community of severe fiscal stress.

The district responses to the standards offer a glimpse into the composition of the communities in which the districts are operating. All three faced the common state policy changes, had similar degrees of requisite organizational change to achieve full compliance with the new graduation requirements, but also served very different local neighborhood communities and had different local fiscal conditions. I first discuss the range of agents and issues followed by the variation of responses and how the responses vary by context. Third, I discuss the district activity in light of the potentially competing expectations from the neighborhood community and the state. Finally, I discuss the duality between constraint and opportunity.

Of import to this study are the variety of agents and issues that have captured the attention of the local educators. The documenting of these agents and messages provide, generally, insight into the community in which the educators operate and, specifically, the different communities in which teachers versus administrators function. District K's teachers and administrators had a very close relationship to its local community, though the central office administrators reported state influence much more frequently than teachers. Teachers only referenced parents, the local media, and the administration as motivators for their activity. Of note, was the apparent contradiction between the teachers' description of the felt pressure from parents to improve test scores (and put up signs congratulating increased scores) and the tangible form of involvement in which parents would request teachers based on teachers years of experience and quality of bulletin boards. District K's administrators, namely the superintendent, had the most direct references to the state as an important agent, though also emphasized the importance of keeping local taxpayers (particularly the wealthiest set) abreast of major fiscal decisions.

District L also had a close relationship with its neighborhood community and had much interaction between the educators and the community. However, the interests of the community were as focused on keeping kids busy after school as they were on improving test scores. The administration and teachers generated after school activities and offered many opportunities for additional academic intervention services. By and large, however, the services were informal and emphasized voluntary participation of students to attend during lunch, a free period, or after school. Coupled with this 'drop-in' model of AIS, was a tangible skepticism among teachers that the community was misplacing attention on test scores resulting in a stigma attached to low school performance. Teachers voiced concern that the new modifications for students (including special education inclusion) slow down the regular academic classes and create boredom for the more academic students. The central administration expanded accountability measures in the tenure review process and worked very closely with local business leaders and community leaders in developing the district budget and local tax levy.

District M, in the midst of its economic struggle, had similar pressures from the same set of agents. As in the other two districts, the teachers felt pressure from their administration and the administration felt pressure from the state. The difference here is that the teachers reported little inter-action with or pressure from parents, and the administration faced the real threat that if the district's numbers did not improve they were facing fur-ther involvement by the state as a SURR school. This intensified pressure resulted in the often mentioned 'trickle down' of pressure and expecta-tions from the state, to the administration to the teachers. District M, unlike the other districts, also made use of the BOCES in expanding their staff development offerings.

The survey findings of educators across New York State offer empirical evidence that the relative involvement of the various agents involved in key decisions varies by location and wealth. Educators in some urban and rural districts and, separately, those serving poor communities are more likely to report involvement of the state and BOCES in key decisions. Alternatively, educators in suburban districts and, separately, serving the wealthiest com-munities seemingly operate in communities with different pressures. How much of this difference can be accounted for by prior district performance is unclear and beyond the scope of this study, though warrants further attention.

In short, the community composition of the three districts is similar, with the local neighborhood and the state playing large roles. However, dif-ferences do exist, some related to local ecological factors. Specifically, Dis-trict M's teachers felt virtually no expectations from the local parents, in direct contrast to District K, though heavy pressure from their administra-tion. District L felt pressure to improve test scores though discounted the community interest as misguided. This resulted in distinctly less intensive AIS services in District L as in District K. District M administrators spoke explicitly of the felt pressure from the state, but also being greatly con-strained by local economics. BOCES, having little interaction with Districts' K and L, provide support for the fiscally constrained District M.

In terms of Arum's (2000) continuum of ecological versus institutional conceptions of a school's community, my qualitative findings support the notion that the important difference in community composition is not so much between districts, though differences exist, but rather between the communities in which teachers and administrators work. The teachers appear more sensitive to local ecological and neighborhood demands while the administrators, particularly central office officials and superin-tendents, function in broader, more consistent institutionalized communi-ties. Similarly, Ogawa and his colleagues (2003) in their study of a single district in CA found teachers making decisions of a technical nature while the higher-level administrators made more decisions of an institutional character.

My survey findings, however, do not match the case findings or those of Ogawa et al. As shown in Figures 1 and 2, the responses of all educators (superintendents, principals, and teachers) reflect variation by district urbanicity and community wealth supporting the importance of ecological dimensions of community. While not shown, I also calculated means for the involvement of the agents categorized by position of the respondent (teachers versus principal versus superintendent). Beyond principals reporting above average involvement of principals, and superintendents reporting above average involvement of superintendents and principals, no differences existed in the reported involvement of the state, BOCES, professional associations, or local community by position in the district. In other words, this evidence does not support the notion that teachers and administrators work in distinctly different communities.

Local school district response to changes in state policy does not take place absent local interests. The decisions of local educators are often made in the vise between state policy levers and local community interests. When the policy and local interest is in agreement (such as in District K), there is little tension within the school district other than finding sufficient resources and technical improvements to meet the common expectations from the environment. However, when the state policy interests differ from the local community interest (such as in District L), the district must move to meet both sets of demands. The third model, in this case District M, includes the strong expectations of the state coupled with very weak (at least academically) expectations from the local community (fiscal expectations, in contrast, were quite strong). Once the district (namely teachers) realized the state-led reform was not going to go away, the district moved quickly to alter its programmatic offerings.

Finally, Giddens' (1984) duality of structure and opportunity helps to explain the apparent contradictions between districts being forced to abide by new state Learning and Graduation standards and the rapid adoption of new practices related to the general expectation that all children will have the opportunity to learn at high levels. In other words, I found strong evidence in these three cases of practices that likely would not have been adopted without the state-imposed constraint to move all students into the Regents academic program. For example, educators in District K explained how it became easier to refer students to a resource room for additional help once the district moved to implement their academic intervention services. Teachers reported many more resources available to students because of the push to implement the new standards. Teachers in District M reported how the process by which to request additional academic services for a student was now much better specified. With the new opportunities for students, came a narrowing of the range of options for special education students in District K who now were universally mainstreamed into regular academic classes. Once again, this structural constraint of mainstreaming also led to a reduction in the number of students classified as special education. The resources freed up by the reduction of classifications resulted in the sense that it was easier to identify students for additional services without the legal and fiscal burdens of special education classification. The local fiscal and state academic constraints even led to a significant change in the teacher contract in District M. In what was described by the central office and teachers alike as a team effort, the contract was altered to remove the specificity of when the school day begins and ends for teachers and replaced it with a simple length of work day provision. This way, teachers could choose to start early or late which had the benefit for students of extending the school day by an hour without extending the work day or week for teachers. This change, it was suggested, would not have happened if the district had not found itself under such tight fiscal constraint from the local community and academic constraint from the state.

If Barley and Tolbert (1997) are correct, institutions are both a product of, and constraint on, the moment-by moment actions of local actors. It is the ongoing and repetitive actions of individuals and organizations interacting recursively with the institutional constraints that allow for a dynamic system of individual, organizational, and institutional change. In one sense, the data from the three cases could tell a story of old practices (remediation and special education) simply being renamed as Academic Intervention Services with no real change taking place. However, I suggest the transformation resulting from the education policy change in 2000 is more complex and substantive than simply putting old wine into new bottles. The reform activities in the districts did involve the renaming of resource room remediation specialists into AIS teachers, but, depending on local fiscal opportunity, they were often converted from part-time to full. Their tasks, the educators also made clear, shifted from simple homework management to more substantive skill development. Finally, the attention to specific student needs became more important and prevalent as greater options and more coherent systems became available for teacher referral to special services.

In New York State, there is little doubt that the educational experience of many students is changing. With each new decision by administrators and teachers to change a label, modify a schedule, and offer additional instruction, the constraints on the decisions are changing. In other words, as rules (institutions) change, practice changes; as practice changes, rule change becomes possible. While we often look for immediate and major changes to practice after formal policy change, real change takes place in much smaller increments.

More students are being educated to higher levels than ever before in New York State. The state policy changes clearly played an important role in modifying the institutional environment of schools by establishing new and common expectations of high school academic programs. However, the interpretation and implementation of these policy changes take place in local communities guided by the interactions of local educators with local and non-local community agents. It is the ongoing interaction between local practice and institutional constraints that allow progress in reforming school practice.

NOTES

1.   The term community has wide and varied meanings. In the literature on schools, community is often conceptualized as internal to the school, (e.g., the school community, creating community in the schools, teachers' professional community), as an external arena of engagement for students (e.g., community service, workforce engagement), or as a variable in the academic success of students. In this paper, I use the term community to refer to the local geography and population included in the catchment's area for the local public schools.

2.   Many scholars have also written about the rise of corporate influence on schools. I do not disagree, though I argue that business influence is exerted locally by local business leaders on schools or at the state or national level by larger consortia of corporate interests (e.g., The Business Roundtable) on governmental leaders (Sipple, 1999; Sipple, Miskel, Matheney, & Kearney, 1997).

3.   For a more complete discussion and definition of AIS services in New York State schools, see (Killeen & Sipple, 2003)

4.   See (Monk et al., 2001) for a more complete description of the methods used.

5.   In order to ensure a 15% sample, we over sampled with the assumption that we would lose some districts. In order for a district to be included in the final analysis, not only would the superintendent have to agree to participate, but also the principal in a high school in the same district and then the teachers within that high school.

6.   See http://www.sri.cornell.edu

7.   Given the purpose of this study we defined high schools as those schools that included a 12th grade. This includes high schools with grades 10–12, 9–12, 7–12, 6–12, 5–12 and K–12. Except in the category of large cities, one high school was randomly chosen from each of the districts that had more than one high school. In the Big Four districts, 2 high schools were chosen out of 4 in Syracuse, 2 of 5 in Yonkers and 2 of 7 in Rochester. In Buffalo, the largest of these districts, 4 high schools were chosen out of 16.

8.   I want to acknowledge the assistance of Kieran Killeen, Miguel Zavala, Lauren Faessler, Terrance Dougherty, Peter Smith, Elaine Little, Leanne Avery, and Lehn Benjamin for their assistance in conducting these cases.

9.   We interviewed a total of 17 people in individual and group interview settings: 11 teachers (7 elementary and 4 secondary), 2 building level administrators, 3 central office administrators (including the Superintendent), and one community leader.

10.   The publication of School Report Card data in local papers was considered instrumental, especially since the district's size makes it easy to identify teachers whose classes did or did not perform well.

11.   A cumulative total of 27 interviews were completed in District L. Participants included seven central office and building level administrators, seven secondary math teachers, nine secondary English teachers and seven community leaders.

12.   We completed 12 individual and 5 group interviews, with a total of 29 interviewees participating. Specifically, the interviewees were 6 junior high school and 9 high school teachers, 6 building administrators, 6 central office leaders (including

administrators, program directors, and district superintendents), and 3 community representatives.

13. This problem, widely described in many of the case districts, has been alleviated somewhat by moving the exam administration earlier in 8th grade and a slightly quicker turnaround in test scoring.

REFERENCES

Arum, R. (2000). School and communities: Ecological and institutional dimensions. *Annual Review of Sociology, 26*, 395–418.

Barley, S. R., & Tolbert, P. S. (1997). Institutionalization and structuration: Studying the links between action and institution. *Organization Studies, 18*(1), 93–117.

Bestor, A. E., Karier, C. J., & McMurray, F. (1985). *Educational wastelands: The retreat from learning in our public schools* (2nd ed.). Urbana: University of Illinois Press.

Bowles, S., & Gintis, H. (1976). *Schooling in capitalist America: Educational reform and the contradictions of economic life.* New York: Basic Books.

Boyd, W. L., & Miretzky, D. (2003). *American educational governance on trial: Change and challenges.* Chicago: National Society for the Study of Education.

Brent, B. O. (2002). Expanding support through district education foundations: A tale of two states. *Leadership and Policy in Schools, 1*(1), 30–51.

Callahan, R. E. (1962). *Education and the cult of efficiency; a study of the social forces that have shaped the administration of the public schools.* Chicago: University of Chicago Press.

Coleman, J. S. (1966). *Equality of educational opportunity* (Report to the President and Congress). Washington, DC: U.S. Office of Education.

DiMaggio, P. J. (1988). Interest and agency in institutional theory. In L. G. Zucker (Ed.), *Institutional patterns in organizations: Culture and environments* (pp. 3–21). Cambridge, MA: Ballinger.

DiMaggio, P. J., & Powell, W. W. (1991). The iron cage revisited: Institutional isomorphism and collective rationality in organizational fields. In W. W. Powell & P. J. DiMaggio (Eds.), *The new institutionalism in organizational analysis* (pp. 63–82). Chicago: University of Chicago Press.

Entwisle, D. R., & Alexander, K. L. (1992). Summer setback: Race, poverty, school composition and mathematics achievement. *American Sociological Review, 57,* 72–84.

Entwisle, D. R., & Alexander, K. L. (1994). Winter setback: The racial composition of schools and learning to read. *American Sociological Review, 59,* 446–460.

Fuhrman, S. (Ed.). (2001). *From the capital to the classroom: Standards-based reform in the states.* Chicago: University of Chicago Press.

Giddens, A. (1979). *Central problems in social theory: Action, structure and contradiction in social analysis.* Berkley, CA: University of California Press.

Giddens, A. (1984). *The constitution of society.* Berkeley: University of California Press.

Greenwood, R., & Hinings, C. R. (1996). Understanding radical organizational change: Bringing together the old and the new institutionalism. *Academy of Management Review, 21*(4), 1022–1054.

Jencks, C. (1972). *Inequality; a reassessment of the effect of family and schooling in America.* New York: Basic Books.

Kaestle, C. (1983). *Pillars of the republic: Common schools and American society.* New York: Hill & Wang.

Killeen, K., & Sipple, J. W. (2002). *How have performance standards changed school district practice? Results from a statewide survey of New York state school districts.* Albany, NY: Educational Finance Research Consortium (available at http://www.albany.edu/edfin).

Killeen, K., & Sipple, J. W. (2003). *The implementation of academic intervention services in New York State school districts: Implications for school organization and instruction.* Albany, NY: New York State Educational Finance Research Consortium (available at http://www.albany.edu/edfin).

Lareau, A. (1987). Social class differences in family-school relationships: The importance of cultural capital. *Sociology of Education, 60*(April), 73–86.

Lareau, A., & Horvat, E. M. (1999). Moments of social inclusion and exclusion: Race, class, and cultural capital in family-school relationships. *Sociology of Education, 72*(January), 37–53.

Meyer, J. W., & Rowan, B. (1977). Institutionalized organizations: Formal structure as myth and ceremony. *American Journal of Sociology, 83*(2), 340–363.

Meyer, J. W., & Rowan, B. (1978). The structure of educational organizations. In M. W. Meyer (Ed.), *Environments and organizations.* San Francisco, CA: Jossey-Bass.

Meyer, J. W., Scott, W. R., Strang, D., & Creighton, A. L. (1988). Bureaucratization without centralization: Changes in the organizational system of U.S. Public education, 1940–80. In L. G. Zucker (Ed.), *Institutional patterns in organizations: Culture and environments* (pp. 139–168). Cambridge, MA: Ballinger.

Monk, D., Sipple, J. W., & Killeen, K. (2001). *Adoption and adaptation: New York State school districts' responses to state imposed high school graduation requirements: An eight-year retrospective.* Albany, NY: New York State Educational Finance Research Consortium (available at http://www.albany.edu/edfin).

Ogawa, R. T. (1994). The institutional sources of educational reform: The case of school-based management. *American Educational Research Journal, 31*(3), 519–548.

Ogawa, R. T., Sandholtz, J. H., Martines-Flores, M., & Scribner, S. P. (2003). The substantive and symbolic consequences of a district's standards-based curriculum. *American Educational Research Journal, 40*(1), 147–176.

Orfield, G., & Kornhaber, M. L. (2001). *Raising standards or raising barriers?: Inequality and high-stakes testing in public education.* New York: Century Foundation Press.

Pallas, A. M., Entwisle, D. R., Alexander, K. L., & Stluka, M. F. (1994). Ability-group effects: Instructional, social or institutional? *Sociology of Education, 76*(1), 27–46.

Parsons, T. (1959). The school class as a social system: Some of its functions in American society. *Harvard Educational Review, 29*(4), 297–318 (269–290).

Ravitch, D. (1974). *The great school wars, New York City, 1805–1973: A history of the public schools as battlefield of societal change.* New York: Basic Books.

Ravitch, D. (2000). *Left back: A century of failed school reforms.* New York: Simon & Schuster.

Rowan, B., & Miskel, C. G. (1999). Institutional theory and the study of educational organizations. In J. Murphy & K. S. Louis (Eds.), *The handbook of educational administration* (2nd ed., pp. 359–383). San Francisco: Jossey-Bass.

Rowan, B. (1982). Organizational structure and institutional environment: The case of public schools. *Administrative Science Quarterly, 32,* 493–511.

Rury, J. L. (2002). *Education and social change.* Mahwah, NJ: Earlbaum Associates.

Scott, W. R., & Meyer, J. W. (1991). The organization of societal sectors: Propositions and early evidence. In W. W. Powell & P. J. DiMaggio (Eds.), *The new institutionalism in organizational analysis* (pp. 108–140). Chicago: University of Chicago Press.

Scott, W. R. (2000). *Institutions and organizations* (2nd ed.). Thousand Oaks: Sage.

Sipple, J. W., Miskel, C. G., Matheney, T. M., & Kearney, C. P. (1997). The creation and development of an interest group: Life at the intersection of big business and education reform. *Educational Administration Quarterly, 33*(4), 440–473.

Sipple, J. W. (1999). Institutional constraints on business involvement in k–12 education policy. *American Educational Research Journal, 36*(3), 447–488.

Spring, J. (1993). *Conflict of interest: The politics of American education* (2nd Ed.). New York: Longman.

Tyack, D. B., & Hansot, E. (1982). *Managers of virtue: Public school leadership in America, 1820–1980.* New York: Basic Books.

Yin, R. K. (1994). *Case study research: Design and methods* (Vol. 5). Thousand Oaks, CA: Sage.

CHAPTER 3

DISTRICT CENTRAL OFFICE-COMMUNITY PARTNERSHIPS
From Contracts to Collaboration to Control

Meredith I. Honig

This paper examines partnerships between district central offices and various "community organizations" such as health and human services and youth development agencies and their forms, functions, and constraining/enabling factors in school improvement. Findings come from an embedded comparative case study of these partnerships in one urban district between 1990 and 2000. Using resource dependence theory and the new institutionalism in sociology as the conceptual framework, this research highlights that central office-community partnerships in this district took three predominant forms—contractual, collaborative, and control relationships—and that functions varied from the provision of new discrete resources to schools to broader capacity building functions for the central office itself. Respondents were likely to report that resource dependencies drove partnership forms and functions. Other findings revealed institutional pressures as primary drivers of the partnerships. Implications relate to how districts and community agencies might work together to create contexts that promote school improvement.

Educational Administration, Policy, and Reform: Research and Measurement
A Volume in: Research and Theory In Educational Administration, pages 59–90.
ISBN: 1-59311-000-0 (hardcover), 1-59311-000-0 (paperback)

INTRODUCTION

District central offices increasingly enter into a variety of formal relation-ships or partnerships with "community organizations"—neighborhood-based health and human services agencies, advocacy groups, and youth development organizations among others that typically operate outside formal school systems—to augment their resources for school improve-ment (Marsh, 2002, 2003). These partnerships—called simply district cen-tral office-community partnerships here—stem in part from the premise that educational systems do not have all the resources students need to achieve high academic standards, and that district central offices' strategic relationships with organizations outside these systems can strengthen stu-dents' opportunities to learn. Recent research on districts reinforces that central offices, particularly in urban areas, lack capacity for basic adminis-trative operations as well as for the implementation of ambitious school improvement strategies (Spillane, 1997). Documentation of education pol-icies that promote school-community collaboration sounds perhaps the loudest call for central office-community partnerships on the grounds that they would enhance implementation of *school*-community partnerships (Cunningham & Mitchell, 1990; David and Lucile Packard Foundation, 1992; Schorr, 1997).

Despite their increasing number in practice and their promise in theory, district central office-community partnerships seldom have been a central feature of research. Educational researchers primarily have examined com-munity partnerships involving schools and states not school district central offices and do not clarify whether lessons from these other partnerships apply to district central offices (e.g., Cibulka & Kritek, 1996; Crowson & Boyd, 1993). In a few studies of school districts, community organizations appear as background, context or impediment to change, rather than as a primary partner in the implementation of educational improvement (David, 1990; Firestone, 1989; Murphy & Hallinger, 1988; Rosenholtz, 1991; Spillane, 1998). The engagement of community residents with dis-trict school boards has received some attention, but these citizen-board interactions hardly resemble the high-profile, big-budget, inter-organiza-tional partnerships currently underway in many districts between district central office bureaucracies and various formal community organizations (Marsh, 2003). Accordingly, central office-community partnerships pro-ceed with limited empirical evidence regarding the conditions under which they might deliver on their promises.

This paper aims to address this practice-research gap and to put district central office-community partnerships on the education research map by examining the following questions:

- What forms do district central office-community partnerships take?

- What functions do these partnerships serve?
- What factors constrain/enable partnership forms and functions over time?
- What are the results and implications for the research and practice of these partnerships, and educational administration more broadly?

I address these questions using findings from a comparative qualitative case study of central office-community partnerships in Oakland, California between 1990 and 2000. Oakland provided a strategic case for this inquiry because conditions there suggested that the central office would demonstrate sustained central office-community partnerships over time with limited interference from conditions that typically frustrate interorganizational relationships. I drew on concepts from resource dependence theory and the new institutionalism in sociology for the theoretical framework for site selection, data collection, and data analysis because these theories illuminate conditions under which organizations interact and various inter-organizational forms, functions, and constraining/ enabling factors over time.

I found that Oakland's district central office-community partnerships varied in terms of their forms and functions over three distinct periods. In the first period, "control by contracts," central office administrators primarily monitored contracts with neighborhood-based community organizations for the provision of health and social services at or near school sites in accordance with central office priorities. In the second period, "collaboration," central office administrators entered into formal collaborative partnerships with a range of community organizations including county health and human services agencies, neighborhood-based non-profit organizations, and a citywide community development organization. In these collaborations, the central office received resources essential to their support of school reform—in this case, partnerships between *schools* and community agencies as a school improvement strategy. In the third period, the district central office limited its contribution of resources to the collaborations and hired its own staff to perform many of the functions previously carried out by community organizations; in response, community organizations curtailed their own participation in partnership activities. I call this period "control by coercion" to emphasize that central office decisions came to dictate the terms of the partnership and that central office administrators operated as though the central office already controlled the resources necessary for implementation of those reform initiatives.

Confirming resource dependence theory the availability of and perceived need for particular resources appeared as a primary influence on partnership forms and functions. The new institutionalism highlights how institutional factors such as organizational and professional norms enabled and constrained these partnerships over time. The paper concludes with implications and future directions for the research and practice of educational administration.

CONCEPTUAL FRAMEWORK

Scholars frequently have drawn on resource dependence theory[1] and the new institutionalism in sociology to explain inter-organizational relationships (e.g., Aldrich, 1976; Gray, 1985; Mawhinney & Smrekar, 1996b; Pfeffer, 1981; Pfeffer & Salancik, 1978; Smylie & Crowson, 1996; Smylie, Crowson, Chou, & Levin, 1994; Van de Ven & Walker, 1979; Weiss, 1987). Taken together these theories provide a set of concepts that can guide empirical inquiry into central office-community partnerships by illuminating why inter-organizational partnerships form, the forms these partnerships take, the functions they serve, and the factors that influence partnership forms and functions over time.

Resource dependence theory posits that inter-organizational partnerships are inevitable. No organization is entirely self-sufficient, and therefore organizations frequently enter into exchanges with each other to enhance their resources essential to their basic operations and their performance. Interdependence depends on at least three factors:

1.   the importance of a particular resource to an organization's survival;
2.   the degree to which that resource is controlled by another organization; and
3.   the marketplace—the extent to which the organization can access the needed resources from other sources (Gray, 1985; Pfeffer & Salancik, 1978; Van de Ven & Walker, 1979; Weiss, 1987). A given organization will be highly dependent on another organization if a resource essential to its production or survival is controlled almost exclusively by that other organization. In this view, organizations are active agents, aware of resource needs and deliberately striving to meet those needs (Aldrich & Pfeffer, 1976). Inter-organizational relationships are primarily contractual and concern the transfer of resources. Organizations themselves are comprised of multiple coalitions or sub-organizations bound together by contracts.

The intensity and frequency of relationships vary in ways that shape the terms of the inter-organizational contracts. For example, an organization may enter into a time-limited contract with another organization for the transfer of a finite set of resources. In such arrangements, that organization typically faces challenges of monitoring or otherwise controlling the contractor's compliance with contract terms. Organizations also may enter into open-ended contracts for the transfer of a variety of unpredictable resources to accomplish future joint tasks—an arrangement sometimes called collaboration or, in extreme cases, merger (Pfeffer, 1972).

The value of a particular resource depends not on an inherent property of the resource but on the extent to which it is in demand relative to its supply. High demand/low supply resources are more valuable than low demand/high supply resources. An organization's power depends on the extent to which an organization controls a valuable resource. Organizations that control market share wield more power than those that do not (Pfeffer, 1981).

Inter-organizational relations inherently are riddled with conflict because organizations typically strive to operate independently but often cannot maintain their independence given such factors as their inability to marshal all the resources necessary for organizational production and the lack of profitability in controlling all the means of production. In this view, conflict is not a barrier to inter-organizational relations to be eliminated but an unavoidable challenge to be managed (Pfeffer, 1981; Pfeffer & Salancik, 1978).

The new institutionalism in sociology provides concepts that help elaborate other dynamics relevant to inter-organizational relationships not attended to by resource dependence theory. First, the new institutionalism allows for a broader range of inter-organizational relationships than only contractual relationships rooted in concerns for organizational production and efficiency. In particular, this line of theory posits that organizations may also establish ties based on values, routines, and taken-for-granted ideas about legitimate organizational activities (DiMaggio, 1991; Friedland & Alford, 1991; March, 1994; Zucker, 1983). The concepts focus attention on these normative bases for inter-organizational partnerships and the explicit and implicit rewards that reinforce certain behaviors. These concepts also suggest that the forms and functions of these partnerships may vary over time and should be treated as an area for empirical investigation rather than as a starting assumption.

Second, the new institutionalism highlights that organizations consist of individuals and groups of professionals who operate within normative systems that shape their day-to-day interactions with each other and individuals from other organizations. Within these systems of norms and standards, scripts or taken-for-granted assumptions about professional practice undergird individual and group interactions (Barley, 1996; DiMaggio, 1991). Scholars who have used these concepts to understand inter-organizational partnerships involving schools highlight that standard educational leadership scripts favor inter-organizational relationships in which educational leaders seek to control community organizations, parents, and others outside schools (Mawhinney & Smrekar, 1996; Smylie & Crowson, 1996; Smylie et al., 1994).

Over time, frequent interactions among organizations contribute not only to interdependence but isomorphism—a process by which organizations come to resemble one another in terms of form, function, and other organizational dimensions (DiMaggio & Powell, 1983; Meyer & Rowan, 1977). Institutional theorists have observed that less legitimate or otherwise dominant organizations come to resemble more legitimate and dominant organizations.

I used these concepts to analyze qualitative data regarding central office-community partnerships' forms, functions, and constraining/enabling factors in several ways. First, these concepts suggested criteria for the selection of a strategic research site—a place that increased my likelihood of observing district central office-community partnerships in action over time and relatively unfettered by conditions that theory already predicts constrain inter-organizational partnerships. As elaborated below, such selection criteria include the supply of particular resources and the recognized need for those resources (i.e., demand); the availability of professional models to guide the individual and organizational practice of partnership participants; and the ability of partnership participants to weather the conflict and power differentials inherent in the endeavor. I treated the latter as a particularly important site selection criterion given decades of research on inter-agency collaboration that highlights political disputes over "turf" as partnership barriers (e.g., Crowson & Boyd, 1993).

Resource dependence theory and the new institutionalism in sociology also focused data collection and analysis on the resource differentials that may prompt the formation of district central office-community partnerships and provided initial concepts for categorizing partnership forms, functions, and factors (e.g., contractual, collaborative, or control relationships; resources provided; and availability of professional scripts). Third, both theories emphasize survival and performance in relation to stated goals as a key indicator of inter-organizational activities and success. Accordingly, I focused my analysis on the persistence of partnerships over time.

METHOD

I used concepts from resource dependency theory and the new institutionalism in sociology to ground a comparative case study of central office-community partnerships in Oakland, California between 1990 and 2000. Such research designs provide opportunities to describe, define, and analyze little understood phenomena such as central office-community partnerships over time (Merton, 1987; Yin, 1989). I drew primarily on interviews, sustained observations, and record data collected between 1998 and 2000 as part of a broader case study of education policy implementation in Oakland during the 1990s (Honig, 2001, 2003).

Site Selection

Oakland, California provided a strategic opportunity for this inquiry. Findings from strategic cases are not generalizable to all partnerships but may generate insights and hypotheses that can inform theory about such partnerships (Hartley, 1994; Merton, 1987) and reveal patterns with such little deviation on a small scale that they could reasonably represent populations (Phillips & Burbules, 2000). Among Oakland's qualifications as a strategic research site, Oakland had a long-standing reputation as the home of resource-rich community organizations—a reputation acknowledged in various publications and confirmed by initial interviews for this study (e.g., McCorry, 1978). Central office administrators reported that they had many years of experience working with various organizations both within the central office and in their previous positions as school principals and community organizers. These conditions suggested that community agency directors and central office administrators would have access to professional scripts that reinforced inter-organizational partnerships regardless of resource demands. This track record also suggested that the community and central office partners likely had the wherewithal to weather a variety of conflicts over time.

Data Sources and Collection

I triangulated three types of data: interviews, observations, and documents. I interviewed 9 central office administrators and 10 community organization representatives who participated in various partnerships between 1990 and 2000. Community organization representatives were directors/staff of neighborhood-based and county health and human services organizations, non-profit youth development agencies, and a citywide non-profit research and advocacy organization. Interview questions focused on individuals' day-to-day work, as well as their perceptions of the forms, functions, and factors affecting central office-community partnerships over time. In addition, I drew on other data from interviews with city council members, school board members, and city and county public agency staff that promised to inform my research questions. Each interview lasted between 60 and 150 minutes and I audio-taped and transcribed most interviews. In all, I analyzed 42 transcripts from interviews with 33 respondents. I also spent countless hours in informal conversations with these respondents about Oakland schools and district central office-community partnerships (Patton, 1990).

Between 1998 and 2000 I directly observed 72.5 hours of meetings between central office administrators and community organization representatives convened to help with implementation of publicly and privately funded initiatives to promote school-community collaboration (reported in the sections on collaboration and control by coercion below). During meeting observations I wrote almost verbatim transcriptions of conversations to capture partnership functions and constraining/enabling factors. I accounted for meetings that predated the start of my data collection through an analysis of meeting minutes from the prior period. These documents covered 39 additional hours of meetings.

I reviewed other documents including newspaper articles and policy reports. I used these documents to better understand education in Oakland especially during the period that predated the start of my data collection.

Data Analysis

I used NUD*IST software to code the interview and observation transcripts and record data. I coded data in several phases. First, analysis proceeded using simple categories suggested by my research questions and theoretical frameworks that required little interpretation: central office activities; community organization activities; joint central office-community activities; central office resources; community organization resources; and constraining/enabling factors related to those activities. In the second stage of coding, I examined data within the activities and resources categories and developed a new set of codes inductively and through constant comparison that indicated the types of specific resources provided through the partnerships: services to schools and fiscal, knowledge-based, and social capital (Miles & Huberman, 1994). I noticed that the provision of these resources varied over time. In my third phase of coding I examined all data with codes corresponding with approximate dates of these variations in resource provisions. I cross referenced these periods with the constraining/enabling conditions to develop a profile of each period in terms of partnership form, functions, and conditions. I tried to fit these patterns to concepts in the literature—"control," "contracts," "collaboration," and "isomorphism"—but found little evidence of isomorphism and forms of control that did not involve contracts. In my final analysis I used the following terms for each partnership period: control by contracts, collaboration, and control by coercion.

FINDINGS

I found that central office-community partnerships took three distinct forms over the 1990s and that functions varied across each of these forms. Resource dependence theory predicted the rationale for these forms as reported by respondents themselves: resource needs and efficiency concerns. However, the new institutionalism offered complementary and sometimes more complete explanations related to taken-for-granted models of central office-community relationships, community organizations' participation in education, and central office administrators' professional practice. I present these findings below in three sections corresponding with these three distinct forms and their attendant functions and constraining/enabling factors.

The first form, control by contracts, featured the district central office entering into formal contracts with neighborhood-based health and human services organizations for the provision of services to school-age children and their families at or near school sites. In these relationships, district central office administrators set and monitored contract terms and the community organizations provided services to schools. Central office administrators met somewhat regularly with heads of county health and human services agencies during this period but these meetings primarily focused on the service contracts. The second form, collaboration, was evident in the mid-1990s. During this period, district central office administrators joined three formal membership organizations that included community organization directors and staff as primary members to support the implementation of school-community partnerships. During implementation, these membership organizations or collaboratives increased the availability of particular resources vital to implementation but unavailable to central office administrators operating alone. At the end of the 1990s, a third form, control by coercion, began to emerge. In this period, the central office did not reinstate contracts but controlled the terms of their relationships with community organizations by withdrawing their own participation in the collaborations of the previous period, by encouraging community organizations to pursue certain avenues, and by taking on many of the functions previously performed by the community organizations.

Control by Contracts

From approximately 1990 through 1992, the district central office primarily had contractual relationships with six neighborhood-based services organizations for the provision of health and human services at fourteen school sites. During this period, these agencies served 572 students and 314 parents—a total that central office administrators regarded as significant particularly given the labor-intensiveness of the service delivery involved.

Also during this period, the Oakland Resources Group[2], a citywide policy research and advocacy organization, convened the superintendent and directors of public county health and human services agencies. One representative from the group of six contractors also participated. Conversations mainly focused on analyzing the number of school-age children utilizing county services and the deployment of service providers to school sites and improving the contracting process. A central office administrator who oversaw this initiative for the central office emphasized that the thrust of the central office-community partnerships was contracted social work case management services and that the central office was the primary driver of this effort:

> So . . . we had social work case managers in all those schools . . . I found 14 schools in the district with the biggest need. And that's where we focused our attention. And the social work case management was the first thrust, first program that we funded.

When asked why district central office-community partnerships took this form and function, respondents typically offered two explanations consistent with concepts from resource dependence theory: the superintendent's beliefs that services provided by community organizations could help improve students' school performance and the availability of data that supported the efficiency and effectiveness of closer working relationships between the district and neighborhood-based services organizations in particular. First, Oakland hired a new superintendent in 1990 whose priorities included a so-called "life circumstances" agenda that emphasized addressing non-academic barriers to students' school success. One central office administrator charged with helping to define and implement this agenda explained that social work case management services emerged as a focal point of this agenda:

> I was brought in by the . . . superintendent . . . to construct a program that dealt with the life circumstances of students and families . . . that prevent students from learning. And he was, I think, very forward looking in that regard. He wasn't quite sure what it all meant, but he just knew that he wanted to. One of the points of his five-year plan was to put together a program that would help students, students and families in need. Whatever their problem was. For the school district to play a central role in addressing the needs and so I . . . did a lot of surveys and research and to make a long story short, my office . . . launched several initiatives including social work case management programs on school sites. The first time they've ever been in Oakland. Where social work case management was actually ON school sites and services provided by non-profit community-based organizations.

Second, many respondents also highlighted a growing awareness that closer working relationships between schools and other youth services organizations could improve the efficiency and effectiveness of each. The Two central office administrators from the early 1990s recalled that a statewide budget crisis prompted a search for strategies to meet their goals. According to one of these respondents:

> The impetus at that early stage was budgetary cutbacks, and some of us began to talk about-we just knew that we were servicing a lot of the same kids and families and yet we haven't worked together. So that was the impetus.

Several respondents highlighted Oakland Resources Group's (ORG's) key role in developing evidence about the efficiency and effectiveness of new relationships between the district (both the central office and schools) and community organizations. ORG formed in the late 1980s, according to its mission statement, to serve as a "policy and advocacy organization" to improve the quality of life of Oakland's low-income children and families. In one of its first citywide campaigns, ORG convened a commission that conducted interviews and focus groups with hundreds of community residents. Primary recommendations from this report included greater community involvement in identifying barriers to student achievement and developing solutions to those challenges. Also during this period, ORG received a grant from a private foundation to work with public county and city agencies and the school district central office to examine the delivery of health and human services to school-age children. Their high profile report revealed that almost two-thirds of all students in focal low-income schools used public services and that one-third of all students in those schools received services from at least two different services programs. Most respondents who recalled this period reported that this survey helped convince many educational leaders to rethink roles between the central office and publicly/privately funded community-based services organizations and that the ORG director at that time was a particularly compelling partnership advocate. One central office administrator recalled:

> And they also did all the data, the research and analysis and then [the ORG director] walked in and sat down with school district officials. She told them more about their schools than they knew. She had all the statistics. She had all the charts.

The superintendent's priorities and a wave of empirical evidence about the potential value of new inter-organizational partnerships suggested a rationale for central office-community partnerships, highlighted by respondents, which reflected concepts from resource dependence theory. Specifically, community organizations had resources that promised to help the central office improve its performance. Resource dependence theory posits that in such cases, power to control contract terms typically rests in the hands of the contractor when resources are in short supply or exclusively controlled by a limited number of organizations. However, in this case, the central office determined the scope of the contracts which suggests an alternative power dynamic—one in which the community organizations were dependent on contracts with the central office to provide their services and otherwise realize their own production goals.

Respondents' comments also suggest strong influences by institutional factors that led central office administrators and other respondents to take for granted that central office-community relationships would be controlled by the central office and that contracts would underlie them. For example, one central office administrator indicated that at that time, advocates for stronger ties between educational and other youth serving organizations such as two prominent private foundation program officers typically promoted social work case management in particular. Social work case management services linked to schools were, according to one central office administrator, "the logical 'in' thing at that time"—a taken-for-granted form of community partnerships—and contracts were the central office's primarily mechanism for entering into such agreements with non-school organizations. In the words of another central office administrator, "These were non profit-employees. How we handled programs like that was we put out an RFP [Request for Proposals] to non-profit agencies and they provided the services." RFPs, typically indicated terms by which services should be provided which from the outset established the central office as the author of contract terms.

Another central office administrator reflected that the idea that community organizations would participate in educational improvement strategies on any terms was "radical enough" at the time and that he and his colleagues spent the majority of their time selling the idea of community organizations' participation rather than debating how the central office and community organizations might work together. As he put it, "I got swatted around pretty quick in the first year [and remember thinking] just really, 'Wow this is going to be a lot harder than I thought!'" In this context, partnerships with community organizations that took forms other than contracts for specific services determined by the central office in this respondent's words, were "not on the table," "a long way down the road," and otherwise considered inappropriate or not possible.

These contracts also reflected traditional notions regarding who decides about educational improvement. Many respondents recalled that the group convened by ORG was dominated by public services agencies in ways that left little room for input from other kinds of community organizations and that within that group the superintendent set the agenda. As one central office administrator reflected:

We had all the big boys and girls at the table, the ones who could [snaps fingers] make a decision. . . . We literally had the [public agency] power brokers at the table who said, I can do that. And you knew they could. . . . [The meetings were formally governed by consensus, but] when superintendent Mesa was at the table—he was initially—and because so much of the effort was— for good or bad—school-centered, people tended to lean more to his word . . . listen more to him and what he thought . . . .

Collaboration

In the mid-1990s the primary form of central office-community relationships changed from contracts to collaboration. As with the previous period, both resource dependence theory and the new institutionalism offer important explanations for this development. Consistent with resource dependence theory, respondents highlighted the need for fiscal resources as a primary prompt for this shift. Other evidence supported concepts from the new institutionalism that emphasized such factors as new staff in the central office that brought with them professional scripts that supported collaborative not contractual relationships.

To elaborate, in the mid 1990s the central office, ORG, neighborhood-based services organizations and others established three formal organizations with central office administrators and community organization directors as primary members: the Interagency Services Team, the Youth Development Taskforce, and the Leadership Council.[3]

- Interagency Services Team. This organization formed out of the largely public interagency partnership described above. In the first year, high ranking central office administrators—an assistant superintendent and division director—represented the central office on the Team. Subsequently, these central office administrators were replaced by their hierarchical subordinates—three program directors from a central office division that handled student services such as safety and drug programs, school nurses, and school-linked services. By 1993, community organizations represented on the Interagency Service Team included an ORG staff person who also served as facilitator and representatives from multiple community organizations including directors of new school-linked family resource centers and staff people from county health, dental, and social services. This group met monthly for the better part of the 1990s.
- Youth Development Taskforce. This organization formed in 1997 and from the outset resembled the second iteration of the Interagency Services Team in terms of its membership: one program director from the central office's student services division, two directors from ORG (who also served as Taskforce staff), six directors/staff of youth development agencies in the process of launching partnerships at Oakland middle schools, various staff from county health and social

services agencies, and a representatives from a county-level inter-agency partnership. This group met at least weekly for two hours until the end of the 1990s.

- Leadership Council. This organization formed shortly after the Youth Development Taskforce and included what many respondents referred to as a first-ever forum for executives of Oakland's major youth-serving agencies. The district superintendent and two school board members represented the school district. Community organization members included the heads of county health and human services agencies, supervisors from the county board, city council members, and directors of several prominent neighborhood-based services organizations. This group met monthly. The Leadership Council was managed by its own full-time staff that operated as a distinct citywide non-profit organization.

Respondents referred to these new organizations as collaboratives. As one central office administrator commented:

> So what has happened is that the school district is still a key player but there are many other players now and many other funding streams. . . . And where we are now is that . . . 'school' is in there but it's not very prominent. Its collaboration . . . So we've really progressed a long way, there's a lot more players, key players in this.

This use of the term "collaboration" is consistent with broader literature that distinguishes a collaboration from other forms of partnerships in that it involves shared goals and joint work across multiple parties (Crowson & Boyd, 1993; Marsh, 2002). Formal statements regarding the purposes of these collaborations (from interviews and documents) confirmed that the joint work during this period involved support for the implementation of school-community partnerships. Multiple data sources suggested that in practice over time these collaboratives to varying degrees served the more specific functions of providing fiscal, knowledge-based, and social capital important to the central offices' support of school-community partnerships but typically unavailable to the district central office.

Fiscal Capital

When asked to explain the functions of the collaboratives and the rationale for their formation, respondents invariably highlighted that both collaboratives made Oakland eligible for funding to seed and support collaborations between schools and community organizations—typically called school-community partnership sites in Oakland—that the central office and community organizations would not have been able to access on their own. Specifically, in the mid 1990s, the federal Health Care Finance Administration in partnership with the State of California launched a program to reimburse school districts for costs associated with certain school-based interventions. The State of California required that participating districts form an interagency collaborative to oversee the disbursement of revenue generated by the program and strongly encouraged the collaborative to use the funding to support school-community partnership sites.[4] The district superintendent designated the individuals already convened by the Oakland Resources Group to serve this purpose. Participants in this group, thereafter named the Interagency Services Team, reported in interviews and at meetings that they subsequently expanded their membership to include directors of new school-community partnership sites—typically staff of neighborhood-based organizations such as school-linked family resource centers.

The central office administrator who tracked the budget for the Interagency Services Team reported when interviewed that this collaborative's annual budget ranged between $100,000 and $150,000. Meeting observations revealed that during at least one year the collaborative oversaw a budget of approximately $300,000. Over the course of the 1990s, the Interagency Services Team used this funding for a variety of purposes related to implementation of school-community partnerships including direct grants to sites for general support, hiring an evaluator to document implementation processes and impacts at Oakland's flagship site, and supporting a consultant to coach site implementation and document lessons learned about site implementation.

Directors of ORG convened the Youth Development Taskforce as part of the application process for a national foundation grant to support the implementation of school-community sites. As the initial and founding community organization in this partnership, ORG directors and staff wrote the grant application and negotiated with the national foundation. In the mid-1990s, the national foundation awarded a planning grant to ORG on behalf of Oakland and subsequently committed approximately $1 million for initial efforts to implement school-community sites at Oakland's 15 middle schools over 3 to 5 years. Importantly, the total dollar amount that this grant promised to generate far exceeded the sum total of the foundation's contribution because as part of the grant agreement, public agencies such as the school district central office committed to redirect other funds to support implementation over the long term. Between 1997 and 2000, central office administrators reported that the central office contributed over $1 million for site implementation from revenue generated from a local parcel tax.

In their first year, the Youth Development Taskforce funded three school-community sites through a competitive grant process. Site directors reported that these discretionary funds were essential to all aspects of their early implementation including helping them to meet their payroll, to support site coordinators, to purchase services otherwise unavailable in their neighborhoods, to develop a management information system, to acquire and renovate facilities, and to provide stipends to parents to participate in site advisory meetings.

In 1997, the Leadership Council formed in response to another national foundation initiative that aimed to produce demonstrable improvements in the health and safety of school-age children by transforming central district, city, and county bureaucracies. The national foundation required that an inter-organizational executive-level board in each of the five participating cities develop a plan to meet the initiative's goals. Under the strong direction of its staff director—who previously had served as director of ORG and as a primary architect of Oakland's plans for the Youth Development Taskforce—the Leadership Council developed a longitudinal plan to reorient the participating public bureaucracies to support the school-community sites seeded by the Youth Development Taskforce. The national foundation conditionally accepted this plan and provided initial funding to the Leadership Council. Unlike the other collaboratives, the Leadership Council did not make grants directly to school-community sites but used their initial funding primarily for staff activities which included working directly with emerging school-community sites on implementation issues and researching which specific bureaucratic reforms might enable their implementation.

Knowledge-Based Capital

Through all three collaboratives, central office administrators accessed new knowledge fundamental to their support of site implementation. While respondents were not likely to report the central office's need for knowledge-based capital as an impetus for founding the collaboratives, their indirect comments and other data sources suggested this resource gap as a primary driver.

Specifically, the design of Oakland's efforts to promote school-community collaboration called for schools and community organizations to work together to make their own decisions about which goals and strategies they would pursue and for central office administrators to help sites to make and implement those decisions. Accordingly, implementation placed demands on central office administrators to develop site knowledge—familiarity with sites' goals, strategies, and experiences. However, central office administrators typically reported limited time for the level of regular engagement with sites they saw as necessary to continually build their site knowledge.

The meetings of the two collaboratives convened by ORG helped central office administrators to build their site knowledge by providing regular opportunities for central office administrators to consult with directors and staff of community organizations who participated directly in the implementation of school-community sites—often a community partner at that level or a site coach. Some central office administrators commented and observations confirmed the importance of these meetings to their site knowledge. "I'll find out about [sites' budgets] on Thursday [at the Youth Development Team meeting] one central office administrator explained when asked how she kept abreast of sites' progress with fund raising.

Interviews and meeting minutes revealed that through collaborative meetings central office administrators had opportunities to learn about such site implementation challenges as fund raising, establishing strong relationships between school and community agency staff, access to facilities, improving the quality of students' opportunities to learn before and after school, and the impacts of neighborhood poverty on site implementation. For example, reports from site representatives about their goals, strategies, and experiences appeared as part of 20 out of 23 documented Youth Development Team meetings in 1999 alone.

During meetings, Leadership Council staff played important knowledge-building roles. Two senior staff members of the Leadership Council participated on the Youth Development Team where they heard frequent reports concerning site implementation. One staff member reported that he spent approximately 25 percent of his time each week at sites "troubleshooting, brainstorming, and learning sort of what they need, what various partners can do." Direct observations and reviews of meeting minutes revealed that these two senior staff members presented information about site implementation issues at almost every Leadership Council meeting through 2000. By 2000, one staff member worked directly with the central office director of student services to survey all Oakland middle schools about their community partnerships to help inform Leadership Council planning.

The collaboratives, especially the community organization representatives who served as staff also increased site knowledge available to central office administrators by serving as primary documenters and disseminators of information about site implementation. For example the Interagency Services Team hired a retired central office administrator to research and document lessons learned about site implementation. This collaborative also kept and disseminated meeting minutes which often included summaries of site implementation accomplishments and barriers.

Social Capital

As with knowledge-based capital, respondents typically did not report central office gaps in social capital—relationships and trust between central offices and sites—as primary drivers of collaboration. However, other data suggested that two of the collaboratives—the Interagency Services Team and the Youth Development Taskforce—served this essential function.[5] To elaborate, respondents frequently pointed to weak social capital between the central office and schools/school-community sites as significant curbs on central office administrators increasing their knowledge of sites' goals, strategies, and experiences essential to the central office's support for implementation as noted above. Sources of weak social capital highlighted by respondents included mistrust that had developed after years of well-publicized incidents of mismanagement and broken promises (both alleged and substantiated) as well as budget crises, changed superintendents (four between 1990 and 2000), and threats of state take over of the district central office that increased the perceived instability and inefficiency of the central office (Coburn & Riley, 2000; Fiscal Crisis and Management Assistance Team, 2000; Gewertz, 2000). Several respondents particularly those participating in the Interagency Services Team emphasized that frequent central office transfers of school principals and competing demands on central office administrators' time challenged the continuity of central office-site relationships. As one central office administrator admitted, "Central office is going to have to find out and develop a strategy that is going to connect with [school-community sites]... but that takes the threat of it [that the central office will impede site implementation] away and that is hard."

Interviews and observations suggested that the Interagency Services Team and Youth Development Taskforce helped strengthen the central office's social capital vis-à-vis school-community partnership sites. For example, when asked about their willingness to share their experiences at collaborative meetings versus directly with central office administrators, site directors reported strong interest in sharing information at collaborative meetings compared to contacting the central office. Many elaborated that because others were present at the collaborative meetings, the collaboratives created, in their words, a sort of "shared accountability" or "watchdog effect" that increased their sense of trust and that the central office administrators would follow through. According to one site director:

> When the school district [central office] is obligated to provide services, who makes sure that happens? The broader policy issue is how do we take heat off sites so you don't have to spend relationship capital to get things resolved that should not require negotiations . . . . It's [been a role for] the [Youth Development Task Force].

One ORG director corroborated this essential role for the Interagency Services Team and Youth Development Taskforce which he and his staff convened when he commented, "We need to be the conscience of the process and the constant face in the face of change."

The Interagency Services Team and Youth Development Taskforce also seemed to strengthen central office-site relationships by coordinating the provision of implementation supports from sources other than the central office. Specifically, each collaborative used its funding to hire or dedicate staff that increased the sheer amount of resources available to sites and otherwise took pressure off the central office to meet all site demands.

An explanation for the shift from contracts to collaboration consistent with resource dependence theory would highlight that changing demands on the central office to access non-traditional resources to meet particular educational objectives upped the ante on the central office to enter into agreements with other organizations that could enhance those resources. Likewise the power of community organizations would have increased thanks to the new resources that they helped the central office access. However, resource dependence theory also suggests that when faced with new resource demands, the central office would have expanded or elaborated its contracts with community organizations to meet these demands—a prediction not substantiated by the Oakland case in which voluntary membership in collaboratives rather than contracts came to undergird district central office-community partnerships. The central office actually curtailed its program of direct contracting for school-based social work case management services and left it up to individual schools to determine whether and how to access these services.

The new institutionalism calls attention to two institutional shifts that seemed to drive the transition from contracts to collaboration: community organizations' increasing legitimacy as participants in educational improvement and new central office staff with professional scripts that supported collaboration. First, data suggested that the legitimacy of community organizations as participants in educational improvement strategies had gained steam and increasingly districts were rewarded for encouraging participation by community organizations. As one central office administrator reflected:

> The partnerships that we have . . . allowed the district to say, yeah, look at this. This is what we are doing. These are the people we are bringing to the table. We kind of leveraged that. We worked on it, though. If you go back to, for me, go back to 1990–91, we can go down and show what is happening. . . . Both [another central office administrator] and I took advantage of that. I wouldn't say exploited it but we took advantage of that there were other partners out there that we could partner with to have outcomes that were win/win. Both for the district and for them. We were good at that. That's what I'm getting at.

One of these rewards was the opportunity to participate in various educational improvement programs that increasingly required collaborative oversight (Honig & Jehl, 2000). As one central office administrator reflected:

> Initially [in the previous period] just . . . I think one of the main thrusts initially was to get the county agencies somehow to site-base staff. We were kind of spending a lot of time, trying to figure out how to tackle this same client issue. . . . MOUs [Memoranda of Understanding, a form of public agency contract]. . . . And so it was a very slow process [of broadening our activities

and members]. After about a year we were moving and lo and behold heard about this thing [a state program to support school-community partnerships] . . . and when we read the first RFP, we were shocked; it was like we wrote it. It was exactly what we were doing; right what we were talking about doing. I actually made some initial strides so all of a sudden all of our attention [whistles, gestures] switched to [community collaboration].

The legitimacy of community organizations as participants in educational improvement also stemmed from mounting concerns that school systems as institutions did not have all the resources they needed to help students meet emerging national and state academic standards and that key roles for community organizations could not necessarily be fashioned in advance in contracts with administrators outside particular neighborhoods. For example, three members of the Interagency Services Team reflected in interviews and a ten-year history of the Interagency Services Team reported that previous community organization participation in education was largely "district-driven" and "school-centered." By this they meant that the school district central office convened community organizations to address the school district's priorities and that community organizations worked *for* the central office not *with* the central office or schools. Meeting minutes especially from early collaborative meetings suggested that members had grown concerned that a stronger voice for community organizations would improve the design and implementation of standards-based school improvement strategies.

Second and perhaps most significantly in the case of the Interagency Services Team and Youth Development Taskforce, new staff members in new central office positions came to represent the district central office in negotiations with community organizations and brought with them institutional scripts that favored collaborative not contractual relationships with community organizations to achieve educational improvement goals. For example, the two main central office representatives to the Interagency Services Team described themselves as "community organizers" with long-term experience with cross-sector collaboration. One previously had worked for a national non-profit family service provider while the other had organized grass-roots political campaigns. The central office representative to the Youth Development Taskforce reported that her primary formative professional experience included almost a decade of work developing a school in an inner city neighborhood on the east coast with strong ties to community organizations. The person hired as director of student services in the late 1990s too had been a long-standing community organizer. These central office administrators described themselves as central office "outsiders" and "movers and shakers" and clarified that they worked "outside the box." They reported that they had been hired specifically to bring non-traditional experience with community collaboration to the district central office. Interviews with assistant superintendents and program directors confirmed that they looked for these qualities in new staff assuming these roles, in institutional theory terms, to bring new professional scripts to bear on central office operations. Even the primary central office representative to the Leadership Council—the interim superintendent—had non-traditional central office experience. He had become interim superintendent after serving as an assistant city manager in Oakland and indicated that his formative professional experiences came when he served as an assistant city manager in an east coast county where he oversaw both education and health and human services (separate jurisdictions in California) and otherwise saw first hand the benefits of closer working relationships between educational and non-educational agencies. He recounted as among his past accomplishments his former county's participation in the national foundation initiative that funded the Leadership Council which he referred to as an important strategy for strengthening cross-sector supports for school-age children.

The creation of new central office positions to specialize in community relationships also marked a turning point in central office-community partnerships. One central office representative recalled that the new central office staff enabled collaboration in part because they served in new, non-traditional centrally office positions dedicated specifically to interactions with community organizations:

> The agency heads [on the precursor to the Interagency Services Team] were replaced in about a year and a half, two with kind of the program managers [assigned specifically to manage collaboration]. I remember we were a little dismayed and we were, seemingly, the interest was on the wane from the top and maybe that might be true, everything's cyclical, you know, you have a, somebody who's got as much on their plate as an agency head it's [snap] What can I do now? And if it isn't then let's move onto another issue or catastrophe or whatever, funding issue, but it was very necessary actually to have the program managers at the table because at that time when you're collaborating, implementing, they're the ones to have there. And it really worked well.

Another central office administrator agreed about this turning point:

> Everybody was enthusiastic [about the initial meetings] but after about a year an a half, pretty soon the big wigs weren't showing up but they sent the middle managers which, quite frankly, now things moved faster when the middle managers came to the table than the bigwigs.

Control by Coercion

By 1999, Oakland entered a third period of central office-community partnerships. The start of this period[6] was marked by the following developments: the Interagency Services Team and Youth Development Taskforce discontinued their meetings and the Leadership Council shifted its focus from school-community partnerships to interventions related to juvenile justice involving primarily public agencies; the district central office hired five new central office employees to provide coaching to school-community sites rather than relying on contractual or collaborative agreements with community organizations for this purpose; and ORG shifted its focus from central office partnerships to direct support for site implementation. I refer to this period as "control by coercion" to capture a predominant dynamic between the district central office and community organizations: central office decisions dictated the terms of the partnerships and strongly influenced decisions by individual community organizations about their participation in school reform.

Specifically, in 1999, the interim superintendent of the central office met with the Interagency Services Team and requested that the collaborative commit 80 percent of its revenue (totaling approximately $300,000 at that time) to cover basic district central office costs. The interim superintendent explained at two Team meetings and in an interview that a significant budget shortfall and a comprehensive state audit had increased state and county pressure on the district central office to curb spending and raise new revenue. The interim superintendent argued that district employees such as school health nurses generated most of the revenue disbursed by the Interagency Services Team; the collaborative's one-time commitment of funds would help the district continue to provide these services and invest in staff that could in turn generate more revenue over the long term. After significant debate and a change in superintendent who also requested the 80 percent commitment, the Interagency Services Team acquiesced to the superintendent's request.

Shortly thereafter, the director of student services, herself a community organizer turned central office administrator, hired five consultants to work as central office staff and coach site implementation—roles traditionally filled by the central office's community partners. Central office administrators assigned to the Interagency Services Team began to play lesser roles in both the Team and other activities related to the implementation of school-community sites. The ORG staff person who convened the Team took a position with another organization after 10 years at ORG and the Team suspended its meetings. During their last meetings, Team members voted to use their remaining funds to hire a consultant who formed a learning network—involving meetings with directors of school-community partnership sites—to help with implementation. This consultant worked out of the ORG office and eventually became an ORG employee. He reported that the new central office consultants occasionally attended these network meetings but that there was no longer a formal partnership between the central office and community organizations.

In 1999, participants in the Youth Development Taskforce voted to reinvent the Taskforce—to replace the Taskforce with two separate working groups, one focused on fiscal sustainability of sites and the other focused on aligning central office, city, and county policy to support sites. As part of the reinvention plan, both groups would establish formal ties to the Leadership Council to enable their work. Shortly thereafter, the interim superintendent transferred the central office representative to a principalship of a high school citing budget cuts and a principal shortage as primary drivers of that decision. Responsibility for central office participation on the Youth Development Taskforce fell to another central office administrator who also oversaw truancy centers, after-school programs, mentoring, parent involvement, and other programs. In an interview, this central office administrator reported significant constraints on his time available for such meetings and that his attendance was sporadic at best:

> Zero. Well, actually maybe five percent. . . . That was about as deep as I was able to get into it last week even though I needed to get deeper. . . . The thing is I am going to meetings [for my other responsibilities]. They might start at 7:30 (a.m.). . . . The next one is at 9:00. The next one is at 11:00. Then there is one at 1:30, one at 3:00 and then when do I get to come in here [to the office]? Maybe at 4:15 I get to come in here and then you have voice mail messages and it takes me 30 minutes to listen to that and then I have got to return those phone calls and that doesn't give me a chance to get to the work.

During this period the interim superintendent himself attended several Taskforce meetings at which he indicated that the central office remained committed to the work in which the Taskforce had been engaged—the implementation of school-community sites. For example, he said, "If I have [school] feeder systems that don't have a [school-community partnership site] then I am doing a disservice to those communities. So the question for me is how to get all systems that need it a [site]." However, he went on to highlight two major barriers to his efforts: limited school capacity for implementing community partnerships and equity concerns. Regarding the latter, the interim superintendent indicated that other community organizations not represented on the Youth Development Taskforce also demanded his support and that investing too much time and resource in the Youth Development Taskforce would be irresponsible. As he explained:

> [School] is a strong collaborative but right now there isn't a square inch of ground to do anything in. In [another school] we have made conscious strategies to make space available . . . but what about other schools in the feeder

system? Do we have a strategy? Is there a movement? How do all the other component parts fit in the movement? I'd like to take it back and chew on it [how the central office will support the Taskforce] . . . . My intent is to put my resources in [school-community partnerships] by hook or by crook. So I think there will be more resources in the pot. . . . I don't have enough information to make a decision right now.

At this meeting the interim superintendent went on to recommend that the collaborative not commit to fund additional sites until members developed a strategy for funding sites district-wide; he indicated that the central office would contribute funding pending the production of an agreeable plan:

So for all of these reasons I find zero support within the district for [site] expansion on philosophical or financial terms until we deal with some of the financial and organizational issues. As part of the discussion we are having here we haven't nailed down the whole issue of goals of the district and goals of [the collaborative] and where there is commonality in those and how they will complement one another. Until that process is complete, the district's position is to delay further [site] implementation until we have answers in all the above areas.

The interim superintendent specified that in his opinion ORG as the fiscal agent for the foundation grant had the right and the responsibility to decide how to proceed with supporting site implementation:

I thought we decided at the last meeting that [ORG] would make the decision about this. We [the central office] are here to provide information. I brought information about space [available on school campuses for launching sites]. That I can't take money away from existing sites to give new sites. And that there are long-term issues. All I came to do is present that information. It's your [ORG's] decision. I never thought I had a role in that decision. Last time I said I didn't even know why we are meeting but you all said you have to meet to get more information.

Subsequently, ORG directors reported to their national funder that they would not support plans to add the additional school-community sites that they had promised the funder in their original implementation plan. At a meeting of the new Youth Development Policy Team, ORG's director indicated that even though his decision jeopardized Oakland's funding from the national foundation, he had committed to make decisions based on the consensus of the collaborative and that consensus suggested freezing site expansion. The citywide non-profit directors charged with staffing the fiscal workgroup never convened its members and the policy team met for several months before ceasing its meetings. ORG entered into renegotiations with the national foundation about the scope if its work.

The Leadership Council continued to negotiate its focus on school-community partnership sites with its national funder. A review of meeting minutes, direct observations, and conversations with staff suggested that such negotiations consumed the better part of a year, after which time the Council voted to stay in tact but to suspend its commitment to school-community sites in favor of a discrete intervention related to juvenile justice. The interim superintendent, the main central office representative on this group, did not receive school board support for his appointment to the superintendency and returned to his post as assistant city manager. The new superintendent attended the partnership meetings though focused most of his initial year as superintendent to instituting a new reading curriculum and launching a cohort of new small autonomous schools.

In sum, the collaborative partnerships of the previous period gave way to central office-community organization dynamics in which the central office controlled the terms of the partnerships and strongly influenced decisions of community organizations, not by dictating contract terms but by example and persuasion—pressures I call, simply, coercion. In particular, members of the Interagency Services Team operated as though they had little choice but to surrender 80 percent of their funding. Events related to the Youth Development Taskforce suggested that the viability of its plans to support school-community sites depended on the central office's decisions regarding its own participation; central office decisions in this context became decisions of the collaborative.

Several respondents offered political explanations for the shift from collaboration to coercive control. For example, one long-time central office administrator commented:

> What happens is that they [central office administrators] get pulled, get siphoned off, when they do other projects and the only thing that's fair to say is that apparently the [school-community partnership] movement is not that important in the overall scheme of things.

Resource dependence theory offers one alternative explanation: central office administrators came to perceive that the central office itself possessed all the resources necessary for site support and that contractual, collaborative or other relationships with community organizations were no longer necessary. In support of this interpretation, central office administrators and other respondents tended to highlight resource needs as primary drivers of the previous period's collaborations—especially funding. Their discontinued participation in the collaboratives corresponded with the central office's acquisition of the Interagency Service Team's funding and limitations on available funding from the Youth Development Taskforce. Also supporting this interpretation, the central office hired community leaders as staff; accordingly central office administrators may have perceived that they no longer needed resources from community organizations because those resources were now on staff.

Other data suggest that this shift in central office-community partnerships may be explained by institutional pressures that reinforced traditional models of central office control over the terms of their partnerships. Central office administrators themselves reported significant external pressures at the end of the 1990s to demonstrate accountability for educational improvement and that predominant accountability models favored single-sector chains of command not collaboration. The following exchange between the chair and member of a special mayor's education commission captures this tension:

> CHAIR: (Considering different educational agendas the commission might recommend that the mayor pursue): See reading is real clear.
>
> COMMISSIONER: [School-community partnerships] is also a possible, clear strategy.
>
> CHAIR: No, voters can't understand them.

Even Oakland's Mayor Jerry Brown, nationally renowned for his advocacy of community involvement in government, lobbied for traditional accountability measures that did not necessarily accommodate community collaboration. As Brown explained to the *Education Week* (Gewertz, 2000):

> I don't accept the word comprehensive [as an organizing idea for educational improvement]. That means you have planners, they write all this stuff up, and nothing happens. [General] Patton didn't have a comprehensive plan. . . . He had a strategy and it was highly focused. Comprehensive can just be the rationale for never achieving . . . . You've got to make stuff happen.

School board members who had previously championed partnerships with community agencies reported that such partnerships were not, in the words of one board member, "responsible government." This board member elaborated: "As long as Oakland is below the national average, we as a board are going to put teachers and textbooks first."

Somewhat ironically, the new central office administrators who in the short term enabled central office-community collaboration, overtime, seemed to impede it by themselves supporting traditional control models between the district central office and others. These new central office employees reported and demonstrated that they brought non-traditional professional scripts to their central office roles, as noted above, but as new central office employees, they also had tenuous job security in civil service systems based on seniority. Comments from these central office administrators suggested that rather than challenging institutional pressures, they acquiesced to them. One former community leader turned county agency representative best captured this shift in perspective of community leaders turned central office staff when he said:

> Its [collaboration is] very difficult when we [in public agencies] have to balance our budget and we have to make all the widgets fall into place, the reporting that's required from the categorical funding. We have to demonstrate all these things to get the money. And those things are based on traditional sort of funding . . . sort of cycles.

One central office administrator who tried to buck these trends and sustain her own participation in the collaboratives reported that she could take such risks because she did not fear losing her job. She said, "I don't care what he [the interim superintendent] says. I don't need this job. I can go always go back [to my school]." Other comments indicated that these central office administrators aimed to fit collaboration into traditional central office accountability systems but that they often did not have the data such accountability systems required. As one central office administrator recalled:

> All we had to do was a little basic arithmetic. . . . Is the county willing [to provide additional site resources]? Not unless we could really prove . . . that it was to their benefit. . . . I don't think that kind of basic work [documentation of site experiences, needs and accomplishments] was ever really accomplished to prove the case.

These data suggest that the very conditions that enabled collaboration in the previous period, over time, may have constrained it.

SUMMARY AND IMPLICATIONS

This article aimed to introduce district central office-community partnerships as a topic for educational research by examining their forms, functions, and enabling/constraining factors in one urban district where conditions boded well for their longevity. Findings demonstrate that community organizations provided resources important to implementing educational improvement strategies, particularly those involving school-community partnerships, and that district central offices can sustain relationships with community agencies over time—at least ten years in the Oakland case. Findings reveal that "central office-community partnerships" can take multiple forms and perform various functions in the same location over time. The Oakland experience suggested that partnerships may fluctuate between relationships in which central office administrators direct or otherwise constrain community organizations' participation (control by contracts and control by coercion) and relationships in which central office administrators and community organization directors and staff work together to set and implement shared goals and strategies (collaboration).

These findings challenge concepts from resource dependence theory, which posit that contracts typically underlie inter-organizational relationships, and point to the importance of both resource dependence theory and the new institutionalism in sociology as important guides for understanding partnership forms, functions, and enabling/constraining factors. In particular, resource dependence theory predicted the rationales respondents were likely to provide for their pursuit of relationships with community organizations but not why the partnerships took particular forms in practice. The new institutionalism in sociology highlighted the taken-for-granted assumptions and professional scripts that seemed to drive how the central office actually related to community organizations.

This analysis has several implications for the research and practice of educational administration. First, this study throws into relief that organizational context matters to educational administrators' participation in inter-organizational partnerships. The partnership patterns revealed here have not been uncovered in studies of partnerships involving educational administrators at state or school levels or among organizations in non-educational sectors. These findings raise a caution about the generalizability of findings about inter-organizational partnerships across government levels.

Second, these findings highlight the importance of professional scripts to central office decisions about how to engage community organizations and that changing central office-community relationships may depend on script shifts. Hiring non-traditional staff may provide one strategy for such shifts at least in the short term. However, in employment systems that offer weak job security for non-traditional employees, the viability of this strategy may be short-lived.

Third, this analysis suggested the importance of using both resource dependence theory and the new institutionalism in sociology as conceptual frameworks for analyzing inter-organizational partnerships. These two theories generally fall within the domains of separate disciplines—with economists and political scientists weighing in on resource dependence theory and sociologists elaborating the branch of the new institutionalism presented here. More cross-disciplinary approaches to partnership studies may help advance the practice of such partnerships and further inform the development of theoretical concepts in each area.

Fourth, this combined theoretical framework highlighted how different data sources lead to divergent conclusions about the factors that influence inter-organizational partnerships. As noted above, respondents' reports tended to align with resource dependence theory's claims that efficiency concerns drive inter-organizational relationships while the new institutionalism in sociology explained other partnership dimensions. Accordingly, these findings reinforce the importance of using multiple data sources in studies of inter-organizational relationships.

This research also raises several questions for future research and practice. First, do other central office-community partnerships follow a similar trajectory or are other patterns apparent? Many studies of inter-organizational partnerships such as those cited above consider partnerships at fixed points in time and do not reveal how such partnerships develop, accumulate experience, evolve, and change. Accordingly, this research tends not to reveal broader institutional patterns that may influence partnerships as they wax and wane and may prematurely conclude that a partnership has ended when it is in the process of taking on a new form. More longitudinal studies of inter-organizational collaboration at various governmental levels may help advance knowledge in this regard.

Second, what forms do central office-community partnerships take when practitioners use research-based guides to inform partnership forms and functions? As noted above, various institutional pressures seemed to lead central office administrators and their community partners to take for granted that partnerships would assume particular forms. Bringing such patterns to the foreground for practitioners may create new conditions for implementation and reveal new patterns that can deepen knowledge about how inter-organizational partnerships play out in practice.

Under what conditions do district central office-community partnerships result in isomorphism—one organization taking on the form and function of another? The new institutionalism in sociology predicted that less legitimate organizations would come to resemble more legitimate organizations in the central office-community partnerships over time. Data from this study did not support this prediction perhaps because the data captured only ten years not the multiple decades typically considered in studies of isomorphism. In addition, the focus of this inquiry was on partnership forms and functions and decisions of the central office and community organizations related to the partnerships not attendant changes in the partner organizations. Nonetheless, the central office's hiring of community members as staff suggested that perhaps over a longer period of time I would have discovered that interactions between central offices and community organizations influenced the practices of each in ways consistent with isomorphic change. Longitudinal studies in other districts might reveal this trend.

In sum, this research may serve as a theoretical and empirical departure for future research and practice of inter-organizational relationships involving district central offices. In the process, it aims to help both researchers and practitioners identify and make sense of the range of factors that constrain or enable such partnerships and otherwise realize the promise of central office-community partnerships to strengthen students' opportunities to learn.

Acknowledgments: The author thanks Julie A. Marsh for the encouragement to write this paper and Morva A. McDonald for helpful comments. A version of this paper was presented at the Annual Meeting of the American Educational Association, Chicago, IL, 2003.

NOTES

1.   Theories that promote the concepts I identify here go by various names, including resource dependence theory including power-dependency model, political economy model, and exchange theory and have many similarities with transaction cost economics (Scott, 2003).

2.   This is a pseudonym.

3.   These are pseudonyms.

4.   The Local Education Agency Medi-Cal Billing Option allowed school districts to recoup their share of the direct and administrative cost of medical services provided by certain school district personnel. Prior to the Billing Option, the state and district split these costs. These services included those mandated by law including school nurses, audiologists, and other specialists.

5.   Data from the Leadership Council did not support this finding.

6.   My data collection ended before a discernable end to this period in practice. Therefore, I refer to data in this section as pertaining to the early part of this period (Cznariawska, 1997).

REFERENCES

Aldrich, H. (1976). Resource dependence and interorganizational relations: Local employment services offices and social services sector organizations. *Administration and Society, 7*, 419–454.

Aldrich, H. E., & Pfeffer, J. (1976). Environments of organizations. *Annual Review of Sociology, 2*, 79–105.

Barley, S. R. (1996). Technicians in the workplace: Ethnographic evidence for bringing work into organization studies. *Administrative Science Quarterly, 41*(3), 404–441.

Cibulka, J. G., & Kritek, W. J. (Eds.). (1996). *Coordination among schools, families, and communities.* Albany, NY: State University of New York Press.

Coburn, K. G., & Riley, P. A. (2000). *Failing grade: Crisis and reform in the Oakland Unified School District.* San Francisco: Pacific Research Institute.

Crowson, R. L., & Boyd, W. L. (1993). Coordinated services for children: Designing arks for storms and seas unknown. *American Journal of Education, 101*(2), 140–179.

Cunningham, L. L., & Mitchell, B. (Eds.). (1990). *Educational leadership and changing contexts in families, communities, and schools. Eighty-ninth yearbook of the National Society for the Study of Education.* Chicago: The National Society for the Study of Education.

Cznariawska, B. (1997). *Narrating the organization.* Chicago: University of Chicago Press.

David and Lucile Packard Foundation (Ed.). (1992). *The future of children: School-linked services* (Vol. 2), Los Altos, CA: Author.

David, J. (1990). Restructuring in progress: Lessons from pioneering districts. In R. F. Elmore & Associates (Eds.), *Restructuring schools: The next generation of education reform* (pp. 209–250). San Francisco: Jossey-Bass.

DiMaggio, P. J. (1991). Constructing an organizational field as a professional project: U.S. art museums, 1920–1940. In P. J. DiMaggio (Ed.), *The new institutionalism in organizational analysis* (pp. 267–292). Chicago: University of Chicago Press.

DiMaggio, P. J., & Powell, W. W. (1983). The iron cage revisited: Institutional isomorphism and collective rationality in organizational fields. *American Sociological Review, 48*(April), 147–160.

Firestone, W. A. (1989). Using reform: Conceptualizing district initiative. *Educational Evaluation and Policy Analysis, 11*(2), 151–164.

Fiscal Crisis and Management Assistance Team. (2000). *Oakland unified school district assessment and recovery plans.* Sacramento, CA: Author.

Friedland, R., & Alford, R. R. (1991). Bringing society back in: Symbols, practices, and institutional contradictions. In W. W. Powell & P. J. DiMaggio (Eds.), *The new institutionalism in organizational analysis* (pp. 232–263). Chicago: The University of Chicago Press.

Gewertz, C. (2000, February 9). Calif. audit cites litany of troubles in Oakland schools. *Education Week,* p. 11.

Gray, B. (1985). Conditions facilitating interorganizational collaboration. *Human Relations, 38*(10), 911–936.

Hartley, J. F. (1994). Case studies in organizational research. In C. Cassell & G. Simons (Eds.), *Qualitative methods in organizational research: A practical guide.* Thousand Oaks, CA: Sage.

Honig, M. I. (2001). *Managing ambiguity: The implementation of complex education policy.* Unpublished Doctoral Dissertation, Stanford University, Stanford, CA.

Honig, M. I. (2003). Building policy from practice: District central office administrators' roles and capacity for implementing collaborative education policy. *Educational Administration Quarterly, 39*(3), 292–338.

Honig, M. I., & Jehl, J. D. (2000). Enhancing federal support for connecting educational improvement strategies and collaborative services. In M. C. Wang & W. L. Boyd (Eds.), *Improving results for children and families: Linking collaborative services with school reform efforts* (pp. 175–198). Greenwich, CT: Information Age.

March, J. G. (1994). *A primer on decision making.* New York: Free Press.

Marsh, J. A. (2002). *Democratic dilemmas: Joint work, education politics, and community.* Unpublished Doctoral Dissertation, Stanford University, Stanford, CA.

Marsh, J. A. (2003, April). *Understanding joint work: District-community partnerships for educational improvement.* Paper presented at the Annual Meeting of the American Educational Research Association, Chicago, IL.

Mawhinney, H. B., & Smrekar, C. (1996). Institutional constraints to advocacy in collaborative services. *Educational Policy, 10*(4), 480–501.

McCorry, J. J. (1978). *Marcus Foster and the Oakland Public Schools: Leadership in an urban bureaucracy.* Berkeley, CA: University of California Press.

Merton, R. K. (1987). Three fragments from a sociologist's notebooks: Establishing the phenomenon, specified ignorance, and strategic research materials. *Annual Review of Sociology, 13*, 1–28.

Meyer, J. W., & Rowan, B. (1977). Institutionalized organizations: Formal structure as myth and ceremony. *American Journal of Sociology, 83*(2), 340–363.

Miles, M. B., & Huberman, A. M. (1994). *Qualitative data analysis: An expanded sourcebook* (2nd ed.). Thousand Oaks, CA: Sage.

Murphy, J., & Hallinger, P. (1988). Characteristics of instructionally effective school districts. *Journal of Educational Research, 81*(3), 175–181.

Patton, M. (1990). *Qualitative evaluation and research methods.* Newbury Park, CA: Sage.

Pfeffer, J. (1972). Merger as a response to organizational interdependence. *Administrative Science Quarterly, 17*, 382–392.

Pfeffer, J. (1981). *Power in organizations.* Marshfield, MA: Pitman.

Pfeffer, J., & Salancik, G. R. (1978). *The external control of organizations.* New York: Harper & Row.

Phillips, D. C., & Burbules, N. C. (2000). *Post positivism and educational research.* Lanham, MA: Rowman & Littlefield.

Rosenholtz, S. J. (1991). *Teacher's workplace: The social organization of schools.* New York: Teachers College Press.

Schorr, L. B. (1997). *Common purpose: Strengthening families and neighborhoods to rebuild America.* New York: Doubleday.

Scott, W. R. (2003). *Organizations* (5th ed.). Upper Saddle River, NJ: Prentice Hall.

Smylie, M. A., & Crowson, R. L. (1996). Working Within the Scripts: Building Institutional Infrastructure for Children's Service Coordination in Schools. *Educational Policy, 10*(1), 3–21.

Smylie, M. A., Crowson, R. L., Chou, V., & Levin, R. A. (1994). The principal and community-school connections in Chicago's Radical Reform. *Educational Administration Quarterly, 30*(3), 342–364.

Spillane, J. P. (1997). Reconstructing conceptions of local capacity: The local educational agency's capacity for ambitious instructional reform. *Educational Evaluation and Policy Analysis, 19*(2), 185–203.

Spillane, J. P. (1998). State policy and the non-monolithic nature of the local school district: Organizational and professional considerations. *American Educational Research Journal, 35*(33–63).

Van de Ven, A. H., & Walker, G. (1979). Coordination patterns within an interorganizational network. *Human Relations, 32*(1), 19–36.

Weiss, J. A. (1987). Pathways to cooperation among public agencies. *Journal of Public Policy Analysis and Management, 7*(1), 94–117.

Yin, R. K. (1989). *Case study research: Design and method.* Thousand Oaks, CA: Sage.

Zucker, L. G. (1983). Organizations as institutions. In S. B. Bacharach (Ed.), *Research in the sociology of organizations.* Greenwich, CT: JAI.

CHAPTER 4

COMMUNITIES OF PRACTICE AND TEACHER QUALITY

Susan M. Printy and Helen M. Marks

Communities of practice have been championed as primary sites for teachers' professional learning. The study conceptualizes high school teachers' communities of practice along two dimensions that might activate learning and, thus, enhance teacher quality: participation and interaction. Using the teacher data file from the Second Follow-Up of the National Education Longitudinal Study of 1988 (NELS:88), the study analyzes the professional impact of community of practice membership on mathematics and science teachers' knowledge, attitudes, and skills. Results of hierarchical linear modeling indicate that community of practice membership, when characterized by full participation and rich interaction, increases teachers' ongoing learning to improve instruction, their sense of competence to meet students' instructional needs, and their use of standards-based pedagogy. At the same time, the study finds evidence that teachers' understandings of instruction are resistant to change.

INTRODUCTION

The expectation that all children meet high academic standards has been an impetus for change in contemporary education (U. S. Department of

Educational Administration, Policy, and Reform: Research and Measurement
A Volume in: Research and Theory In Educational Administration, pages 91–122.
Copyright © 2004 by Information Age Publishing, Inc.
All rights of reproduction in any form reserved.
ISBN: 1-59311-000-0 (hardcover), 1-59311-000-0 (paperback)

Education, 1993, 2002). Most educators agree that, in order to meet such standards, students must be engaged in activities that cause them to exercise higher order thinking skills—to solve problems, to construct knowledge, and to connect to the world beyond the classroom (National Council of Teachers of Mathematics, 1989, 1991, 1995, 2000; National Research Council, 1996; Newmann & Associates, 1996). However, traditional text-based instruction delivered through lecture and discussion still typifies most mathematics and science classrooms (Weiss, Banilower, McMahon, & Smith, 2001). Even though teachers of these subjects have been encouraged toward constructivist, student-centered pedagogy by the mathematics and science disciplinary standards (NCTM, 1989, 1991, 1995, 2000; NRC, 1996), they frequently question the advisability of focusing on deeper coverage of fewer topics and struggle with the belief that students at all stages of schooling can engage complex material (Weiss, et al., 2001).

Those who study teacher quality acknowledge that teacher learning is a necessary condition for change in teaching practice (Darling-Hammond & Sykes, 1999; Feiman-Nemser, 2001). Teachers need to develop a greater ability to analyze their students' current knowledge and find ways to expand that knowledge (Darling-Hammond, Wise, & Klein, 1995). Beyond enhancing their own content knowledge and pedagogical skills, teachers must also examine, and often change, their underlying attitudes, beliefs, and values about the nature of knowledge and the abilities of students.

Policy documents supporting the professionalization of teaching advocate lifelong learning and encourage "job-embedded" learning tied closely to the classroom. Analyzing how they instruct students in their classrooms encourages teachers to refine new teaching skills and to examine the beliefs, attitudes and assumptions they bring to their work (Interstate New Teacher Assessment and Support Consortium, 1992; Interstate School Leaders Licensure Consortium, 1996; National Board for Professional Teaching Standards, 1994). Such development efforts focus on teachers' communities of practice rather than on individual teachers, and they encourage the collective solving of specific problems of practice and the sharing of knowledge. As evidenced by early ethnographic studies in organizations other than schools, communities of practice can be instrumental in developing organizational competence and devising innovative solutions (Orr, 1996). The learning of teachers in their communities of practice and the potential of that learning for enhancing teachers' knowledge, dispositions, and skills is the focus of this paper.

"Community of practice," as used here, refers to a group of teachers engaged in an educational endeavor in which they share common interests and about which they have developed common understandings (see, for example, Lave & Wenger, 1991; Wenger, 1998). As teachers interact regularly with a group of colleagues, they shape their practice: they determine the purpose of their joint work, they come to understand what activities are valued, and they establish social norms for relationships among members (Wenger, 1998).

As used commonly in educational literature, however, the term "community of practice" can be misleading for several reasons. First, the word "community" suggests that teachers who work, or practice, together always constitute a tightly-bonded social group, when, in fact, research on schools has repeatedly shown this not to be the case, particularly in high schools (Huberman, 1993; Firestone & Herriott, 1982; Louis, Marks, & Kruse, 1996; Powell, Farrar, & Cohen, 1985; Siskin, 1994; Sizer, 1984). Second, communities of practice, are potential sites for learning, but there is no assurance that what members learn will increase their productivity or effectiveness. While communities of practice in schools, as in other organizations, may be vehicles for improvement, they have a full range of other organizational impacts. They can perpetuate stereotypes, prejudice, and destructive practices as much as they result in productive change and innovation (Wenger, 1998). Communities of practice should not be romanticized: as an entity, they are value neutral, not intrinsically beneficial or harmful (Wenger, 1998).

Because of the learning possibilities inherent in communities of practice, they are an organizational form worthy of study. In schools, communities of practice can potentially improve teacher quality as well as bring needed change to educational processes. Informed by both qualitative and quantitative studies of the social organization of schools, this study has two purposes: first, to conceptualize dynamics of high school teachers' communities of practice that might be related to productive or improvement-oriented practice; and second, using national data, to investigate the professional impact of productive communities of practice on teachers' approach to their work as measured in three domains:

1. *Knowledge*—teachers' ongoing learning to improve instruction;
2. *Attitudes*—teachers' sense of their competence in meeting the instructional needs of all their students; and
3. *Skills*—teachers' use of standards-based pedagogy.

The study draws on data collected from 2,718 high school science and mathematics teachers who were part of a larger sample of 5,657 teachers participating in the Second Follow-Up of the *National Education Longitudinal Study of 1988* (NELS:88) (National Center for Education Statistics, 1994). While not a random sample of U.S. high schools, the 420 schools from which these teachers were sampled represent a cross-section of school sectors—public, Catholic, and National Association of Independent Schools (NAIS)—and geographic locations—urban, suburban, and rural. Because these data are multilevel, i.e., the teachers are nested in schools, the study employs hierarchical linear modeling (HLM) as its primary analytic technique.

THEORETICAL FRAMEWORK

Communities of practice consist of members who come together as a result of shared values, who engage in shared activity, and who produce shared resources in the process (Wenger, 1998). "Communities of practice," as first conceptualized by Lave and Wenger (1991), captures a theory of social learning based on the assumption that social practice—that is, participation with others in valued enterprises—is the fundamental process by which individuals learn, develop their identities, and make sense of the situations in which they find themselves. As teachers interact with other teachers in the course of their work, they are learning. Learning is situated in activity and is "ubiquitous" there (Lave, 1993; Lave & Wenger, 1991).

Wenger (1998), in further delineating the initial conceptualization, indicated that "practice" gives coherence to the "community." Three dimensions define communities of practice according to the relationship among participants: mutual engagement, joint enterprise, and shared repertoire.

Mutual engagement means that members of the community take part in activities that matter to them, and, collectively, they make sense of their situation. The "practice" of such communities is the process of participation: doing things, working out relationships, inventing, interpreting, producing, or resolving (Lave, 1988). For members of a mathematics department community of practice, for example, teachers participate when they attend in-service together, coordinate what should be taught in each course, invent ways to reward or sanction members, interpret standards documents, produce a curriculum, and resolve disputes over course assignments. Practice exists because the teachers engage in actions with each other and negotiate meanings pertinent to the actions. These negotiations can range from a conscious process of give and take involving all members to a more subtle, almost unconscious process of mutual adaptation by individuals over time. While factors such as proximity or allegiance can facilitate interaction, mutual engagement depends on being actively involved with others in the work community members are there to do (Wenger, 1998).

Being included in what matters is a requirement for being engaged in a community of practice. Certainly this means being actively involved in the work of the community, but it also refers to the social relations among community members. In order to be mutually engaged, members must participate in ways that are acknowledged as legitimate. Members understand that newcomers will take part in a peripheral way before they move to participating in core community activities as full members. Each member develops his or her way to contribute to the practice, even as the community develops shared ways of doing things (Wenger, 1998). For instance, for science teachers working collectively to improve instruction, one community member might be the acknowledged expert in creating strategies for cooperative student work and another in securing resources by writing grants.

Joint enterprise refers to the negotiated understanding of what the practice is about—what the members of the community of practice intend to accomplish. Joint enterprise develops from a collective process of negotiation as members respond to their situation. For example, mathematics teachers, after noting the difficulty their students have in responding to open-ended questions on state proficiency tests, might collectively agree that having students write about mathematics will be a fundamental part of their practice. Making such a change, the community of mathematics teachers shapes the enterprise at the same time they pursue it. Perfect agreement may not exist among community members about this practice, but disagreement is a natural part of finding ways of working together (Lave, 1988; Wenger, 1998).

Communities of practice do not exist as isolated entities; they are embedded within organizational and environmental influences and conditions. However, the power that external forces have over the practice of a community is always mediated by the community's production of its practice. Community members decide what is important and what is not, what to do and what not to do, what to pay attention to and what to ignore (Wenger, 1998). In the example just given, mathematics teachers decided that having students write about mathematics is important to students' understanding of the subject. The process of selection that went into making this decision creates a sense among community members of what they are accountable for, in the sense that they are accountable to other members of the community. After a period of time, the mathematics teachers might decide that the resources spent on writing in their classrooms have not resulted in sufficient benefit to continue the practice. Writing about mathematics, then, might be de-emphasized. The joint enterprise is more than a statement of purpose; it is a dynamic process that "pushes the practice forward as much as it keeps it in check" (Wenger, 1998, p. 82).

Shared repertoire refers to the resources (e.g. routines, policies, processes, concepts, symbols) produced by the community to negotiate meaning and to coordinate multiple activities (Wenger, 1998). The mathematics department where teachers have students write about their understanding of mathematics concepts adopted a policy, which was probably written into a document. Curriculum objectives and teachers' lesson plans reflect the implementation of this policy. After a period of time, teachers negotiated a modification of this practice. As this example shows, the resources have a history or shared points of reference known to community members, yet they are also ambiguous in that they can take on new interpretations as negotiated by the community. In a sense, the resources are artifacts of the practice around which new learning develops. The inherent flux in the repertoire of a practice makes coordination and communication challenging, yet it opens the practice to the generation of new meanings.

Research on Teachers' Communities

Multiple streams of research have demonstrated the importance of teachers' collegial relationships in their professional lives. Teachers' communities have been conceptualized in three general ways: as school-wide professional communities (Bryk, Camburn, & Louis, 1999; Kruse, Louis, & Bryk, 1995), as subject department communities (Bidwell, Frank, & Quiroz, 1997; McLaughlin & Talbert, 2001; Rowan, Raudenbush, & Kang, 1991; Siskin, 1994; Siskin & Little, 1995; Talbert, 1995), or as sub-groups consisting of small numbers of like-minded teachers (Bidwell et al., 1997; Bidwell & Yasumoto, 1999; Siskin, 1994).

Researchers at the Center for the Organization and Restructuring of Schools (CORS) found that school-wide teacher communities are more likely to occur in elementary schools (Louis, Kruse, & Associates, 1995; Louis et al., 1996). In contrast, researchers at the Center for Research on the Context of Secondary School Teaching (CRC) found that the departmental community is likely to be more salient for high school teachers, although the complexion of department communities varies widely, even within the same school (McLaughlin & Talbert, 2001; Siskin, 1994). In the strong traditional communities, teachers enacted their practice according to long standing, common understandings about the ways students learn and the best ways to teach different subjects. In the strong innovative communities, teachers departed from subject paradigms and fit the course work to the needs, interests, and academic ability of their students.

Teachers' understandings of their subject and the nature of the discipline itself also proved important in the way departmental communities emerged. Mathematics is regarded as a defined, sequential, and static subject (Stodolsky & Grossman, 1995). As a *defined* subject, the boundaries are clear. Generally, high school mathematics teachers will have had similar undergraduate preparation programs and they will be prepared to teach a number of subjects in the department. As a *sequential* subject, mathematics is taught in a certain order, as prior student learning is a prerequisite for later learning. For the most part, mathematics is a *static* subject, that is, stable and unchanging. These characteristics encourage mathematics teachers toward departmental collegial interaction. They are likely to coordinate curricular content and to have extensive knowledge of one another's practices and curricular approach. Mathematics teachers might also have less autonomy in choosing instructional techniques and materials and might be hesitant to make dramatic change to their teaching practice.

Science is a less-defined, non-sequential, and dynamic subject (Stodolsky & Grossman, 1995). Science teachers generally study *specialized* subjects (e.g. chemistry, biology, physics), and are regarded as "experts" in a particular field of science. As a result, they are unlikely to teach a wide variety of courses. Because science subjects are quite different, courses are *non-sequential* and do not require close coordination. Unlike mathematics, science is *dynamic,* often changing. New knowledge appears regularly, and in an effort to stay up to date, science teachers are often willing to seek out experts outside of the school. All of these characteristics discourage broad departmental interaction. Close collegial interaction among science teachers is often limited to a sub-group, for instance, a small number of teachers who teach biology (Bidwell et al., 1997; Bidwell & Yasumoto, 1999).

At whatever level the community of teachers is enacted—school-wide, department, or a small group of close colleagues—teachers are members of communities of practice. More accurately, teachers probably hold overlapping membership in multiple communities of practice; that is, they interact with different groups of teachers around varying interests. In regular interaction with any one group of colleagues, teachers come to understand what it is to be a teacher within that specific community: they establish a purpose for their work together, they develop clarity about what is valued, and they accommodate to the normative relationships among members (Wenger, 1998).

Communities of Practice and Productivity

The learning that occurs within communities of practice is generally a stabilizing force (Wenger, 1998). As teachers come to understand what is valued by the community and how they can contribute to the work of the community, expectations and norms for behavior are collectively shaped. Over time, these norms define the status quo. Without some deliberate intervention or a cultural norm oriented toward innovation, high school departmental communities of practice will likely support the status quo, making at best small, incremental improvements in core practices within the department. Departmental boundaries, when impermeable, divide the school and reduce the chance that productive changes occurring within a department will diffuse widely throughout the school (Hargreaves & Macmillan, 1995). It is for these reasons that teachers often continue to teach as they have always taught, arguably as they themselves were taught.

If the community of practice perspective is to prove useful for activating teacher learning that results in improved practice, it is important to identify specific dynamics that might characterize teachers' community of practice membership as *productive*—that is, contributing to beneficial change in the core technology of schools. We argue that productive community of practice membership involves teachers in social learning that is likely to make them better teachers. Productive membership is characterized by full participation in departmental and school activities and rich interaction with a wide range of school members.

Participation

Professional certification or licensure positions a teacher to take part in a practice, such as high school mathematics or science instruction. Through training and socialization, a teacher acquires the valued core knowledge and instructional strategies common to the discipline as well as general assumptions about how students will best learn subject content. Although a certain element of legitimacy accompanies a teacher's initial hiring, what matters for participation in communities of practice is the legitimacy colleagues grant (Lave & Wenger, 1991; Wenger, 1998). Access to the activities of a practice provides opportunities for teachers to learn and, through learning, to enhance their knowledge and skills. Teachers learn as they move from peripheral to full participation.

When new teachers enter a practice, they are immediately responsible for instructing students. Their participation is peripheral because they receive assignments that demand the least amount of time and skill, based on the complexity of the subject knowledge to be conveyed (Lave & Wenger, 1991; Siskin, 1994). Beginning teachers often teach classes at the lower levels of the subject hierarchy, such as general or remedial classes or those for freshmen students (Siskin, 1994; Weiss. Matti, & Smith., 1994). In high schools, the practice of tracking students for instruction, therefore, might minimize the potential for legitimate participation.

Like other members of the department, new teachers participate in activities that occur at the end of the production process—instructing students in classrooms—but their participation is not full. Unlike veteran teachers, however, new teachers have not engaged in the many necessary activities that occur before teachers walk into classrooms with their lesson plans. They did not decide which students would be in which class, select the textbooks for use, or plan the scope and sequence for the courses they teach. They did not contribute to the overall organization of the departmental curriculum. Over time, as new teachers learn through observation, experience, and interaction with others, they come to understand the student population and contribute to collective understandings of how the department can best organize instruction. With greater competence, teachers begin to teach classes requiring more extensive knowledge of subject matter or more complex pedagogical skills. As they gain experience and take more responsibility, they move to the center of the community where they may help set the foundation for instruction in the department (Lave & Wenger, 1991; Wenger, 1998).

Interaction

Interaction with teachers who have different ideas is essential if schools are to draw on their best resources for improvement, teachers themselves (Hargreaves & Macmillan, 1995). Participation in communities of practice, through a process of social learning, allows teachers to continually test their understandings and ideas against those held by other members of the community (Bandura, 1977; Wenger, 1998). Learning also occurs through exposure to the beliefs and practices represented in other communities of practice, either through overlapping membership, when an individual belongs to more than one community, or through boundary encounters, when individuals in different communities come into contact (Wenger, 1998).

Studies of organizational behavior indicate that individuals who interact frequently share the same preferences and make similar decisions based on those preferences (March & Olsen, 1976; Scott & Cohen, 1995; Van Maanen & Barley, 1984). As a result, among departmental colleagues, high school teachers find support for continuing practices that have worked for them in the past. When teachers interact only with others like themselves, conformity and perpetuation are the likely results (Van Maanen & Schein, 1979). On the other hand, innovation is likely to occur when learning

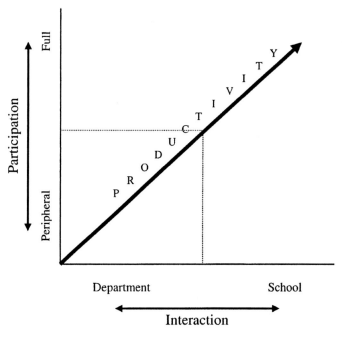

FIGURE 1
Dimensions of Productive Communites of Practice

experiences involve a variety (similar and dissimilar) of other organizational members (Van Maanen & Schein, 1979). Because organizational gains result from diversity, groups benefit from having heterogeneous group members (March, 1991). These findings from organizational research indicate that teachers' interactions with school members outside of the department, in concert with interactions within the department, are likely to result in changes to teachers' beliefs and practices (Grossman, Wineburg, & Woolworth, 2001).

As teachers participate in the practices of a community, their knowledge and skill deepens with increasing involvement in the group's central activities. When teachers' interact with others inside and outside the subject department, they encounter a range of opinions, some similar to their own and some different. With each new experience, with each new idea, teachers learn something with consequences for their own individual practices. These learnings also feed back into the understandings held by the community of practice (Wenger, 1998). When both dynamics, participation and interaction, bear on teachers' communities of practice, the likelihood of productivity increases (Figure 1). Productive practice is that which enhances teachers' knowledge, attitudes, and skills.

Teacher Learning, Competence, and Use of Pedagogy

Teacher Learning

Research has shown the connection between teachers' collegial relationships and teachers' learning. Studies in Chicago schools indicate the positive relationship between teachers' participation in collegial activity and self-reports of improvement in their instruction (Camburn, 1997). School-wide professional community, similarly, has a strong association with a general orientation of a school's faculty toward experimentation and innovation (Bryk et al., 1999), which may accelerate professional learning in the organization. An important contributing factor in the Chicago studies was social trust, perhaps necessary to overcome the norms of autonomy that are so much a part of teaching (Hargreaves, 1991). Similarly, a recent qualitative study by Grossman, Wineburg, and Woolworth (2001) documented the importance of trust and reciprocity to community members' learning.

Pedagogical Competence

School effectiveness research has shown that teachers' attitudes are instrumental in how they instruct students and in how students respond to instruction (Brophy, 1986; Cooper & Tom, 1984; Raudenbush, 1984). One such attitude, teachers' belief in their pedagogical competence, is actually socially-constructed through interactions within their communities (Wenger, 1998). When teachers perceive that they can accomplish a task, they are willing to put forth more effort and to persist through stressful or difficult situations. Teachers' pedagogical competence—the sense that they can affect student learning through their instructional practices—is closely tied to their assumptions about whether students can learn and to their own ability to modify how they teach.

Other researchers have investigated teachers' sense of their ability to affect student learning, as "self-efficacy" and "collective efficacy" (Ashton & Webb, 1986; Goddard, Hoy, & Woolfolk, 2000; Tschannen-Moran, M., Woolfolk Hoy, A., & Hoy, W. K., 1998). Competence also refers to teachers' accountability to other community members for helping students learn, a notion of accountability that has also been investigated elsewhere, as teachers' "collective responsibility" for student learning (Little, 1990; Louis, Kruse, & Associates, 1995; Lee & Smith, 1996; Marks & Louis, 1997). Responsibility, as an attribute of teachers, emphasizes the shared conviction among a school's teachers that all students can and will learn if given opportunity and support (Lee & Smith, 1996). Collective responsibility for students has been empirically shown to result from school-wide professional community (Marks & Louis, 1997).

Use of Standards-Based Pedagogy

A series of documents developed under the guidance of the National Council of Teachers of Mathematics (NCTM) and the National Research Council (NRC) set guidelines and procedures for curriculum, instruction, professional development, and assessment for mathematics and science teachers respectively. Representing a change from traditional, teacher-centered, didactic instructional techniques, standards documents take a systemic approach to reform and have a number of features in common, including a focus on understanding, an emphasis on comprehension of material rather than rote memorization of facts, and support for depth of knowledge about fundamental mathematics and science processes (National Education Goals Panel, 1997).

Regardless of subject, the learning inherent in social interaction around standards-based reform initiatives is likely to increase teachers' use of instructional methods consistent with the disciplinary standards. Social learning can also equip teachers to use effectively practices consistent with reform, though this effectiveness develops slowly over time (Bidwell, 2001; Coburn, 2001). Those who study how teachers incorporate standards-based practices seem to agree. Evidence indicates that when teachers analyze instructional practices and materials within their communities, they will learn how to use them (National Education Goals Panel, 1997; Marks & Louis, 1997; Camburn, 1997; Bidwell & Yasumoto, 1999; Bidwell et al., 1997).

CONCEPTUAL MODEL AND HYPOTHESIS

Drawing on the theoretical framework indicating that the effectiveness of teachers' community participation relates directly to the extent to which members of the community share a common purpose, engage in common activities, and experience open social relations, we have developed a conceptual model as the basis for evaluating the relationship of teachers' participation in communities of practice and three professional outcomes:

1. teacher learning,
2. pedagogical competence, and
3. teachers' use of standards-based pedagogy.

We control for teachers' gender and race, which, based on previous research, might contribute to the professional outcomes independently of their community of practice membership (Louis et al., 1996). Because teachers' subject area and the curricular level of the teaching assignment may also affect these outcomes, as well as their participation in communities of practice, as our earlier discussion has suggested, the model controls for teaching subject and predominant curricular track. Teachers' years of experience in the school lead to fuller participation in communities of practice, and, thus, is included in the model. Teachers' satisfaction with their school controls for possible positive response bias. Because school demographics (i.e., sector, geographical location, size) may also influence the professional outcomes under study (Lee & Bryk, 1989; Lee & Smith, 1995), the model also posits their relationship to the outcomes.

Hypothesis

Teachers' participation in communities of practice, to the extent that it is characterized by full participation in purposeful activities focused on instruction and by rich interactions among school members, will positively affect teacher quality as measured by teachers' ongoing learning, their sense of competence to meet students' instructional needs, and their use of pedagogy that aligns with the national science and mathematics disciplinary standards.

METHOD

Sample and Data

This cross-sectional analysis uses the teacher data file from the Second Follow-up to the National Educational Longitudinal Study of 1988 (NELS:88). Completed in 1992, the Second Follow-up collected survey responses of mathematics and science teachers sampled from the 1,500 U.S. public, Catholic, and elite private (NAIS) high schools enrolling NELS:88 seniors who were targeted by the National Center for Education Statistics (NCES) for contextual data collection (NCES, 1994). Because the survey items specifically inquired about teacher participation within the department or outside of the department, these data are particularly appropriate for studying high school teachers' communities of practice. The original teacher sample numbered 5,657 teachers, of whom 2,718 representing 420 high schools were eligible for inclusion in the sub-sample for the present study. Eligibility rested on two criteria: (1) availability of school and teacher data on the variables of interest in this study, and (2) the participation in NELS:88 of at least five of the school's teachers. Establishing this somewhat arbitrary cut-off number of a minimum of five reflects our assumption that these randomly selected teachers are representative of their peers.

Measures

Measures for the study, except where noted, were constructed using the Rasch model (Wright & Masters, 1982). The Rasch model provides a simple way to construct linear measures for ordered nominal data (Likert scores) by transforming the data into probabilities that respondents will endorse attitudes or behaviors represented by the scale item. Derived in this way, measures rank responses hierarchically—that is, items with the lowest scores are frequent in teachers' practice and items with the highest scores are rare. Therefore, higher rankings are given to items representing participation in core community activities (full participation) and interaction outside of the department. This ordering of items is consistent with the dimensions of social learning identified as contributing to productive community of practice participation. The Rasch model provides a person separation reliability, which indicates that the measure adequately "sorts out" responses of individuals so as to rank them hierarchically and adds a measure of reliability beyond the fit statistics of the scales. (For a complete discussion of the use of the Rasch method in this study, see Printy, 2002.)

Teacher learning is one of three dependent measures. Constructed as a Rasch scale, teacher learning suggests the extent to which teachers believe that their pedagogy has improved through interaction around instruction with a school teaching colleague or administrator. Teachers indicated on a four point scale the extent to which their instruction benefited through interaction with:

  a.   Teachers outside of the department;
  b.   Teachers in the department;

    c.   Department chair;
    d.   Principal; or
    e.   Another administrator.

A standardized measure (M = 0, SD = 1), its person separation reliability is .62 and its reliability as measured by Cronbach's alpha (i.e., internal consistency) is .70.

Pedagogical competence, also a dependent measure, reflects teachers' sense that they can respond adequately to students' instructional needs. Constructed as a Rasch scale, pedagogical competence comprises six survey items, measured on a four point scale, referring to the respondents' beliefs that he or she:

    a.   Can get through to difficult students;
    b.   Makes a difference in students' lives;
    c.   Can do little to affect achievement (reversed);
    d.   Changes approach if students not doing well;
    e.   Is responsible to prevent dropouts; and
    f.   That different teacher methods can affect achievement.

A standardized measure, (M = 0, SD = 1), the person separation reliability for pedagogical competence is .68 and the Cronbach's alpha is .66.

Use of standards-based pedagogy, the final dependent measure, is constructed as an index and includes separate measures for mathematics and science that reflect student-centered, problem-based instruction aligned with national mathematics and science standards. Because the extent of use rather than a hierarchical ranking of items is its focus, the measure is constructed as a sum of teacher responses rather than a Rasch scale. Combined into a single index for standards-based pedagogy and standardized (M = 0, SD = 1), the mathematics and science measures and their component items follow:

1.   *Mathematics standards-based pedagogy* incorporates ten responses from mathematics teachers. Seven survey items, with a four point scale, queried teachers about the extent to which their instruction emphasized:
    a. The nature of proofs;
    b. Representing problems;
    c. Integrating math branches;
    d. Multiple approaches to problems;
    e. Solving problems;
    f. Raising questions/conjectures; and
    g. Raising students' interest in math.
    Three items, using a five point scale, asked about the frequency of teachers' use of:

    h. Student-led discussions;

    i. Cooperative groups; and

    j. Oral reports.

    A standardized measure (M = 0, SD = 1), its Cronbach's alpha is .72.

2. *Science standards-based pedagogy* draws ten items from the teacher survey to create an index. Seven items from the teacher survey, using a four point scale, inquired about science teachers' emphasis on:

    a. Developing lab skills;

    b. Scientific methods;

    c. Problem solving or inquiry skills;

    d. Further study in science;

    e. Student interest in science;

    f. Importance of science in daily life; and

    g. Relating science to the environment. Three items asked about the frequency of use for instructional practices, on a five point scale:

    h. Student-led discussions;

    i. Cooperative groups; and

    j. Oral reports.

    Standardized (M = 0, SD = 1), the Cronbach's alpha is .70 for Science standards-based pedagogy.

The independent variables include a measure of Communities of Practice, the organizational form whose relationship to teacher quality is evaluated in the analysis, and a set of measures to control for characteristics of teachers and their schools which might influence learning, pedagogical competence, and the use of standards-based pedagogy apart from teachers' involvement in communities of practice.

Communities of Practice, constructed as an index of three Rasch scales, reflects the social learning inherent in teachers' purposeful activity with a broad range of school members around curriculum, instruction, and student performance. Each of the three component measures, mutual engagement, joint enterprise, and shared repertoire, is standardized (M = 0, SD = 1). The components, described below, are summed and standardized to create the index. The Cronbach's alpha for the index is .71.

1. *Mutual engagement*, a Rasch measure, taps the interaction of science and mathematics teachers with others both in and out of the subject department around curriculum, instruction, testing, and student performance. The measure includes responses of teachers to ten survey items. Two of the items queried teachers about how much time they spent with

    a. Teachers in the department and

    b. Teachers outside of the department. Four items asked whether teachers discussed with their colleagues (yes or no) the following:

c. Instructional techniques;
d. Subject area curriculum;
e. Curriculum for a course; and
f. Testing procedures.

Three questions asked teachers if they discussed curriculum with other teachers (yes or no):

g. In the department;
h. Outside of the department; or
i. Outside the school.

A standardized measure (M = 0, SD = 1) *mutual engagement* has a person separation reliability of .72 and a Cronbach's alpha of .69.

2. *Joint enterprise*, a Rasch measure comprising of five items, indicates the extent to which teachers, reporting on a four point scale, share departmental goals and a school mission and are oriented to learning and instructional experimentation:

a. The respondent is encouraged to experiment with teaching;
b. Teachers in the department continuously learn;
c. Teachers in the department share beliefs about the mission;
d. Goals and priorities in the department are clear; and
e. There is agreement among the faculty about the school mission.

A standardized measure (M = 0, SD = 1, *joint enterprise* has a person separation reliability of .73 and a Cronbach's alpha of .74.

3. *Shared repertoire*, a Rasch scale employs eight component items to measure teachers' cooperative and coordinated participation in valued departmental and school activities. Each teaches indicated (on a four point scale) the extent to which he or she:

a. Is familiar with the content of others' courses;
b. Coordinates his or her course with teachers in the department;
c. Coordinates his or her course with teachers outside of the department;
d. Agrees that there is cooperative effort among staff;
e. Agrees that grading practices are consistent and fair. Three items asked (yes or no) whether the teacher participated:
f. In a school wide curriculum committee;
g. In a departmental curriculum committee; or
h. In another committee.

A standardized measure (M = 0, SD = 1), shared repertoire has a person separation reliability of .69 and a Cronbach's alpha of .65.

Teachers' Background and School Demographics

Teachers' social background variables include two dummy-coded variables, *Female* (Yes = 1, No = 0) and *African American* (Yes = 1, No = 0), and two continuous variables, *Satisfaction with their teaching situation* and *Years of experience in the school*, each standardized (M = 0, SD = 1). Teachers' professional background includes three dummy-coded variables. Teaching subject area is a dummy-coded variable for *Mathematics* with science as the comparison group (Yes = 1, No = 0). Teachers' track assignment is indicated by two dummy-coded variables: *Academic* (Yes = 1, No = 0) and *Remedial* (Yes = 1, No = 0) with General/vocational track teaching as the comparison group. School demographic variables, employed as statistical controls, include two sector dummy variables, *Catholic* (Yes = 1, No = 0) and *NAIS* (Yes = 1, No = 0), with public schools as the comparison group. School location is also indicated by dummy codes, *Urban* (Yes = 1, No = 0) and *Rural* (Yes = 1, No = 0), with suburban schools as the comparison group. *Size* represents the number of students the school enrolls, as reported by the school administrator. *Average student family SES*, a composite measure constructed from parent reports of father's educational level, mother's educational level, father's occupation, mother's occupation, and family income, is provided by NCES for use with NELS:88 Second Follow-up data. School *size* and *average family SES* are standardized measures (M = 0, SD = 1).

Analytic Approach

The first analysis is descriptive, employing Two-way Analysis of Variance (ANOVA) to examine whether significant observed differences exist by subject area and teaching assignment for three sets of measures:

1. dependent variables—teacher learning, pedagogical competence, and use of standards-based pedagogy;
2. the extent of teachers participation in communities of practice, which we have hypothesized to influence the professional outcomes positively; and
3. the social and professional characteristics of teachers employed as controls.

The analysis tests, as well, for any subject matter by track interactions involving these variables. Should such interactions occur, we will construct interaction (i.e., product) terms and test their significance in the multivariate analyses.

To evaluate the relationship of teachers' participation in communities of practice to the professional outcomes in a model fully adjusted for potentially confounding covariates, we use a multilevel analytic technique, hierarchical linear modeling (HLM) (Bryk & Raudenbush, 1992). HLM is an appropriate analytic technique to use with nested data, such as NELS:88, in which the subjects (i.e., the mathematics and science teachers) are nested within schools.

The first step in an HLM analysis is to compute a fully unconditional model, i.e., one that has no predictors at any level, to estimate the within- and between-school variance components for each of the dependent variables. Based on these estimates, we calculate the interclass correlation coefficient (ICC) or the proportion of variance in each outcome that exists between schools and that is potentially explainable by school features, once within-school differences among the teachers and their participation in communities of practice are taken into account. The unconditional model also provides an HLM reliability statistic, a measure of the relationship of the estimated between-school variance in the dependent variable to its true variance.

We then conduct separate within-school HLM analyses to estimate the unique contribution of communities of practice to each dependent variable, net of the modeled teacher characteristics and any interactions existing between these background attributes. The third set of HLM analyses, adjusted for within-school differences among teachers, investigates the relationship of the school demographic characteristics to the professional outcomes. We calculate the proportion of variance in the outcomes explained by the within- and between-school models.

RESULTS

Observed Differences

The social and professional characteristics of teachers differ significantly according to their teaching subject and the curricular track of their focal teaching assignment, but no significant interactions occur in the relationships (Table 1). Women comprise just over half of the mathematics teachers in the sample, but represent only a third of the science teachers. The gender of teachers does not vary significantly across curricular tracks. African American teachers constitute a similar proportion of mathematics (4 percent) and science (2 percent) teachers, but a significantly greater proportion of remedial (9 percent) teachers relative to academic (3 percent) and general/vocational (4 percent) teachers.

The distribution of teachers by subject across curricular track varies significantly. Of teachers of academic and general/vocational courses, nearly 60 percent are mathematics teachers. For all remedial teachers, however, over 73 percent are mathematics teachers. For the full number of mathematics and science teachers in the sample, the relative distribution of each subset across curricular tracks is much the same.

Mathematics and science teachers report an equal number of years experience (12) in their present school. Teachers in the academic track have the most seniority (13 years) and teachers in the remedial track have

TABLE 1

Observed Differences in Study Variables by Subject and Curricular Track: Two-way Analysis of Variance with Interactions

	Mathematics	Science	Academic	General/Vocational	Remedial	Interaction
N	1618	1091	1654	939	116	
% Female	50.4**	33.7	44.1	41.0	54.3	n.s.
% African American	3.8	2.4	2.6	3.6	8.6***	n.s.
% Mathematics Teachers			59.7	58.1	73.3**	
% Academic	61.0	61.1				
% General/Vocational	33.8	36.1				
% Remedial	5.2	2.8				
Experience in present school in years	12.2	12.2	12.8***	11.4	10.0	n.s.
Satisfaction with the teaching situation[a]	-.01	.01	.09***	-.16	-.06	n.s.
Communities of Practice[a]	.10***	-.15	.07***	-.11	-.03	*
Teacher Learning[a]	.06***	-.09	-.01	-.00	.19	n.s.
Pedagogical competence[a]	-.02	.03	.03	-.08	.14***	n.s.
Use of Standards-Based Pedagogy[a]	-.14	.21***	.18***	-.22	-.71	***

Notes: [a]Standardized variable (mean = 0, SD = 1)

$^{***}p < .001;\ ^{**}p < .01;\ ^{*}p < .05$

the least (10 years). The level of satisfaction with the teaching situation expressed by mathematics teachers does not differ significantly from the level expressed by science teachers. Academic teachers, however, report significantly higher levels of satisfaction with teaching than general/vocational teachers (.3 SD) and remedial teachers (.2 SD).

Communities of practice also vary significantly across subject and curricular track. Participation of mathematics teachers in communities of practice is fuller than among science teachers (.3 SD) while academic teachers' participation exceeds that of general/vocational teachers (.2 SD) and remedial teachers (.1 SD). Moreover, teachers' levels of involvement in communities of practice according to subject area interact significantly with their curricular track teaching assignment.

Teachers' professional outcomes vary significantly either by subject or track, or both. While mathematics teachers are significantly more likely to benefit from the expert advice of their school colleagues than science teachers (.2 SD), teacher learning does not vary significantly across curricular tracks. Subject area and curricular track do not interact. Pedagogical competence is equivalent across subject areas; however, teachers in the remedial track report significantly more competence than do teachers in the general/vocational (.2 SD) and academic (.1 SD) tracks. Significant interactions are not evident.

Teachers' use of pedagogical techniques in line with the national disciplinary standards varies by subject and track assignment. Science teachers tend to use standards-based pedagogy more than do mathematics teachers (.4 SD). Academic teachers use more of these instructional methods than do general/vocational teachers (.4 SD) or remedial teachers (.9 SD). Standards-based pedagogy interacts significantly with subject area and teaching assignment.

HLM

Unconditional models

Using the fully unconditional models, we calculated the ICC for each professional outcome: Teacher learning, 7.4; Pedagogical competence, 3.0; and Use of standards-based pedagogy, 1.1. (See Table 2 for the psychometric properties of the dependent measures.) The HLM reliability statistic indicates the reliability of the sample mean as an estimate of the true school mean. Calculated as a function of the between-school variance in relation to the within-school variance and sample size, the reliability will be low to the extent that the ICC or proportion of explainable between-school variance is low: Teacher learning, .34; Pedagogical competence, .16, and Use of standards-based pedagogy, .06.

TABLE 2
Professional Outcomes: Psychometric Properties

	Teacher Learning	*Pedagogical Competence*	*Use of Standards-based Pedagogy*
ICC	7.40	2.97	1.05
HLM Reliability	.34	.16	.06
Person Separation Reliability	.62	.68	—
Cronbach's Alpha	.70	.66	.72 (M)
			.70 (S)

Within-school models

We fit a within-school model for each of the three professional outcome measures (Table 3). All of the social and professional attributes of teachers contribute significantly to at least one of the dependent measures although, for many, the magnitude of effects is small. Race has a positive relationship with pedagogical competence (.4 SD) and the use of standards-based pedagogy (.4 SD). Gender is a significant factor only in women's more frequent use of standards-based pedagogy (.1 SD). Teachers' experience in the school has a significant negative relationship with teacher learning (–.1 SD) and pedagogical competence (–.1 SD). Teachers' satisfaction with their teaching situation contributes significantly to teacher learning (.1 SD), pedagogical competence (.2 SD), and standards-based pedagogy (.1 SD).

Mathematics teachers are significantly less likely to report competence (–.1 SD) and to use standards-based instruction (–.7 SD). Academic teachers, on average, are significantly less inclined to learn from colleagues (–.04 SD). Remedial teachers are significantly less likely than academic teachers (.6 SD) or general/vocational teachers (.5 SD) to use student-centered methods. Subject by track interaction terms are also included in the pedagogy models. The significant effect for academic mathematics teachers (.5 SD) indicates that they use standards-based pedagogy to a greater degree than their mathematics colleagues who teach general/vocational classes. No significant difference is detected for remedial mathematics teachers.

For each dependent variable, community of practice participation results in a significant, positive increase in the professional outcomes. For a one-standard deviation increase in teachers' participation in communities of practice, teacher learning increases by nearly one-half of a standard deviation, pedagogical competence by over one-fifth of a standard deviation, and standards-based pedagogy by one-fifth of a standard deviation. These findings support our hypothesis that community of practice membership, when characterized by full participation and rich interaction,

TABLE 3
The Professional Impact of Participation in Communities of Practice:
Within-school Influences on Teacher Learning, Pedagogical Competence,
and Use of Standards-based Pedagogy

Dependent Variables:	Teacher Learning[a]	Pedagogical Competence[a]	Use of Standards-based Pedagogy[a]
Intercept	.05	.01	.16**
Teacher			
African American	.01	.36***	.40***
Female	−.05	.06	.13***
Experience[a]	−.11***	−.05**	−.03
Satisfaction[a]	.06***	.18***	.11***
Mathematics	.04	−.12**	−.70***
Academic	−.04*	.04	.07
Remedial	.10	.18*	−.51**
Math*Academic	—	—	.48***
Math*Remedial	—	—	.08
Communities of Practice[a]	.47***	.22***	.20***
CoP*Mathematics	−.03	−.05	.06
CoP*Academic	−.03	.04	−.08*
CoP*Remedial	−.01	.17*	−.08
Within-school Variance Explained	20.4%	10.9%	16.2%

Notes: [a]Variable standardized, M = 0, SD = 1
*** p<.001; ** p<.01; * p<.05

enhances teachers' knowledge, competence, and pedagogical skills. Productive community participation provides teachers ample opportunities to learn from those with expertise. Within productive communities, members establish normative expectations that teachers will offer responsive instruction. Community membership enables teachers to make sense of the disciplinary policy documents and plan strategies to implement them.

Because the Two-way ANOVA analysis indicated significant interactions between subject and track related to teachers' level of community of practice involvement, interaction terms (i.e., communities of practice by mathematics, communities of practice by academic, and communities of practice by remedial) are included in each of the three within-school models. The subject interaction term does not gain significance in any model. The track interaction terms, however, do gain significance for two of the outcomes. Among teachers who report high levels of community of practice participation, academic teachers are significantly less likely to use standards-based instructional practices (–.1 SD) than general/vocational teachers. Within the same group of high-involvement practitioners, remedial teachers are significantly more likely to have a sense of pedagogical competence (.2 SD) than their general/vocational colleagues.

The significance of the various interaction terms in the models suggests the complex nature of social learning within communities of practice. The analyses support increased participation and interaction as contributing to teacher quality, measured by teachers' on-going learning, pedagogical competence, and standards-based instructional skills. However, the effects of social learning vary at different levels of community involvement, across curricular tracks of the teaching assignment. While remedial teachers have a significantly higher level of pedagogical competence, on average, than other teachers, this effect is even stronger for those teachers who are full members of productive communities of practice. At high levels of community participation, academic teachers, on average, are less likely to embrace standards-based instructional practices than other fully participating teachers. This finding suggests that productive participation might mean that teachers challenge proposed change, leading to slow rather than quick adoption of innovative practices.

The total amount of within-school variance explained is 20 percent for teacher learning, 11 percent for pedagogical competence, and 16 percent for standards-based pedagogy (Table 3).

Between-school models

Although the explainable variance is small, we also fit a between-school demographic model for each dependent variable to examine the presence of differences according to school sector, urbanicity, size, and average SES (Table 4).

Teacher learning, which has the greatest amount of between-school variation of the three outcomes, is significantly influenced by most of the school level covariates. Teachers in NAIS private schools learn less from their colleagues than teachers in Catholic (.2 SD) or public school (.3 SD). Teachers in urban and rural schools are equivalent in gaining knowledge from colleagues, at a level that is significantly greater than the learning reported by suburban teachers (.1 SD). Large school size constrains the ability of teachers' to benefit from other teachers' expertise (.1 SD), though perhaps only marginally. School level factors do not directly affect pedagogical competence. Variation in this outcome relates only to differences among teachers.

Teachers' use of standards-based pedagogy has the smallest amount of between-school variation of the three dependent measures. Even so, two school level variables reach significance. Teachers in rural schools use student-centered, problem-based instructional practices more often than

TABLE 4
The Professional Impact of Participation in Communities of Practice:
Between-school Influences on Teacher Learning, Pedagogical
Competence, and Standards-based Pedagogy

Dependent Variables:	Teacher Learning[a]	Pedagogical Competence[a]	Use of Standards-based Pedagogy[a]
Intercept	−.03	−.03	.13*
School			
Catholic	−.11	−.07	−.16
NAIS	−.28**	.11	−.06
Urban	.11*	.00	.02
Rural	.10*	.06	.13**
Size[a]	−.05*	−.01	.06**
Student			
Family SES[a]	−.03	−.01	−.03
Between-school			
Variance Explained	35.0%	19.7%	0%

Notes: Level-2 models are fully-adjusted for within-school differences
[a]Variable standardized, M=0, SD=1
*** p<.001; ** p<.01; * p<.05

teachers in suburban (.1 SD) or urban (.2 SD) schools. Large school size is positively related to increases in teachers' use of standards-based techniques (.1 SD).

DISCUSSION

As conceptualized for the study detailed here, communities of practice reflect the natural participation and interaction patterns of high school mathematics and science teachers with their departmental colleagues, but they also represent the learning potential of participation and interaction beyond what is most familiar, including participation in school level activities and interaction with a broad range of school members. Essentially, teachers have membership in multiple communities. Such productive community membership provides teachers with opportunities for learning of the sort that appears to significantly enhance teachers' knowledge, attitudes, and skills.

Personal Traits

African American teachers, women teachers, and those who are satisfied with their teaching situation report higher levels on one of more of the professional outcomes generally. While we might speculate on the reasons why this might be the case, there is nothing in these data to support more than supposition. However, future investigations into the relationships among teachers' personal traits, their community of practice participation, and the resulting professional consequences might be fruitful.

Teacher Learning

From one way of thinking, teacher learning represents a straight-forward exchange of information. Teachers report that their instruction has improved because they have learned things from other school colleagues. Set against the norms of autonomy so often associated with high school teaching, however, teacher learning also perhaps taps the willingness of teachers to open their practice to examination by another teacher or an administrator. Community of practice participation increases teachers' propensity for doing so.

School differences appear more consequential for teacher learning than any of the other professional outcomes. Teachers in NAIS schools report learning at a lower level than their public or Catholic school counterparts. It is possible that teachers in NAIS schools are "independent artisans" who learn alone (Huberman, 1993).

In urban schools, teachers might face a greater need for learning as a result of the challenges presented by low-achieving students. Urban schools might also provide teachers with greater internal resources, access to educational specialists or consultants, for example. In general, small school size, which makes interaction and formation of strong social relations easier, is associated with learning. Teachers in rural schools, which are smaller on average, also tend to learn more. Faculty in rural schools may also be more open or engage in more positive social relations.

Pedagogical Competence

Teachers' pedagogical competence, as defined for this study, derives its meaning from students' achievement. Competence incorporates teachers' acknowledgement that their teaching affects how students learn as well as their disposition to adapt their instruction as needed to insure that students learn. This conceptualization, admittedly, is at odds with a variety of other goals of education (e.g. credentialing) or purposes of instruction (e.g. controlling students). Community of practice membership increases the likelihood that teachers will embrace the meaning of pedagogical competence used in this study. This effect appears most consequential for teachers of remedial classes.

Participation in productive communities, however, does not counter the resistance of experienced teachers and mathematics teachers to modify their instruction. While pedagogical competence increases overall as a result of community of practice membership, the collective understandings of the community could even reinforce the notion that veteran members of the community, as expert teachers, have less need than other teachers to change their practices. It is possible that the community of practice acknowledges the correctness of mathematics teachers' defined and sequential approach to instruction even as community participation encourages these teachers' to make changes to instruction.

Use of Standards-based Pedagogy

Teachers' use of standards-based pedagogy represents a specific set of student-centered, inquiry-based instructional practices that reflect the principles of the national mathematics and standards documents. As such, the pedagogy outcome reflects the implementation of a national policy initiative as well as the use of innovative teaching practice. Participation in a productive community of practice contributes to higher use of these student-centered practices. Within their communities of practice, teachers can make sense of such policies and devise appropriate strategies for instruction.

The strongest influences on teachers' use of standards-based pedagogy relate to the paradigmatic differences between subjects that are entrenched, or institutionalized, in common understandings about instruction (Grossman & Stodolsky, 1995; Meyer & Rowan, 1977; Stodolsky & Grossman, 1995). Science teachers, with a commitment to the scientific method, appear to have a greater natural affinity for problem-based instruction. Mathematics teachers' acknowledged concern with coverage of basic facts and preparation of students for subsequent courses leaves them little room to try out the new instructional approaches associated with the standards. It is possible that the national conversation about standards encouraged science teachers in the study sample to try these practices more than it did mathematics teachers, an effect shown in earlier research (Bidwell & Yasumoto, 1999).

The contrasting effects for tracking-related terms might derive as much from external influences related to students as to the operational contexts of subjects. Standards-based practices are student-centered, collaborative approaches rather than teacher-centered, didactic approaches. Teachers with remedial classes might have greater need (or perceived need) for control oriented strategies than teachers of academic classes (Cusick, 1992; McNeil, 1986). Among mathematics teachers, those who teach academic classes to more capable students perhaps do not have as much need for control and are more amenable to using standards-based instructional techniques.

The size of the community of practice coefficient (.2 SD) relative to the size of the mathematics coefficient (–.7 SD) and the remedial coefficient (–.5 SD) suggests the stability of the secondary educational system. The organization of mathematics instruction as teacher-centered and sequential, from these data, appears to be extremely resilient to change. The organization of secondary instruction according to ability level tracks is equally embedded in the institutionalized structure of secondary schools. Teachers of academic subjects who have many opportunities to learn through participation and interaction report significantly less use of standards-based pedagogy than highly involved general/vocational teachers. It appears that teachers at this academic level reach ongoing, collective understandings that standards-based instructional practices do not best serve their instructional goals. This evidence suggests that the job-embedded learning work of teachers, while having a positive influence on the use of non-traditional and, therefore, innovative instructional methods will not result in a quick turn-around of teachers' understandings of instruction.

School contexts do have some influence on instructional practices. Teachers in rural schools report higher use of standards-based pedagogy, perhaps reflecting a hands-on versus passive orientation that better serves a manual work-oriented culture. The association of pedagogy with large school size might represent more differentiated curricular-tracking in larger schools.

CONCLUSION

When teachers regularly contribute to a range of valuable work-related activities and interact with school members in and out of the subject department, they have on-going opportunities for learning. An increase in the occasions for learning increases the probability that teachers' community of practice membership will be productive. Productive membership brings teachers into contact with other teachers and administrators from whom they can learn. Participating with their colleagues on important tasks, teachers have opportunities to draw on others' expertise and to test their own ideas and ways of doing things against the experiences of others. Productive membership provides teachers the opportunities to look at students from different perspectives than they are accustomed to and to develop skills for working with diverse students. In doing shared work with a wider range of colleagues, teachers might open to inquiry their notions of what it means to be competent and, perhaps, re-negotiate new understandings that will prove beneficial to students. Productive membership allows teachers to make sense of policy initiatives that challenge their habitual practice. Consideration of new ideas from a different mindset—one resulting from productive community membership—increases the likelihood that these ideas will be considered on their merit rather than from the perspective of institutionalized beliefs.

Even so, focusing attention on teacher learning within communities of practice will not change the quality of teachers or the effectiveness of schools in short order. Examining individual teachers' communities, McLaughlin and Talbert (2001) suggest that strong communities either maintain traditional practices or innovate in order to engage students. In mediating the influences from the external environment on teachers' work, the community serves as a stabilizing force or a force for change. Bidwell (2001) argues that informal networks of faculty members stabilize formal structures of schooling while they also provide mechanisms for adaptation of those structures in response to uncertainties and local circumstance. The findings of this study support Bidwell's dual argument, as tendencies of community participation toward adapting and stabilizing are both evident. Teacher's communities of practice maintain the institutional understandings associated with the disciplines even as they enhance teachers' knowledge, modify their beliefs, and increase their use of innovative instructional techniques. In essence, teachers' communities of practice help the school maintain legitimacy while helping teachers adapt, as necessary, in response to external influences. These stabilizing effects are apparent both for differences related to subject and differences related to tracking. The results of this study indicate that instructional improvement will not result from short-term strategies that leave unexamined the systemic forces that affect the ways in which teachers work together and that ultimately find their way into teachers' classrooms in the form of instruction (McLaughlin & Talbert, 2001).

Because communities of practice are acknowledged to have a range of organizational impacts, it is important that teachers appreciate the factors that distinguish teachers' community participation as productive. In some measure, adopting this orientation requires that teachers take on additional responsibilities and expend greater effort in activities that pay dividends in terms of improved instruction and, potentially, increases in students' achievement. For example, cognizant of the learning opportunities inherent in participation and interaction, veteran teachers might establish social relationships with newcomers, invite them to take part in committees, or might arrange for close mentoring for colleagues teaching courses for the first time. For their part, new teachers might take more initiative to seek the expertise of mature teachers. Departments might give serious thought to rotating course assignments and assuring that teachers have opportunities for working with different groups of students. The study findings indicate how important it is for teachers to take a broad view of schooling, beyond their own classrooms and subject departments. At minimum, teachers in a school need to get to know one another. Strong affiliative relationships can help to counteract norms of autonomy that keep teachers isolated in their classrooms.

Whether teachers realize it or not, they do exercise social influence within their communities of practice (Smylie, Conley, & Marks, 2002). When teachers acknowledge their influence and use it consciously while keeping student learning at the center of their negotiations, their efforts are more likely to make an impact. As teachers' learning efforts within their departmental communities of practice cohere, and as these efforts are integrated across the school, a critical mass builds with potential to move the school forward in reforming its educational processes and increasing its effectiveness.

Acknowledgments: A report of this study was presented in November, 2002, at the annual meeting of the University Council for Educational Administration, Pittsburgh, PA. We thank Rodney Ogawa and Wayne Hoy who read an earlier draft of this paper and made helpful suggestions for its final development.

REFERENCES

Ashton, P. T., & Webb, R. B. (1986). *Making a difference: Teachers' sense of efficacy and student achievement.* New York: Longman.

Bandura, A. (1977). *Social learning theory.* Englewood Cliffs, NJ: Prentice Hall.

Bidwell, C. E. (2001). Analyzing schools as organizations: Long-term permanence and short-term change. *Sociology of Education, 74*(5), 100–114.

Bidwell, C. E., Frank, K. A., & Quiroz, P. A. (1997). Teacher types, workplace controls and the organization of schools. *Sociology of Education, 70*(4), 285–307.

Bidwell, C. E., & Yasumoto, J. Y. (1999). The collegial focus: Teaching fields, collegial relationships, and instructional practice in American high schools. *Sociology of Education, 72*(4), 234–256.

Brophy, J. E. (1986). *Socializing students' motivation to learn.* East Lansing: Michigan State University Press.

Bryk, A., Camburn, E., & Louis, K. S. (1999). Professional community in Chicago elementary schools: Facilitating factors and organizational consequences. *Educational Administration Quarterly, 35*(Supplemental), 751–782.

Bryk, A. S., & Raudenbush, S. W. (1992). *Hierarchical linear models: Applications and data analysis.* Newbury Park, CA: Sage.

Camburn, E. (1997). *The impact of professional community on teacher learning and instructional practice.* Unpublished dissertation, University of Chicago, Chicago, IL.

Coburn, C. E. (2001). Collective sensemaking about reading: How teachers mediate reading policy in their professional communities. *Educational Evaluation and Policy Analysis, 23*(2), 145–170.

Cooper, H. M., & Tom, D. Y. (1984). Teacher expectation research: A review with implications for classroom instruction. *Elementary School Journal, 85*(1), 77–89.

Cusick, P. (1992). *The educational system: Its nature and logic.* New York: McGraw-Hill.

Darling-Hammond, L., & Sykes, G. (Eds.). (1999). *Teaching as the learning profession: Handbook of policy and practice.* San Francisco: Jossey-Bass.

Darling-Hammond, L., Wise, A. E., & Klein, S. P. (1995). *A license to teach: Building a profession for 21st-century schools.* Boulder, CO: Westview Press.

Feiman-Nemser, S. (2001). From preparation to practice: Designing a continuum to strengthen and sustain teaching. *Teachers College Record, 103*(6), 1013–1055.

Firestone, W. A., & Herriott, R. W. (1982). Two images of schools as organizations: An explication and illustrative empirical test. *Educational Administration Quarterly, 18*(2), 39–59.

Goddard, R. D., Hoy, W. K., & Woolfolk, A. (2000). Collective teacher efficacy: Its meaning, measure, and effect on student achievement. *American Education Research Journal, 37*(2), 479–507.

Grossman, P. L., & Stodolsky, S. S. (1995). Content as context: The role of school subjects in secondary school teaching. *Educational Researcher, 24*(8), 5–11.

Grossman, P., Wineburg, S., & Woolworth, S. (2001). Toward a theory of teacher community. *Teachers College Record, 103*(6), 942–1012.

Hargreaves, A. (1991). Contrived collegiality: The micro-politics of teacher collaboration. In J. Blase (Ed.), *The politics of life in schools* (pp. 46–72). New York: Sage.

Hargreaves, A., & Macmillan, R. (1995). The balkanization of secondary school teaching. In L. S. Siskin & J. W. Little (Eds.), *The subjects in question* (pp. 141–171). New York: Teachers College Press.

Huberman, M. (1993). The model of the independent artisan in teachers' professional relations. In J. W. Little & M. W. McLaughlin (Eds.), *Teachers' work: Individuals, colleagues, and contexts* (pp. 11–50). New York: Teachers College Press.

Interstate New Teacher Assessment and Support Consortium (1992). *INTASC model core standards.* Washington, DC: Council of Chief State School Officers.

Interstate School Leaders Licensure Consortium (1996). *ISLLC standards for school leaders.* Washington, DC: Council of Chief State School Officers.

Kruse, S., Louis, K. S., & Bryk, A. S. (1995). An emerging framework for analyzing school-based professional community. In K. S. Louis & S. Kruse (Eds.), *Professionalism and community: Perspectives on reforming urban schools* (pp. 23–44). Newbury Park, CA: Corwin.

Lave, J. (1998). *Cognition in practice.* Cambridge, UK: Cambridge University Press.

Lave, J. (1993). The practice of learning. In S. L. Chaiklin, J. (Ed.), *Understanding practice: Perspectives on activity and context* (pp. 3–34). Cambridge, UK: Cambridge University Press.

Lave, J., & Wenger, E. (1991). *Situated learning: Legitimate peripheral participation.* New York: Cambridge University Press.

Lee, V. E. & Bryk, A. S. (1989). A multi-level model of the social distribution of high school achievement. *Sociology of Education, 62*(3), 172–292.

Lee, V. E., & Smith, J. B. (1995). Effects of high school restructuring and size on early gains in achievement and engagement. *Sociology of Education, 68*(4), 241–270.

Lee, V. E., & Smith, J. B. (1996). Collective responsibility for learning and its effects on gains in achievement for early secondary school students. *American Journal of Education, 104*(2), 103–147.

Little, J. W. (1990). The persistence of privacy: Autonomy and initiative in teachers' personal relations. *Teachers College Record, 91*(4), 509–536.

Louis, K. S., Kruse, S., & Associates. (1995). *Professionalism and community: Perspectives on reforming urban schools.* Thousand Oaks, CA: Corwin Press.

Louis, K. S., Marks, H. M., & Kruse, S. (1996). Teachers' professional community in restructuring schools. *American Educational Research Journal, 33*(4), 757–798.

March, J. G. (1991). Exploration and exploitation in organizational learning. *Organization Science, 2*(1), 71–87.

March, J. G., & Olsen, J. P. (1976). *Ambiguity and choice in organizations.* Bergen, Norway: Universitetsforlaget.

Marks, H. M., & Louis, K. S. (1997). Does teacher empowerment affect the classroom? The implications of teacher empowerment for instructional practice and student academic performance. *Educational Evaluation and Policy Analysis, 19*(3), 245–275.

McLaughlin, M. W., & Talbert, J. E. (2001). *Professional communities and the work of high school teaching.* Chicago: University of Chicago Press.

McNeill, L. (1986). *Contradictions of control: School structure and school knowledge.* New York: Routledge & Kegan Paul.

Meyer, J. W., & Rowan, B. (1977). Institutionalized organizations: Formal structures as myth and ceremony. *American Journal of Sociology, 83*(2), 340–363.

National Board for the Professionalization of Teaching Standards (1994). *What teachers should know and be able to do.* Arlington, VA: NBPTS.

National Center for Education Statistics (1994). *National Education Longitudinal Study of 1988.* Washington, DC: U. S. Department of Education.

National Council of Teachers of Mathematics (1989). *Curriculum and evaluation standards for school mathematics.* Reston, VA: National Council of Teachers of Mathematics.

National Council of Teachers of Mathematics (1991). *Professional standards for teaching mathematics.* Reston, VA: National Council of Teachers of Mathematics.

National Council of Teachers of Mathematics (1995). *Assessment standards for school mathematics.* Reston, VA: National Council of Teachers of Mathematics.

National Council of Teachers of Mathematics (2000). *Principles and standards for school mathematics.* Reston, VA: The National Council of Teachers of Mathematics, Inc.

National Education Goals Panel (1997). *Improving student learning in mathematics and science: The role of national standards in state policy.* Washington, DC: National Education Goals Panel.

National Research Council. (1996). *National Science Education Standards.* Washington, DC: National Academy Press.

Newmann, F. M., & Associates. (1996). *Authentic achievement: Restructuring schools for intellectual quality.* San Francisco, CA: Jossey-Bass.

Orr, J. (1996). *Talking about machines: An ethnography of a modern job.* Ithaca, NY: Cornell University Press.

Powell, A. G., Farrar, E., & Cohen, D. C. (1985). *The shopping mall high school.* Boston, MA: Houghton Mifflin.

Printy, S. M. (2002). *Communities of practice: Participation patterns and professional impact for high school mathematics and science teachers.* Unpublished dissertation. Columbus, OH: The Ohio State University.

Raudenbush, S. W. (1984). Magnitude of teacher expectancy effects on pupil IQ as a function of the credibility of expectancy induction: A synthesis of findings from 18 experiments. *Journal of Educational Psychology, 76*(1), 85–97.

Rowan, B., Raudenbush, S. W., & Kang, S. (1991). Organizational design in high schools: A multilevel analysis. *American Journal of Education, 99*(2), 238–266.

Scott, W. R., & Cohen, R. C. (1995). Work-units in organizations: Ransacking the literature. In L. S. Siskin & J. W. Little (Eds.), *The subjects in question: Departmental organization and the high school.* New York: Teachers College Press.

Siskin, L. S. (1994). *Realms of knowledge: Academic departments in secondary schools.* Washington, DC: Falmer Press.

Siskin, L. S. & Little, J. W. (Eds.). (1995). *The subjects in question: Departmental organization and the high school.* New York: Teachers College Press.

Sizer, T. R. (1984). *Horace's compromise: The dilemma of the American high school.* Boston, MA: Houghton Mifflin.

Smylie, M. A., Conley, S., & Marks, H. M. (2002). Exploring new approaches to teacher leadership for school improvement. In J. Murphy (Ed.), *The educational leadership challenge: Redefining leadership for the 21st century* (pp. 162–188). Chicago: University of Chicago Press.

Stodolsky, S. S., & Grossman, P. (1995). The impact of subject matter on curricular activity: An analysis of five academic subjects. *American Educational Research Journal, 32*(2), 227–249.

Talbert, J. (1995). Boundaries of teachers' professional communities in U.S. high schools: Power and precariousness of the subject department. In L. S. Siskin & J. W. Little (Eds.), *The subjects in question: Departmental organization and the high school* (pp. 68–94). New York: Teachers College Press.

Tschannen-Moran, M., Woolfolk-Hoy, A., & Hoy, W. K. (1998). Teacher efficacy: Its meaning and measure. *Review of Educational Research, 68*(2), 202–248.

U. S. Department of Education (1993). *Standards for all: A vision for education in the 21st century: High standards for all students. Goals 2000: Educate America.*

U. S. Department of Education (2002). *No child left behind act of 2001: Reauthorization of the elementary and secondary education act.* Washington, DC: U. S. Department of Education.

Van Maanen, J., & Barley, S. (1984). Occupational communities: Culture and control in organizations. *Research in Organizational Behavior, 6,* 287–365.

Van Maanen, J., & Schein, E. (1979). Toward a theory of organizational socialization. In B. M. Staw (Ed.), *Research in organizational behavior* (Vol. 1, pp. 209–264). Greenwich, CT: JAI.

Weiss, I. R., Banilower, E. R., McMahon, K. C., & Smith, P. S. (2001). *Report of the 2000 national survey of science and mathematics education.* Chapel Hill, NC: Horizon Research, Inc.

Weiss, I. R., Matti, M. C., & Smith, P. S. (1994). *A profile of science and mathematics education in the United States, 1993.* Chapel Hill, NC: Horizon Research, Inc.

Wenger, E. (1998). *Communities of practice: Learning, meaning, and identity.* New York: Cambridge University Press.

Wright, B. D., & Masters, G. N. (1982). *Rating scale analysis: Rasch measurement.* Chicago: Mesa.

CHAPTER 5

ESTIMATING THE EFFECTS OF ACADEMIC DEPARTMENTS ON ORGANIC DESIGN IN HIGH SCHOOLS

A Crossed-Multilevel Analysis

Sang-Jin Kang, Brian Rowan, & Stephen W. Raudenbush

This paper uses a "crossed" multilevel statistical model to estimate the percentage of variance in three measures of organic management lying within and between academic departments in a sample of approximately 340 public and Catholic high schools in the United States. The results show that academic departments account for about 9% of the total observed variance in the measure of principal leadership used in this study, about 8% of the variance in the measure of staff cooperation used here, and about 8% of the variance in the measure of teacher control used here. These results suggest that departments account for only a small proportion of the *total* variance in measures of organic management. However, since the academic departments could have more influence on dimensions of organizational structure or climate not measured, we recommend additional research to examine department effects on a wider range of organizational outcomes.

Educational Administration, Policy, and Reform: Research and Measurement
A Volume in: Research and Theory In Educational Administration, pages 123–152.
Copyright © 2004 by Information Age Publishing, Inc.
All rights of reproduction in any form reserved.
ISBN: 1-59311-000-0 (hardcover), 1-59311-000-0 (paperback)

INTRODUCTION

Academic departments exist in remarkably similar form in most large high schools in the United States. However, the extent to which these departments affect school management and teachers' work remains in dispute. Cusick (1983) suggested that academic departments exist mostly as a matter of administrative convenience, not as academic sub-units vested with substantive authority over the educational process in high schools. However, more recent analyses contradict this view, suggesting that departments have important effects inside high schools (e.g., Johnson, 1988).

Among the recent analyses affirming the importance of academic departments are a set of studies showing how the disciplinary subcultures around which departments are formed define and shape teachers' instructional practices and workload conditions (Ball, 1987, Little 1982; Little & McLaughlin, 1993; Siskin, 1991). A related set of studies show that departments housing different disciplines display very different patterns of instructional management, including differing levels of control over instructional decision making, different patterns of collegial support, and different patterns of sequencing and coordinating students' course work over time (Bidwell & Yasumoto, 1999; Grossman & Stodolsky, 1994; Stodolsky & Grossman, 1995 ; Rowan, Raudenbush, & Kang, 1991; Raudenbush, Rowan, & Kang, 1991). Finally, it appears that departments can play a key role in mediating the impact of external, educational reforms on teaching practice (Ball, 1987; McLaughlin, 1987).

There is a problem with most research on academic departments in high schools, however. In both qualitative and quantitative research, scholars have been unable to disentangle the confounding array of factors that might lead to a finding of department effects on management or teaching practices inside high schools. We know, for example, that one reason teachers working in different departments report very different patterns of school organization and climate, and use different teaching practices, is that their departments are organized around different disciplines. But disciplines are *not* departments. Instead of being organizational sub-units of specific schools, academic disciplines exist as large, complex, and highly institutionalized structures that are organized and operate in society at large. Thus, a subject-area department within a typical school will usually be organized in reference to a disciplinary society and its affiliated institutions, a complex of organizations that is formed and operates outside of schools.

In fact, there is a large literature on disciplinary subcultures in society, and much attention to the effects of these subcultures on substantive educational processes inside of schools. This work originates in C.P. Snow's (1959) classic discussion of the two cultures of science, continues through Philip Jackson's (1986) seminal discussion of the ways in which disciplinary subcultures affect the practice of teaching, and culminates in more recent empirical studies of disciplinary differences among teachers in how they understand the nature of teaching, enact it, and work as colleagues to manage it (see, for example, Stodolsky, 1988; Stodolsky & Grossman, 1995; Rowan, Raudenbush, and Cheong, 1993; Rowan, 2002a).

In much of this literature, academic disciplines are seen as deeply institutionalized structures. For example, a given academic discipline is seen as being constituted by a set of epistemological beliefs about the nature of knowledge and how it can be transmitted, and these beliefs are seen as being formulated and maintained by disciplinary societies and associations operating outside of schools and passed on to members through various forms of socialization. From this perspective, it makes sense to expect that academic disciplines—operating as large, institutionalized complexes in society—will have the kinds cognitive, normative, and regulatory effects on educational practice that institutional theorists have hypothesized to be true of a variety of institutionalized structures in society (for a review of this issue, see Rowan and Miskel, 1999).

However, the effects of disciplines on organizational processes should not to be confused with departmental effects. To see this, consider the evidence of disciplinary effects on educational practice in elementary schools (which are not departmentalized). These studies show that patterns of teaching practice and instructional management vary greatly across disciplines. For example, Stodolsky (1988) found that elementary school teachers (with generalist assignments) used very different instructional formats when teaching mathematics as opposed to social studies. Moreover, instructional management practices in elementary schools have been found to vary across different subjects (for a review, see Spillane and Bursch, n.d.). Mathematics and language arts, for example, are more subject to test-based accountability, have more uniform curricular definition, and show more sequential coordination than do disciplines such as social studies, science, or art. Yet, all of this academic differentiation is taking place within a type of organization (the elementary school) that is *not* departmentalized. Thus, the effects being observed in elementary schools are best conceptualized as resulting from the cognitive, normative, and regulatory influence of disciplines, not from the actions of local departments.

On the other hand, it would be a mistake to generalize these results from elementary schools and to argue that *all* history departments, or *all* mathematics departments, will be the same, no matter what high school they are located in. To be sure, any academic department within a particular high school will be affected by the disciplinary structure within which it is embedded, but the ways in which academic departments housing the same discipline are organized and managed across a variety of high schools, and how teachers enact their teaching roles within these departments, have been found to be shaped by a host of other influences that interact with, and modify, the influences of disciplinary structures on practice. The best way to see this is in research comparing departments housing the same disciplines in different high schools. Following the lead of Talbert and McLaughlin (1994), Gutierrez (1996) and Donnelly (2000) conducted this kind of research. Gutierrez found that mathematics departments in different high schools varied in their work practices and general climate dimensions, showing different patterns of curriculum sequencing, different levels of academic press, differing modal patterns of teaching, and different degrees of collegiality. Similar findings were reported in Donnelly's study of science departments. In this study, science departments in different high schools were found to differ in managerial practices, attention to and connections with disciplinary organizations, and various conceptions of work.

The studies just reviewed offered a variety of explanations for why departments housing the same disciplines might operate differently across schools, explanations that can be classified along three primary dimensions. First, characteristics of the schools in which the departments were embedded seem to shape the ways in which departments operate, with differences in staff and student composition, market sector, and geographic location having the potential to affect departmental dynamics. In addition, the pre-dispositions and professional commitments of department members, arising out differences in their social and occupational backgrounds, might affect how individuals enact their roles as department members. And finally, characteristics of the departments themselves—their size, relative power within the school, unique view of their mission, and unique organizational histories—can shape departmental effects on educational practice.

All of this leaves us in a quandary. Although many educational researchers think academic departments in high schools are an important locus of school organization, there are skeptics (e.g., Cusick, 1983). As a result, there is a need to establish whether or not academic departments *do* exercise an important influence on substantive educational processes in high schools. Surprisingly, close inspection of existing research shows that clear evidence on this point has not yet been published. Most of the quantitative research on academic departments, for example, has modeled the effects of disciplines (not departments) on organizational outcomes. Moreover, while a lively case study literature has focused squarely on departments, there is evidence in that literature that departments organized around the same disciplines can operate quite differently depending on the schools in which they are located, the individuals who hold membership in the departments, and the structural features of the departments themselves. More importantly, case studies are best suited to capturing patterns of local activities and meanings within specific sites, but they do not provide evidence of either the existence or size of average "departmental effects" across large numbers of cases. As a result, prior research and theory give us sound reason to expect that departments play an important role in shaping educational processes in secondary schools, but a strategy for establishing such effects—especially in quantitative studies of schooling—is needed.

APPROACH

This paper generates quantitative evidence of departmental effects on management processes in high schools by capitalizing on a recent advance in multi-level statistical modeling—the use of what Goldstein (1987) called "crossed" multi-level modeling (for the first empirical application of this approach in educational research, see Raudenbush 1993; for a general discussion of such models, see Raudenbush and Bryk, 2002). The specific purpose of this paper is to estimate departmental effects on patterns of school management in high schools using a "crossed" multi-level statistical model developed by Kang (1992a; 1992b). As an initial step in this agenda, we formulate a statistical model in which individual teachers are viewed as members of two cross-classified, higher level units—academic disciplines and particular schools (which, together, define an individual teacher's departmental membership). Then, building on a long line of work by Rowan and colleagues on the development of "organic" management within secondary schools (see, for example, Miller and Rowan, 2003; Raudenbush, Rowan, and Kang, 1991; Rowan, Raudenbush, and Kang, 1991; Rowan, Raudenbush, & Cheong, 1993; Rowan, 2002b), we show how this crossed multilevel model can be used to estimate the effects of individuals, disciplines, schools, and departments on teachers' perceptions of organic management in high schools.

BACKGROUND

The problem of how to estimate department effects on patterns of organic management in high schools is relevant to two lines of work in educational administration. The first is a program of research on "organic" management in schools conducted by Rowan and colleagues in order to test hypotheses drawn from contingency theory (for a theoretical rationale for this program, see Rowan, 1990; for empirical studies, see Raudenbush, Rowan, & Kang, 1991; Rowan, Raudenbush, & Kang, 1991; Rowan, Raudenbush & Cheong, 1993; Rowan, 2002a, 2002b; and Miller & Rowan, 2003). In a series of studies, these researchers measured organic management in terms of three, strongly associated dimensions of organizational design—the presence of supportive school leadership, the presence of strong teacher control over decision making, and the presence of supportive collegial relationships among the teaching staff. Then, in a body of research spanning more than a decade, Rowan and colleagues studied why patterns of organic management differed within and across schools, and whether differences in the degree of organic management within and between schools was associated with differences in school and/or teacher effectiveness. A good summary of this research can be found in Miller and Rowan (2003).

The research reported here is relevant to a broader literature on school organization and climate as well. This body of research (like the work of Rowan and colleagues on organic management) uses questionnaire responses from individual teachers to measure the structural and climate properties of schools. For decades, the use of individual teacher responses in research on school organization and climate created controversy about the appropriate unit of analysis. Many researchers in educational administration and other fields argued that in research on schools as organizations, individual teacher's responses should be aggregated to the school level, with all analyses of teachers' responses being conducted as purely between-schools analyses. The justification advanced for this view was that the theoretical constructs under study were organizational, not individual (for a review, see Miskel and Ogawa, 1988). However, other researchers criticized this approach, arguing that purely between-schools analyses of teachers' responses necessarily ignored the large (and substantively interesting) variation in reports about organizational structure and climate existing among teachers within the same school. These researchers called for purely between-teachers analyses of school organization and climate measures (see, for example, Pallas, 1988; James and Jones, 1974).

With the widespread availability of multilevel statistical computing packages such as HLM5 (Ruadenbush, Bryk, Cheong, & Congdon, 2000), debates about the appropriate unit of analysis in such studies have become moot. Within a nested, multilevel framework, it is possible to model teachers' reports about properties of schools at both the individual level of analysis *and* the school level of analysis, and to do so within the framework of a nested, multilevel statistical model (for a general treatment, see Raudenbush & Bryk, 2002). In fact, multilevel models of school climate invariably produce substantively interesting findings. For example, in the research on organic management conducted by Rowan and colleagues, it has been found that teachers' perceptions of administrative leadership, staff cooperation, and control over decision making vary significantly within and between schools. In most analyses, somewhere between 70–80% of the variance in teachers' perceptions of organic management lies within schools, and about 20–30% lies among schools. Moreover, variance at both these levels can be explained on theoretical grounds. For example, Rowan and colleagues found that private schools, elementary schools, and smaller schools tend to be rated by teachers as more organic in form than larger, public, and secondary schools. In addition, Rowan and colleagues explained why teachers' perceptions of organic management vary within the same school. In particular, they developed the idea that large, complex organizations are characterized by "micro-climates" that develop among individuals who share common sub-unit membership and/or common working conditions within the academic division of labor in schools (Rowan, Raudenbush, & Kang, 1991). Especially important for the purposes of this paper has been the consistent finding—across a range of data sets and studies—of discipline effects on patterns of organic management within schools. For example, in a series of analyses, Rowan and colleagues have found that a teacher's disciplinary assignment affects that teacher's perception of school leadership, teacher control over decision making, and staff cooperation, as well as teachers' task perceptions and pedagogical beliefs (Rowan, Raudenbush, & Kang, 1991; Rowan, Raudenbush, & Cheong, 1993; Rowan, 2002a; Miller and Rowan, 2003).

The problem with this research, however, is that *departments* were never formally developed as a unit of analysis in the research program, despite the expressed interest in studying "micro-climates" within schools. As in much other research, Rowan and colleagues did identify important effects of disciplinary memberships on teachers' perceptions of organizational properties, but they did not nest teachers into departments within schools or cross-classify individuals into discipline-by-school units in order to estimate and model an explicit "department" variance component in their analyses. By contrast, that is the problem taken up here.

A CROSSED-MULTILEVEL STATISTICAL
MODEL OF DEPARTMENT EFFECTS

To estimate department effects on organic management within high schools, this paper employs a "crossed-multilevel" statistical model developed by Kang (1992a, 1992b). This model differs from the more commonly-used, "nested" multi-level models that readers might be familiar with. In the "crossed" multi-level model developed here, individual teachers are viewed as holding memberships in two higher-level units that are cross classified—schools and academic disciplines—and the cross-classification of these two macro factors defines a set of cells in which teachers are nested that we label as departments. Goldstein (1987) called the procedure we are using to classify individuals into groups a "crossed-multilevel" data structure. It would be possible, of course, to model department memberships within what Goldstein (1987) called a "nested-multilevel" data structure. For example, we could view individual teachers as being nested within departments, which were in turn nested within schools. But that is not the argument we are making here. Instead, we use the cross-classification units for teachers as an index of departmental membership in assessing the size of departmental effects on the three dimensions of organic management discussed earlier.

Base Model

In conducting the analysis, we call our simplest model the base model. This model is akin to the usual "unconditional" model in hierarchical linear models in that it partitions variance in our dependent measures into teacher, discipline, school, and department components before entry of any independent variables. As in a standard, nested, two-level hierarchical linear model, the crossed multilevel model we present takes the form of within- and between-group models. The first model represents a within-department regression model without any predictors:

$$Y_{ijk} = \beta_{jk} + e_{ijk} \tag{1}$$

where Y_{ijk} represents the value of a school management variable perceived by ith teacher in school j, teaching kth subject for $i = 1, 2, \ldots, n_{jk}, j = 1,2, \ldots, J, k = 1,2, \ldots, K$; where β_{jk} is the mean value of an outcome in each department, and e_{ijk} is a random error with mean zero and variance σ^2. The sub notation of n_{jk} implies the unbalanced design characteristics, in which the number of teachers within departments is not the same in all schools. Equation (1) simply states that the level of an organic management measure perceived by an individual teacher is composed of the true value of that teacher's departmental mean, plus individual error.

In the between-department model, the parameter, β_{jk}, which is the departmental mean of teachers' perceptions of a school management variable, is seen as varying as a result of the random effects associated with the schools where departments are located, the subjects around which departments are formed, and the unique effect of each department as an organization within schools. To model this, we write:

$$\beta_{jk} = \mu + a_j + b_k + c_{jk} \tag{2}$$

where μ is the grand mean for all schools; a_j, b_k, and c_{jk} are the random effects of a school j, a discipline k, and a department jk identified by the discipline k a teacher taught within a school j. The three random factors of school (denoted a_j), discipline (denoted b_j), and department (denoted c_{jk}) are assumed to have a distribution with mean zero and variances T_a, T_b, and T_c respectively.

The model allows the option of defining each of the two main factors (schools and disciplines) as having either fixed or random effects. Because this study uses only the academic disciplines of English, mathematics, social studies, and science, it is appropriate to consider the discipline effect, b_k, as having a fixed effect, since the results of our analyses are not be applicable to teachers who teach subjects other than the four academic-subjects under study here. Using the strategy of dummy variable coding in a regression model, we can therefore specify $K - 1$ subject dummy indicator variables in Equation (2a), which would be:

$$\beta_{jk} = \mu_k + \sum_{k=1}^{K-1} \gamma_k D_k + a_j + c_{jk} \qquad (2a)$$

where μ_k becomes the mean for the teachers teaching Kth subject (say mathematics), γ_k is the effect of subject k indicated by each dummy variable of D_k,(i.e., social studies, English, and science), and the other terms remain the same as in Equation (2). So, equation (1) is the within-department model in our analysis, and equation (2) or (2a) is the between-department model in the analysis, with both equations together constituting the crossed-multilevel model. In particular Equation (1) and (2) as a pair can be called a crossed random-effects multilevel model while Equation (1) and (2a) can be called a crossed mixed-effects multilevel model. This study uses the mixed-effects model, and discussions in the following pages are limited to that model.

Looking more closely at the base model defined by equations (1) and (2a), we can see that there are three random parameters, each with its own variance. The within-department variance, σ^2, reflects the magnitude of differences among teachers' perceptions within departments. The between-school variance, T_a, reflects the magnitude of differences among schools in teachers' perceptions of organic management. And, the between-department variance, T_c, provides information about the magnitude of differences among departments in the same school on the measures of organic management. Now, the reader will recall that we are treating the effects of disciplines as fixed effects in the current model, so there is no unique variance component for disciplines in the model. But that is not the main point of the analysis, which is instead designed to investigate T_c, the variance in perceptions of organic management due to departments.

The variances provide useful information about the expected spread of organic management features around the means for various units of analysis in the model. But from these, we can also derive several intra-class correlations that describe the relative amount of total (random) variation at each level of analysis in the model. For example, the intra-department correlation, $T_c/(\sigma^2 + T_a + T_c)$, tells us the percentage of variance in teachers' perceptions of organic management lying among departments within schools, while the intra-school correlation, $T_a/(\sigma^2 + T_a + T_c)$ tells us the percentage of variance in teachers' perceptions lying among schools. Typically, researchers view intra-class correlations of this sort as initial evidence about the importance of some analytic unit in producing variation in the dependent variable, that is, as initial evidence of the size of that unit's "effect" on the dependent variable. For example, in the current study, if the proportion of variance in organic management lying among departments within schools is high, we will have initial evidence that academic departments are important in shaping the outcome under study.

An additional piece of diagnostic information that can be obtained from the base model is an estimate of the reliability with which organic management can be measured at various units in the analysis. In the crossed multilevel model being estimated here, the parameter of each cell mean, β_{jk} is seen as a function of each subject mean and the random effect of school j and department jk. If an estimate, $\hat{\beta}_{jk}$, is used instead $\hat{\beta}_{jk}$, then the reliability for our estimates of department means is:

$$\alpha_{jk} = \frac{\beta_{jk}}{\hat{\beta}_{jk}} = \frac{\tau_a + \tau_a}{\tau_a + \tau_c + \sigma^2/n_{jk}} \tag{3}$$

where n_{jk} is the sample size for department jk. When differentiation within schools due to departments is ignored and the outcome measures are aggregated into school means, then the reliability of the aggregated school mean, β_j, is:

$$\alpha_j = \frac{Var(\beta_j)}{Var(\hat{\beta}_j)} = \frac{\tau_a}{\tau_a + \tau_c/K + \sigma^2/\left(\sum_{k=1}^{K} n_{jk}\right)} \tag{3a}$$

The reliabilities just discussed also provide important diagnostic information about whether to directly model departmental variation in organic management within schools. As Rowan, Raudenbush, and Kang (1991a) pointed out, "a decision to aggregate the perceptions of individuals into [some higher level] measures of climate should depend ... on the estimated reliability of [the means of] the perceptual measure" at different levels of analysis. In the present analysis, for example, if the reliability of department means is sufficiently high, it makes sense to proceed to an explanatory modeling stage. If it is extremely low, however, such modeling will be difficult, since a low reliability will indicate that it is very difficult to reliably discriminate among mean scores across departments.

In summary, the base model just discussed provides important information about any set of organizational measures built up from individuals' responses. Using the estimated variance components σ^2, T_a, and T_c, we can obtain initial diagnostic information about the relative importance of processes occurring at various levels of analysis in producing the outcome, and we can assess our ability to reliably discriminate in levels of the dependent variable at higher levels of analysis in the model.

Explanatory Model

As in any multilevel model, the base model just discussed can be expanded to include independent (or predictor) variables. These might include variables measuring the characteristics of individual teachers, the characteristics of schools, or the characteristics of departments. For example, suppose we want to model the effects of individual teachers' backgrounds on their perceptions of organic management. Then we could formulate the within-department regression model as:

$$Y_{ijk} = \beta_{0jk} + \sum_{p=1}^{p} \beta_{pjk} X_{pijk} + e_{ijk} \tag{4}$$

where β_{pjk} is the effect of pth predictor variable of ith teacher. The random error component, e_{ijk}, is the residual error distributed with mean zero and variance σ^2 after accounting for the effects of P variables on the outcome variable Y_{ijk}. The essential feature of the multilevel approach is that those within-department parameters, or the effects of individual characteristics, $\beta_{0jk}, \beta_{1jk}, \ldots, \beta_{Pjk}$ may or may not vary across the departments. In this study, we assume that these effects are fixed and that only the intercepts are random. Thus, the intercept parameter can be conceived as the adjusted mean value of teachers' perceptions on an outcome variable within each department.

We can also expand the between-department model to include independent variables. For example, when the intercept parameter, is random across schools and departments but not for disciplines, as in our mixed-effects crossed multilevel model, then we can formulate the between-department model as:

$$\beta_{0jk} = \gamma_{00} + \sum_{k=1}^{3} \gamma_{0k} D_k + \sum_{q=4}^{Q} \gamma_{0q} W_{qij} + a_{0j} + c_{0jk} \tag{5}$$

where γ_{0k} are the effects of the disciplines teachers taught, as indicated by the three dummy variables of D_k, and γ_{0q} are the effects school and department characteristics, W_{qjk}, on the random parameter β_{0jk}. The two residual error terms in Equation (5), a_j and c_{jk}, are assumed to have distributions with mean zero and variances of T_a and T_c respectively. If the random intercept, now the adjusted average perception of teachers, β_{0jk}, varies across schools but not departments after accounting for the effects of the discipline teachers taught and the characteristics of schools, we can set the last random part, c_{jk}, to zero. A comprehensive description of this modeling strategy appears in the first author's dissertation (Kang, 1992a).

DATA

Data for this study were taken from the 1984 Administrator Teacher Survey (ATS) of schools in the High School and Beyond study (HSB) (Jones, et al., 1983), with data on predictor variables taken from both the ATS and HSB data files. The ATS sample consisted of 538 public and private secondary schools that participated in the 1982 HSB study. In the ATS data, a random sample of up to 30 teachers was administered a questionnaire within each school. In schools with fewer than 30 eligible teachers, all eligible teachers were sampled. In the present study, we use data *only* for teachers who taught one of the four major academic subjects of mathematics, social studies, English, and science and who worked in public and Catholic high schools.[1]

Analytic Sample

Not all of these sampled teachers completed all of the ATS survey items used to construct our measures. Thus, there was missing data at the teacher level. Teachers who provided incomplete data for any of the component items used to develop the three measures of organic management examined in this study were dropped from the sample. Moreover, data were also missing on teachers within the HSB data files. This left us with an analytic sample of 4107 teachers from 339 schools.

Table 1 shows the number of teachers, departments, and schools classified by market sector (public vs. Catholic), geographic region of the U.S., and academic subject. There are 3627 teachers from 288 public high schools and 480 teachers from fifty-one Catholic high schools, or on average of 12.59 and 9.41 teachers of public and Catholic high schools respectively. The total number of academic departments in the sample is 1,267, or on average, 3.24 teachers per department. The number of teachers per school ranged from one to twelve.

TABLE 1
Number of Teachers (Departments) and of Schools in the Sample
Classified by Sector, Region, and Academic Subjects

| | Number of Teachers (Departments) | | | | | Schools |
Sector/Region	Math	Social Studies	English	Science	Subtotal	(N)
Public						
Urban	289	301	214	205	1009	73
	(68)	(72)	(70)	(71)	(281)	
Suburban	465	492	360	346	1663	129
	(125)	(126)	(125)	(119)	(495)	
Rural	288	297	174	196	955	86
	(82)	(78)	(75)	(80)	(315)	
Subtotal	1042	1090	748	747	3627	288
	(275)	(276)	(270)	(270)	(1091)	
Catholic						
Urban	16	40	21	22	99	13
	(8)	(12)	(11)	(11)	(42)	
Suburban	47	111	80	96	334	32
	(24)	(30)	(31)	(31)	(115)	
Rural	4	15	14	14	47	6
	(3)	(5)	(5)	(5)	(18)	
Subtotal	67	166	115	132	480	51
	(35)	(47)	(47)	(47)	(176)	
Total	1109	1256	863	879	4107	339
	(310)	(323)	(317)	(317)	(1267)	

Measures of Organic Management

The dependent variables in the analysis are three measures of organic management originally developed by Pallas (1988) and used by Rowan, Raudenbush, and Kang (1991) in their earlier analysis of ATS data. The measures index the nature of leadership exercised by school principals, the amount of cooperation among teachers in a school, and the amount of control teachers have over decisions over school policies. The ATS items used to construct these scales are listed here in Appendix A.

Scales were constructed by standardizing all items and then summing component items for each scale to construct a unique score for each teacher on each scale. *Principal Leadership* is a 14-item scale measuring the principal's administrative leadership that contains items consistent with

TABLE 2
Descriptive Statistics and Alpha Reliability of the Three Organic
Management Measures Classified by Four Academic Subjects

	Mean	*SD*	*Reliability*	*Items (N)*
Principal Leadership (Total)	−.586	9.946	.92	14
Math	.126	9.732		
Social Studies	−.861	10.373		
English	−1.190	10.033		
Science	−.498	9.450		
Staff Cooperation (Total)	−.090	5.328	.84	8
Math	.456	5.119		
Social Studies	−.531	5.773		
English	−.655	5.201		
Science	.404	4.926		
Teacher Control (Total)	−.179	5.250	.77	9
Math	.288	4.888		
Social Studies	.024	5.316		
English	−.881	5.544		
Science	−.367	5.227		

Rosenholtz's (1985) view of supportive leadership as exercised in effective schools. *Staff Cooperation* is an eight-item scale measuring the extent of cooperation among school staff consistent with current views about cooperative professional communities in high schools. *Teacher Control* is a nine-item scale measuring the extent to which teachers have control over or participation in the formation of school and classroom policies. Table 2 shows the descriptive statistics for these three measures for teachers in each of the four academic subjects under study. The internal consistencies of the scales (as measured by Cronbach's alpha) are .92 for principal leadership, .84 for staff cooperation, and .77 teacher control. In later stages of the analysis, we also will present data on the reliabilities of these measures at the school and department levels of our analysis.

Teacher-Level Variables

Following earlier work, we expect that teachers' perceptions of organic management are shaped by various experiences associated with their social and professional backgrounds. As a result, our explanatory model includes a variety of teacher-level variables that could lead to different socialization experiences. The operational meaning and coding system for each of these variables is listed below:

> *Race:* a dummy variable that stands for teacher's ethnic background, where black = 0 and other = 1;
>
> *Sex:* a dummy variable of a teacher's gender, where female = 0 and male = 1;
>
> *Years of Education:* an ordinal variable transformed from the years of education possessed by a teacher, where 0 = less than master's, 1 = master's, 2 = beyond master's.
>
> *Years of Experience:* a continuous variable measuring the total number of years of teaching experience of a teacher.
>
> An additional variable takes into account a teacher's location within the academic division of labor of departments within high schools. That variable is:
>
> *Track:* an ordinal variable used as a proxy for a teacher's track assignment, as indicated by a teacher's estimate of the percentage of students in his/her class that are above or below the average achievement level of the school. It is coded on a 10-point scale with 0 = 0–9 percent, and 10 = 90–100 percent above school average.

Discipline Indicators

As discussed earlier, previous research on academic departments often failed to disentangle the effects of disciplinary cultures from department effects. To avoid this problem, and to test substantively interesting questions about the effects of disciplinary cultures on school management, this study includes a set of dummy-coded variables indexing the main academic subject a teacher reported teaching. The academic disciplines are coded as below.

> *Social Studies:* a dummy variable coded 1 if a teacher's most frequently taught course was in a social science discipline, otherwise coded 0.
>
> *English:* a dummy variable coded 1 if a teacher's most frequently taught course was in English or a related subject, otherwise coded 0.
>
> *Science:* a dummy variable coded 1 if a teacher's most frequently taught course was in a natural science, otherwise coded 0.
>
> *Math:* the contrast variable captured by an intercept indicating the teachers whose most frequently teaching course was in mathematics.

School-Level Variables

Our analysis also included several properties of schools found in previous research to account for school-to-school variation in organic management. These variables, taken from the 1980 HSB data files, were:

Sector: a dummy variable coded 0 for public schools and 1 for Catholic schools.

School Size: a continuous variable representing the total student enrollment at a school.

Percentage Minority: a continuous variable representing the percentage of black and Hispanic students at a school.

Percentage Disadvantaged: an ordinal variable representing the percentage of disadvantaged students. The values ranged from 0 = 0–9 percent to 9 = 90–100 percent.

School Mean Achievement: a continuous variable consisting of a school mean computed from the HSB base-year tests of sophomores and seniors.

School Mean SES: a continuous variable that aggregated HSB base-year measures of the socioeconomic status of sophomores and seniors at a school.

Rural: a dummy variable coded 1 if schools were located in a rural area, otherwise coded 0.

Urban: a dummy variable coded 1 if schools were located in an urban area, otherwise coded 0.

Suburban: a reference variable for the school location of Rural and Urban, captured as an intercept parameter.

RESULTS

The results of the study are presented in two stages: (1) a variance decomposition and analysis of the psychometric properties of measures of organic management derived from estimating the base model and (2) an analysis of the effects of all independent variables on the measures of organic management derived from estimating the explanatory model.

Variance Decomposition and Psychometric Properties

Table 3 reports the variance components for each of the random effects in the base model (σ^2, the variance lying among teachers within depart-

TABLE 3

Psychometric Properties of the Three Organic Management Measures

	Principal Leadership	*Staff Cooperation*	*TeacherControl*
Variance Decomposition			
Teacher Level	68.481	22.110	20.985
Department Level	8.996	2.262	2.169
School Level	23.288	4.351	4.915
Total	100.765	28.723	28.068
Intraclass Correlations			
Department Level[a1]	8.9	7.9	7.7
School Level[a2]	23.1	15.1	17.5
Total	32.0	23.0	25.2
Reliability			
School Level[b1]	.76	.66	.69
Department Level[b2]	.60	.49	.52
Number of Items	14	8	9

Notes: [a1]Intraclass correlation at the department level is measured by
$\rho = \tau_c/(\tau_a + \tau_c + \sigma^2)$, where τ_a, τ_c and σ^2 are the variances attributable to the differences of schools, departments, and individual teachers.
[a2] Intraclass correlation at the school level: $\rho = \tau_c/(\tau_a + \tau_c + \sigma^2)$.

[b1]Reliability of the school mean of teacher perceptions: $\alpha = (\sum_{j=1}^{J} a_j)/J$, where a_j

$= \tau_a/(\tau_a + \tau_c/k_j + \sigma^2/\Sigma_{njk})$, where k_j is the number of departments within each school of j, njk is the number of k teachers within each department.
[b2] Reliability of the departmental mean of teacher perceptions :

$\alpha = \left(\sum_j \sum_k \alpha_{jk}\right)/G$, where $\alpha_{jk} = (\tau_a + \tau_c)/(\tau_a + \tau_c/k_j + \sigma^2/n_{jk})$, G is the

total number of departments in the sample ($G = 1267$).

ments, T_c, the variance lying among departments within schools, and T_a, the variance lying among schools). Each of these variance components is a unique estimate that separates out the effects of other components, and that controls for the fixed effects of disciplines.

The main point of this analysis is to quantify the effects of departments on patterns of organic management in schools. As a result, we turn now to the second panel in Table 3, where the percentage of total variance in each of the three outcome measures accounted for by schools and departments is reported. The data show that departments account for about 9% of the total observed variance in our measure of principal leadership, about 8% of the variance in our measure of staff cooperation, and about 8% of the variance in our measure of teacher control. It is important to note that these estimates are *not* confounded with school effects, nor are they confounded with the effects of disciplinary cultures on the measures. Instead, the results are showing the unique contribution of departments—as distinctive sub-units within schools—to variation in organic management.

Table 3 also shows the percentage of variance in measures of organic management that lies among schools. Schools account for about 23% of the total variance in principal leadership, about 15% of the total variance in staff cooperation, and about 18% of the total variance in teacher control. Finally, if we add together the percentages of variance accounted for by schools and departments together (as the row labeled "total" in panel 2 of Table 3 does) we get a sense of how much our two organizational factors (schools and departments) contribute to variation in perceptions of organic management. Further, we can subtract that number from 100 to arrive at the percentage of variance in our measures that lies among teachers within departments. As in most previous analyses, the percentage of variance among teachers is quite large, about 68% for principal leadership, about 77% for staff cooperation, and about 75% for teacher control.

The final panel of Table 3 reports the reliabilities for our measures of organic management at the teacher, department, and school levels of analysis. The data in Table 3 show that the reliabilities for departmental means on principal leadership, staff cooperation, and teacher control are .60, .49, and .52 respectively, while for school means on these same measures, the reliabilities are .76, .66, and .69 respectively. These are moderate reliabilities, but they reflect two main features of the analysis—first, the relatively small variance across departments and schools in comparison to the relatively large variance in teachers perceptions lying among teachers within a given department, and second, the small numbers of teachers per department and school in the analyses (about 3 teachers per department, and about 12 teachers per school). In our view, the reliabilities reported here are large enough to warrant further analyses at both the school and department levels.

Table 4 reports an additional component of the base model—the fixed-effects of the four academic subjects on the organic management measures. These fixed effects are reported in terms of regression coefficients, with the standard error of these coefficients shown in parentheses. Recall that these effects were estimated through the inclusion of three dummy variables in the model. As a result, the intercept in the base model is the mean value of an organic management variable for all of the teachers in the sample who reported teaching mathematics most frequently. The other coefficients for social studies, English, and science are the mean differences from the mean of the reference group, in this case, mathematics teachers. Thus, each of these regression coefficients should be interpreted in conjunction with the value of the intercept.

TABLE 4

Fixed Effects Estimates (Standard Errors) of Academic Subjects on the
Organic Management Measures

Academic Subjects	Principal Leadership	Staff Cooperation	Teacher Control
Intercept (Math)	−.55 (.431)	.33 (.219)	−.31 (.219)
Social Studies	1.00* (.467)	.30 (.255)	.67* (.249)
English	−.44 (.452)	−.87**(.248)	.41 (.242)
Science	−.46 (.481)	−.91**(.264)	−.42 (.258)

Notes: *Coefficient is larger than twice of standard error.
　　　　**Coefficient is larger than three times of standard error.

One important feature of the estimates shown in Table 4 is that they are not confounded with teachers' departmental membership. This is unlike the estimates reported in many previous studies, which often reported strong disciplinary effects on a variety of organizational outcomes (see, especially, Rowan, Raudenbush, & Kang, 1991; Raudenbush, Rowan, & Kang, 1991; Strodolsky & Grossman, 1995). Since those estimates were confounded with department effects, however, the results reported here represent a step forward in the analysis of disciplinary effects on school management processes.

Looking closely at Table 4, we see that there *are* discipline effects on school management. But the pattern of effects varies across the three dimensions of organic management and defies easy description. Past studies of disciplinary cultures and their effects on school management have been based on two main theoretical perspectives. One line of work was derived from contingency theory as illustrated in a variety of analyses presented by Rowan (*2002a; Miller and Rowan, 2003). There, the focus was on relative levels of task uncertainty and task variety affecting teachers' need to build organic forms of management in schools, and the assumption was that math and science teachers worked in a more routine task environment than social studies and English teachers. On this basis, the prediction from contingency theory would be that math and science teachers should report lower levels of organic management in their immediate environments than English and social studies teachers.

An alternative perspective is found in the work of Siskin (1991) and Stodolsky and Grossman (1995). Here, the emphasis has been on the uniformity of professional training among teachers and the sequential interdependence of high school coursework in a discipline. In this view, mathematics teachers share a common body of subject matter knowledge, and depend critically on each others' teaching for success due to the sequential ordering of coursework in their field. All of this is assumed to increase the amount of cooperation among mathematics teachers, but to decrease their levels of control over school policies, which are constrained by heavily institutionalized understandings of the discipline. Meanwhile, teachers in the other disciplines are assumed to have diverse professional training, and course work within these disciplines is seen as inherently less sequentially interdependent than course work in mathematics. As a result, teachers in these disciplines are predicted to show lower levels of staff cooperation, but higher levels of control over decision making. It should be noted that, in contrast to contingency theory, this perspective is silent on the effects of disciplines on teachers' perceptions of principal leadership.

In point of fact, neither of these hypotheses seems well-confirmed by the data in Table 4, and so it is perhaps best to summarize the results simply by saying that the data in Table 4 show distinctive disciplinary profiles that, as yet, are not adequately predicted by theory. For example, social studies teachers consistently report the highest levels of organic management. In Table 4, for example, they report the highest levels of supportive leadership, the highest levels of control over school decision making, and (along with mathematics teachers) the highest levels of staff cooperation. By contrast, English and science teachers show the lowest levels of staff cooperation of all academic teachers, but are otherwise like math teachers in their perceptions of principal leadership and control over school decisions. Finally, along with social studies teachers, math teachers show the highest levels of staff cooperation.

Results from the Explanatory Model

The next step in the analysis was to include the other independent variables in the model in order to explain variation in the three measures of organic management at the individual, department, and school levels of analysis. Table 5 shows the results of this analysis, which estimates a specific form of the explanatory model described in Equations (4) and (5). For each dependent variable in our analysis, Table 5 reports the effects of each independent variable, where the entries in the table are the regression coefficients for each independent variable (with standard errors in parentheses). Please note that the predictor variables are grouped into three sections in the table: school-level predictors, subject indicators, and teacher-level predictors.

School-Level Predictors

The results in Table 5 are consistent with past studies of organic management in schools (see, for example, Miller & Rowan, 2003). In particular, as in past research, the sector in which a school is located has large

TABLE 5
Fixed Effects Estimates (Standard Errors) of School- and Teacher-level
Predictors on the Three Organic Management Measures

	Principal Leadership *Effect (SE)*	*Staff Cooperation* *Effect (SE)*	*Teacher Control* *Effect (SG)*
School Level Predictors			
Sector	3.886*	2.737**	2.726**
	(1.010)	(.459)	(.424)
Urban	−1.060	−.453	−1.612**
	(.825)	(.370)	(.341)
Rural	−1.771*	−.632	−.179
	(.799)	(.359)	(.330)
Disadvan	−.186	−.040	−.042
	(.193)	(.087)	(.080)
Avmiron	.022	.0007	−.019*
	(.015)	(.007)	(.006)
School Size	−.0005	−.0004*	−.0005*
	(.0004)	(.0002)	(.0002)
Mean SES	1.046	.708 (.494)	.155 (.455)
	(1.098)		
Mean Achievement	−.084 (.104)	−.067	−.042
		(.047)	(.043)
Subject Indicators			
Intercept (Math & Sub-urban)	7.700	5.588	3.996
Social Studies	1.511**	.381	1.192***
	(.474)	(.259)	(.251)
English	−.199	−.984**	.575*
	(.458)	(.251)	(.243)
Science	−.062	−.761*	−.072
	(.481)	(.264)	(.256)
Teacher Level Predictors			
Experience	.164	.389**	−.014
	(.117)	(.065)	(.063)
Sex	−.469	−.740**	−.502**
	(.303)	(.169)	(.164)
Education	−.673**	−.389**	−.157
	(.214)	(.119)	(.115)
Race	−2.620**	−.448	−.799**
	(.538)	(.300)	(.294)
Track	.652**	.028	.639***
	(.150)	(.084)	(.082)

Notes: *Coefficient is larger than twice of standard error.
          ** Coefficient is larger than three times of standard error.

effects on each of the measures of organic management in the analysis (see also Bryk & Driscoll (1988), Chubb & Moe (1990), and Rowan, Raudenbush, and Kang (1991) for similar findings using ATS/HSB data). By contrast, the effects of other school-level variables on organic management are less consistent than the effects of school sector, although they are, in the main, consistent with previous findings reported by Rowan, Raudenbush and Kang (1991) using ATS data and Miller and Rowan (2003) using Schools and Staffing Survey (SASS) data. Perhaps the most consistent finding is that larger schools generally show lower levels of organic management (although the negative effect of school size on principal leadership is not statistically significant in the data presented in this paper). Otherwise, the geographic location of schools and their student body composition had only occasional effects on the outcome measures, a finding consistent with our previous analyses of ATS data (Rowan, Raudenbush, & Kang, 1991), but inconsistent with findings from analyses using SASS data (Miller & Rowan, 2003), which included a much larger sample of schools and teachers.

Subject Indicators

The second group of results in Table 5 once again show the effects of the four academic subjects, this time adjusted for the addition of teacher and school characteristics. The results are only slightly different from those shown in Table 4, the main difference being that English teachers' now have a statistically significant advantage over mathematics teachers in their reported levels of teacher control. Again these effects are not confounded with teachers' school or department memberships, and so are important to the argument about disciplinary effects on management practices. In contrast to Table 4, then, the estimates of discipline effects reported in Table 5 come from a model that explicitly controls for the effects of school and teacher characteristics on patterns of organic management.

Teacher-Level Variables

The final panel shows the effects of teacher characteristics on teachers' perceptions of organic management. These results are virtually identical to those reported in the earlier analysis of ATS data presented by Rowan, Raudenbush, and Kang (1991), and are only slightly different from those reported by Miller and Rowan (2003) in their analysis of SASS data. The data show that more highly educated teachers generally report lower levels of organic management, while teachers working with high track students, minority teachers, and female teachers report generally higher levels of organic management (although the coefficients for each of these independent variables is not always statistically significant across all of the dependent variables).

Portion of Explained Variance

The final step in the analysis was to examine the proportions of variance explained by the prediction model at each level in the model. Table 6 reports these findings, which are derived by subtracting residual variance at each level of the prediction model from the variance at each level of analysis estimated via the base model.

The top panel in Table 6 shows the residual variance components estimated for each level of analysis in the explanatory model, while the lower panel shows the percentage of variance at each level explained by the model. We can see from the table that our model explains very little (less than 2%) of the variance in measures of organic management lying among teachers within departments, although some of the residual variance at this level of analysis undoubtedly reflects measurement error that cannot be explained. The explanatory model does a much better job of explaining between-school variance, however. For example, nearly 54% of the between school variance in measures of teacher control is explained by the prediction model, about 32% of the between school variance in staff cooperation is explained, and about 19% of the variance in teacher control is explained. Finally (and not surprisingly, given that we did not include specific properties of departments as predictors in our analyses), the explanatory model accounts for very little of the between-department variance found in the base model. About 4% of the between-department variance in principal leadership is explained away by the entry of teacher and school characteristics into the prediction model. That same figure is about 3% for staff cooperation, and about 7% for teacher control. In fact, these small percentages represent an important finding, for they suggest that depart-

TABLE 6
Residual Variance and % of Explained for the
Three Organic Management Measures

	Principal Leadership	*Staff Cooperation*	*Teacher Control*
Residual Variance Decomposition			
Teacher Level	67.67	21.78	20.60
Department Level	8.67	2.20	2.02
School Level	18.84	2.96	2.27
Total	95.17	26.94	24.89
Variance Explained %			
Teacher Level	1.2%	1.5%	1.8%
Department Level	3.7%	2.6%	7.0%
School Level	19.1%	31.9%	53.8%

ment effects on organic patterns of management are not much explained by differences among departments in the background characteristics of members, or by the specific characteristics of the schools where they are located.

One final observation about Table 6 is warranted. The analysis presented here used the same data as were used in the earlier analysis of organic management in high schools reported by Rowan, Raudenbush, and Kang (1991). A major difference in the two analyses, however, is that the earlier analysis used a two-level, nested, hierarchical linear model while the present analysis used the crossed, multilevel model. It is therefore interesting to observe the differences in variance components found in the two studies. In comparison to the earlier study, the prediction model used in the present study explained a greater proportion of variance at school level but less variance at teacher-level than the earlier analysis. But this simply signals that the variance estimates in the earlier study were confounded with the effects of departments as internal units within schools.

DISCUSSION

The purpose of this study was to examine the common hypothesis that academic departments play an important role in the management of American high schools. To examine this hypothesis, we conceptualized and estimated a crossed multilevel model that allowed us to estimate separate variance components representing the effects of teachers, schools, and departments on teachers' perceptions of organic management in a large sample of high schools included in the High School and Beyond Study. With respect to the main purpose of the study, we found that the academic department in which teachers held membership accounted for less than 10% of the variance in the three measures of organic management analyzed in this study. We also found that department means on these measures could be estimated with modest reliability (ranging from around .40 to .60 depending on the measure), although the reliabilities of department means on the dependent variables were clearly limited by the small number of teachers per department in the data set.

The chief question is whether these results support recent arguments about the important role played by academic departments in the management and operations of high schools. We would argue that the results reported here do not suggest *large* effects of departments on school management processes, although they do provide at least some evidence of department-specific micro climates within schools. However, this conclusion should be tempered by several additional observations about the findings.

First, departmental effects are estimated here only *after* controlling for a variety of confounding effects. For one, our model controls for disciplinary differences among departments in the same school, and as we have seen, disciplinary cultures have meaningful effects on school management processes, even if these effects are not currently well-explained by theory. Further, the effects we are estimating control for the individual characteristics and track assignments of teachers in each of department within a school, as well for the location of a particular department within a specific school. Thus, the effects we are reporting are the *unique* effects of departments as sub-units within a school. Thus, they are not disciplinary effects, nor are they are a reflection of differences in staff composition and work assignments operating within departments. From this perspective, there *do* appear to be unique effects of departments in the shaping of school management features.

Second, we earlier argued that the proportion of variance in organic management lying among departments was relatively small in relation to *total* variance. But if we instead examine the contribution of department-to-department differences within schools to just the percentage of the variance in organic management due to organizational units in our model, we can make a different interpretation of the findings. For example, consider only the variance in organic management due to the random effects of schools and departments, and not variance due to the random effects of teachers or the fixed effects of teacher characteristics. Now, if we ask what percentage of this organizational variance is accounted for by departments, we get a somewhat different picture of the importance of departments in the overall organizational design of high schools. From Table 3, for example, we see that the proportion of marginal between-organizational variance accounted for by departments ranges from about 27% for principal leadership, through about 30% for teacher control, to about 34% for staff cooperation. This suggests that among the effects on organic management resulting from individuals' locations within organizational units in high schools, location within a specific department is relatively important, although still less important than an individual's location within a specific school.

Third, previous qualitative studies have shown that there can be school-to-school differences in the roles of academic departments (e.g., Cusick, 1983; Donnelly, 2000; Gutierrez, 1996; Siskin, 1991). In this light, it is important to remember that what we are reporting here are average estimates of departmental effects on school management, estimates that obviously do not describe every case. Thus, there remains a role for qualitative studies in research on academic departments, if for no other reason than to explore the conditions under which departmental differences in organic design are larger or smaller in particular schools.

Fourth, departmental effects were estimated in this study only for the four academic subjects in the analysis, and thus they account only for variance in organic management that exists across these types of departments within schools. We would expect larger departmental variances than were found here if we were to conduct a study that included non-academic teachers in the analysis. Indeed, in the results reported by Miller and Rowan (2003), it was precisely the contrast among academic and non-academic teachers that showed the largest effects in the within-school portions of models predicting organic management in schools.

Fifth, it is important to remember that we investigated the effects of departments on a single dimension of organizational design in high schools—the presence of organic patterns of management. The effects of departments on other dimensions of organizational structure or management, or the departmental effects on various dimensions of school climate, could be quite different than those found here. Thus, we recommend further studies designed to examine department effects on a wider range of organizational outcomes.

CONCLUSION

If the recommendation is to conduct further studies of department effects on organizational structure and climate in high schools, we urge researchers to follow our lead in developing statistical models that are better suited to the problem than the ones used in the past. As discussed in this paper, the crossed multilevel model employed here has several desirable features in studies of departmental effects. For one, traditional studies of school organization and climate conducted at a single level of analysis, as well as the two-level, "nested" hierarchical linear models used in much previous research (including our own) have never adequately taken into account the department as a distinctive unit within the overall structure of high schools. By contrast, the statistical model presented here does that. Moreover, the crossed multilevel model specified here was designed to disentangle the confounding effects of differences among departments in teacher composition, disciplinary affiliation, and school location in estimating the unique effects of departments on organic management in schools. In this sense, the crossed multilevel model employed here has both methodological and theoretical advantages, and its use in future studies of departmental effects on organization structure and climate should be considered by other researchers.

NOTE

1.   Teachers teaching subjects other than the four academic subjects and working in non-Catholic private schools were not included in the sample. These teachers are not clearly defined in their departmental memberships and quite

heterogeneous. The inclusion of these non-academic subject teachers would increase the complexity of the analysis substantively.

REFERENCES

Ball, S. J. (1987). *The micro politics of the school.* London: Methuen.

Bidwell, C. E., & Yasumoto, J. Y. (1999). The collegial focus: Teaching fields, collegial relationship, and instructional practice in American high schools. *Sociology of Education, 72*(4), 234–256.

Bryk, A. S., & Driscoll, M. E. (1988). *The school as community: Theoretical foundations, contextual influences, and consequences for teachers and students.* Madison: University of Wisconsin, National Center on Effective Secondary Schools.

Chubb, J.E., & Moe, T.E. (1990). *Politics, markets, and America's Schools.* Washington, DC: Brookings Institute.

Cusick, P. A. (1983). *The Egalitarian Ideal and the American High School.* New York: Longman.

Donnelly, J. (2000). Departmental characteristics and the experience of secondary science teaching. *Educational Research, 42*(3), 261–273.

Goldstein, H. (1987). *Multilevel models in educational and social research.* London: Charles Griffin.

Grossman, P. L., & Stodolsky, S.S. (1994). Considerations of content and the circumstances of secondary school teaching. *Review of Research in Education, 20,* 179–221.

Gutierrez, R. (1996). Practices, beliefs, and cultures of high school mathematics departments: Understanding their influence on student advancement. *Journal of Curriculum Studies, 28*(5), 495–529.

Jackson, P. (1986). *The Practice of Teaching.* New York: Teachers College Press.

James, L. R., & Jones, A. P. (1974). Organizational climate: A review of theory and research. *Psychology Bulletin, 81,* 1096–1112.

Johnson, S. M. (1988). *The primary and potential of high school departments.* Stanford, CA: Center for Research on the Context of Secondary Teaching, School of Education, Stanford University.

Jones, C., Martin, F., Tourangeau, R., McWilliams, H., & O'Brien, F. (1983). *High school and beyond first follow-up(1982) school questionnaire data file user's manual.* Washington, DC: National Center for Education Statistics.

Kang, S. J .(1992a). *A mixed linear model with two-way crossed random effects and estimation via the EM Algorithm.* Unpublished doctoral dissertation. East Lansing, MI: Michigan State University.

Kang, S. J. (1992b). *A crossed-multilevel model for educational research.* Paper presented at the annual meeting of American Educational Research Association. San Francisco, CA.

Little, J. W. (1982). Norms of collegiality and experimentation: Workplace conditions of school success. *American Educational Research Journal, 19,* 325–340.

Little, J. W., & McLaughlin, M. W. (1993). *Teachers' work: Individuals, colleagues, and contexts.* New York: Teachers College Press.

McLaughlin, M. W. (1987). Learning from experience: Lessons from policy implementation: *Educational Evaluation and Policy Analysis, 9,* 171–178.

Miller, R. J., & Rowan, B. (2003). Sources and consequences of organic management in elementary and high schools. In, Hoy, W. & Miskel, C. (Eds.), *Theory and research in educational administration*, Volume 2, (pp.51–89). Greenwich, CT: Information Age Publishing.

Miskel, C., & Ogawa, R. (1988). Work Motivation, Job Satisfaction, and Climate. In N. Boyan (Ed.), *Handbook of Educational Administration*. New York: Longman.

Pallas, A. (1988). School climate in American high schools. *Teachers College Record, 89*, 541–53.

Raudenbush, S. W. (1993). A crossed random effects model for unbalanced data with applications in cross-sectional and longitudinal research. *Journal of Educational Statistics, 18*(4), 321–349.

Raudenbush, S. W., & Bryk, A.S. (2002). *Hierarchical linear models: Applications and data analysis methods.* Thousand Oaks, CA: Sage

Raudenbush, S. W., Bryk, A. S., Cheong, Y. F., & Congdon, R. T. (2000). *HLM 5: Hierarchical linear and non-linear modeling.* Chicago: Scientific Software International.

Raudenbush, S. W., Rowan, B., & Kang, S. J. (1991). A multilevel, multivariate model for study school climate with estimation via the EM algorithm and application to U.S. high school data. *Journal of Educational Statistics, 16*, 295–330.

Rowan, B. (1990). Commitment and control: Alternative strategies for the organizational design of schools. *Review of Research in Education, 16*, 353–389.

Rowan, B. (2002a). Teachers' work and instructional management, part I: Alternative views of the task of teaching. In Hoy, W. & Miskel, C. (Eds.), *Theory and Research in Educational Administration*, Volume 2, (pp. 129–149). Greenwich, CT: Information Age.

Rowan, B. (2002b). Teachers' work and instructional management, part II: Does organic management promote expert teaching. In Hoy, W. & Miskel, C. (Eds.), *Theory and Research in Educational Administration*, Volume 2 (pp. 151–168). Greenwich, CT: Information Age.

Rowan, B., & Miskel, C. (1999). Institutional theory and the study of educational organizations. In Murphy, J. & Louis, K.S. (Eds.), *Handbook of Research in Educational Administration*. San Francisco: Jossey Bass.

Rowan, B., Raudenbush, S. W., and Cheong, Y. F. (1993). Teaching as a non-routine task: Implications for the management of schools. *Educational Administration Quarterly, 29*, 479–500.

Rowan, B., Raudenbush, S. W., & Kang, S. J. (1991). Organizational design in high schools: A multilevel analysis. *American Journal of Education, 99*, 238–66.

Rosenholtz, S. J. (1985). Effective schools: Interpreting the evidence. *American Journal of Education, 93*, 352–388.

Siskin, L. S. (1991). Departments as different worlds: Subject subcultures in secondary schools. *Educational Administration Quarterly, 2*, 134–160.

Snow, C.P. (1959). *The two cultures and the scientific revolution.* New York: Cambridge University Press.

Spillane, J. & Burch, P. (n.d.). *Policy, administration, and instructional practice: "Loose coupling" revisited.* Unpublished manuscript, School of Education and Social Policy, Northwestern University.

Stodolsky, S. (1988). *The subject matters.* Chicago: University of Chicago Press.

Stodolsky, S. & Grossman, P. (1995). The impact of subject matter on curricular activity: An analysis of five academic subjects. *American Educational Research Journal 32*, 227–249.

Talbert, J. E., & McLaughlin, M. W. (1994). Teacher professionalism in local school contexts. *American Journal of Education, 102*(4), 123–153.

APPENDIX: COMPONENT ITEMS FOR THE THREE ORGANIC MANAGEMENT SCALES FROM THE ADMINISTRATOR AND TEACHER SURVEY 1984 (ATS84) DATA FILES

Principal Leadership (14 Items)

T19I The principal does a poor job of getting resources for this school.

T19J The principal deals effectively with pressures from outside the school that might interfere with my teaching.

T19K The principal sets priorities, makes plans, and sees that they are carried out.

T19M Goals and priorities for the school are clear.

T19O Staff members are recognized for a job well done.

T19Q Staff are involved in making decisions that affect them.

T19R The principal knows what kind of school he/she wants and has communicated it to the staff.

T19S This school administration knows the problems faced by the staff.

T19T In this school, I am encouraged to experiment with my teaching.

T19W The school administration's behavior toward the staff is supportive and encouraging.

T19Y The principal seldom consults with staff members before he/she makes decisions that affect us.

T19BB In this school the teachers and the administration are in close agreement on school discipline policy.

T19HH The principal lets staff members know what is expected of them.

T19JJ The principal is interested in innovation and new ideas.

Staff Cooperation (8 items)

T19B Staff members in this school generally don't have much school spirit.

T19D You can count on most staff members to help out anywhere, anytime—even though it may not be part of their official assignment.

T19E Most of my colleagues share my beliefs and values about what the central mission of the school should be.

T19V I feel accepted and respected as a colleague by most staff members.

T19X Teachers in this school are continually learning and seeking new ideas.

T19DD There is a great deal of cooperative effort among staff members.

T19EE Staff members maintain high standards of performance for themselves.

T19GG This school seems like a big family everyone is so close and cordial.

Teacher Control/Teacher Influence (9 items)

T01A Determining student behavior codes.

T01B Determining the content of in-service programs.

T01C Setting policy on grouping students in classes by ability.

T01D Establishing the school curriculum.

T02A Selecting textbooks and other instructional materials.

T02B Selecting content, topics, and skills to be taught.

T02C Selecting teaching techniques.

T02D Disciplining students

T02E Determining the amount of homework to be assigned.

CHAPTER 6

IMPLEMENTING TEACHER EVALUATION SYSTEMS

How Principals Make Sense of Complex Artifacts to Shape Local Instructional Practice[1]

Richard Halverson, Carolyn Kelley, & Steven Kimball[2]

This study examines how local school leaders make sense of complex programs designed to evaluate teachers and teaching. New standards-based teacher evaluation policies promise to provide school leaders and teachers with a common framework that can serve as a basis for improving teaching and learning in schools (Danielson & McGreal, 2000; Odden & Kelley, 2002). However, implementation research suggests that the ways in which local actors make sense of and use such policies determines the nature of the changes that actually occur in schools (Desimone, 2002; Spillane, Reiser, & Reimer, 2002). In this paper, case studies of schools in a large school district are used to examine school-level implementation of a standards-based teacher evaluation system. Specifically, we examine the ways in which school and district leaders emphasize and select from the many features of a teacher evaluation framework in the implementation process. We then discuss the

Educational Administration, Policy, and Reform: Research and Measurement
A Volume in: Research and Theory In Educational Administration, pages 153–188.
Copyright © 2004 by Information Age Publishing, Inc.
All rights of reproduction in any form reserved.
ISBN: 1-59311-000-0 (hardcover), 1-59311-000-0 (paperback)

ways in which key features of the process were co-opted, ignored, or adapted in accordance with school context, and we point to how the resulting teacher evaluation practices help to create conditions for more substantive conversations about reforming teaching practice.

INTRODUCTION

While it is generally acknowledged that teachers exert great influence over the improvement of student learning (Darling-Hammond & Ball, 1997; Wright, Horn & Sanders, 1997), the role that school leaders play in shaping system capacity for successful teaching and learning is often underappreciated (Elmore 2002; ; Hallinger & Heck 1996; Murphy, 1994). For the most part, principals affect instruction indirectly, through practices such as the acquisition and allocation of resources, supporting and encouraging staff, enforcing rules for student conduct, or taking personal interest in the professional development process (Berends, et. al., 2002; Peterson, 1989). However, principals can also affect teaching practice directly through teacher supervision and evaluation. Evaluation is a formal means for school leaders to communicate organizational goals, conceptions of teaching, standards, and values to teachers (Wise, Darling-Hammond, McLaughlin, & Bernstein, 1984).

TEACHER EVALUATION FRAMEWORKS

Teacher evaluation is a common, often mandatory practice in schools. The traditional programs and practices of teacher evaluation, however, are based on limited or competing conceptions of teaching (Darling-Hammond, Wise, & Klein, 1999), and are often characterized by inaccuracy, lack of support (Peterson, 1995) and insufficient training (Loup, Garland, Ellett, & Rugutt, 1996). Traditional teacher evaluation practices tend to preserve the loose coupling between administration and instructional practices, consequently limiting the ability of principals to foster improvements in teaching and learning (Rowan 1990; Weick, 1976, 1996). Rather than being used as tools for instructional leadership, traditional evaluation programs are often seen as perfunctory and treated by both teachers and principals as an administrative burden. Teacher assessment has frequently been used to weed out the poorest performing teachers rather than to hold all teachers accountable or to improve the performance of all teachers (Darling-Hammond et al., 1999; Haney, Madaus, & Kreitzer, 1987). Because of these traditional limits on scope and efficacy, teacher evaluation has had a limited impact on teacher performance and learning (Darling-Hammond, Wise, & Pease, 1983; Peterson, 1995).

A number of districts developed evaluation systems based on teaching standards to address these concerns. These new systems focus evaluation on a common vision of teaching elaborated across broad domains of practice, comprehensive standards and rubrics, and multiple-sources of evidence (Davis, Pool, & Mits-Cash, 2000; Kimball, 2002; Milanowski & Heneman, 2001). One such model, Danielson's (1996) *Enhancing Professional Practice: A Framework for Teaching*, develops standards to assess and promote teacher development across career stages, school levels, subject matter fields, and performance levels. The framework is organized into four domains of planning and preparation, the classroom environment, instruction, and professional responsibilities. These domains include 22 components spelled out by 66 elements to specify a range of appropriate behaviors. Each element includes rubrics to assess unsatisfactory, basic, proficient, and distinguished performance. The framework is also intended to foster teachers' development by specifying techniques for assessing each aspect of practice, a program of evaluator training, and emphasis on using the framework to include formative as well as summative evaluation (Danielson & McGreal, 2000).

Prior research on the implementation of this type of standards-based teacher evaluation system has examined the initial perceptions of teacher and administrator acceptance (Davis, Pool, & Mits-Cash, 2000; Milanowski & Heneman, 2001), the nature of feedback, enabling conditions and fairness perceptions (Kimball, 2002) and the relationship of these evaluation systems to student achievement (Gallagher, 2002). Yet we know relatively little about how local school leaders actually use such systems in practice, which features they select from the frameworks to emphasize in their evaluations, and how they adapt the systems to existing evaluation practices. In this paper, we use sense making theory as a lens to examine how local school leaders use the framework to shape teaching practices in schools. This knowledge will help policy makers and school leaders to better understand both obstacles and opportunities afforded by comprehensive teacher evaluation frameworks.

SENSEMAKING

Sensemaking theory addresses the cognitive dimensions of change in people and organizations (Spillane, Reiser, & Reimer, 2002; Weick, 1996). Sensemaking begins with the constructivist assumption that learning is shaped by prior experience (Confrey, 1990; Greeno, Collins, & Resnick, 1996). Through experience, people build mental models to anticipate regular patterns of action in the world (Gentner & Stevens 1983; Hammer & Elby

2002). Mental models act as perceptual filters that help to determine both what we notice, and how it is interpreted (Starbuck & Milliken, 1988). Our models shape what we notice in new experiences, and can override the potential of new ideas to transform behavior (Cohen & Barnes, 1993). The impact of new ideas can be either marginalized or co-opted by preexisting practices and ideas (Chinn & Brewer, 1993; Keisler & Sproull, 1982). The tendency to interpret the new in terms of the old may lead people to attend to the surface similarities of new concepts and practices instead of attending to the deeper, structural differences (Gentner, Ratterman, & Forbus, 1993; Ross, 1987). People also tend to retain practices they value, and value the practices they retain.

The sense we make of new information is also shaped by our social and situational context (Greeno, 1998). Organizations and institutions routinize existing models through policies, programs, and traditions. Thus, the intended effects of innovations are not necessarily altered by the malice or laziness of implementers, but instead by the best efforts of local actors seeking to satisfy conflicting goals (Fischoff 1975; March & Simon, 1958; Spillane, Reiser, & Reimer 2002). Actors make sense of new practices within their existing social and situational context, and often adjust the meaning of the new in terms of their established context of meaning.

Our cognitive models, however, are not rigid structures that determine what we notice and name. Rather, our models interact with our perceptions and experience in an iterative process through which new experiences can come to shape our existing models. Successful learning requires an active process of readjusting mental schema to what we already know (Carey, 1985; Schank & Abelson, 1977). The tenacious hold our existing ideas have on what we notice and name can require an experience of expectation failure to jolt us into reconstructing our network of assumptions (Schank, 1982). In organizations, new policies and programs can provide this jolt to existing practice, encouraging practitioners to reframe their practice in terms of the new expectations. The ways that practitioners make sense of new initiatives in terms of pre-existing models make the implementation of new, complex programs a far from linear and predictable process.

Artifacts as a Window on Sensemaking

Because of its iterative and transitory nature, the sensemaking process has proven to be difficult to research. One way to access sensemaking is to identify occasions when existing models are perturbed by interventions (Bronfenbrenner, 1979). Leaders and policy-makers introduce policies and programs into organizations to reshape existing practices. In these cases, policies and programs can be understood as sophisticated *artifacts* intended to shape or reform existing practices in an institutional context (Halverson & Zoltners, 2001; Norman, 1993; Pea, 1993; Wartofsky, 1979). Organizational artifacts originate from different locations. Artifacts such as district policies, state and federal programs, and teacher professional networks originate outside the local school context, whereas other artifacts originate within the school as locally designed efforts to resolve emergent and/or recurrent problems of practice (Halverson, 2002). Taken together, the network of received and locally designed artifacts composes a local situation that both facilitates and constitutes local leadership and teaching practice (Spillane, Halverson, & Diamond, 2001).

Artifacts have several features important for understanding sensemaking. First, artifacts are designed in order to shape practice in certain ways. The consequent effect on practice, however, is not a direct translation of artifact features to desired outcomes. Those who use artifacts perceive certain features as *affordances* (Gibson, 1986; Norman, 1993) that support a certain range of actions. Affordances are an actor's perception of the ways the artifact can be used in practice. The actual use of a complex artifact, such as a teacher evaluation policy, depends not only on the features built into the design of the artifact, but also on affordances of artifact use perceived by actors. The affordances perceived by local actors determine which features of the artifact are implemented. For example, an artifact that features evaluation in multiple domains of practice can afford a more comprehensive approach to teacher assessment by addressing out-of-classroom as well as classroom practice. The availability of these features does not mean the artifact will be used as intended. For example, an evaluator could focus only on classroom teaching behaviors while effectively ignoring out-of-classroom behaviors. In the hands of another evaluator, however, the evaluation artifact could afford a better-rounded assessment of professional practice. Artifacts can also serve to *constrain* behavior (Norman, 1993). Like affordances, constraints are perceptions of artifact features that limit or qualify behaviors. Teacher union contracts, for example, often constrain evaluator action by permitting a maximum of two formal observation occasions during the school year. While certain affordances and constraints are built into artifacts by design, the challenge of implementation rests on the interests and abilities of local actors to identify and exploit the intended artifact features.

An artifact-based approach to the analysis of implementation focuses on how local leaders select certain features of complex artifacts as affordances and consider other features as constraints. Policy artifacts are introduced into schools not only to alter existing practices, but also to enhance the capacity of local actors to understand their work in new ways and to alter the organizational conditions of the work. A sensemaking perspective highlights how the introduction of complex artifacts draws upon and contributes to the evolution and interaction of individual understanding and local capacity.

School principals play a key role in how evaluation artifacts are implemented. In many school districts, administrative certification is required for performing teacher evaluations. Principals shoulder most of the burden of teacher evaluation processes. We use the concepts of principal will and skill and organizational structure to capture the interplay between actors and the school context.[3] The principal's capacity for innovation is measured in terms of individual *will* and *skill* to enact new practices. *Will* refers to the level of motivation of the local leader to implement the artifact. Leaders who have had a role or stake in the development of the artifact, and those who view instructional leadership as core to their role may be more likely to embrace the artifact, emphasizing its affordances and deemphasizing the constraints it may impose. *Skill* is the ability of leaders to engage in the intended practice. From a sensemaking perspective, skill levels are determined by the relevant experience of the leader as well as by the training received for the intended practice. Will and skill are not generic capacities appropriately activated in predictable ways. From a sense making perspective, the availability of will and skill depends critically on how actors interpret the need for action in a given situation.

In addition to the will and skill of individuals, local leadership capacity is framed by the context of organizational *structures,* such as pre-existing practices and available resources, to support innovative practice. Leadership capacity is determined by the prior context of practice, including pre-existing similar practices, constraints on innovation, and multiple professional responsibilities. Our sensemaking perspective emphasizes how a leader's perception of structural possibilities, in the form of artifact affordances and constraints, bears on implementation. In the example of teacher evaluation offered above, the perceived needs and capacity of the local situation help to shape both a local leader's will to enact difficult features of a complex evaluation program, and her skill in fully implementing the artifact. Organizational capacity is both shown and determined through the material and temporal resources perceived necessary to support the implementation process.

METHODOLOGY

This study focuses on the ways that school leaders make sense of a complex district teacher evaluation artifact in their local school setting. We chose a case study approach to collect, interpret and present our data. Case studies provide opportunities to explore practices in depth, and to understand the complex interactions that characterize local systems (Stake, 1995). In order to make comparisons across cases, we chose to develop three cases of schools within a single district, faced with similar pressures to implement district policies.

Site Selection

The study takes place in a large school district in the Western United States, which we refer to as Valle Verde Unified.[4] The district was chosen because it has made a substantial effort to implement a standards-based teacher evaluation system based on the framework for teaching (Danielson, 1996). The framework interested the district because it addressed criticisms of traditional teacher evaluation models by incorporating more sophisticated and elaborate evidence gathering and by providing feedback to enhance teaching practice for teachers at all skill levels and career stages.

We adopted a multi-dimensional approach to investigating how school leaders made sense of the teacher evaluation system. The data collected for the study include:

- interviews with district leaders and with principals and teachers from 7 elementary, 4 middle and 3 high schools in the district, for a total of 14 schools;
- written teacher evaluations in each school; and
- data describing the local demographic environment and instructional contexts.

Fourteen schools were selected from the district's elementary, middle and high schools. We consulted with a district representative to choose schools with a range of socioeconomic contexts and perceived levels of acceptance of the evaluation reform. Other schools were randomly sampled from among the remaining schools available.

Data Analysis

We began our analysis by examining themes that emerged from interviews conducted in all 14 schools. We searched for patterns in how the artifact was used to support the principal's role as evaluator and instructional leader. The triangulation of principal self-reports with (a) teacher and district administrator interviews, (b) teacher assessment scores, and (c) written (narrative) teacher evaluations provide multiple sources of data to understand principal perceptions of the constraints and affordances presented by the evaluation framework.

Analysis of the data collected from the 14 schools shaped our selection of an elementary, middle and high school for more detailed case analysis of leadership sense making. We developed a coding scheme iteratively to allow patterns to emerge from the data. The coding scheme enabled us to explore the programmatic context, characteristics of the implementation process, local perceptions of artifact affordances and constraints, the impact of the evaluation system on principals, teachers and on the school, and local perceptions of artifact utility. After coding the data, we constructed three school cases to describe the implementation process in each school. The cases were then analyzed to reveal shared and unique characteristics of the sensemaking and implementation process.

FINDINGS

In the following sections, we present a summary of findings from the teacher evaluation experiences in the 14 schools sampled in the district, including perceptions of administrators and teachers of system features and implementation. Following an analysis of the experiences across the schools, we provide illustrative case descriptions of the ways in which three Valle Verde schools implemented the new teacher evaluation framework. Each school case includes a brief demographic background, a description of the evaluator's perspective, an outline of the evaluation process, a summary of the written evaluation forms, and an account of the evaluators' and teachers' perceptions of the utility of the process.

Experiences across the District

The evaluation system at Valle Verde, based on the *Framework for Teaching* (Danielson, 1996), was implemented in 2000 following three years of planning and field-testing. In contrast to the prior system, the new approach represented a more comprehensive set of teaching standards, with explicit performance rubrics, and multiple sources of evidence. The new district policy required that all teachers participate an evaluation cycle of (a) a goal setting meeting, (b) a pre-observation meeting, (c) the observation, and (d) discussion of the observation write-up. The cycle was organized around the district-developed evaluation model. The number of observations ranged from nine times per year for beginning, or probationary, teachers to single observations for experienced, or post-probationary, teachers. More details about the district evaluation policy are available in Appendix A. Key findings relating to principal and teacher interview responses, written evaluations and evaluation decision-making in the 14 schools are summarized below.

Principal Responses

Teachers and school leaders alike felt the evaluation system provided the opportunity to observe and reflect on teaching practice. Principal perceptions of the evaluation system ranged from an opportunity to develop morale or team building in the school to a significant time-management problem or a mandate that needed accommodation. Compared to the previous, open-ended system at Valle Verde, principals who viewed themselves as strong instructional leaders felt constrained by the specificity of the new system. Other principals liked the clarity of the new system for providing guidance on the focus of evaluation. Most principals viewed evaluation as a time management challenge, with increased meetings required and more paperwork requirements. Some made adjustments by streamlining their evaluation approach or cutting back on the amount and types of evaluation evidence. Others made changes to build in more time at school for evaluation activities. Many gave up significant personal time to complete all of the evaluations. Each principal saw merits in the system despite the widespread belief that teacher evaluation itself was not a primary force improving teaching. Most evaluators adhered to the basic evaluation procedures and tried to complete the goal-setting session, the required number of observations, and the post-observation conferences.

Teacher Responses

Teachers were largely positive about the feedback they received as a result of evaluation. With a few exceptions, feedback was seen as frequent, timely, and positive. Teachers cited specific examples of feedback that they utilized to change aspects of their instruction. Most said that their evaluator was qualified to provide feedback. However, in a few cases, teachers felt their evaluators were not adequately qualified to evaluate content-based pedagogy. In particular, evaluators who lacked instructional skills (e.g., those with a background in physical education, special education, or business) were not perceived as having the ability to evaluate instructional content decisions or pedagogical content knowledge. Few claimed dramatic change in instructional practice as a result of the evaluation process, but teachers were positive about the specific changes to theirs practice such as better questioning techniques, use of materials, and improved student engagement.

Overall, teachers were positive about interactions with their principals and other evaluators. Several post-probationary teachers remarked that their ability to select their evaluation domain contributed to the fairness, but not necessarily the accuracy of the evaluation. Others said that the principal or other evaluator set the stage for fairness by actively seeking dialogue with the teacher about the evaluation rating and getting the teachers' input. Several spoke of the principal encouraging teachers to offer other evidence if they disagreed with a rating.

Nature of Evidence Used in the Evaluation

There was variation in the evidence gathered across evaluators. The evidence primarily consisted of class observations and related discussions. Although lesson plans and student artifacts were required to be collected, they did not appear to be systematically gathered or analyzed. In addition, some evaluators skipped the goal-setting session and either left out the goal-setting process or combined it with the observation conferences (for the next series of observations).

The evaluation system was perceived as a low-stakes, formative artifact. Principals emphasized praise in written evaluations and provided 'gentle' criticisms if they criticized teachers at all. The district evaluation form contained an area for rating based on a number of rubrics and space for a narrative evaluation. Very little critical feedback was provided either through evaluation scores or in narratives. Principals did not assign an unsatisfactory rating in any of the 485 written evaluations we reviewed. For evaluation decisions, some principals evaluated teacher performance by comparing the teacher's practice to the proficient level (Level 2), and adjusted scores as evidence warranted. Others allowed scores to evolve more naturally from their analysis of the evidence. Narrative feedback was affirmative and seemed intended to foster reflection and growth. Written evaluations provided by elementary and middle school principals in many cases included longer narratives, despite often having more staff to evaluate than middle or high school principals. High school evaluations contained minimal written feedback, usually one to three sentences, even though the evaluation role was shared in high schools. Most evaluators allowed considerable teacher input into what would be observed and into the performance ratings (e.g., teachers could bring additional evidence to bear in the decision).

The analysis of the data from across the district revealed a substantial investment by district and local school leaders in designing and implementing the teacher evaluation framework. Many teachers and leaders were grateful for the opportunity to talk about teaching. However, the reception of the artifact into local school contexts caused several conflicts. The evaluation program required a considerable amount of time. The time pressures, as we shall see in our cases, forced leaders to select which artifact features to implement. While the artifact was intended by designers to give local leaders a tool to improve teaching, most leaders did not use the artifact to disturb existing administrator-teacher relations. Praise rather than critique, and high scores rather than low, characterized the written feedback provided by evaluators. In the next section, we provide three cases to illustrate themes of how principals made sense of the artifact in their local school contexts.

La Esperanza Elementary School

La Esperanza Elementary is a K–6 school in the heart of the largest city in the Valle Verde district. Principal Susan Richards and her staff see the education of students learning English as a second language as the main challenge for the school. La Esperanza's 36 teachers are organized into grade-level teams throughout the school. 81 percent of the 690 students are members of a minority group (primarily Latino), and 84 percent of the students qualify for free and reduced lunch. Nearly half are classified as English as a Second Language (ESL) students. The school is currently under significant accountability pressure from the state and is being monitored and assisted in the effort to improve student academic performance.

The teachers interviewed at *La Esperanza* included one first grade, one second grade, and two third grade teachers. Three of the four teachers did not have substantial teaching experience, while the fourth had been teaching for more than a decade at the school. All four of these teachers (along with the rest of the faculty) were evaluated by the principal. All of the teachers interviewed and the principal agreed that *La Esperanza* had challenges not faced by other district schools. Principally, the presence of significant numbers of non-English speaking students meant that teachers must be patient with and accommodate students.

Evaluator Characteristics

Principal Richards had been at the school for four years. Before coming to *La Esperanza* elementary, she worked for eight years as a fourth grade teacher, served as a teacher leader, and a trainer for the district initiatives in writing and math. In addition, she worked as a dean of students for four and a half years and as an elementary school principal for three years. Part of her prior work was on a Native American reservation, working with a highly at-risk student population.

Richards viewed her role as an instructional coach for the faculty. She believed that her experience with the district provided her with the knowledge and skills she needs to identify appropriate teaching techniques and make helpful suggestions. She recognized the potential stress associated with a summative evaluation system that attempts to provide formative feedback to teachers, and works with teachers to reassure them that the system is formative and an opportunity for growth, rather than for humiliation and anger:

> My goal is to make them, to help them feel more comfortable, that I am not just an evaluator but I am also a coach. That is my role. That is the role I want. I want to be a supervisory coach. And so we work hard at trying to establish that kind of rapport. And we are getting there. It has taken four

years of trust to know that I am not going to beat them up . . . and destroy them.

Teacher interviews corroborated Richards' description. All four teachers commented on their positive and upbeat interactions with Richards. One teacher said that "she truly is there to help us. I mean, not to criticize or anything like that . . . I love it when she would come in because I know she is watching me to help me improve what I am doing."

Evaluation Process

Richards estimated that she spent approximately fifteen hours per year on each teacher's evaluation. (With 36 teachers, this is the equivalent of fully a third of the academic year spent on observation, evaluation, and feedback). The evaluations were based on evidence collected through formal observations and intermittent informal observations, such as walk-throughs, throughout the year. The principal also gathered information regarding teacher performance during other committee meetings and professional gatherings. She viewed the new evaluation system as flexible in its use. For example, this past year she chose to emphasize teacher goal-setting and required all teachers to submit their goals in the first month of the school year. As part of goal-setting sessions, teachers evaluated themselves and then discussed her evaluation of their performance. Richards connected the evaluation process to how teachers met their goals.

In her classroom observations, Richards split her time between scripting part of the lesson and observing classroom dynamics. This process allowed her to get a sense of how the classroom worked while using examples of classroom conversation and activity in her report. She focused on teacher skills in questioning and responding to students. After recording her reflections on the observation form, Richards dropped the written evaluation off for the teacher to sign and arranged for a post-observation conference. During the conference, she asked about the strengths and weaknesses of the lesson and what the teacher might do differently. She offered positive feedback to highlight the successful aspects of the lesson. Richards reminded teachers of needed changes in a positive manner "until the third time, that is my key, a third time . . . if I have asked you three times to clarify your lesson plans . . . and they are still not clarified, then it becomes an evaluative measure... that is all lettered and documented."

Summary of Written Evaluations

An analysis of the evaluations revealed that the mean score for the faculty across evaluation domains at La Esperanza was between "proficient" and "area of strength" on the district scale. No teacher received an unsatisfactory rating. This indicated that, according to the principal, most teachers are performing at or above a proficient level.

Richards included a significant number of written comments on the teacher evaluation forms. The narrative section averaged just over 24 sentences per evaluation. The majority of the narratives were composed of excerpts from Richards' scripted observation notes. Each evaluation had a final summative paragraph, which expressed the high value that person added to the school. In addition, this final paragraph always included a sentence saying that the teacher was an important member of the *La Esperanza* family. For example, she described one teacher as being a "wonderful asset for La Esperanza."

There was no clear relationship between the assigned scores and the amount and content of the written narratives. For example, there were several instances where a score of a 1 was given, but there was little or no discussion of the rationale for the low score in the narrative. Information gathered from the teacher and principal interviews suggested that substantial dialogue was taking place between the principal and the teachers that was not documented in the evaluation forms. For example, one teacher reported that, after an observation, the principal gave her a recommendation about how to improve her questioning and answering techniques with her students. This recommendation could not be found in the written evaluation narrative. The teachers also reported that they regularly received verbal suggestions from the principal throughout the school year.

Perceptions of the Evaluation Process

All four of the teachers interviewed indicated that Richards' written evaluations are extremely affirmative, emphasizing many positive aspects of their teaching. As the principal said, "I try to find their highlights . . . and then I will make one recommendation. I won't beat a dead horse, but I will make one recommendation because that is what I should do and to assist my teachers." The principal indicated that teachers have been positive about the evaluation process. She gave the following example of a positive response from teachers as a result of the evaluation process:

> I was in a first grade classroom and I saw a lot of the same writings hung up on a wall that had been there all year. And I didn't have. . . a problem with that but I was curious for the teacher to tell me what was the purpose to maintain those? And their reasoning was excellent. Based on this reading training that we had which is the children go around and they read familiar print continuously so that they have success with finding the writings and it is also finding words and they do word writing. So that kind of conversation is really good so I understand what they are doing. And they also are aware of what is going on in the classroom.

The principal's focus on positive feedback and coaching, along with the team-based instruction throughout the school, helped to create a climate of openness to observation, evaluation, and feedback among teachers.

Teamed teachers often worked together to address evaluation goals. While the evaluation was not a primary focus, teamed teachers typically discussed with one another their evaluation goals as they planned their work for the year.

Despite the large time commitment and teacher reception to the evaluation system, Richards did not believe that the evaluation process was a good tool to improve teaching in her school. When asked whether the evaluation system could change teaching, she said,

> On average, no. I don't think so. . . . I think it can be very disheartening. I think evaluations can either encourage and give teachers a pat on the back that they don't often get or it can totally destroy them. It is just how you approach it. And I have seen both things happen. It is a very hard thing to do. And I don't think it changes people. I think it can stop people. I don't think it changes them.

While the evaluation system itself may not have led to deep change, the principal described how state accountability requirements provided pressure to change.

> I think what changes us, what drives change here for my teachers will be, well, it really comes down from the State Department beating us up. And then as a team, it is a total team effort, we get together and look at our scores, look and what we are doing, and then we look at what we need to change and how to implement change.

Richards' low estimate of the impact of the evaluation system contrasted with teacher's views. Teachers provided several examples of how Richards' evaluation feedback enhanced their teaching. Newer teachers remarked how the evaluations helped to improve classroom management. A veteran teacher offered an example of feedback regarding pedagogical content in math. Much of this feedback was specific and not directly connected to the evaluation framework. For example, one teacher indicated that the principal suggested using a microphone at the next student presentation and having a master of ceremonies to host the show. Another recommendation focused on increasing wait time after questioning students, or shifting the balance of large and small group time to improve student discussion. Teachers did not mention evaluation rubrics in their comments about principal feedback.

Several new teachers believed that the framework itself provided a "progress map" to identify areas for improvement. One teacher said that the system "kind of gives you the direction to go to or work towards." While these new teachers noted the effect of the system on their practice, one veteran teacher did not think that the system caused teacher change. However, the veteran teacher did say that the system provided a good "method to track" what type of professional development she would seek. All four teachers believed that the system was fair. The teachers reported considerable input into what went into the final evaluation. One teacher said that she can "discuss with her why I feel I am at a 2 and maybe at a 1 there. She is very fair about taking my suggestions into her reasoning."

Woods Middle School

Woods Middle School serves about 1000 7th and 8th graders in a large city in the Valle Verde district. In 2001–02, 17% of Woods students were Latino, and 28% qualified for free or reduced-price lunch. Student performance in reading, language arts, and mathematics is above national norms for eighth grade students; however, significant gaps exist between the test scores of white and ESL students. The school staff included 42 teachers, five special education teachers, and five additional teaching staff. The teachers interviewed at Woods included one probationary teacher, two teachers on major evaluations, and two on minor evaluations. The probationary teacher was in his first year, the two major evaluation teachers had been teaching for less than five years, and the two minor evaluation teachers had been at Woods for at least eight years. Two taught math and three taught English.

The school was organized around a cohort model that grouped students and teachers together as they passed through grade levels. This structure gave teachers opportunities to get to know their students well, and established structures for common instructional planning time. While several of the veteran teachers mentioned this structure as an occasion to share strategies about instruction, other teachers designed and taught their lesson plans independently.

Evaluator Characteristics

The Woods administrative team included Principal John Storm, an assistant principal and a dean of students. Storm was in his seventh year at Woods Middle School, his third year as principal. After an earlier career as a managing partner of a private sector business, Storm has spent his past twelve years as an educator in the district. Storm feels that his main strength as a principal has been his ability to listen to teachers, students, and parents and to solve problems as they emerge in the school. This blend of problem-solving and listening has enabled him to use the evaluation system to point out potential instructional issues while being sensitive to teacher's professional context:

> Because then I can point out problems to (the teachers) . . . and that requires a little bit of discussion. Some of it just comes from personal experience. I have been doing this long enough where I happen to know that so

and so is working on their master's degree. I don't have to ask them. I just know they are doing it.

Principal Storm saw the teacher evaluation framework as an important, if burdensome, supplement to his role as school instructional leader. Storm felt the evaluation system was particularly useful as a tool to help or dismiss probationary teachers. His approach to the new evaluation program was informed by his own six-point system for what constitutes good teaching:

> The first is that the objective is clearly stated . . . and the kids have to know what it is they are supposed to learn. The lesson has to have a clearly defined structure. You can't just do this and that. They all have to be related. I expect to see most of the students actively participating in their learning, not just sitting there and listening. I expect to see a teacher checking for understanding frequently so that they don't keep teaching after they have lost their kids. And then I expect to see teacher/student, student/student interactions to be appropriate. And any misbehavior I expect the teacher to respond to appropriately.

Teachers reported that Storm's six-point system characterized their experience of the evaluation process. Four of the five teachers interviewed reported that the principal's concerns with checking for understanding, classroom management, and clearly defined organization structure came across in the evaluation process. When asked to provide a specific example of feedback, four of the teachers mentioned Storm's review of their questioning practices. The teachers did not seem to differentiate between Storm's established checklist and the new framework. One veteran teacher noted that Storm's focus on questioning technique flowed from "the evaluation form he always uses."

Evaluation Process

Storm used the new evaluation system as a complement to his existing informal system of formative feedback. Storm began the evaluation process with brief visits to each classroom within the first several weeks of school. "Leading up to that I spent some time in the classroom informally, two times that I documented, and then two or three times just walking around getting into the classroom." His multiple observation practice enabled him to get a sense of where potential problems might occur in the school as well as to introduce himself to students and teachers throughout the school.

Storm considered the observations themselves to be an important component of the evaluation process. Allocating sufficient time to observe all teachers requires annual planning. "What I do is I reserve 25 percent of my day, one period a day, to do observations. And then I will sit down with the teacher's schedule . . . and I will actually book observations a month in advance." His time commitment to the evaluation process—fully 25% of his time—is corroborated by the 114 formal visits recorded on the official evaluation forms.

The annual cycle began with an opportunity for teachers to rate themselves using the evaluation system:

> At the beginning of the year I ask the teachers to go through the rubric and self-evaluate. And then when they sit down with me to go through their goals for the year, I will ask them about their self-evaluation . . . .I find teachers to be pretty much on target. They know where they are.

Storm then scheduled individual teacher observations. He used a laptop to record his observations of classroom practice. Storm's ability to write-up his comments in the class enabled him to provide feedback to teachers by the end of the school day. These comments serve as a rough draft for the final evaluation report, and give teachers the chance to discuss the main points of the report before it takes final form.

Storm relied on his past experience as an evaluator as well as the observation data to make his judgment about the quality of teaching. Storm began each rating at Level Two, the proficient level of performance. If the teacher has met the Level Two criterion, Storm moves to Level Three. "Level Three is just a little extension of Level Two. In fact, most of the rubric is written, take Level Two, and then add a little component to it." Level One ratings provide a special challenge in writing the final report. Storm commented: "Level One is poor teaching even though it is satisfactory, it is still poor teaching." Storm felt that the level of documentation must be much greater in a Level One evaluation, as it is directed toward remediation or to establish grounds for termination. Consequently, Storm reported that teachers with Level One evaluations received more substantive feedback for their observations.

Summary of Written Evaluations

Forty-eight Woods teachers were evaluated during the 2001–2002 school year. Average scores ranged between "proficient" and "area of strength" across the four evaluation domains. No teachers received an unsatisfactory rating in any domain. Limited narrative feedback was provided for each teacher. Forms for post-probationary teachers included an average of 9.7 sentences per domain area, while the probationary teachers received 10.2 per area. Most of the narratives included a balance of descriptive and laudatory sentences. There was an average of less than one sentence per evaluation directed toward either suggestions or critiques of teaching. Although both the teachers and the evaluators remarked on the value of the scripted comments made in class, these scripted comments were not present in the written evaluation forms. Over half of the evaluations included sentences commending the teacher's contribution to the local school culture, hard work, or participation in extra-curricular activities.

Perceptions of the Evaluation Process

Teachers were generally more positive than Storm about the potential effect of the evaluation process on their teaching. One teacher commented how the rubrics and domain structure of the evaluation program "helps create a common sense of good teaching" among the staff. Another teacher mentioned that the framework offers a structured opportunity to reflect on practice that "helps me strengthen my content knowledge." Teachers differed about their assessment of Storm's time investment. Two teachers noted that, even though the time taken by the observation and evaluation process signified administrative interest in teaching, the principal did not spend enough time in their classroom to really make a difference.

Even though he questioned the effect of the new system on shared perceptions of teaching, Principal Storm saw the teacher evaluation program as an improvement on the system it replaced. The older system focused on nine "topics" of teaching, and allowed teachers to pick three topics on a major evaluation, and one topic for a minor. The disadvantage of that system was that it allowed teachers to "focus on one area and just ignore everything else." The new system:

> Forces you to look at a broad range of teacher skills. And in that respect it is very, very good. Because, as an administrator, I am looking at this, boy, they have a lot of stuff they have to do as teachers. And it helps me remember the things that I am supposed to be looking for.

In Storm's view, the new system was particularly helpful in documenting poor performance and for helping new teachers. These affordances of the system accorded with Storm's belief in the importance of working with probationary teachers. The system rubrics provided a common reference for communicating about substandard teaching practice. Storm offered an example of how:

> In Domain Three, under grouping of students, if I were to tell a teacher that his or her instructional groups are inappropriate to the students or the instructional goals, that is unsatisfactory. Now, if a teacher knew that, then they could go to this rubric and say, well, what is satisfactory? . . . So, for someone who is doing poorly, it is very beneficial."

The system helped Storm and the teachers frame formative programs to improve their teaching. Storm described a teacher evaluated as unsatisfactory several years before: "I was very, very specific in the areas and had very concrete evidence as to why he was unsatisfactory. And I have worked with him for four years now and I would say this year he has made some real improvements."

According to Storm, the capacity of the system for identifying and helping poor teaching did not seem to apply equally well to good teaching. Because he spent the most time with newer or poorer performing teachers, good teaching received relatively less feedback. Storm contrasted the value of the system for probationary and proficient teachers:

> But I view this system as extremely effective for an unsatisfactory or a Level One teacher. For a teacher who is proficient or a very strong teacher, we are just documenting the fact that they are good teachers.

Storm did not feel that the new evaluation system supported the establishment of agreement about what good teaching means: "I think every teacher thinks that their teaching is good. Whatever they do is good. And they haven't tailored their teaching style to meet the rubric." The novelty of the system may mean that it has not had a chance to create a shared sense of agreement. Storm commented, "You have to remember . . . these teachers weren't brought up in this system. This system has been imposed on teachers that have been here a long, long time." It is interesting to note that while Principal Storm emphasized the value of the evaluation process for novice and poor teachers, it was the veteran teachers with relatively higher scores who reported the most benefit to their teaching. Two veteran teachers valued the opportunity to reflect on their teaching afforded by the process. One teacher mentioned that the "rubrics helped me understand the difference between Level 2 and Level 3 teaching," and that the rubrics gave him something to aim toward in his teaching.

Storm's final point concerned the lack of feedback he has received on being an evaluator. While he noted that he received valuable training to conduct evaluations, he has received no feedback on his own evaluation practices. In his words:

> I have never gotten any feedback from anyone on [whether] I am doing a good job as an evaluator . . . . I mean, my bosses never ever talk to me about the evaluations that I have written. I don't think my boss has ever read my evaluations. So, I wouldn't mind getting some feedback to know whether or not I am meeting the district standard.

Jaye High School

The Jaye High School context presents special challenges for understanding how evaluators make sense of the evaluation process. In 2001–02 the largely upper-middle class student population at Jaye included 1,880 students. The student transience rate was 16 percent, 6.8 percent were labeled as special education students, 3.1 percent of the students were English-language learners, and the free/reduced price lunch population was 11.2 percent. Student performance on a national norm-referenced test was higher than the average performance of other district high schools. The 93 teachers on staff included 10 probationary teachers. The teachers and principal commonly reflected upon two features of the school context during the interviews. The first involved efforts to involve staff across the curriculum in setting school goals. The second, and a related factor, was a strong sense of collegiality in the school.

Teachers interviewed at Jaye included a veteran English teacher, a mid-career biology teacher, an early/mid-career history teacher, and a novice mathematics teacher. Principal Jennifer Fredericks was in her third year at the school and had extensive experience as a teacher and administrator. The four other administrators who acted as evaluators were not interviewed.

Evaluator Characteristics

Fredericks sought to develop department and school-based instructional goals, using a consensus-building approach. She explained that from her first day in the school, she worked to get the school to focus on data (e.g., student test scores) to set goals and to monitor progress. She encouraged teachers to share best practices during staff meetings. These processes were intended to develop a "common building belief system of what we are doing as a community, the sense of community to serve the students."

Principal Fredericks supported the new teacher evaluation system and was willing to invest the time and effort to make it productive. She asserted that the system fit with their "school wide belief system in rubrics. . . . It gives you a verbal picture of what you want to see." Her active support of the evaluation system capitalized on her instructional expertise and was reflected in how she structured the evaluation process. Fredericks described the evaluation system as fitting her philosophy on instructional leadership and incorporated the rubrics into her "own contextual belief system." She compared her leadership approach to the four domains of the evaluation system by planning what she wanted to do before she became a principal (reflecting domain 1); creating an environment "where people felt free to interact with me, to interact with one another," (modeling domain 2); then implementing the plan or plans (domain 3); and finally, giving back to her school community by working and sharing with each other through best practices during faculty meetings (domain 4). As she summarized, "We have actually role-modeled the [evaluation system]" as school leaders.

Fredericks explained that her experience, training, and practice as a teacher made her a good evaluator. Before she became an administrator, she attended Madeline Hunter training sessions and developed her skills in scripting classroom observations. In addition to the skills needed to conduct evaluations, Fredericks asserted that her credibility as a classroom teacher was a critical attribute for her legitimacy as an evaluator. As a principal, she saw her most important strength as her "ability to see all sides of the situation and to put myself in the shoes of the other person, whether it be a parent, a student, a teacher; to understand where everyone is coming from. And not to take anything personally."

Despite the increased demands of the evaluation system, Fredericks said she was able to manage the process because, "I am a pretty good time manager . . . I look over a semester and I can figure out where I have to be." To handle the time and workload demands, she planned one semester at a time and began with the probationary teachers, who required more time due to the structure of the evaluation system and their uncertainty in practice. Then she worked with teachers on the major evaluation and finally addressed the minor evaluations, " . . . because they take less time." She lamented that the time dedicated to probationary teachers, although necessary, limited how much she could work with other teachers.

Evaluation Process

The evaluation process described by the principal was similar to that described by teachers who had other evaluators. Fredericks held pre-observation conferences to meet with the teachers before the evaluation process began. During the meetings, she went through the evaluation rubrics and procedures to explain the process. She asked where teachers saw themselves in the rubrics. If a specific rubric lacked clarity, she would discuss what she believed it was trying to get at. When the questions were resolved, the focus of the evaluation was selected (i.e., domain(s), components, and elements). Teachers set a target for growth for each domain. Teachers chose a growth goal for each domain on which they were evaluated. Probationary teachers prepared one goal for each of the four domains. The targets of growth served as the focus for the written evaluation.

Fredericks structured her evaluation approach to focus on probationary teachers and centered her efforts on maximizing formative feedback to these novice teachers. She assigned herself a larger share of probationary teachers than the other evaluators. As she explained, "I want the new teachers I hire to have that connection with me and . . . I think that is a very formative time." She saw probationary teachers as vulnerable and was concerned about attrition, because new teachers typically "are just not mentored and encouraged."

To lower teacher anxiety about the process, Fredericks told teachers to feel free to make mistakes and not to worry about her being in the room. She also gave them flexibility in scheduling observations. As she stated, "I am not there to look at a perfect lesson . . . so I try to put them at ease ...

because I see this role as a helping role, not to go in there and catch them doing something wrong." She also tried to make sure that teachers were aware that what was being written down would be in the evaluation. As she explained, "There is never anything in the evaluation that I do that surprises. There is never anything in writing or checks in those boxes that the teacher has not been with me [and discussed] . . . And I try to always find something to commend them on." She explained that she was careful about what she wrote and how she phrased written comments in order to prevent teachers from reacting negatively to evaluations. When she first started doing evaluations as an administrator, she ". . . was amazed that the use of a word could make somebody very anxious." So, ". . . I am more careful about using words like 'very' or 'often' or 'frequently' or 'occasionally.'" During conferences, she asked teachers to talk about instructional artifacts (planning documents, test results, etc.) involved in the lesson. Consistent with the leadership approach discussed above, teamwork and school wide goals re-emerged during evaluation discussions.

Fredericks tried to foster self-reflection and monitoring/correcting and used constructive criticism, trying to help teachers think about the observed situation ". . . and go back to it in their mind and think about how they might do it differently. And then I will say 'or you could have . . . ' but I don't say 'this is the way it should always be done.' There is never one way to do anything." She tried to encourage teachers to have interactive classes, where kids are major participants.

Summary of Written Evaluations

The evaluation context at Jaye is made more complex because of the multiple evaluators involved. Thus, even though Fredericks played an important role in making sense of the evaluation artifact for the school program, the other evaluators brought their own assumptions to the process. Thus it is not surprising that both the written evaluations by evaluators and the teacher reactions to their evaluations at Jaye varied considerably. Two of the evaluators (including the principal) provided detailed written commentary, with evidence described and specific recommendations for improvement. In contrast, the other evaluators provided very brief descriptions of performance, with only a few sentences, little if any evidence reported and few recommendations for improvement.

Individual teacher evaluation scores on the 79 evaluations provided by the district averaged between "proficient" and "area of strength" on the district scale. Although five teachers received level one ratings in particular domains, there was no written description of why the rating was given or how the teacher could improve on the element. Despite the prompt on the evaluation form (and implied requirement of the system) to offer specific evidence for the ratings, it was rare for evaluators to offer such evidence or to provide recommendations to improve. It was also difficult to find negative feedback in either the write-ups or from the interview transcripts. Evaluators delivered criticism in a positive fashion (if critique was provided) or first pointed out positive aspects of performance and characteristics of the teacher.

Written evaluations documented positive aspects of teacher performance. In some cases, recommendations for improvement were provided. For example, one evaluator commented that, "teacher uses goals suitable for most students." This same evaluator had three recommendations for the teacher, including the following: "When planning lectures, provide as many opportunities to engage as many students as possible throughout the lecture." The written evaluations also allowed evaluators to document praise for how teachers had taken on extra school responsibilities. For several of the teachers interviewed, more feedback seemed to be provided during discussions with the evaluator than was reflected in the written evaluations. However, other teachers reported receiving minimal feedback in either written or verbal form.

Perceptions of the Evaluation Process
Principal Fredericks thought the comprehensive standards and rubrics of the evaluation system helped to promote a common and continuing dialog with teachers. Fredericks believed the system provided a framework for teachers to think about their work and a process for them to interact, get help and talk about their practice, and be recognized for their efforts. Most teachers also preferred the new system to the prior one, which required an extensive written evaluation but did not have the level of knowledge and skill elaboration of the current system. One teacher, however, preferred the old system, where ". . . you could sit down and talk and you could read it and pick it out and read it again if you need a little pat on the back." Other teachers valued the potential for objectivity of the new system's detailed rubrics.

Jaye staff had mixed reactions about the impact of the evaluation process on their instruction. The principal believed that the evaluation system led some teachers to change their practice. For example, a special education teacher who had relied on lectures changed his practice to get students more actively involved. After evaluation discussions, Fredericks noted ". . . his room is full of colored pens and pencils and the kids have no books and the kids are keeping these forms . . . And he loves it." Two teachers mentioned the evaluation process improved their teaching through better planning and classroom management, keeping students on task and increased use of reflection. Two other teachers were not as positive. One commented that her evaluator (not the principal) had little or no teaching experience: "I was evaluated by someone who didn't teach school, who has never taught school. [He] went from the world of work, business, into education, into administration." This teacher reported a better experience with a different evaluator the prior year. The other teacher consistently received high ratings and was rarely offered feedback specific to the content he taught. Teachers commented that the evaluation system required more paperwork and effort than the prior system, but it was more burdensome for evaluators than for teachers. One teacher said that, "I think what happens is [the administrators] get up against the time when all the evaluations are due and things get really hectic." Two teachers explained the system was more work intensive than the prior system, but was worth the effort and more objective.

Fredericks expressed that evaluator training offered by the district could be improved. The trainers took a minimalist approach focused on getting evaluations done efficiently rather than well. As she stated, "Basically, the person was saying, 'this is how you can get them done the fastest. You don't really have to do this. And you don't really have to do that. And you can just whip them out." She suspected that evaluators varied considerably in how accurately they evaluated teachers and how well they provided growth-directed feedback. She suggested the district should have master evaluators help beginning administrators, to "go in until they have a comfort zone of performing evaluations and the process."

ANALYSIS

Investigating the way that local leaders make sense of a complex artifact such as a new teacher evaluation highlights the selection of artifact affordances, from among the many possible features of the artifact, and helps us to understand how leaders adapt new practices to their existing contexts. The interaction of leaders' will, skill and their perceptions of organization structure organize our comments about sensemaking.

Will

Most principals wanted to make this system work and tried hard to comply with the system requirements for numbers of observations and write-ups. However, it was apparent that the evaluation system was extremely time-consuming, absorbing as much as 25% of the principal's time. We saw principals address the time issue by complex scheduling and by investing significant amounts of personal time. Evaluators satisfied the time requirements through brief classroom visits, writing up the observation while observing the class, and in stealing a few minutes before and after class for the pre- and post-observation meetings. Despite this significant time investment, some teachers felt that an insufficient amount of time was invested in the system to provide meaningful feedback on teaching practice. In many schools, most evaluations were dated all on the same day at the end of the evaluation cycle, suggesting that many evaluation forms were completed at the last minute.

The considerable time investment required to conduct observations and complete the evaluations narrowed the range of cognitive and structural resources available to implement the full range of artifact features. The artifact design relies on evaluators to collect multiple kinds of evidence to document the different components of teaching practice as specified in the rubrics. The elaborate system of rubrics and evidence requirements challenged evaluators to move beyond classroom observation in order to develop fundamentally new evidentiary bases. Our study suggests that although evaluators stretched their professional and personal time to observe all teachers, the evaluations lacked evidence grounded in the rubrics. The evaluation criteria included, for example, "reflecting on teaching" and "communicating with families," but no evidence was provided by evaluators for ratings in these domains. Simply complying with the district policy to conduct observations of all faculty seemed challenging enough. To take full advantage of the evaluation program, evaluators and teachers need more time and training on how to collect, reflect upon, and present evidence to maximize the potential of the evaluation system for promoting better teaching practice.

Skill

We found that the written evaluations lacked either formative or critical feedback. The majority of written comments focused on scripting of classroom activities, classroom management and generic comments pointing to the important role the teacher had played in the school. While several of the principals used the evaluation process to suggest new practices and to encourage staff collaboration, few examples of specific, evidence-based suggestions grounded in the rubrics found their way into the written evaluations. The focus on classroom management was reflected in the views of new teachers who expressed a more positive view of the potential impact of the system on improving their teaching practice. Veteran teachers, presumably more familiar with classroom management practices, were more reserved in their praise.

The evidence from our case study schools suggest that evaluators lacked the skills to provide valuable feedback, particularly with accomplished teachers. Evaluators instead used evaluation as an opportunity to work with novice teachers and to build a positive school culture rather than as an opportunity to push instructional practices to the highest levels. However, we cannot discern from our study whether this lack of skill was a cause or an effect of evaluator priorities. In other words, the perceived lack of skill in providing formative feedback to accomplished teachers was qualified by the competing, and perhaps more legitimate, goal of enlisting the support of veteran teachers for the new evaluation initiative. Concerns about the politics of evaluation and maintenance of strong social relations among faculty and evaluators may have led evaluators to provide nearly exclusively positive and largely low level, narrow and specific feedback to teachers.

The lack of critical comments and the inconsistencies between the reported value of feedback and the written instruments suggest the importance of attending to the political context for evaluation. While the lack of "unsatisfactory" ratings in the case-study schools and the narrative feedback might suggest a high quality of teaching across the schools, all principals described instances of sub-standard teacher performance. Clearly, the evaluation process was not fully represented by the written components alone. Performance appraisal research suggests that negative feedback is difficult to convey and often avoided for fear of depressing employee motivation (Ilgen & Davis, 2000), and the political nature of formal appraisals may result in lenient evaluation ratings in order to motivate employee performance (Longenecker, Sims & Gioia, 1987; Murphy & Cleveland, 1995). In such cases, evaluation systems may send mixed messages about organizational goals for rating accuracy and performance improvement through evaluations (Kozlowski, Chao & Morrison, 1999). Written negative comments carry great weight in organizational cultures, and supervisors interested in maintaining long-standing, collaborative relationships with employees are often reluctant to use formal instruments to provide negative feedback.

The absence of critical feedback in most written evaluations might not mean the complete absence of such feedback. Recall Principal Storm's comment that the specificity of the rubrics was valuable for helping to dismiss incompetent staff, yet these critical messages were not reflected in the written evaluations. If teachers receive the most meaningful feedback verbally, then the written instruments could be used to preserve the delicate organizational culture of trust and collaboration between evaluator and teacher. At the same time, neglecting to document specific instances of low performance blunts a central intention of the evaluation program. Without critical feedback, the artifact becomes a tool to maintain a positive sense of community rather than a tool to distinguish levels of practice, and to foster improvement and reflection on teaching practice.

Structure

Structure here refers to the personal, professional and institutional traditions that shape local practice. Our analysis showed the power of the self-perceived role of evaluators as instructional leaders on the evaluation process. Self-imposed role definitions reflected the skills of the evaluator, and seemed to enhance or constrain their will for selecting and implementing certain features of the artifact. The roles chosen by evaluators had significant effect on the affordances of the artifact selected for implementation. For example, Jaye's Principal Fredericks actively modeled her instructional leadership approach around the vision of performance represented in the evaluation domains. At *La Esperanza*, Richards' role as an instructional coach was reflected in her team-building messages of encouragement and inspiration on her written narrative evaluations. Richards' belief that critical evaluation feedback could be devastating to teachers shaped her role as an evaluator to encourage rather than to criticize her teachers. She downplayed the summative, critical features of the artifact in order to fit the artifact to her perceived role in the school.

Woods Principal John Storm perceived the evaluation artifact differently. His role as an instructional leader involved communicating a consistent message about his six key indicators of good teaching. While not inconsistent with the evaluation model, it was these indicators—and not the evaluation system itself—that guided his observations. Storm relied on his model to guide the Woods evaluation process and to give specific feedback to struggling teachers. In this case Storm replaced designed features with his own conception of good teaching, and used the new district initiative to flesh out his previously developed evaluation practices. While full implementation of the artifact may require a redefinition the self-perceived role of the evaluator, the expertise of the evaluator as an instructional leader depends on the very role-perception in need of alteration. Implementing more of the artifact features would require evaluators to "see" their instructional leadership roles differently to allow for a more critical perspective on evaluation practice.

CONCLUSIONS AND IMPLICATIONS

In this study of sensemaking and implementation of a knowledge and skills-based teacher evaluation system, we found that the features of the artifact that potentially enhance the opportunity to improve teacher quality were filtered through pre-existing perceptions, knowledge, and structures. Consistent with the literature on sensemaking and implementation, we found that local implementation of the evaluation system varied substantially from school to school, and was shaped by the ways in which principals understood their own role, their context, and the evaluation artifact. Principal sensemaking seemed to be primarily a function of principal self-perception of their role as a leader and the knowledge and skills they bring to that role; prior evaluation practices in the school and district; and school context factors such as teacher morale and existing challenges facing the school (e.g., student population risk factors, external accountability pressures).

We found that there was a strong desire of local leaders to use teacher evaluation practices for two central purposes: one, to maintain a community of good will with teachers, and two, to help novice teachers improve or remove those unable to perform at a basic level. In each case, the affordances exploited by leaders seemed to extend the functions of the previous evaluation system. Further, these uses seemed to inhibit the recognition and use of other features intended to provide specific, critical, and formative feedback to veteran teachers.

A key question in the implementation of complex artifacts is whether features have sufficient power to change the embedded organizational culture. From a compliance perspective, the amount of time spent to implement the teacher evaluation framework should be judged a huge success at Valle Verde. However, implementation of the full range of artifact features seems hindered by time constraints and school cultures and professional practices that reinforce the separation of instructional and supervisory practices. The gap between supervision and instruction that constitutes the organizational culture of many schools is difficult to cross (Hazi 1994; Rowan, 1990). Closing this gap takes time. A condition for closing this gap might be to develop both common practices for teachers and leaders to interact around instruction, and a common language to facilitate the conversations. The district framework for teaching includes features to facilitate both processes. Since the framework is already in place at Valle Verde, and since teachers and principals view it as a useful process, there already is significant movement toward these ends. The framework is being used widely across the district, and appears to be helping to develop the capacity for teachers and evaluators to engage in regular conversations about instruction. District leaders could push implementation further and capitalize on this newfound capacity in order to more tightly couple instructional and supervision practices in the school culture. Over time, this capacity may have the power to change instructional culture.

Thinking of implementation as a long-term process of reshaping prior knowledge, skills, and beliefs will require district leaders to focus on the key "teachable moments" currently emerging for district evaluators and teachers, such as the desire of evaluators to receive district feedback on their own evaluation practice. We hypothesize that the increasing experience with evaluation and feedback might make principals more likely to identify and focus on the instructional improvement features of the evaluation system. Taking advantage of the ways evaluators learn from their experience may change the features principals select in the artifact, and therefore modify the implementation of specific features of the artifact to enhance its instructional improvement outcomes. Specifically, our analysis suggests the following five areas of focus for continued attention.

Providing a Clearer Conceptual Connection between the Teacher Evaluation Framework and Enhanced Student Learning

A key intention in the district design was to use the evaluation artifact to improve student learning. However, few principals and teachers viewed the evaluation process as having a direct relationship to student achievement, accountability goals, or even as a pathway to significantly improving teacher quality. To make this link explicit, evaluators may need additional training in content-based pedagogy and evaluation feedback. Enhanced skills alone may help evaluators recognize the opportunity for instructional improvement that the evaluation artifact provides, and thereby encourage them to use evaluation as a means to work with teachers at all skill levels to significantly improve instructional practice.

Tying Feedback to the Evaluation Standards

Training for evaluators could also focus on building understandings about how evaluation rubrics enhance teaching practices and improve student learning. Although teachers are asked to set goals for one or two specific elements in the domains on which they are evaluated, written feedback is seldom specifically tied to the standards. Maintaining a focus on the evaluation standards beyond the goal setting process could help to more directly link goal-setting, evaluation feedback, and overall improvement in the teacher evaluation system. Training in providing evidence-based feedback, such as evidence needed to demonstrate content-specific pedagogy, could extend existing training and support relationships in order to create shared understandings of evaluation as a tool to promote instructional improvement. Teachers could more clearly see a connection between formative recommendations and improvement on the rubrics in the evaluation system.

Coordinating the Structural Requirements of the Program

With three years of implementation, the routinization of the evaluation process provides a foundation for further development. District leaders need to familiarize themselves with the evaluation process, and better understand the various roles that goal setting, observation, and verbal and written feedback play. In doing so, the district could provide feedback on the existing evaluation process in local schools, and evaluators could develop networks to share practices on how to provide effective and efficient evaluations. Once district and school leaders realize how far they have come, their insights can be used to build on these newly developed capacities.

Recognizing and Accommodating the Political Contexts of Evaluation

The politics of evaluation were evident in a variety of features of the evaluation artifact. For example, district training for evaluators in time management suggests awareness by the district of school-level reactions to the time-consuming nature of the evaluation process. In addition, the politics of supervisor-teacher relations at the school level shaped the nature of written evaluation feedback, which was almost uniformly positive, even when teachers received relatively low scores on specific rubrics.

Recognition of the political nature of evaluation might help to untangle how issues of training and skill development combine with existing political and cultural expectations for the evaluation process. Political response is rational and appropriate if it facilitates implementation of the evaluation system. Recognition of the political nature of implementation could enable district and school leaders to view political response as a part of the process on the way to full implementation of the evaluation artifact, and not the final destination. Explicit attention to the political nature of evaluation and an examination of the features of the evaluation artifact could enhance the ability to use evaluation to provide constructive feedback in a dynamic political and cultural organizational context.

The Valle Verde Unified approach to implementing a new teacher evaluation system relied on a low-stakes, developmental model that depended heavily on the ability of local evaluators to extend their prior evaluation experience to meet the requirements of the new system. Our study of the resulting implementation suggests that the district has developed local capacity to use the framework for teaching to support richer teacher and leader interaction around instruction. While much sensemaking research looks backward to investigate the relation of the past to the present, our perspective suggests that a sensemaking perspective can also point to areas for subsequent development. Future research is needed to understand how leaders might choose and exploit the potentially transformative features of evaluation system and integrate these features into new practices of teacher evaluation.

NOTES

1. A previous version of this paper was presented at the 2003 Annual Meeting of the American Educational Research Association, Chicago, Illinois, April 2003. The research reported in this paper was supported in part by a grant from the U.S. Department of Education, Office of Educational Research and Improvement, National institute on Educational governance, Finance, Policy-Making and Management, to the Consortium for Policy Research in Education (CPRE) and the Wisconsin Center for Education Research, School of Education, University of Wisconsin-Madison (Grant No. OERI-R3086A60003). The opinions expressed are those of the authors and do not necessarily reflect the view of the National Institute on Educational Governance, Finance, Policy-Making and Management, office of Educational Research and Improvement, U.S. Department of Education, the institutional partners of CPRE, or the Wisconsin Center for Education Research.

2. The authors would like to thank Gary Zehrbach, Bill Thornton, and Terry Fowler for their contributions to data collection and analysis on the project.

3. The will, skill, and structure elements are adapted from Rowan (1996), who describes teacher knowledge and skills (skill), teacher motivation (will), and the situation or context in which teachers work (structure) as critical factors influencing teacher and student performance.

4. Names of the school district, schools, and educators have been disguised.

REFERENCES

Berends, M., Bodilly, S., & Kirby, S. N. (2002). Looking back over a decade of whole-school reform: The experience of new American schools. *Phi Delta Kappan, 84*(2), 168–175.

Bronfenbrenner, U. (1979). *The ecology of human development: Experiments by nature and design.* Cambridge, MA: Harvard University Press.

Carey, S. (1985). *Conceptual change in childhood.* Cambridge, MA: MIT Press

Chinn, C. A., & Brewer, W. F. (1993). The role of anomalous data in knowledge acquisition: A theoretical framework and implications for science instruction. *Review of Educational Research, 63,* 1–49.

Cohen, D. K., & Barnes, C. A. (1993). Pedagogy and policy. In D. K. Cohen, M. W. McLaughlin, & J. E. Talbert (Eds.), *Teaching for understanding: Challenges for policy and practice* (pp. 207–239). San Francisco: Jossey-Bass.

Confrey J. (1990). A review of the research on students conceptions in mathematics, science, and programming. In: Courtney C. (Ed.), *Review of Research in Education* (pp. 3–56). American Educational Research Association.

Danielson, C. (1996). *Enhancing professional practice: A framework for teaching.* Alexandria, VA: Association for Supervision and Curriculum Development.

Danielson, C., & McGreal, T. L. (2000). *Teacher evaluation to enhance professional practice.* Alexandria, VA: Association for Supervision and Curriculum Development.

Darling-Hammond, L., & Ball, D. L. (1997). *Teaching for high standards: What policymakers need to know and be able to do* [Electronic version]. National Education

Goals Panel, June, 1997. Retrieved September 12, 2003 from http://www.negp.gov/reports/highstds.htm

Darling-Hammond, L., Wise, A. E., & Klein, S. P. (1999). *A license to teach: Raising standards for teaching.* San Francisco, CA: Jossey-Bass.

Darling-Hammond, L., Wise, A. E., & Pease, S. R. (1983). Teacher evaluation in the organizational context: A review of the literature. *Review of Educational Research, 53*(3), 285–328.

Davis, D. R., Pool, J. E., & Mits-Cash, M. (2000). Issues in implementing a new teacher assessment system in a large urban school district: Results of a qualitative field study. *Journal of Personnel Evaluation in Education, 14*(4), 285–306.

Desimone, L (2002). How can comprehensive school reform models be successfully implemented? *Review of Educational Research, 72*(3), 433–479.

Elmore, R. (2002). Bridging the gap between standards and achievement: The imperative for professional development in education. Washington, DC: Albert Shanker Institute.

Fischoff, B. (1975). Hindsight foresight: The effect of outcome knowledge on judgment under uncertainty. *Journal of Experimental Psychology: Human Perception and Performance, 1,* 288–299.

Gallagher, H. A. (2002). Vaughn Elementary's innovative teacher evaluation system: Are teacher evaluation scores related to growth in student achievement? Madison: University of Wisconsin, Wisconsin Center for Education Research, Consortium for Policy Research in Education.

Genter D., Rattermann M. J., & Forbus, K. D. (1993). The roles of similarity in transfer: Separating retrievability from inferential soundness. *Cognitive Psychology, 25*(4), 524–575.

Gentner, D. & Stevens, A. L. (Eds.). (1983). *Mental models.* Hillsdale, NJ: Erlbaum.

Gibson, J. J. (1986). *The ecological approach to visual perception.* Mahwah, NJ: Erlbaum.

Greeno, J. G. (1998). The situativity of knowing, learning, and research. *American Psychologist, 53*(1), 5, 26.

Greeno, J. G., Collins, A. M., & Resnick, L. B. (1996). Cognition and learning. In D. Berliner & R. Calfee (Eds.), *Handbook of educational psychology* (pp. 15–46). New York: Simon & Schuster Macmillan.

Hallinger, P., & Heck, R. H. (1996). Reassessing the principal's role in school effectiveness: A review of empirical research, 1980–1995. *Educational Administration Quarterly, 32*(1), 5–44.

Halverson, R. (2002). *Representing phronesis: Supporting instructional leadership practice in schools.* Evanston, IL, Northwestern University. Unpublished dissertation.

Halverson, R., & Zoltners, J. (2001). Distribution across artifacts: How designed artifacts illustrate school leadership practice. Paper for the 2001 American Educational Research Association, Seattle, WA.

Hammer, D., & Elby, A. (2002). On the form of a personal epistemology. In B. K. Hofer & P. R. Pintrich (Eds.), *Personal epistemology: The psychology of beliefs about knowledge and knowing* (pp. 169–190). Mahwah, NJ: Erlbaum.

Haney, W., Madaus, G., & Kreitzer, A. (1987). Charms talismanic: Testing teachers for the improvement of American education. In E. Z. Rothkopf (Ed.), *Review of Research in Education* (pp. 169–238). Washington, DC: American Educational Research Association.

Hazi, H. M. (1994). The teacher evaluation-supervision dilemma: A case of entanglements and irreconcilable differences. *Journal of Curriculum & Supervision, 9*(2), 195–216.

Ilgen, D. R., & Davis, C. A. (2000). Bearing bad news: Reactions to negative performance feedback. *Applied Psychology: An International Review, 49*(3), 550–565.

Keisler, S., & Sproull, L. (1982). Managerial response to changing. *Administrative Science Quarterly, 27,* 548–570.

Kimball, S. M. (2002). Analysis of feedback, enabling conditions and fairness perceptions of teachers in three school districts with new standards-based evaluation systems. *Journal of Personnel Evaluation in Education, 16(4), 241–269.*

Kozlowski, S. W. J., Chao, G. T., & Morrison, R. F. (1999). Games raters play: Politics, strategies, and impresson management in performance appraisal. In J. W. Smither, (Ed.) *Performance Appraisal: State of the Art in Practice* (pp. 163–205). San Francisco, CA: Jossey-Bass.

Longenecker, C. O., Sims, H. P., & Gioia, D. A. (1987). Behind the mask: The politics of employee appraisal. *The Academy of Management Executive, 1*(3), 183–193.

Loup, K. S., Garland, J. S., Ellett, C. D., & Rugutt, J. K. (1996). Ten years later: Findings from a replication of a study of teacher evaluation practices in our 100 largest school districts. *Journal of Personnel Evaluation in Education, 10,* 203–226.

March, J. G., & Simon, H. A. (1958). *Organizations.* New York: Wiley.

Milanowski, A. T., & Heneman, H. G., III. (2001). Assessment of teacher reactions to a standards-based teacher evaluation system: A pilot study. *Journal of Personnel Evaluation in Education, 15*(3), 193–212.

Murphy, J. (1994). Transformational change and the evolving role of the principal: Early empirical evidence. In J. Murphy & K. S. Louis (Eds.). *Reshaping the principalship: Insights from transformational change efforts* (pp. 20–53). Newbury Park, CA: Corwin.

Murphy, K. R., & Cleveland, J. N. (1995). *Understanding performance appraisal: Social, organizational and goal-based perspectives.* London: Sage.

Norman, D. A. (1993). *Things that make us smart: defending human attributes in the age of the machine.* Reading, MA: Addison-Wesley.

Odden, A., & Kelley, C. (2002). *Paying teachers for what they know and do: New and smarter compensation strategies to improve schools* (2nd ed.). Thousand Oaks, CA: Corwin.

Pea, R. D. (1993). Practices of distributed intelligence and designs for education. In Salomon, G. (Ed.). *Distributed cognitions: Psychological and educational considerations* (pp. 47–87). Cambridge, UK: Cambridge University Press.

Peterson, K. D. (1989). *Secondary principals and instructional leadership: Complexities in a diverse role.* Madison, WI: The National Center for Effective Secondary Schools.

Peterson, K. D. (1995). *Teacher evaluation: A comprehensive guide to new directions and practices.* Thousand Oaks, CA: Corwin.

Ross, B. H. (1987). This is like that: The use of earlier problems and the separation of similarity effects. *Journal of Experimental Psychology: Learning, Memory, and Cognition, 13,* 629–639.

Rowan, B. (1990). Commitment and control: Alternative strategies for the organizational design of schools. *Review of Research in Education, 16,* 353–389.

Rowan, B. (1996). Standards and incentives for instructional reform. In S. H. Fuhrman & J. O'Day (Eds.), *Rewards and reform: Creating educational incentives that work* (pp. 195–225). San Francisco: Jossey-Bass.

Schank, R. C. (1982). *Dynamic memory: A theory of reminding and learning in computers and people.* New York: Cambridge University Press.

Schank, R. C., & Abelson, R. P. (1977). *Scripts, plans, goals, and understanding.* Hillsdale, NJ: Erlbaum.

Simon, H. A. (1996). *The sciences of the artificial.* Cambridge, Mass., MIT Press.

Spillane, J., Halverson, R., & Diamond, J. (2001). Investigating school leadership practice: A distributed perspective. *Educational Researcher, 30*(3), 23–28.

Spillane, J., Reiser, B. J., & Reimer, T. (2002). Policy implementation and cognition: Reframing and refocusing implementation research. *Review of Educational Research, 72*(3). 387–431

Stake, R. E. (1995). *The art of case research.* London: Sage.

Starbuck, W., & Milliken, F. (1988). Executives' perceptual filters: What they notice and how they make sense. In Hambrick, D. (Ed.) *The Executive effect: Concepts and methods for studying top managers* (pp. 35–65). Greenwich, CT: JAI.

Wartofsky, M. W. (1979). *Models: Representation and the scientific understanding.* Dordrecht, Holland; Boston, D. Reidel.

Weick, K. E. (1976). Educational organizations as loosely coupled systems. *Administrative Science Quarterly, 21*(1), 1–19.

Weick, K. E. (1996). *Sensemaking in organizations.* London: Sage.

Wise, A. E., Darling-Hammond, L., McLaughlin, M. W., & Bernstein, H. T. (1984). *Teacher evaluation: A study of effective practices.* Santa Monica, CA: Rand.

Wright, P. S., Horn, S. P., & Sanders, W. L. (1997). Teacher and classroom context effects on student achievement: Implications for teacher evaluation. *Journal of Personnel Evaluation in Education, 11*, 57–67.

APPENDIX A:
DISTRICT OVERVIEW AND EVALUATION SYSTEM SUMMARY

The school district is the second largest in the state and includes 85 schools, approximately 60,000 students, 3,700 certified staff, and 270 administrators. Thirty-eight percent of the student population is non-white, with Hispanic students making up the largest part of the non-majority group. Although the district had recently revised aspects of its teacher evaluation system, the district and teachers' association agreed in 1997 that more comprehensive evaluation reforms were needed.

The new teacher evaluation system includes all of the standards and many of the suggested sources of evidence included in the *Framework for Teaching* (Danielson, 1996). There are four domains of practice with 23 components and 68 elements elaborating behavioral descriptions of the components. The domains are Planning and Preparation, Classroom Environment, Instruction, and Professional Responsibilities. Each element includes separate descriptions of teaching performance on a four-level rubric: unsatisfactory, target for growth (level 1), proficient (level 2), and area of strength (level 3). Table 1 includes an example of one set of rubrics for one of the 68 elements.

Multiple sources of evidence are called for to assess performance relative to the standards. Evidence may include a teacher self-assessment, a pre-observation data sheet (lesson plan), classroom observations, pre- and post-observation conferences, other observations of teaching practice (e.g., parent-teacher meetings or collegial discussions), samples of teaching work and instructional artifacts, reflection sheets, three-week unit plan, and logs of professional activities. Unlike the suggestions in the Framework for Teaching, instructional portfolios are not required as part of the evaluation evidence.

Similar to the district's prior system, teachers are evaluated annually and specific procedures exist depending on where teachers are in three evaluation stages: probationary, post-probationary major, and post-probationary minor. Probationary teachers are those who are novice teachers or who taught previously in another district. Probationary teachers are observed at least nine times over three periods of the year and are provided a written evaluation at the end of each period. If they don't advance after their first year, probationary teachers undergo a second probationary year. If their performance is unsatisfactory, they may be dismissed.

Teachers in post-probationary status are evaluated in a major evaluation based on two of the performance domains, one selected by the teacher and the other by the evaluator. Formal observations occur three times over the

TABLE 1

Example of Rubric for Domain 1: Planning and Preparation; Component 1b: Demonstrating Knowledge of Students

Element	*Unsatisfactory*	*Target for Growth/Level 1*	*Proficient/ Level 2*	*Area of Strength/ Level 3*
Knowledge of Students' Varied Approaches to Learning	Teacher is unfamiliar with the different approaches to learning that students exhibit, such as learning styles, modalities, and different intelligences.	"Teacher displays general understanding of the different approaches to learning that students exhibit, and includes a limited variety in lesson planning.	Teacher displays solid understanding of the different approaches to learning that different students exhibit and occasionally uses those approaches.	Teacher uses, where appropriate, knowledge of students' varied approaches to learning in instructional planning, as an integral part of their instructional planning repertoire.

course of the year and a written evaluation is provided toward the end of the year. After a successful major evaluation, teachers move to a two-year minor evaluation phase.

Teachers on the post-probationary minor cycle are evaluated on one domain and receive one formal observation, resulting in one written evaluation at the end of the year. The process is repeated during the next year, with one new evaluation domain selected. An optional minor evaluation process is available to teachers who have at least five years experience in the district and have been successfully evaluated under the major phase. Teachers in the alternative minor process may choose from six professional growth options (e.g., pursuit of National Board Certification, supervising a student teacher or engaging in an action research project). These options must still be tied to an evaluation domain, but are less structured than typical minor evaluations.

The written evaluations include a cover sheet with the teacher's name and basic demographic information (hire date, school, grade/subject, type of contract), whether the teacher is on the probationary and post-probationary cycle, and when the evaluation and observations occurred. Pursuant to state law, the form also indicates whether the complete evaluation was satisfactory or unsatisfactory. The form ends with evaluator and teacher signatures.

Evaluators are to mark the appropriate performance level on the four-level rubric for each element of each domain evaluated. Following the scores, the evaluators are required to provide a narrative description of the evaluation. The narrative is to include a separate description for any element receiving an unsatisfactory rating, with evidence cited from observations, and recommendations. For domains with scores above unsatisfactory (level 1–3), the form calls for "one complete narrative mentioning data for each, commendations, and recommendations." Any evaluation standard rated unsatisfactory results in an unsatisfactory evaluation and the teacher undergoes an intervention process. Teachers in the intervention process work with their administrator to establish an assistance plan and are evaluated on all performance standards that are not being satisfactorily met. When all objectives of the assistance plan are met, teachers may go back into the regular evaluation cycle.

CHAPTER 7

WE MUST MODEL
HOW WE TEACH

Learning to Lead with Compelling Models of Professional Development[1]

Ellen Goldring and Nancy Vye

This paper presents the results of a research study that explored the implementation and impact of a multimedia, case-based professional development program for practicing school leaders. The new multimedia, case-based leadership training program, *The Institute for School Leadership,* specifically links leadership to learning following the National Research Council report, *How People Learn* (Bransford, Brown, & Cocking, 1999). Participants' knowledge and understanding of information related to effective school leadership improved significantly as a result of their participation in the ISL. Participants also indicated that the Institute curriculum and delivery strongly adheres to the *How People Learn* Framework. There are striking differences between the initial and later responses to challenge questions as well. The results suggest technology can provide powerful avenues for professional development that are rooted in practice, and can help address the transfer of knowledge and the development of expertise.

Educational Administration, Policy, and Reform: Research and Measurement
A Volume in: Research and Theory In Educational Administration, pages 189–217.
Copyright © 2004 by Information Age Publishing, Inc.
All rights of reproduction in any form reserved.
ISBN: 1-59311-000-0 (hardcover), 1-59311-000-0 (paperback)

INTRODUCTION

Educational leaders are more aware today than at any time in the field's history of the complexities and challenges of public education, and of the importance of effective educational leadership to the enduring success of schools and all children (Goldring & Greenfeld, 2002; Murphy & Seashore Louis, 1999). Key to realizing this success is opportunities for high quality professional development. Professional development programs for educational leaders have been highly criticized over the past decades for emphasizing management rather than instructional leadership, providing activities and content unrelated to student learning and school improvement, and designing learning goals disconnected to the realities of professional practice (Kochan, Bredeson, & Riehl, 2002). Moreover, the roles for school leaders have changed substantially over the past decade. A renewed focus on instructional improvement and accountability requires that professional development address domains that have been largely left out of typical principal preparation programs.

Compounding these issues are concerns related to the underlying instructional models that typify professional development programs. Recent work in the learning sciences indicates that traditional modes of instruction often result in limited transfer of learning from the workshop classroom to the real world of schools (Bransford, Brown, & Cocking, 1999). There is a critical need to change instructional delivery models in ways that enhance the probability that school leaders can put their new learnings into practice.

The purpose of this paper is to describe a multimedia case-based, leadership training program, *The Institute for School Leadership* (hereafter ISL) that specifically addresses both the need for compelling models of professional development for school leaders that link leadership to learning and focus on instructional improvement for children. Furthermore, the ISL is designed according to state-of-the-art principles of teaching and learning as described in a recent National Research Council report entitled, *How People Learn* (Bransford, Brown, & Cocking, 1999).

The paper also presents the results of research accompanying the ISL. Specifically, the research addresses the following questions:

- What do participants learn from the ISL?
- How do ISL participants' beliefs about school leadership change?
- To what extent does the training exemplify principles of effective teaching and learning as described in the *How People Learn* framework?

THE NEED FOR NEW MODELS OF
PROFESSIONAL DEVELOPMENT

A core challenge facing America's schools is the improvement of student learning; America's youth do not perform as well as their counterparts in many other, often less-developed nations (National Center for Education Statistics, 2000). However, meeting this challenge will depend on substantial improvements in the quality of instruction in America's schools and change in teachers' practices in the classroom. Schools with shared, focused visions about instruction, norms of collaboration, collective responsibility for students' academic success, and an ongoing reflective dialogue among staff about practice create incentives and opportunities for improving teachers' practice (Bryk & Driscoll, 1985; Hallinger & Heck, 1996; Newman & Wehlage, 1995; Purkey & Smith, 1983). Sustained coherence and alignment among resources, learning communities, and external constituencies are also essential components of school improvement (Knapp, Copland, & Talbert, 2003).

School leadership is essential for the development and maintenance of these conditions. Unless school leaders practice in ways that support teacher learning, recent federal and state reform initiatives are likely to have, at best, a marginal effect on teaching and learning. Professional development and training programs are crucial for refocusing school leadership on teaching and learning and helping principals change instructional practices.

Most school leaders are ill-prepared to create and sustain these conditions (Goldring & Cohen-Vogel, 2000). The lack of preparation is even more salient because the nature of instruction is changing to ensure all children can learn. Since the effective schools movement, radically differing views of teaching and learning have emerged. Partly in response to lackluster results on the National Assessment of Educational Progress tests and the involvement of cognitive scientists in the debate about learning, the nature of classroom teaching is changing. Educational reformers advocate altering teaching and learning to take into account how students learn, good pedagogical practice, and the nature of the content or discipline (Stevenson, 1996). New models of teaching and learning are placing greater emphasis on content, subject matter, and authentic pedagogies. Simultaneously, state level curricula frameworks accompanied by high stakes testing and school accountability expectations, are placing principals at the center of instructional reform efforts. The nature and expectations for teaching and learning have changed due to standard based reforms. Reforms across the curricula are emphasizing content and authentic achievement, placing new emphases on the importance of a deep understanding of subject matter. New teaching strategies emphasize changing roles for teachers and students where teachers are facilitators of instruction and students are active learners: In considering new curriculum reforms in California, Cohen (1991) remarks:

> In order to teach math as the new Framework intends, most teachers would have to learn an entirely new version for the subject. . . .They would have to acquire a new way of thinking about mathematics, and a new approach to learning it. They would have to additionally cultivate strategies of problem solving that seem to be quite unusual. They would have to learn to treat mathematical knowledge as something that is constructed, tested and explored, rather than as something they broadcast, and that students accept and accumulate. Finally, they would have to un-learn the mathematics they have known. (p. 120)

In addition, teachers report being only moderately prepared to implement content standards and address the special learning needs of a diverse student body. A 1998 survey of 4,000 teachers in the United States indicated that while 71% reported being very prepared to maintain order and discipline in the classroom, 41% felt the same about implementing new teaching methods, and just over a third (36%) about implementing new curriculum and performance standards (U.S. Department of Education, 1999). Furthermore, just one-fifth of teachers surveyed indicated being very well prepared to address the needs of a diverse student body and to integrate educational technology into their teaching.

This lack of confidence is perpetuated by teacher turnover and teacher shortfalls that force schools to hire emergency-certified and out-of-subject instructors. According to Shen (1997), over 7.5% of all public school teachers in 1993–4 were alternatively-certified nationally; in the Northeast, that number was 14%. In addition, it is common practice, particularly in secondary schools throughout the United States, to hire teachers in an understaffed area to teach in fields that do not match their training (Ingersoll, 1997). Approximately one-fifth, one-quarter, and one-half of public school students between the grades of 7 and 12 who are enrolled in English, mathematics, and history courses, respectively, are taught by teachers without even an in-field minor (Ingersoll, 1996).

A teaching force only marginally prepared to meet new instructional demands coupled with instructional reforms call out for strong instructional leadership. Instructional leadership focuses on how principals influence processes that subsequently impact student learning (Hallinger & Heck, 1996); it captures the principal's involvement in teaching and learning (Beck & Murphy, 1993). Coined during the effective schools movement, principal instructional leadership is demonstrated through identifying a "mission" for the school; spending considerable time on monitoring instruction and supervising teachers; emphasizing the use of instructional time; paying particular attention to the individual and collective achievement of students; and holding high expectations for students and teachers alike (Bossert et al., 1982; Hallinger & Murphy, 1986; Wimpleberg, 1987). Research has confirmed that effective principals are highly involved in the instructional program of the school. Additionally, research has shown that school principals have great impact on instruction and student outcomes by supervising teacher practices (Hallinger & Heck, 1998). A recent analysis examining principals' contributions to fourth grade reading exposes the importance of the principal's work with teachers (Hallinger & Heck, 1998). The authors conclude that "the effects of principal leadership on school outcomes were almost completely indirect through supervising teachers' classroom practices" (p. 184). Whatever the specifics, the instructional leadership role brings principals into the classrooms.

Are school leaders prepared for instructional leadership roles that emphasize a new vision of teaching and learning? Analyses of principal and teacher responses to the *Schools and Staffing Survey* (SASS), a nationally representative survey administered by the U.S. Department of Education, suggest that most principals have narrow exposure to subject area knowledge and limited influence over the curriculum (Goldring & Cohen-Vogel, 2000). On an item which asked teachers to rate their agreement with the statement "My principal talks with me frequently about my instructional practices," less than 10% strongly agreed and well over twice that strongly disagreed. The remaining 67% of respondents were split fairly evenly between the two other response categories. Just under 33% of teachers somewhat agreed and another 34% somewhat disagreed that their principals spoke with them about their instructional practices on frequent occasions.

Furthermore, in the recent administration (1999–2000) of the *Schools and Staffing Survey*, school principals were asked how often they engaged in a number of activities during the past year. By and large, public school principals spend more time on administration than on instructional leadership. Only 50% of public school principals indicated that they facilitated student learning everyday; forty-six percent supervised teachers everyday, while 82% of principals managed school facilities and maintained physical security everyday (this was prior to September 11th). In fact, public school principals reported spending more time on developing public relations than on developing curriculum. Principals may organize professional development for teachers, "but they rarely provide intellectual leadership for growth in teaching skill" (Resnick & Glennan, Jr., 2002, p. 160).

THE CURRICULUM: CORE LEARNING PRINCIPLES

The *Institute of School Leadership* (ISL), funded with a grant from the Bill and Melinda Gates Foundation and the State of Tennessee, uses a blended, case-based instructional approach to provide professional development opportunities to propel teaching and learning. The core learning principles or guiding instructional philosophy of the Institute, as set forth by the *How People Learn* framework, focuses on teaching and learning that is learner-centered, community-centered, assessment-centered, and knowledge-centered. Learned-centered teaching environments take into account the pre-existing knowledge that all learners have. Bransford et al. (1999), relying on such learning theorists as Cobb (1994), Piaget (1952, 1973a, 1973b, 1977, 1978), and Vygotsky (1962, 1978) note, "in the most general sense, the contemporary view of learning is that people construct new knowledge and understandings based on what they already know and believe" (p. 10). They continue:

> A logical extension of the view that new knowledge must be constructed from existing knowledge is that teachers need to pay attention to the incomplete understandings, the false beliefs, and the naïve renditions of concepts that learners bring with them to a given subject. Teachers need to build on these ideas in ways that help each student achieve a more mature understanding. If students' initial ideas and beliefs are ignored, the understandings they develop can be very different from what the teacher intends. (Bransford et al, 1999, p. 10)

Learners' preconceptions—developed from their everyday experiences— are many times at odds with current assumptions and knowledge comprising mature disciplines. If learners' preconceptions are not directly addressed, they often memorize classroom content, yet still use their experience-based preconceptions to act on the world.

However, it is not sufficient to simply 'start where the learner is.' Teaching and learning must be steeped in specific, "well-organized bodies of knowledge . . .that lead to understanding and subsequent transfer" (Bransford et al., 1999 p. 136). Although it seems obvious that learning involves the goal of acquiring new knowledge, the important point that emerges from the research literature is the need to emphasize "connected" knowledge that is organized around foundational ideas of a discipline. Courses are often organized in ways that fail to develop the kind of connected knowledge structures that support activities such as reasoning and problem solving. For example, textbooks broadcast facts and conclusions, but are limited in their ability to provide learners with the experience of constructing conclusions in the first place. Knowledge-centered environments provide access to and multiple opportunities for learners experience using foundational knowledge to solve problems, thereby enabling the learning to develop a mature understanding of the knowledge domain that is connected and adaptive for use.

Vygotsky (1978) suggested that all learning is culturally-mediated, historically developing and arising from cultural activity. One implication of this perspective is that providing supportive settings where people can learn from one another is essential for optimal learning. Community-centered approaches to learning require the development of norms that promote learning communities. Learning communities provide structures that facilitate learning, and also shape and determine what learning is valued. Strong learning communities facilitate collaboration, where collective problem solving strategies and continual improvement can be modeled.

Lastly, assessment-centered learning environments provide feedback to teachers and learners so that they can revise their current thinking and problem solving approaches and improve their performances. A number of studies show that providing opportunities for feedback and revision greatly helps learning (Barron et al., 1998; Black & William, 1998). In addition, helping learners self-assess is especially important for learning because ultimately learners need to develop the habits of mind to reflect on their own progress rather than always rely on others for feedback. Assessment-centered environments help learners come to value the processes of revising their own thinking and providing feedback to others in a collective problem solving group.

THE CURRICULUM: FACILITATING
LEARNING AND THE TRANSFER OF KNOWLEDGE

At the core of the *Institute for School Leadership* (ISL) program is a set of five multi-media cases depicting realistic situations and problems that school leaders are likely to face in their schools, and information resources that are used to address the cases. A major goal of case-based instruction is to promote transfer of learning from the classroom to worlds outside of the classroom by integrating the learning of domain knowledge with problem solving (Barrows, 1985; Bransford et al., 1999; Hmelo, 1995; Williams, 1992). Case-based instruction provides learners with the chance to become familiar with the types of situations and problems that they are likely to encounter outside of the classroom. It also enables learners to learn important domain knowledge. As noted previously, recent research suggests that domain knowledge is very important to developing problem solving expertise. Bransford (1993) suggests that "an important component of effective problem-solving involves access to a great deal of well-organized, domain-specific knowledge" (p. 172). He continues, "It is still easy to overlook the need to emphasize specific knowledge rather than look only at general expertise" (p. 173).

In traditional instruction, domain knowledge is usually first learned through didactic modes, and then *applied* to solve problems. In case-based instruction as implemented in the ISL, learners learn content *in order to* solve problems. Case-based instruction places the problem or challenge at the center of teaching. Cases "function as environments that are to be explored and that allow students to see the need to acquire new concepts and skills" (Bransford, 1993, p. 182). Recent research suggests that attempting to solve a case creates the "need to know" in a learner and best prepares the learner for learning new knowledge (Bransford & Schwartz, 1999).

THE TECHNOLOGY PLATFORM

The Institute curriculum is composed of five multi-media case modules delivered in a computer environment called STAR Legacy (Schwartz, Lin, Brophy, & Bransford, 1999). The Legacy interface is depicted in Figure 1.

Legacy was developed for case-based instruction and embodies the principles of *How People Learn* framework, that is, supports learner-, knowledge-, assessment-, and community-centered instruction. In Legacy, learners first review a case and respond to its associated problem or "challenge" on the basis of their preconceptions and initial thoughts (learner-centered). In the next step, they are offered expert resources to provide foundational knowledge, insights and alternate ways of thinking about the problem or challenge (knowledge-centered). Note that not all learners use the resources in exactly the same ways; they use a resource more or less depending on their prior knowledge and skills (learner-centered). Expert

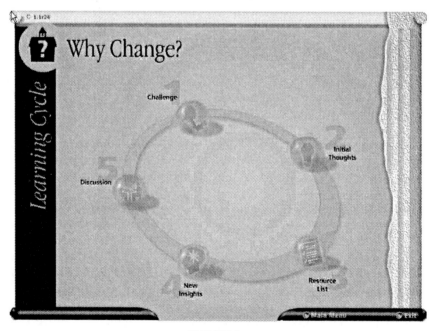

FIGURE 1
Learning Cycle

resources may include published research and visual aids, but most frequently focus on targeted interviews with leaders in their respective fields (see, Schwartz, Lin, Brophy, & Bransford, 1999). Finally, learners are asked to reevaluate the problem in the context of what they have learned through the resources and discussion with their peers (assessment-centered). They share what they have learned, how they have revised their initial thoughts, and what new insights they have gained in a group presentation (community- centered). This combination of pre-assessment, resource consultation, and post-assessment has proven to be an enormously powerful learning tool.

The STAR Legacy model as implemented in the ISL allows learners to interact with real-world problems in a much more sophisticated manner than is possible with a written description of a case, no matter how elaborate and detailed. The multi-media cases anchor and situate the problems in real contexts and thus "involve complex situations that require students to formulate and solve a set of interconnected sub problems" that can be viewed from multiple perspectives (Bransford, 1993, p. 182).

In summary, the core tenets of the ISL framework as implemented through multimedia cases are geared toward facilitating learning that activates existing knowledge as a foundation for new knowledge, demonstrates new knowledge, helps the learner apply the new knowledge, and assists the learner in integrating this new knowledge into his/her school setting.

PROGRAM IMPLEMENTATION

The curriculum and program for the *Institute for School Leadership* were developed by a collaborative design team, including a group of highly experienced practitioners from throughout the State of Tennessee, an interdisciplinary team from Vanderbilt University, and a multimedia learning group. The curriculum was designed and piloted extensively before implementation. Practicing principals and superintendents as well as leaders from the State Department of Education were called upon to review, critique, and test the new curricula materials.

The ISL is a 3-day training workshop that is held in various locations across the state of Tennessee. Facilitators, who have been extensively trained by the Vanderbilt faculty and educators that developed the training modules, conduct the workshops. They travel throughout the State with mobile computer labs for each of the training workshops. Participants of the workshop are each given a laptop computer to use for the duration of the training. They are seated in small groups, with individual laptops, although at times the facilitators project from the front of the room.

The five case modules are used over the 3 day-training program. Each case module consists of a complete STAR Legacy cycle with extensive resources. The Institute curriculum covers five key topics: the need for change, how people learn, data-based decision making, leading change, and school improvement planning. Modules 1 and 2 are completed during the first day of training. Module 3 takes up the whole second day, while Modules 4 and 5 comprise the curriculum of the third day.

The modules are wrapped around The *Standards for School Leaders,* developed by the Interstate School Leaders Licensure Consortium (ISLLC) standards. The ISLLC Standards are standards for leadership preparation, licensure assessment, and professional development adopted by many states, including the State of Tennessee. The Standards are clearly focused on school improvement, teaching and learning, and instructional leadership with the clear purpose of developing leadership for student learning. Other roles, such as managerial leadership, are placed in the service of propelling student learning. Each of the six standards articulate what principals need to know and understand (mastery), do and implement (behavior, actions), and value and believe (dispositions). Administrators in the State of Tennessee must complete 72 hours of ISLLC–based training every five years to keep the Professional Administrator License. The ISL is part of the ISLLC training required for ongoing professional development.

The first module is called, Why Change? This module introduces the participants to the main protagonist, Principal Jonathan Edwards. Principal Edwards works in a school that has improved over the years. But, in the words of his superintendent, Principal Edwards' school "is a good school, but not good enough." The school has average achievement overall, but there are gaps among students of different ethnicities. This challenge requires participants to explore what is happening in the educational arena at the national, state, and local levels that are requiring schools to change drastically. Key challenge questions include: To what degree are you sympathetic with Principal Edwards? What would you suggest to Principal Edwards about how he should react to the superintendent's comments? Why might the superintendent have said Principal Edwards' school is good, but no longer good enough? The superintendent has explained the need for Principal Edwards to meet new standards. What would be the difference between Principal Edwards simply complying with these new standards or embracing them?

The second module, Change to What? presents Principal Edwards realizing he needs to change the teaching and learning at his school, but questioning, what is effective teaching and learning? What is a compelling vision for a different type of learning and teaching? This module helps school leaders revisit research-based concepts of teaching and learning based on the core tenets of *How People Learn.* This module provides the participants with an instructional perspective focused on learning that can drive school improvement in their schools. The key challenge questions are: What are the advantages and possible disadvantages of schools that are focused on standards and high stakes assessments? Is it really reasonable to assure all students can succeed? What do we know about learning and teaching that could help Principal Edwards ensure that students learn effectively?

The third module, Where is my School Now? focuses on data-based decision making. Principal Edwards acknowledges his school needs to change and has a better understanding of instruction and curriculum that embrace high quality teaching and learning. But now he asks, how do I know where to focus my efforts? How can I clarify and prioritize areas of high need? This module presents a comprehensive look at using and understanding data for school improvement. The key challenge questions include: What kinds of information and data would you advise Principal Edwards to use and collect? Once he has access to data, how can Principal Edwards use it to identify his schools strengths and weaknesses? The resources include actual data sets, such as standardized achievement assessments as well as school climate inventories, and formative assessments, with narration and graphic displays of how to interpret and use data to build a shared sense of understanding and focus school improvement.

The fourth module explicates the process of change, How do I Lead the Way? Principal Edwards is now poised to embark upon a change process. This module explores how school leaders can lead change through a very clear understanding of collaboration as a major tool of effective community involvement. The module presents the varied and sophisticated skill set needed to implement student-centered learning. The resources include discussions of the importance of a focused vision, the change process, communication, creating and managing a culture of learning, involving the community and understanding the political, social and legal issues of change.

The final module, What's Next?, brings the learning to the participants' own schools. The challenge recounts Principal Edwards' journey of change and asks the participants to begin a plan of improving student learning in their schools by first addressing a set of challenge questions that reviews the four subsequent learning cycles. These questions include: Do you think you can motivate people in your school community to "embrace" change, rather than simply "comply" with new regulations? How? (Challenge 1); How might you define and structure "opportunities for success" so that all students can succeed? (Challenge 2); What are several sources of available data that you will consult to learn more about your school? (Challenge 3); and, What are some 'bumpy' features of the change process that you can anticipate and how will you deal with them? (Challenge 4).

The resources embedded in each module are varied and are grouped into the topics that address each of the challenge questions. Resources typically include video clips from practicing school professionals speaking to specific issues that were raised in the challenge. There are also video clips of experts and academics that help provide new knowledge. There are data charts and narration, and other graphic displays of material, as well as links to further reading and articles. Participants work through the resources as individuals, in groups or in a 'jigsaw' fashion, with an emphasis on processing, applying, and understanding and discussing the resources. At the end of the resource section, groups synthesize and discuss their new insights to challenge questions. Each group also prepares a presentation to the other participants, geared toward synthesizing new learning as well as providing another opportunity for application, synthesis and feedback.

We now turn to the research that accompanied the program implementation.

THE RESEARCH

Participants

This paper presents data based on 14 separate workshops, conducted from January through March 2003. A total of 394 participants attended these workshops. The participants represent leadership personnel from rural, suburban, and urban school districts across the State of Tennessee. Forty-five percent of the participants work in rural districts, 31% are from suburban districts, while the remaining leaders are from urban school districts. The participants include a majority of school principals, as well as assistant principals and central office superintendents and curriculum coordinators (see Table 1).

Methods

The research team implemented a pre-test, post-test design with multiple replications for each cohort of ISL participants. Training workshops were conducted throughout the State of Tennessee with approximately 30 school leaders participating in each workshop. Participants registered for the training via the State's webpage and received ongoing professional development credits for their participation. Data collection was conducted

TABLE 1
Institute Participants

School Leadership Role:	N = 347		Average Years of Experience
Principal	190	54.8%	8.2
Assistant Principal	81	23.3%	5.1
Central Office Personnel	76	21.9%	8.3

via the Legacy program and uploaded to a centralized database, enabling us to conduct multiple replications of all data collection, across all participants. The pre-post data collection is embedded in the training materials. At the beginning of each workshop participants logged onto their laptop computers and responded to a pre-test, at the end of the three day training they once again responded to a post-test, as well as an institute evaluation.

Variables

Three sources of data were collected. First, before and after the workshop participants responded to an adapted version of The *ISLLC School Leadership Self Inventory* (National Policy Board for Educational Administration, 2000), a self-report inventory consisting of Likert scale items. We chose this instrument because it was directly tied to the ISLLC standards, as is the ISL curriculum, and it focused on leadership for learning. As mentioned above, the Standards have been adopted by a large majority of states and key professional associations, and are part of the standards for school administrators' licensure in the State of Tennessee.

The ISLLC inventory was prepared to assess participants' knowledge and understanding (mastery), beliefs (dispositions) and actual behaviors (application) related to each of the six Standards for School Leaders established by the Interstate School Leaders Licensure Consortium. There are separate sub-scales that assess respondents' knowledge and understanding (mastery), beliefs (dispositions), and behaviors (application) related to each standard.[2] For example, Standard 2 states: "A school administrator is an educational leader who promotes the success of all students by advocating, nurturing, and sustaining a school culture and instructional program conducive to student learning and staff professional growth." An item examining mastery related to Standard 2 asks, "To what extent do you have personal mastery (knowledge and understanding) about principles of effective instruction, curriculum design, implementation, evaluation, and refinement." An item examining beliefs related to Standard 2 asks, "To what extent do you believe, value, and have commitment to the variety of ways in which students can learn."

To the best of our knowledge, this instrument had not undergone any specific psychometric testing. Therefore, we pilot-tested and revised the instrument after extensive psychometric considerations, including factor analyses and reliability analyses. Exploratory and confirmatory factor analyses were conducted for each scale to examine departure from a one-factor structure. The initial instrument was extremely long (118 items). Thus, another goal of the psychometric testing was to make the scales shorter. Unless the second factor extracted from the exploratory analysis explained a relatively large proportion of total variances (more than 10%), we did not break down the scales to sub-scales. Rather, the focus was to find the set of items that best reflects the main factor and simultaneously achieve high reliability with fewer items. All the scales extracted only one factor except for four scales. In those scales, none of the secondary or third factors explained more than 10% of all variances. Confirmatory Factor Analyses for all scales suggested good fit of the one factor structure; Normed Fit Index and Tucker-Lewis Index exceed .95 in all cases. The revised inventory consists of 89 items. Reliabilities for the revised scales range from .77 to .94 (see Appendix A for item examples).

In order to determine scale validity, we asked a group of experts involved in both the development and implementation of the Institute to rate each of the original 118 items in terms of the extent to which the content of the item is addressed in the Institute curriculum. The revised inventory includes only items rated as valid by experts.

A second data collection mechanism was an institute evaluation collected on another instrument, *Experiences and Benefits from this Course* (Cordray & Pion, 2002). The inventory surveys types of teaching and learning activities used in classrooms, workshops and professional development and was developed in conjunction with others who have assessed and evaluated instruction using the *How People Learn* framework (see Appendix B). This instrument was administered at post-test, immediately at the end of the three day Institute and provides information about the extent to which participants' training experiences were consistent with *How People Learn* principles of learning. Specifically, this assessment asked the extent to which the training was assessment-centered, learner- centered, knowledge-centered and community- centered. All four subscales had high reliability, in the .9 range. This instrument has undergone extensive psychometric development by its developers. Furthermore, its validity was ascertained in the context of our own study in two ways. Facilitators each completed an implementation check list that also assessed the extent to which they reported their level of implementation of the *How People Learn* framework at each institute workshop. In addition, program developers and professionals from the State Department of Education observed various workshops to ascertain implementation fidelity. We triangulated data from all three sources.

Third, we analyzed *Challenge Responses*. Throughout the training, participants are asked to write down responses to various challenges and questions. There is an initial challenge at the beginning of the training and a final challenge that asks the participants to apply what they have learned to the challenge again. We analyze a sample of participants' initial responses and compare them to their final responses to assess participant learning. In particular we focus on whether participants have changed in 'stance,' knowledge and values about leadership and learning, and are better able to delineate a process of school improvement. These analyses are used to begin to understand how and what leaders learn.

WHAT ARE PARTICIPANTS LEARNING?

How Did Participants' Beliefs about School Leadership Change?

Participants' knowledge and understanding of information related to effective school leadership improved significantly as a result of their participation in the training as indicated by matched pair t-tests. Participants from *all* the Institute workshops showed statistically significant *knowledge* gains (self-reported) from pre-test to post-test on the Mastery scales for all 6 ISLLC standards. As presented in Figure 2, all participants gained more than one standard deviation in their mastery of the core knowledge base necessary to implement the ISLLC standards. On average, participants moved from indicating they had sufficient knowledge and understanding (mean = 3) to having quite a bit of knowledge and understanding (mean = 4) regarding the knowledge base needed to be an effective school leader. The largest gains were reported in regard to Standard 3, 'promoting the success of all students by ensuring the management, organization, operations, and resources for a safe, efficient, and effective learning environment' (t = –18.27, p < .00), and Standard 4, "promoting the success of all students by collaborating with families and community members, respond-

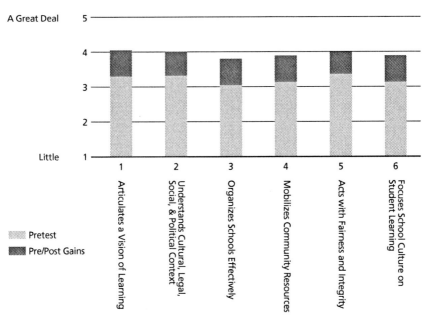

FIGURE 2
Mastery Pre-Post Gains on ISLLC Standards

ing to diverse community interests and needs and mobilizing community resources" (t = −17.36, p < .00).[3]

We further analyzed the mastery pre-post gains to determine if there was a relationship between amount learned and years of experience. We hypothesized that those with more years of experience may be less likely to report increases in their mastery of knowledge base related to the ISLLC standards. We calculated correlations between mastery gains and years of experience for each of the six ISLLC standards separately for school level leaders (principals and vice-principals) and central office personnel (e.g., superintendents and curriculum coordinators). There was only one significant, moderate correlation for central office personnel: the greater the years of experience, the *more* they gained on mastery of Standard 3—organizing schools for effective instruction (r = .23, p < .05). This finding supports the need for ongoing professional development in terms of refocusing leadership on learning.

Participants' beliefs were generally aligned with the ISLLC standards at the beginning of the ISL and as a result, the mean pretest to posttest change observed on these scales was less than what we saw on the Mastery/ Knowledge scales (see Figure 3). Overall, participants' mean ratings were higher on the *Beliefs* scales than on the *Mastery* scales. In other words, participants were less sure about their knowledge and understanding than they were about their beliefs related to the standards. [4] On average, participants have a great deal of commitment to the beliefs and values attached to the ISLLC standards, gaining approximately one-half of a standard deviation pre-to post-test, all statistically significant gains. The largest pre-post change in beliefs was on Standard 6, "a school administrator is an educational leader who promotes the success of all students by understanding, responding to, and influencing the larger political, social economic, legal and cultural context" (t = −7.34, p < .01).

There was one significant, moderate correlation between change in beliefs and years of experience, only on Standard 2, for central office personnel. Specifically, central office personnel with more years of experience were less likely to change their beliefs about 'promoting the success of all students by advocating, nurturing, and sustaining a school culture and instructional program conducive to student learning and staff professional growth' (r = −.23, p < .05). This may be a case where highly experienced practitioners insist they already hold this value.

Another way to understand what participants are learning during the Institute is to examine their responses to challenge questions immediately after reviewing the multi-media case, the pre-test or what we called initial thoughts, and compare this response to their new insights, written after reviewing the resources. By way of example, we present the responses of one of the participants to the first challenge question posed for Module 3, Where is My School Now? "What kinds of information and data would you advise Jonathan to use and collect?" the challenge asked. One respondent

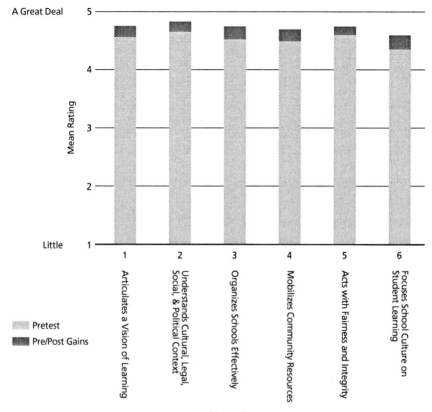

FIGURE 3

Pre-Post Changes in Beliefs on the ISLCC Standards

wrote in his initial thoughts, "He needs to disaggregate the scores on TCAP and look at what students are not making progress. Look at sex, ethnic groups, grade levels, and academic areas. Trends over several years can be helpful also."

The same participant wrote the following to the same challenge questions after viewing and interacting with the resources: "Lots of summative tests data is available but the formative testing can give the most help to students. Assessing the school climate can also give valuable information. The State Department is a wonderful resource for test information and disaggregated scores. It would also be valuable for your school to do a community-mapping project to assess resources."

Another challenge question for the same module asked, "Once Jonathan has access to data, how can he use it to identify his school's strengths and weaknesses? One response to the initial thoughts was: "Once

Jonathan has the information, he needs to look for trends over time to identify areas of need and areas of strength. He can then plan to address those areas through staff development, collaboration with principals and the evaluation process." The new insights response from the same participant, after reviewing the resources, was

> Jonathan needs to involve his teachers in examining the data and finding trends, patterns, etc. They need to have ownership of the data. He also needs to consider the other areas that will contribute to the effectiveness of his school: school climate, how can it be structured or restructured to support school improvement? How can he involve the community making the school improvement plan one they support and how can he use community knowledge to enhance student learning? He must also keep in mind that this data is simply that: data. It is a tool to use to improve test scores. As he works with his teachers, they need to understand he believes there are many things about the school that are not assessed and are still valuable components of the school identity.

We note a number of observations about the changes in the pre-post responses to challenge questions. First and most obvious is the sheer depth in the new insight responses compared to the initial thoughts. In addition, of note, is the reference to a much wider array of knowledge and the use of more 'expert' terminology such as 'community mapping,' 'formative and summative assessments,' as well as the limits of test data, in this case, types of data. In the first challenge question, the respondent could only reference the state standardized test, TCAP, while in the new insights, the respondent has an expanded repertoire that includes formative assessment measures and measures of school climate and the broader community context. The respondent also had more of a sense of how to use the knowledge in the second response, after interacting with the resources.

In Challenge 4, How do I Lead the Way, the challenge question asked, "How might Jonathan go about building and sustaining a new mission and vision for his school?" One respondent wrote his initial thoughts: "This is going to take lots of collaboration. He can't just develop a vision and mission all by himself." The same respondent's new insights, after interacting with the resources was considerably more developed: "His task is complicated, but he can very easily reach this goal. He needs to begin by collaborating/ brainstorming with people within his school. As the instructional leader of his school, he should take the initiative to share his ideas, learn from those who have different viewpoints, and seek an integrated view of where the school is headed. He should also contact all community members who share in the education of the children at Adams. The insights offered by people outside the school looking in are crucial and essential to developing a successful mission and vision. To sustain this vision and mission it has to belong to the community members. Ownership of the vision/ mission is essential to maintaining it. And change is OK."

Similarly, one respondent wrote initial thoughts, "1. He should start by facilitating dialogue among his staff so that everyone shares a common vision. 2. All stakeholders including businesses, parent groups, and the central office staff need to be included in taking ownership in moving toward the vision," while adding a much broader, nuanced discussion in new insights:

1. He should take a look at restructuring time within the school day. Finding time for collaboration and dialogue is a critical first step.
2. Listening to resistance is important in establishing healthy communication during the process. This also treats everyone as professionals and helps everyone get on board.
3. Practicing selective abandonment is critical in moving teachers to change. When they think something is being added and not taken away they become overwhelmed and resist.

Another respondent specifically referred to his/her first response in addressing the challenge question after reviewing the resources and engaging in a group discussion. Initially the respondent said, "Jonathan must start with his own staff. He must make his staff understand what his mission is and share with them what changes must be made. Not necessarily the whole program but the basis of what is involved. In my opinion his greatest task is to get the support of his staff." Later on, s/he added the following to new insights:

In my initial statement only one group was mentioned. There are many other situations that must be addressed. A communication plan must be devised, developing ownership from all involved, building teams of leaders, develop a plan of what and how you want to assess this change, make plans for resistance to change and be able to decide what you can do with that part. Focus on your goal and be willing to change if needed.

Some respondents referred to specific resources in their new insights. For example:

Bob Eaker's section on the characteristics of a professional learning community was awesome. There must be shared mission, vision, and values. I especially liked what he said about clear sense of values in that the faculty must be willing to make a commitment to each other in terms of how their going to behave to become the kind of school they want to become. Collaboration, collective inquiry (seeking out best practices), engaging in action research (trying things out and does it work?), and evaluating and assessing efforts based on results were key points. I also liked the three questions that every teacher should ask about every single lesson.

These excerpts suggest several conclusions about participants' learning. First, participants' new insights are "better" than their initial thoughts in that they contain more relevant ideas on an issue and these new ideas tend to be focused in nature. These new ideas relate to concepts introduced in the Legacy resources, and so we conclude that participants most likely learned them from these sources. Furthermore, participants are not "rote learning" the information—parroting it back in its original form—but are interpreting the information and connecting it with the problems at hand. Research indicates that this level of information processing will likely produce longer-term learning and retention (Bransford, 1979).

In addition, the language used by participants to articulate their thoughts tends to be solution-focused and action-oriented, for example, "he should also contact all community members who share in the education of the children at Adams". From this standpoint, participants understand new concepts as tools for solving problems—not as rote learned, isolated concepts—and they are more likely to transfer their learning when solving similar problems in their own schools. As discussed earlier, this is a key learning goal of case-based instruction.

TO WHAT EXTENT DOES THE TRAINING IMPLEMENT THE *HOW PEOPLE LEARN* FRAMEWORK?

Participants also indicated that the Institute curriculum and delivery strongly adheres to the *How People Learn* framework. As presented in Figure 4, participants rated the professional development at the end of the Institute as being learned-centered, community-centered, knowledge-centered and assessment-centered "Almost Always" on the *Experiences and Benefits from this Course* (Cordray & Pion, 2002) instrument (The means ranged from 4. 2 to 4.4, SD = .7 –.8). These items go beyond the typical ratings of participant satisfaction that are often used to evaluate professional development. This provides a measure of treatment implementation or fidelity. In other words, we can begin to attribute the learning gains presented above to the implementation of the *How People Learn* framework.

DISCUSSION

The results overwhelmingly suggest that participants benefited in important ways from participating in the ISL. Participants' knowledge and understanding of information related to effective school leadership improved significantly as a result of their participation in the training. Furthermore,

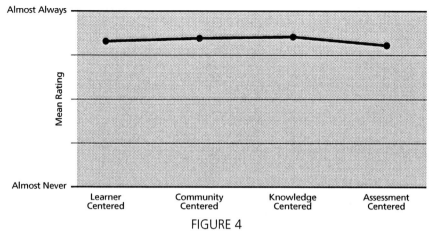

FIGURE 4
Evaluation of How People Learn Aspects of the Institute

knowledge gains were obtained for all cohorts of ISL participants on all 6 ISLLC standards. Although the changes were more modest on the Beliefs scales—most likely because of ceiling effects at pre-test—they too were statistically reliable.

Of course, one threat to the validity of these conclusions is that the ISLLC is a self-report measure; participants may be giving socially desirable responses at post-test because they feel generally positive about their workshop experiences. Although this cannot be ruled out, participants' initial and final responses to the challenge questions suggest that this is not the case and that the reported pre-to-post changes in knowledge are real. Participants' responses to new insights (the challenge post-test questions) reflected knowledge they had acquired by reviewing and working with the resources. Furthermore, their responses suggested that they had processed the information deeply and were connecting it to the problems at hand.

There has been continuous widespread criticism of professional programs for school principals and the over reliance on licensing (Hess, 2002). Many programs are characterized as being marginal and piecemeal (Peterson & Kelly, 2002). Along with this criticism is the claim that one-shot, short-term workshops cannot contribute to real learning. In fact, short-term workshops are often mentioned in terms of being useful mechanisms for self-renewal, rather than having an impact on the knowledge base (Peterson & Kelly, 2002). Amongst the important implications of the model of learning implemented in the *Institute for School Leadership* is that it suggests that high-quality professional development based on models of teaching and learning can impact the knowledge-base, even if they are of short-term in duration. This was evidenced by both the ISLLC inventory and the pre-post challenge responses. It may be that most short-term, one shot workshops do not implement any specific model based on principles of learning and therefore it is the pedagogy and content of the short-term workshops that make them ineffective, rather than merely the duration.

We are not suggesting that a three-day workshop is the answer to providing professional development that is substantive, coherent, and challenging. Nor are we suggesting this model provides adequate opportunities for implementation, practice and reflection—all hallmarks of high quality professional development. Our results do indicate that this mode of professional development can serve as an important component for 'setting the stage' or 'seeding the culture' for a focused agenda around impacting instruction.

Furthermore, the combination of a technology platform using case-based instruction, embedded resources, and trained facilitators puts forth the foundations of a model of professional development that can reach numerous educational leaders across a wide geographic area. The participants reported high levels of 'treatment fidelity,' that is, they indicated that the Institute implements learner-centered, knowledge-centered, assessment-centered, and community-centered instruction. This finding suggests that there are ways to addresses the need to build capacity around leadership development, especially leadership focused on student learning.

Although the ISL as designed and implemented appears to have successfully met its goal of being a compelling program that links leadership to learning and focuses on instructional improvement for children, one may ask whether it will impact what school leaders do in their schools? Will they apply what they learn to help them solve problems in their own schools? This is an empirical question that we plan to address through follow-up interviews with a sample of workshop participants and with the analysis of pre-test, post-test results of the ISLCC inventory where participants are reporting their activities.

However, as Kelly and Peterson (2002) note:

> Leadership preparation is not simply a matter of developing a set of discrete skills and building isolated bits of knowledge. Instead it means embedding skills and knowledge in a complex, analytical "mental map" that can be applied to complex, varied and uncertain situations. Leaders facing complex situations need complex mental maps to address those situations. . . .Leadership preparation programs need to provide learning experiences that develop complex mental maps and models for action in specific contexts (p. 270).

This type of professional development can be accomplished if the learning model focuses on problems in context.

Why is solving problems in context so important and why is modeling this type of teaching and learning during professional development for school principals so crucial? The reason is that learning new knowledge from the perspective of how to put it into practice will enable leaders to develop a connected knowledge base that is adaptive for solving their schools' problems—compared with professional development that is more didactic in nature; ISL-trained leaders are in a better position to effectively use what they learned in professional development. In addition, the principles of teaching and learning that are modeled in the ISL are precisely aligned with new standards for classroom teaching and learning. In this way, school leaders have experienced first hand a clearly-articulated model of effective teaching and learning that, in their role of instructional leader, they can promote among their faculty and thereby contribute to the improvement of student learning in schools.

NOTES

1.   The *Institute for School Leadership* was developed with generous support from the Bill and Melinda Gates Foundation and The State of Tennessee in collaboration with John Bransford, James Guthrie and Pearl Sims. The research for this program was supported by the Learning Sciences Institute, Vanderbilt University. We acknowledge the research assistances of Cynthia Mayfield and Kristie Rowley.

2.   Behaviors (actions) are being post-tested after six months and hence are not reported in this paper. The total number of items includes those for the behavior scales.

3.   We analyzed the data first to determine if there were any differences among the cohorts of the individual workshops. There were highly consistent findings across all implementations of the ISL workshop and no significant differences. Therefore, we aggregated the data.

4.   We acknowledge the beliefs scales are more likely to suffer from social desirability and hence there is a ceiling effect.

REFERENCES

Barron, B., Schwartz, D. Vye, N., Moore, A., Petrosino, A., Zech, L., Bransford, J., & CTGV (1998). Doing with understanding: Lessons from research on problem and project-based learning. *Journal of the Learning Sciences, 3 & 4,* 271–312.

Barrows, H. S. (1985). *How to design a problem-based curriculum for the preclinical years.* New York: Springer-Verlag.

Beck, L. G., & Murphy, J. (1993). *Understanding the principalship.* New York: Teacher College Press.

Black, P., & William, D. (1998). Assessment and classroom learning. *Assessment and Education, 5*(1), 7–75.

Bossert, S., Dwyer, R., Rowan, B., & Lee, G. (1982). The instructional management role of the principal. *Educational Administration Quarterly, 18,* 34–63.

Bransford, J. (1979). *Human cognition.* Belmont, CA: Wadsworth.

Bransford, J. (1993). Who ya gonna call? Thoughts about teaching problem-solving. In P. Hallinger, K. Leithwood, & J. Murphy (Eds), *Cognitive perspectives on educational leadership* (pp. 171–191). New York: Teachers College Press.

Bransford, J., & Schwartz, D. (1999). Rethinking transfer: A simple proposal with multiple implications. In A. Iran-Nejad & D. Pearson (Eds.), *Review of Research in Education, 24,* 61–100. Washington, DC: American Educational Research Association.

Bransford, J. D., Brown, A. L., & Cocking, R. (1999). *How people learn: Brain, mind, experience, and school.* Washington, DC: National Academy Press.

Bryk A. S., & Driscoll, M. E. (1985). *An empirical investigation of the school as community.* Chicago: University of Chicago, Department of Education.

Cobb, P. (1994). *Theories of mathematical learning and constructivism: A personal view.* Paper presented at the Symposium on Trends and Perspectives in Mathematics Education, Institute for Mathematics, University of Klagenfurt, Austria.

Cohen, D. K (1991). Revolution in one classroom. In S. H. Fuhrman and B. Malen (Eds.), *The politics of curriculum and testing* (pp. 103–124). New York: Falmer.

Cordary, D., & Pion, G. (2002) *Experiences and benefits from challenge-based learning.* Unpublished manuscript, Vanderbilt University.

Goldring, E., & Cohen-Vogel, L (2000). *Supporting environments for instructional reform: What's a principal to do?* Paper presented at the annual meeting of the American Educational Research Association, Montreal, Canada.

Goldring, E., & Greenfield, W. (2002). Understanding the evolving concept of leadership in education: Roles, expectations and dilemmas. In J. Murphy (Ed.) *The educational leadership challenge: Redefining leadership in the 21st century,* NSSE Yearbook. Chicago: University of Chicago Press.

Hallinger, P., & Heck, R. H. (1996). Reassessing the principal's role in school effectiveness: A review of empirical research, 1980–1995. *Educational Administration Quarterly, 32*(1), 5–44.

Hallinger, P., & Heck, R. H. (1998). Exploring the principals' contributions to school effectiveness: 1980–1995. *School Effectiveness and School Improvement, 9,* 157–191.

Hallinger, P., & Murphy, J. (1986). The social context of effective schools. *American Journal of Education, 94,* 28–35.

Hess, F. (2002). *Lifting the Barrier.* Washington, DC: American Enterprise Institute.

Hmelo, C. E. (1995). Problem-based learning: Development of knowledge and reasoning strategies. *Proceedings of the seventeenth annual conference of the Cognitive Science Society* (pp. 404–408). Pittsburgh, PA: Erlbaum.

Ingersoll, R. M. (1996). Teacher quality and inequality. *Proceedings of the American Statistical Association,* Chicago, IL.

Ingersoll, R. M. (1997). Teacher turnover and teacher quality: The recurring myth of teacher shortages. *Teachers College Record, 99*(1), 41–44.

Kelley, C., & Peterson, K. D. (2002). The work of principals and their prepration. In M. Tucker & J. B. Codding (Eds.), *The principal challenge. Leading and managing schools in an era of accountability.* San Francisco: Jossey-Bass.

Knapp, M., Copland, M., &Talbert, J. E. (2003). *Leading for learning: Reflective tools for schools and district leaders.* Seattle: Center for the Study of Teaching and Policy, University of Washington in collaboration with The Wallace Foundation.

Kochan, F. K., Bredeson, P., & Riehl, C. (2002). Rethinking the professional development of school leaders. In J. Murphy (Ed.), *The educational leadership challenge: Redefining leadership in the 21st century,* NSSE Yearbook. Chicago: University of Chicago Press.

Murphy, J., & Seashore Louis, K. (1999). *Handbook of research on educational administration.* San Francisco: Jossey-Bass.

National Center for Education Statistics, U.S. Department of Education (2000). *Pursuing excellence: Comparisons of international eighth-grade mathematics and science achievement from a U.S. perspective, 1995 and 1999.* P. Gonzales, C. Calsyn, L. Jocelyn, K. Mak, D. Kastberg, S. Arafeh, T. Williams, and W. Tsen. NCES 2001-028. Washington, DC: U.S. Government Printing Office.

National Policy Board for Educational Administration. (2000). *Collaborative professional development process for school leaders.* The Interstate School leaders Licensure Consortium.

Newmann, F., & Wehlage, G. (1995). *Successful school restructuring: A report to the public and educations by the Center on Organization and Restructuring of Schools.* Alexandria, VA and Reston, VA: Association for Supervision and Curriculum Development, and the National Association for Secondary school Principals.

Peterson, K. D., & Kelley, C. (2002). Principal In-Service Programs. A portrait of diversity and promise. In M. Tucker & J. B. Codding (Eds.), *The principal challenge. Leading and managing schools in an era of accountability.* San Francisco: Jossey-Bass.

Piaget, J. (1978). *Success and understanding.* Cambridge, MA: Harvard University Press.

Piaget, J. (1977). *The grasp of consciousness.* London: Routledge and Kegan Paul.

Piaget, J. (1973a). *The child and reality: Problems of genetic psychology.* New York: Grossman.

Piaget, J. (1973b). *The language and thought of the child.* London: Routledge and Kegan Paul.

Piaget, J. (1952). *The origins of intelligence in children.* M. Cook, trans. New York: International Universities Press.

Purkey, S. C., & Smith, M. S., (1983). Effective schools: A review. *The Elementary School Journal, 83*(4), 427–452.

Resnick, L. B., & Glennan, T. K. (2002). Leadership for learning: A Theory of action for urban schools districts. In A. Hightower, M. Knapp, J. A. Marsh, & M. W. McLaughlin (Eds.), *School districts and instructional renewal.* New York: Teachers College Press.

Schwartz, D., Lin, X., Brophy, S., & Bransford, J. (1999). Toward the development of flexibly adaptive instructional designs. In. C. Reigeluth (Ed.). *Instructional design theories and models* (Vol. 2, pp.183–213). Mahwah, NJ: Lawrence Erlbaum.

Shen, J. (1997). Has the alternative certification policy materialized its promise? A comparison between traditionally and alternatively certified teachers in public schools. *Educational Evaluation and Policy Analysis, 19*(3), 276–283.

Stevenson, R. B. (1996). Knowledge-in-use: Reconceptualizing the use of knowledge in school decision making. In S. L. Jacobson, E. S. Hickcox, & R. B. Stevenson (Eds.), *School administration: Persistent dilemmas in preparation and practice.* Westport, CT: Praeger.

U.S. Department of Education. (1999). *Teacher quality: A report on the preparation and qualification of public school teachers.* Washington, D.C.: USDE.

Vygotsky, L.S. (1962). *Thought and language.* Cambridge, MA: MIT Press.

Vygotsky, L.S. (1978). *Mind in society: The development of the higher psychological processes.* Cambridge, MA: The Harvard University Press. (Originally published 1930, New York: Oxford University Press.)

Williams, S. M. (1992). Putting case-based instruction into context: Examples from legal and medical education. *The Journal of the Learning Sciences, 2*, 367–427.

Wimpleberg, R. (1987). The dilemma of instructional leadership and a central role for central office. In W. Greenfield (Ed.), *Instructional leadership: concepts, issues and controversies.* Boston: Allyn and Bacon

APPENDIX A:
THE ISLLC SCHOOL LEADERSHIP SELF INVENTORY AND SAMPLE ITEMS

Standard 1: "A school administrator is an educational leader who promotes the success of all students by facilitating the development, articulation, implementation, and stewardship of a vision of learning that is shared and supported by the school community."

Mastery: To what extent do I currently have PERSONAL MASTERY (KNOWLEDGE & UNDERSTANDING) of the following:

- information sources, data collection, and data analysis strategies
- learning goals in a pluralistic society

Beliefs: To what extent do I currently BELIEVE, VALUE AND HAVE COMMITMENT to the following:

- a school vision of high standards of learning
- continuous school improvement

Standard 2: "A school administrator is an educational leader who promotes the success of all students by advocating, nurturing, and sustaining a school culture and instructional program conducive to student learning and staff professional growth."

Mastery: To what extent do I currently have PERSONAL MASTERY (KNOWLEDGE & UNDERSTANDING) of the following:

- principles of effective instruction
- curriculum design, implementation, evaluation, and refinement

Beliefs: To what extent do I currently BELIEVE, VALUE AND HAVE COMMITMENT to the following:

- student learning as the fundamental purpose of schooling
- the variety of ways in which students can learn

Standard 3: "A school administrator is an educational leader who promotes the success of all students by ensuring management of the organization, operations, and resources for a safe, efficient, and effective learning environment."

Mastery: To what extent do I currently have PERSONAL MASTERY (KNOWLEDGE & UNDERSTANDING) of the following:

- legal issues impacting school operations
- theories & models of organizations & principles of organizational development

Beliefs: To what extent do I currently BELIEVE, VALUE AND HAVE COMMITMENT to the following:

- making management decision to enhance learning and teaching
- high-quality standards, expectation, and performances

Standard 4: "A school administrator is an educational leader who promotes the success of all students by collaborating with families and community members, responding to diverse community interests and needs and mobilizing community resources."

Mastery: To what extent do I currently have PERSONAL MASTERY (KNOWLEDGE & UNDERSTANDING) of the following:

- community relations and marketing strategies and processes
- the conditions and dynamics of the diverse school community

Beliefs: To what extent do I currently BELIEVE, VALUE AND HAVE COMMITMENT to the following:

- families as partners in the education of their children
- schools operating as an integral part of the larger community

Standard 5: "A school administrator is an educational leader who promotes the success of all students by acting with integrity, fairness, and in an ethical manner."

Mastery: To what extent do I currently have PERSONAL MASTERY (KNOWLEDGE & UNDERSTANDING) of the following:

- the values of the diverse school community
- the purpose of education and the role of leadership in modern society

Beliefs: To what extent do I currently BELIEVE, VALUE AND HAVE COMMITMENT to the following:

- the ideal of the common good
- development of a caring school community

Standard 6: "A school administrator is an educational leader who promotes the success of all students by understanding, responding to, and influencing the larger political, social economic, legal, and cultural context."

Mastery: To what extent do I currently have PERSONAL MASTERY (KNOWLEDGE & UNDERSTANDING) of the following:

- the role of public education in developing and renewing a democratic society and an economically productive nation
- global issues and forces affecting teaching and learning

Beliefs: To what extent do I currently BELIEVE, VALUE AND HAVE COMMITMENT to the following:

- recognizing a variety of ideas, values, and cultures
- importance of a continuing dialogue with other decision makers affecting education

APPENDIX B:
EXAMPLES OF ITEMS EXAMINING IMPLEMENTATION OF HOW PEOPLE LEARN FRAMEWORK

HPL- Learner Centered

I learned how to solve real-life problems.
What I learned connects well with what I know already.

HPL-Community Centered

Asked participants to help each other to understand ideas or concepts.
Formed "discussion groups" to facilitate learning.

Asked participants to share ideas and experiences with others whose backgrounds and viewpoints differ from their own.

HPL-Knowledge Centered

Simulated participants to intellectual effort beyond that required by most professional development.
Asked participants to explain the basis for their answers to questions.
Encouraged participants to use multiple resources to improve their understanding.

HPL-Assessment Centered

I was encouraged to evaluate my work.
I got feedback about my performance that helped me to improve my thinking or understanding of the subject area or understanding of the subject area.
I was encouraged to evaluate how effective my own learning strategies are.

CHAPTER 8

PUTTING TAB A INTO SLOT B

A Reliable Method for Identifying Subsystem Advocacy Coalitions[1]

Thomas V. Shepley

For decades, policy scholars have searched for ways to generate a reliable understanding of how policymaking takes place. Even though a host of policy theories have been proposed, none has been able to fully explain the complex nature of policy creation in representative democracies. One promising generalized and testable policy theory, the Advocacy Coalition Framework (ACF), attempts to unify several approaches to policy analysis. However, there remains some question about the appropriate methods for testing the ACF. Relying on a new approach for identifying advocacy coalitions, this study focuses on elite reading policy actors in the states of California (n = 52) and Texas (n = 46). Using interview transcripts, the beliefs and relationships of these actors are quantified. These two factors are then used to divide the subsystems' participants into coalitions. Analyses indicate support for the use of this new approach in identifying subsystem coalitions. Not only does the new approach address both policy actor activity and beliefs the method is sensitive enough to detect multiple coalitions in at least two state subsystems. Taken as a whole, the findings of this study support the claim that the ACF is a useful way of interpreting coalition cohesion in a variety of subsystems,

Educational Administration, Policy, and Reform: Research and Measurement
A Volume in: Research and Theory In Educational Administration, pages 219–249.
Copyright © 2004 by Information Age Publishing, Inc.
ISBN: 1-59311-000-0 (hardcover), 1-59311-000-0 (paperback)

including that of state-level reading policy. Future research using similar methods is needed to confirm the efficacy of this new approach for identifying coalitions in a variety of policy subsystems.

PROBLEM, RESEARCH PERSPECTIVES, AND IMPORTANCE

Policy analysis is like a hot dog—the contents of both are generally suspect and variable (Stewart, 1991). Even with this criticism, policy researchers have long searched for ways to generate powerful descriptions and explanations of how policymaking takes place. Building upon and unifying the strengths of other policy analysis models, Sabatier and Jenkins-Smith proffered in 1993 and revised in 1999 a generalized and testable theory called the Advocacy Coalition Framework (ACF). The utility of the ACF has been tested in such disparate arenas as North American environmental, energy, airline, education, and federal communications policy. This framework has also been found to be helpful in explaining policy change in Europe, Asia, and Australia as well (Sabatier & Jenkins-Smith, 1999). Generally, these studies from around the world, found that the ACF approach to dividing subsystems into coalitions was a useful way of analyzing the policymaking process.

Finding a valid and reliable method to measure subsystem coalitions, however, has eluded ACF researchers for some time now. This is mainly due to the three assumptions about policy analysis grounding the ACF. First, to understand the relationship between policy-oriented learning and policy change, a study must be longitudinal, spanning a decade or more. Second, the best way to understand policy change over time is to establish how policy actors work together in coalitions and thus seek to influence decisions at a variety of governmental levels. Third, to understand both the actions of policy actors as well as public policies, one must identify the values-component inherent in each; suggesting that within any particular policy, value priorities and causal assumptions are embedded and act as the underpinnings of the policy. In combination, these three assumptions have proven to make measurement of the ACF components and studying subsystem coalitions quite difficult. Of particular difficulty has been creating a reliable method to place policy actors that have worked together into appropriate coalitions that are adhered by policy beliefs. Hence, as with the paper models of my childhood, it has been difficult to put "Tab A" into "Slot B," and thus create a reliable method for identifying advocacy coalitions.

Broad Overview of ACF Terminology

As Sabatier and Jenkins-Smith (1999) report, the ACF focuses on understanding policy change by subdividing the larger policy community into subsystems—those actors that are involved in a particular area of policy.

When a topic has permeated the subsystem to such an extent that policy actors try to influence policy concerning that topic, the subsystem is said to have reached maturity. Within these mature subsystems, policy actors from various and diverse backgrounds group themselves into coalitions over long periods of time, glued together by similar beliefs. Each coalition works within a subsystem to put into place policies that reflect those beliefs. To enhance their efforts, coalition members learn about the policy area through research findings and real-world experiences. This policy-oriented learning is more likely to take place within subsystems that can be more accurately measured or where there are clear causal factors for a problem area. Important individuals known as policy brokers also can have an impact on the subsystem if they learn from subsystem outputs and change their beliefs. Professional fora, where scientists in the field or members of academia come together to reason through a policy problem, are another means for the dissemination of knowledge concerning the policy area and thus can be a conduit for policy-oriented learning. These types of learning can change secondary aspects of a coalition's or individual's beliefs, but for a major change in policy or beliefs to happen, a perturbation of external parameters is generally needed.

Advocacy Coalitions and Belief Systems

Wildavsky (1962) observed that within policymaking systems, a variety of policy actors form coalitions. Wildavsky suggested that these coalitions are made up of groups and individuals who advocate distinct policy viewpoints. Sabatier and Jenkins-Smith (1993) emphasized that members of these coalitions share similar values concerning problem causal beliefs. In addition, the authors opined that these coalition members often work together in order to support those values within the policy process. Sabatier and Jenkins-Smith contend that this general agreement within a coalition concerning belief systems focuses the attention of the group on particular types of problems in an attempt to better understand the world around them and establish policies consistent with their beliefs. The authors also maintain that these common beliefs will lead policy actors to work in a coordinated manner, forming an advocacy coalition.

Since advocacy coalitions are made up of policy elites, Sabatier and Jenkins-Smith (1993) relied on a mix of theories to identify coalition beliefs based on the beliefs of policy elites. The authors agreed with Sabatier and Hunter (1989) that belief systems of policy actors cannot be easily associated with simple ideological stances. This seems particularly true in education policy. Mazmanian and Sabatier (1983) were able to show that starting in the late 1960s, liberal members of the national education subsystem began to question the validity of some compensatory education programs. Instead of using a linear ideological construct to define belief systems,

Sabatier (1988) emphasized that the concept of beliefs to be used in the ACF would need to be grounded in Ajzen and Fishbein's (1980) theory of reasoned action (actors weigh alternatives in reference to a set of goals) and March and Simon's (1958) bounded rationality (satisficing and the limits of cognitive information), as well as Axelrod's (1976) views on the relative complexity and internal consistency of elite beliefs. Sabatier (1988) went on to note, though, that these authors spoke only to the existence of belief systems and not to how those systems would react when confronted with inaccuracies or inconsistencies. For this, Sabatier suggested Lakatos's (1971) approach, which differentiated between core beliefs and other types of beliefs.

Lakatos (1971) described scientific development as a product of competing research programs. Lakatos noted that most research programs are based on a hard core of unchallenged premises, with certain theoretical modifications to a program being made over time. Therefore, when changes in a theory allow for expanded explanative power and greater empirical corroboration, scientific progress occurs and theory is altered accordingly. Using Lakatos's work as a foundation, Sabatier and Jenkins-Smith (1993) outlined three categories in the ACF that coalition member beliefs fall into, including a deep core, a policy core and a series of secondary aspects. Deep core beliefs are fundamental values that can apply to all policy areas. Contained within the deep core is the relative priority of such values as freedom, power, privacy, and liberty. The policy core contains values that relate more specifically to the policies of the subsystem and a few interrelated subsystems. Within the policy core are values that relate to the relative place of government and markets in the policies of the subsystem as well as views on the appropriate level of governmental jurisdiction over the subsystem and a general position on subsystem policy conflict areas. Secondary aspects are completely specific to the policies of the subsystem and are related to particular positions on administrative rules, funding allocations and the interpretation of regulations.

Coalitions and Belief Systems in Policy Subsystems

For the most part, Sabatier and Jenkins-Smith (1993) hypothesize that coalitions are aligned around policy beliefs for long periods of time, though the coalitions may have less agreement about secondary aspects. A profusion of studies that address coalition belief systems have shown great promise for this feature of the ACF (Abrar, Lovenduski, & Margetts, 2000; Ellison, 1998; Mawhinney, 1993; Mintrom & Vergari, 1996; Zafonte & Sabatier, 1998). However, researchers have investigated the ACF using varied methodological techniques. Sabatier and Jenkins-Smith (1993) prescribed their own two-step approach to create reliable measures of beliefs over time. The use of this clustering approach has weaknesses though

(Shepley, 2003), one of which is that the approach fails to show that subsystem coalition members work together in a nontrivial manner (Sabatier & Jenkins-Smith, 1999). A second group of approaches to testing the ACF use unspecified case study methods. By "unspecified," I mean that the methods for analyzing individual cases through the lens of the ACF vary and are generally not described within the context of the study. Most often, researchers offer no descriptions of what data sources were used, how the data were collected and analyzed, and what methods were used in deciding to accept or reject ACF hypotheses. Case studies lacking in rigorous methods, while useful in looking for historical trends, are not replicable approaches to studying policy in all subsystems. Hence, there remains some question about the appropriate methods for testing the ACF.

A New Approach to Identifying Subsystem Coalitions

Relying solely on the clustering approach or solely on an unspecified case study approach clearly offers inadequate methods for testing the ACF in policy subsystems. Hence, I employ a new approach to identify subsystem coalitions. In the spirit that Sabatier and Jenkins-Smith (1993) proposed a generalized theory of policy change, this article builds upon the strengths of the empirical work in the field of policy study by using a new approach to defining subsystem coalitions. The new approach uses the strengths of multiple techniques (e.g., social network analysis, interview data analysis, comparison of means analysis, and analysis of variance) to detect policy coalitions in state reading policy subsystems. Instead of utilizing document analysis to determine belief variables, I use numerical data assigned to statements from interviews. In this article, these interview data not only represent the policy beliefs of elite actors in the subsystems but also repair the flaw in Sabatier and Jenkins-Smith's (1993) traditional clustering approach by assessing the policy network interactions of those actors. This requires, first, grouping subsystem actors using a social network approach, into two groups: the core (dominant coalition) and the periphery (nondominant coalition). This is followed by a comparison of beliefs means between these two groups. In doing so, the new approach to policy analysis improves on the validity of the approaches used by other ACF scholars in the past and provides a more appropriate method for measuring subsystem coalitions that can be used by policy scholars in the future.

STATE READING POLICY SUBSYSTEMS AS A TESTING GROUND

In order to assess this new approach to defining coalitions, I chose state level reading policy subsystems as a testing ground—in this case, California and Texas. Both California and Texas have seen dramatic shifts in reading policy over the last decade. In the early 1990s, California policymakers and educators responded to the perception of a reading achievement problem by creating a whole host of reading policy programs and initiatives (California Department of Education, 1995; Goodman, 1998). Nearly every branch and section of the California government dealing with education took part in the creation of these new reading policies. This multifaceted, collaborative effort to improve reading achievement is called the California Reading Initiative (CRI). During the late 1990s, Texas policymakers and educators built upon a long history of using education standards and testing by focusing on early reading as an area for investment and intervention. This led to the creation of the Texas Reading Initiative (TRI), the state model of school accountability and the student promotion policy known as the Texas Student Success Initiative (Brooks, 1997; Garner, 2000; Lindsay, 1997).

Broad changes to policy and large reallocations of money in a field can best be explained by the use of a generalized theory of policy change such as the Advocacy Coalition Framework. Hence, state reading policy subsystems are excellent venues for testing the new approach to identifying coalitions proposed by this article. I now turn to reviewing the relevant policy factors important for understanding coalition formation in state reading policy subsystems.

BASIC ATTRIBUTES OF THE
PROBLEM AREA IN READING

Larger issues that take place outside or across a subsystem can affect policy subsystems and provide the foundation for policy beliefs that link policy actors into coalitions. Of the four relatively stable external parameters that Sabatier and Jenkins-Smith (1993) note can affect policy beliefs and systems, the parameter most important for testing a new method of coalition definition is the basic attributes of the problem area. These basic attributes are helpful in identifying how coalitions are bound together by beliefs about reading policy. The three stable attributes discussed here are reading standards, reading assessments and instructional approaches in reading. The use of the word *stable* does not mean unchanging; rather it refers to the fact that these three areas are aspects consistently used when defining a reading achievement problem. How these three aspects of the problem area are defined, manipulated, and used in causal theories will be of great importance in understanding how coalitions are bound together. This section places these three basic aspects of the problem area within a context of state reading policy changes in California and Texas, offering them as possible belief areas that might serve as "glue" for state reading policy coalitions.

Reading Standards

Throughout the 1980s, California worked to fully implement a systemic model of educational reform. The creation of a progressive, English-Language Arts Framework in 1987 was part of this model of reform. Dissatisfaction with this literature-based series of standards, which deemphasized direct instruction in letter-sound relationships, led to revisions to the state reading standards in the 1990s. In 1997, the California State Board of Education adopted a new set of English and Language Arts standards, which reemphasized more traditional approaches to reading instruction (Carlos & Kirst, 1997).

As Horn (2001) pointed out, Texas began its work with reading standards long before the call for educational change through systemic reform. In order to identify and assess the basic goals of education, Governor John Connally created the Governor's Commission on Public School Education in 1968. By 1975, Texas education standards (what were then called objectives) had been developed in reading and math. In 1984, state standards were revised in order to create what was termed the Essential Elements of Instruction, but these were again revised in 1994, to make the standards more specific and rigorous. These new standards were called the Texas Essential Knowledge and Skills (TEKS) (Denton, 1997).

State standards have certainly changed over the last few decades, but the stable aspect of this problem-area attribute is that standards in reading are now a continuous part of the policy subsystem. Statewide reading standards in both California and Texas have been used for several decades. Setting a standard level of reading achievement is the first aspect in understanding a defined underachievement problem in both the California and Texas reading subsystems in the last decade. By setting standards, policymakers in both states were able to point to a specific goal in reading that was going unmet. Given this, beliefs concerning reading standards may play an important role in grouping policy actors into coalitions.

Reading Assessments

California has encouraged the use of standardized reading assessments since 1961 (California Department of Education, 1998). It was not until 1972, however, when the California Assembly mandated the use of the California Assessment Program (CAP), that a common statewide test of reading achievement was used in California. Given the fact that the CAP was not created to produce individual student scores and in response to changes in the state standards, a new generation of assessments called the California Learning Assessment System (CLAS) was implemented in 1991. The new system of assessment was plagued with a variety of validity problems though, and in 1994 Governor George Deukmejian terminated the use of the CLAS. In 1995, an interim measure for student assessment was created, called the Pupil Incentive Testing Program (PITP). In 1997, following the passage of Senate Bill 376 (sponsored by Senator Dede Albert, D-San Diego) and the creation of the Standardized Testing and Reporting program (STAR), the State Board of Education designated the Stanford Achievement Test Series, ninth edition, Form T (Stanford 9) as the sole statewide, standardized measure of reading achievement in the state (Charter School Development Center, 1999).

As Alford (2001) confirmed, Texas has been involved in statewide testing in reading for nearly a quarter of a century as well. The first program for assessing reading and other subjects on a statewide level was adopted in 1979—1980. Though the Texas Assessment of Basic Skills (TABS) was created as a diagnostic tool for teachers, in response to the recommendations of the Perot Commission Report, the Texas Educational Assessment of Minimum Skills (TEAMS) replaced the TABS in 1984. This minimum skills test became, in 1987, a mandatory exit skills exam. Three years after that, the Texas Assessment of Academic Skills (TAAS) was created to replace the TEAMS as a standards-based assessment. The TAAS has been used in high-stakes testing to assure content knowledge in the areas of reading and math at certain gateway grades. Most recently, the TAAS was replaced with the Texas Assessment of Knowledge and Skills (TAKS), which has been heralded as an assessment that is both more challenging than the TAAS and in better alignment with the state standards.

While there have been a vast number of different types of assessments in the last quarter century, assessment in reading is a continuous part of the policy subsystem and is thus a stable aspect. Statewide assessment systems in both California and Texas have been running for several decades. Testing and assessing reading achievement levels is an important aspect in understanding a defined underachievement problem in both the California and Texas reading subsystems in the last decade. By using state or national assessments, policymakers in both states were able to provide further evidence that the specific goals in the reading standards were going unmet. Poor test scores in reading would build the foundation for new policies that would seek to address poor reading achievement levels in the state. Hence, beliefs concerning reading tests could also play an important role in grouping policy actors into coalitions.

Reading Instructional Approaches

As Aukerman (1971) has suggested, reading teachers, theorists, and scholars in the English-speaking world have for several centuries sought the most effective method for teaching children to read. Two methods of reading instruction have been the predominant approaches, one known as the code-emphasis, or phonics, approach and the other as the meaning-emphasis, or whole language, approach. Determining which of these instructional methods is most effective or appropriate for advancing child-hood literacy has been a consistent aspect of the debate concerning reading for quite a long time.

Up through the first half of the 19th century, reading was predominantly taught in the United States using a method that was based on instruction of phonic concepts—first teaching letter names, then letter sounds and later focusing on appropriate elocution (Ravitch, 2000; Smith, 1934). An alternate whole-word method was advanced by certain educational reformers, including Horace Mann, and became very popular in the United States between 1845 and 1945 (Ravitch, 2000). With the publication of *Why Johnny Can't Read,* by Rudolph Flesch (1955), reaction against the look-say or whole-word method became pronounced, enflaming what has since been referred to as the Reading Wars. Flesch's book, which lasted for 30 weeks on the nation's best-sellers list, blamed the so-called literacy crisis of the 1950s on the use of the whole-word method. Flesch (1955) emphasized in no uncertain terms that the whole-word method was illogical and was the wrong way to teach reading. As a solution to the reading problem in America, Flesch insisted "systemic phonics is *the* way to teach reading" (p. 121, original emphasis).

At the height of these Reading Wars, the Carnegie Corporation commissioned Jeanne Chall to review all research in the area of reading instruction and early reading methods (Adams, 1998; Chall, 1996; Ravitch, 2000). Chall's review concluded that direct decoding instruction enhanced reading achievement. Shortly after Chall's review of the research, Frank Smith (1971) and later Kenneth S. Goodman (1986) heralded the return of the whole-word or look-say method, which they termed the Whole Language Philosophy. Balmuth (1982) confirmed that Smith and Goodman's Whole Language Philosophy was not a totally new idea but rather a direct descendant of the earlier logographic approaches of whole-word and look-say. Defining the Whole Language Philosophy has been a challenge to reading researchers, partly because its proponents claim that it is more than a reading method or approach; but rather they say it has theoretical and political components as well (Edelsky, 1990). Bergeron's (1990) meta-analysis and Moorman, Blanton and McLaughlin's (1994) follow-up work in defining whole language is very useful here. These researchers reviewed works concerned with the Whole Language Philosophy to determine what the common aspects were. They noted that most whole language researchers point to the naturalness of reading, that literacy instruction should enhance students' personal ownership of the text and that whole language practitioners resist the artificial instruction found in basal readers as well as any attempts by outside authorities to control the class curriculum. In addition, the researchers suggested that beliefs on direct instruction of the alphabetic system vary from those who feel that this type of instruction is not necessary (Goodman, 1993; Weaver, 1994) to those who see it as a necessity for some students (Routman, 1996). These differing forms of whole language instruction spread to many of the nation's classrooms through the late 1970s and into the 1980s.

There have been multiple attempts at calling a truce in the Reading Wars. This has only led to a renewed battlefront, this time over the middle ground of the Reading Wars and attempts to define what has been termed a Balanced Approach. Pressley (1998) defines this as an approach that is somewhere between a bottom-up (traditional pro-phonics) approach to reading instruction and a top-down (whole language) one. Which instructional technique is most effective in teaching young children to read—phonics, whole language, balanced—continues to be a point of contention within reading policy communities across the United States. Researchers like Moats (2000) reject the call for a balanced approach, suggesting that this is simply whole language in disguise. Those researchers from the whole language camp, like Goodman (1995), deny this position, suggesting that whole language has always been a balanced approach to reading instruction.

These Reading Wars have played out in state subsystems all over the country. In California, the 1987 English Language-Arts Frameworks or state standards were largely seen as a whole language document. Legislation in California was passed requiring the use of phonics to teach reading, and the revised standards required knowledge of decoding and phonics skills (Young, 2002). In Texas a similar transition took place, as a move toward more phonics-based instruction was encouraged by the Office of the Governor, the Texas Education Agency, and the State Board of Education. The passage of new standards in Texas mirrored the changes in the California state reading standards, requiring knowledge of phonics skills and concepts (Shepley, 2002).

Certainly, this pendulum of reading instructional approach has a dynamic aspect, but the stable aspect of this problem area attribute is that instructional approach to reading is a continuous part of defining reading achievement as a problem area. Debates over how to best teach children to read have been going on even longer than the standards and assessment aspects. These reading debates have been going on in both California and Texas for several decades as well. The method of teaching reading is an important aspect in understanding a defined underachievement problem in both the California and Texas reading subsystems in the last decade. By focusing on the instructional approach to reading, policy-makers in both states were able to provide a remedy to the unmet standards revealed by testing results. Beliefs concerning reading instructional approach may also be a logical approach for grouping policy actors into coalitions.

In sum, any method for identifying subsystem coalitions must take into account a variety of attributes that are basic to the problem area; in this case defining underachievement in reading. The three stable attributes discussed here are reading standards, reading assessments and instructional approaches in reading. These three basic attributes will be helpful in proposing how coalitions are bound together by beliefs about reading policy. I now turn to reviewing the relevant aspect of the ACF important for understanding coalition formation in state reading policy subsystems.

ADVOCACY COALITIONS AND BELIEF SYSTEMS

Using Lakatos's (1971) work as a foundation, Sabatier and Jenkins-Smith (1993) outlined three categories in the ACF that coalition member beliefs fall into, including a deep core, a policy core, and a series of secondary aspects. Deep core beliefs are fundamental values that can apply to all policy areas. Contained within the deep core is the relative priority of such values as freedom, power, privacy, and liberty. The policy core contains values that relate more specifically to the policies of the subsystem and a few interrelated subsystems. Within the policy core are values that relate to the relative place of government and markets in the policies of the subsystem as well as views on the appropriate level of governmental jurisdiction over the subsystem and a general position on subsystem policy conflict areas. Secondary aspects are completely specific to the policies of the subsystem and are related to particular positions on administrative rules, funding allocations and the interpretation of regulations.

For the most part, Sabatier and Jenkins-Smith (1993) hypothesize that coalitions are aligned around policy beliefs for long periods of time, though the coalitions may have less agreement about secondary aspects. A profusion of studies that address coalition belief systems have shown great promise for this feature of the ACF (e.g., Abrar, Lovenduski & Margetts, 2000; Chen, 2000; Heintz, 1988; Lertzman, Rayner, & Wilson, 1996; Mawhinney, 1993; Sato, 1999; Zafonte & Sabatier, 1998) However, few of these studies look both at coalition member beliefs and at coalition member interactions. While studies like that of Zafonte and Sabatier (1998) have shown reliable, replicable evidence that coalition members do indeed work together to alter policy based on beliefs, their findings show that coalitions may not necessarily be based on policy beliefs, but may be "glued" together by secondary beliefs. Hence, since there remains some question about this aspect of the ACF, I propose testing a new approach to identifying coalitions.

USING A NEW APPROACH TO FIND COALITIONS IN STATE READING POLICY SUBSYSTEMS

In order to identify coalitions in state reading policy subsystems, it is first important to determine whether active members of the subsystem have actually worked together in any fashion. Research by a colleague of mine in the area of state level reading policy is of great use here. In her analysis of state reading policy domains, Song (2003) was able to measure the interactions and influence levels of policy actors in a variety of states, including California and Texas. Using a social network approach, Song found that the policy actors in both states were grouped into a core/periphery structure. In describing this structure, Song emphasized the fact that those policy actors in the core of the domain were more influential and thus more powerful than those at the periphery. Given this distinction between core and peripheral actors, it seems logical to assume that those actors in the core of the policy domain make up the dominant coalition within a subsystem and that those in the periphery make up one or more nondominant coalitions in the subsystem. Most ACF studies have found just two coalitions within subsystems. Given this, I will work on the premise that in both California and Texas the actors in the network core make up one coalition, while actors in the periphery make up another. However, it is important to keep in mind that there is no limitation to the number of nondominant coalitions within the periphery. Therefore, during all examinations of coalition data, it will be important to remain open-minded to the consideration that there are more than two coalitions.

The second important aspect of coalition formation is that members of a coalition share common policy beliefs, though they may show less agreement on secondary beliefs. In terms of state reading policy subsystems, the most likely areas concerning policy beliefs would be reading standards, assessment, and instructional methods. It remains unclear if one, two or all three of these belief areas are the glue that holds reading policy coalitions together. Debate in state reading policy subsystems has remained focused around reading standards, reading assessments and the appropriate method for reading instruction for a significant period of time. Changes in the types of standards and assessments used in California and Texas have been argued about for several decades. Among all of these, though, the field of reading has been divided most by stances on reading methods. On this topic, battles have raged for well over a century. This division is alive and well in the exchanges between researchers and scholars like Coles (2000), Lyon (1997), Moats (2000), and Taylor (1998). It is logical that this sort of division would be witnessed in state reading policy subsystems as well, surrounding not only the question of reading methods but also other policy issues that relate to literacy, such as reading standards and assessments. Therefore, I propose the following hypothesis with three exploratory subheadings as a test of measuring coalition boundaries in state reading policy subsystem:

Hypothesis 1. There will be significant differences between coalition means of actors' belief statements with regard to: (a) reading instructional methods or (b) reading assessments or (c) reading standards within state reading policy subsystems.

METHODS

Sampling Procedures

The unit of analysis for this study was the state reading policy subsystems, specifically in California and Texas. In order to delineate a sufficient policy subsystem for each state, a wide variety of policy actors who might have had an impact on reading policy were identified. Policy actors were defined as individuals working alone or in any one of the following formal or informal groups:

a. citizen groups,
b. educational associations,
c. educational institutions (e.g., K–12 school systems, higher education institutions),
d. government agencies,
e. labor unions,
f. the media,
g. non-education associations,
h. philanthropic foundations,
i. private/for-profit firms,
j. think tanks, and
k. policy institutes.

To identify the initial sample our research group followed the procedures used by Heinz, Laumann, Nelson, and Salisbury (1993). Heinz et al. insist that individuals and groups should be selected because of their substantive concerns in setting policy. Through searches of published reports, the Internet, state archives, and newspapers, we generated initial lists of possible interviewees who had been active in state reading policy. Working with consultants knowledgeable about reading policy activities in the states, we augmented and refined these lists of interviewees. At least one individual from each of the identified interest groups or policy organizations was contacted for inclusion in the study. In addition, a snowballing (Kingdon, 1995) or sequential sampling (Heinz et al., 1993) technique was used. That is, during the interviews, individuals were asked to identify other key individuals and/or groups in the reading policy subsystem that had been omitted from the list of interviewees. Given this, the sample of policy actors was expanded to include these additional individuals and/or groups. The aim was to reach elite policy actors and their organizations in the reading policy community or those in close contact with elite policymakers who could serve as knowledgeable informants. The ultimate goal was to obtain a representative sample of the reading policy subsystems in California and Texas.

In California, representatives of 40 organizations (sometimes more than one per organization) and 6 individual actors who were acting on their own were identified as important members of the reading policy subsystem in that state. Of the 59 policy actors we contacted, 52 participated, yielding a response rate of 88%. In Texas, representatives of 42 organizations (again, sometimes more than one per organization) were identified as important members of the reading policy subsystem in that state. Of the 63 policy actors we contacted, 46 agreed to be interviewed, producing a 73% response rate. To utilize Song's (2003) work on the policy network in California to separate policy groups into dominant and nondominant coalitions for hypothesis 1, alterations were made reducing the size of the sample. A total of 49 elite policy actor interviews from 37 policy organizations were used, including interviews from 13 government officials, 27 interest group members, 3 members of the media, and 6 individual actors. To separate Texas policy groups into dominant and nondominant coalitions, alterations to the Texas sample were made as well. A total of 44 elite policy actor interviews from 30 organizations were used, including interviews from 16 government officials, 27 interest group members, and 1 member of the media.

Data Collection and Management

Interview data were collected from individuals through three standard, open-ended schedules: policymakers, interest groups, and media. Each potential interviewee was contacted by letter and asked to participate in the study. A letter was followed by a telephone call requesting an appointment for the interview. The interviews, generally lasting from 30 to 45 minutes, were conducted either by telephone or, when an appointment could be scheduled, in face-to-face meetings. The interviews were tape-recorded and transcribed, except for one interview in California that was conducted by email and then was followed up by a phone interview for additional questions.

Interview data were digitized and stored in an electronic database. A computer software program called ATLAS.ti (Scientific Software Development, 2001) was used in building and indexing the interview database. A hermeneutic unit was created for each state to store the data related to that state's policy actor's interviews. Excel (Microsoft Corporation, 1999) was used in compiling the quantitative database. A spreadsheet was created for each state to store the data related to that state's policy actors.

Measurement

Testing the hypothesis required that policy actors' beliefs regarding three pertinent policy issues in state subsystems (i.e., reading approach, reading standards, and testing in reading) are measured through the interviews of elite policy actors in California and Texas. The interviews included questions specifically designed to elicit statements on their views concerning appropriate methods for reading instruction as well as state standards and state tests. Ideally, this study would have had not only a scope of a decade or more, but actually would have used data collected at intermittent points throughout this time period and beyond. This, however, was not possible. The data collected did include the responses of policy actors regarding the events in state reading policy over the last two decades.

To ascertain the beliefs of policy actors concerning appropriate reading methods, they were asked, "Should reading instruction be based primarily on phonics, whole language, balanced approach, integrated approach, or some other approach?" To gauge the beliefs of policy actors on the topic of state standards, the question, "Do you support state standards for reading?" was proffered. Likewise, to gain an understanding of their beliefs on state testing, policy actors were asked, "Do you support state tests for reading?" After each question, the interviewer requested that the policy actor explain his or her position in further detail, if the interviewee had not already done so.[2]

Narrative Coding Process

The process of coding the interview transcripts for policy beliefs was completed in the following manner. Two researchers coded each interview through the use of the computer program ATLAS.ti (Scientific Software Development, 2001). Each researcher identified narrative statements that conveyed a complete thought related to the relevant topics; in this case, beliefs about appropriate methods of teaching reading as well as the importance of state standards and state tests in reading. The chosen narrative statement could be of any length, ranging from a sentence to a paragraph or two. To find information on any particular coding topic, the researchers paid close attention to the questions asked to elicit a response for each category. The researchers also looked for additional codable moments for each category topic throughout the interview. Researchers coded only those statements that could justifiably be understood as the opinion or belief of the respondent or organization. Once each researcher had completed the initial coding process, the two aggregated all statements related to each coding topic, using ATLAS.ti. Working together, the two researchers reached consensus on each coded narrative statement, assuring that both researchers were in agreement that each narrative statement fit into each category.

Statement-Level Extent Coding Process

The interview data in each belief category (i.e., methods, standards, testing) were then coded on an ordinal extent scale ranging from one to five. To gauge beliefs in the area of reading methods, a ranking of one was given to statements that showed a strong preference for phonics or if negative references were made about whole language. For example, the following statement made by a participant was ranked as a one: "We have been pushing phonics and I think that point has been made very clear." A ranking of three was given when statements showed a preference for a balanced, comprehensive, integrated, individualized, or similar type of program. A ranking of five was given when statements showed a strong preference for whole language or if a strong negative reference or a relatively large number of negative references were made toward phonics or scientifically based research. For example, a five was given to the following statement: "First of all, whole language is more effective and there is tons of research to show it." The intermediate rankings of two and four were assigned to statements that showed a mild preference for phonics or whole language, respectively. Similar extent scale ratings were assigned to statements concerning reading standards and testing. Those statements most in favor of reading standards or the use of reading tests were assigned a ranking of five, while those most opposed to these policies were assigned a one. Neutral or balanced statements regarding reading standards or tests were assigned a ranking of three.

Reliability

Working separately once more, the two researchers read, analyzed, and made judgments of which extent category within the coding topic best described the statements on that particular topic. Both intra-coder and inter-coder reliability levels were checked through the use of 30 randomly selected transcripts. Since some interviewees made more than one statement concerning the belief areas, the total number of statements assessed varied based on the number of codable moments in each interview.

Intra-coder levels were assessed by having the same two researchers recode randomly selected transcripts one week after the initial coding. Levels of intra-coder reliability were quite high, ranging from 100% agreement in Methods Coder 1 ($r = 1$) to a lower end of agreement at 87% by Standards-Coder 2 ($r = .95$). Inter-coder reliability was assessed by comparing the agreement of the two researchers' coding decisions on randomly selected interview documents. These levels ranged from a high of 90% agreement in the Assessment Belief Codes to a low of 72% agreement in the Standards Belief Codes. Still, the level of correlation was quite high, with all coefficients above $r = 0.9$. After estimating the reliability levels, two researchers coded each of the statements through a consensus process. The disagreements that occurred during the independent extent coding process were settled through discussion and consultation during the consensus-coding phase. However, for the remainder of this study, interview level extent coding data were used.

The researchers, working separately once again, read the statements concerning the beliefs of each participant. Taking all the participant's statements as a whole, the researchers assigned an ordinal extent scale ranging from one to five to every interview in the three coding areas. Hence, every interviewee was assigned a beliefs extent level in the areas of reading methods, standards and testing based on the totality of their statements in the area. Working together again, the two researchers consensus-coded the interview level extent codes for each of the three belief areas. The disagreements that occurred during the independent, interview-level extent coding process were settled through discussion and consultation during the consensus-coding phase. Results from the interview-level consensus coding process were used in all subsequent analyses.

ANALYSIS

To test hypothesis 1, the extent levels of statements concerning reading methods, reading standards and reading testing were categorized in Excel (Microsoft Corporation, 1999) by state (California and Texas) and coalition (dominant and nondominant). Data concerning the belief systems of policy elites in the two states were grouped by coalitions and were analyzed using a two-tailed t-test of means differences. All together, six analyses of means differences were completed, comparing the following:

a. methods belief means of California dominant and nondominant coalitions,
b. standards belief means of California dominant and nondominant coalitions,
c. testing belief means of California dominant and nondominant coalitions,
d. methods belief means of Texas dominant and nondominant coalitions,
e. standards belief means of Texas dominant and nondominant coalitions and
f. testing belief means of Texas dominant and nondominant coalitions.

Since hypothesis 1 is stated as a set of three possible coalition "adhesives," to accept the hypothesis, statistical significance ($p < .05$) will need to be reached in one or more of the California tests (a–c) and one or more of the Texas tests (d–f). The reason for this is that while coalitions may share similar core beliefs, agreement around only one set of beliefs is required for coalition formation.

RESULTS FOR THE
CALIFORNIA SUBSYSTEM

As described by Song (2003), the California policy network can be subdivided into a core, or dominant, group of policy actors and a periphery, or nondominant, group of actors. Applying the ACF concept of dominant and nondominant coalitions, I grouped the California reading subsystem along similar lines, resulting in the coalitions presented in Table 1.

Grouping the policy actors who belonged to each of these policy organizations into the two coalitions, I tested hypothesis 1 in the California reading subsystem using a two-tailed t-test of means differences. All together, three analyses of means differences were completed, comparing the following:

a. methods belief means of California dominant and nondominant coalitions,
b. standards belief means of California dominant and nondominant coalitions and
c. testing belief means of California dominant and nondominant coalitions.

Table 2 shows the results of these t-tests.

TABLE 1
Membership of the California Dominant and Nondominant Coalitions

Dominant Core	*Nondominant Periphery*
• Association of California School Administrators	• Individual Policy Actor (Academic-A)
• American Publishers Association	• Individual Policy Actor (Academic-B)
• California Assembly Education Committee	• Individual Policy Actor (Academic-C)
• California County Superintendents Educational Services Association	• Individual Policy Actor (Academic-D)
• California Commission on Teacher Credentialing	• Individual Policy Actor (Academic-E)
• California Federation of Teachers	• California Association of Bilingual Educators
• California Office of the Governor/ Secretary for Education	• California Association for the Education of Young Children
• Consortium of Reading Excellence	• California Association of Teachers of English
• California Reading Association	• California Reads Roundtable
• California Reading and Literature Project	• California State University's Institute for Education Reform
• California School Boards Association	• Individual Policy Actor (Lobbyist)
• California State Board of Education	• National Center to Improve the Tools of Educators
• California State Department of Education	• PACE Institute
• California Senate Education Committee	• Pacific Research Institute
• California State Parent and Teachers Association	• Sacramento City Unified School District
• California Teachers Association	• West Ed
• Los Angeles Times	• William D. Lynch Foundation for Children
• Sacramento Bee	• Whole Language Umbrella
• Sacramento County Office of Education	•

The results of the means tests show preliminary support for hypothesis 1 in the California reading subsystem. The dominant coalition within the California reading subsystem is markedly more in favor of a phonics approach to reading instruction than is the nondominant coalition. This

TABLE 2

Mean Differences in Beliefs of Dominant and Nondominant Coalitions in the California Reading Subsystem

	Reading Methods		Reading Standards		Reading Testing	
	Dominant	Non-dominant	Dominant	Non-dominant	Dominant	Non-dominant
Mean	2.07	3.11	4.71	3.63	4.11	3.11
Variance	0.67	1.43	0.21	1.80	0.80	2.10
Cells	27	19	28	19	27	18
df	29		21		26	
t	−3.30**		3.38**		2.61**	

Notes: *p < .05 ** p < .01 *** p < .001

statistically significant difference holds up in the area of reading standards and testing as well, where members of the dominant coalition tend to favor both policies more than do members of the nondominant coalition. These results suggest that the dominant coalition is held together by similar policy beliefs concerning reading methods, standards and testing.

Testing for Multiple Coalitions

An assumption of hypothesis 1 was that there are only two coalitions within the California reading subsystem: one dominant and one nondominant. While the results presented in Table 2 do support the assertion that there are statistically significant differences between these two proposed California coalitions in all three belief areas, further examination of the data counters this simple use of dominance and nondominance for coalition boundary definition in California. As can be seen in Table 2, variance in nondominant coalition member beliefs ranges from 1.43 in reading methods to over 2.10 in reading testing, while variance in the dominant coalition never exceeded 0.80. The relatively extreme variability in the nondominant coalition suggests a need for further examination.

One possibility is that in actuality, there are two or more nondominant coalitions. At least two ACF studies (Ellison, 1998; Sabatier & Zafonte, 1995) found subsystems that have more than two coalitions. As previously mentioned, the first clue to multiple coalitions is seen in the variance of the nondominant coalition. To determine the likelihood that multiple coalitions exist in the California reading subsystem, I examined the descriptive statistics in each coalition. The results, presented in Table 3, show that the range of scores in the nondominant coalition is far greater than the range

TABLE 3

Descriptive Statistics for Dominant and Nondominant Coalitions in the California Reading Subsystem

	Reading Methods		Reading Standards		Reading Testing	
	Dominant	Non-dominant	Dominant	Non-dominant	Dominant	Non-dominant
Mean	2.07	3.11	4.71	3.63	4.11	3.11
Min.	1	1	4	1	2	1
Max.	3	5	5	5	5	5
Range	2	4	1	4	3	4

of belief scores in the dominant coalition across all three policy belief areas measured. In fact, scores supporting both extremes of each belief scale were found in the nondominant coalition. The range of scores in the dominant coalition was much lower in both reading methods and standards. The data point to the possibility that while there is one dominant coalition bound by beliefs on reading methods and/or reading standards (with less agreement on reading testing), there does appear to be more than one nondominant coalition within the California reading subsystem.

Looking for ways to identify a boundary between the two nondominant coalitions, I reexamined Song's (2003) data and found that a small group of three academics (A, B, and D) and two interest groups with a curricular focus (Whole Language Umbrella and the California Association of Bilingual Educators) formed what seemed to be a subgroup within the nondominant coalition. The three academics had worked with each other with regard to reading policy, and the interest groups, taken together, had worked with all three of the academics. This information supported the first part of Sabatier and Jenkins-Smith's (1999) definition of coalition boundary, i.e., those members of a coalition must have worked together in the policy subsystem. This would result in three California coalitions: the same dominant coalition as before, and two nondominant coalitions. Nondominant coalition #1 would have the same membership as previously listed, except now five members (Academics A, B, D, the California Association of Bilingual Educators and the Whole Language Umbrella) would make up nondominant coalition #2.

The next step was to test whether these three coalitions would hold up to statistical testing of belief means. In order to reexamine the data for the three coalitions, I performed a one-factor analysis of variance (ANOVA) on the California reading policy subsystem. The output from this ANOVA is presented in Table 4. It shows statistically significant differences between the three coalitions in each of the belief areas.

TABLE 4

Results of the ANOVA on a Three Coalition California Reading Policy Subsystem

Source	Sum of Squares		Degrees of Freedom		Mean Square		F
	Between	Within	Between	Within	Between	Within	
Methods	31.35	22.15	2	43	15.67	0.52	30.4***
Standards	31.33	20.07	2	44	15.67	0.46	34.3***
Testing	31.07	36.17	2	42	15.54	0.86	18.0***

Notes: *p < .05 ** p < .01 *** p < .001

I also examined the descriptive statistics of each of these new coalitions. The results, presented in Table 5, show that the range of standards and testing belief scores are greater than the range of methods belief scores. For example, the range of reading methods scores within coalitions is never greater than 2. In the reading standards and testing scores within coalitions, the range reaches 3. Even more importantly, the coalitions based on reading methods beliefs suggest a Phonics-Leaning (Dominant) Coalition, a Balanced-Leaning (Nondominant #1) Coalition, and a Pro-Whole Language (Nondominant #2) Coalition. Trying to group coalitions by beliefs concerning reading standards and or testing does not hold together as well. For instance, Nondominant Coalition #2 would include actors who are strongly opposed to state reading standards along with policy actors who give this policy qualified support. Grouping three coalitions around beliefs about reading testing is also problematic, as the Dominant Coalition and Nondominant Coalitions would each contain members who highly favor state testing in reading and those who are negative toward state reading tests.

In sum, of the three possible reading beliefs presented in hypothesis 1, the results of the ANOVA support hypothesis 1a (reading instruction

TABLE 5

Descriptive Statistics of a Three-Coalition California Reading Policy Subsystem

	Reading Methods			Reading Standards			Reading Testing		
	Dom.	ND#1	ND#2	Dom.	ND#1	ND#2	Dom.	ND#1	ND#2
Mean	2.08	2.50	4.80	4.71	4.21	2.0	4.11	3.77	1.40
Min	1	1	4	4	3	1	2	2	1
Max	3	3	5	5	5	4	5	5	2
Range	2	2	1	1	2	3	3	3	1

beliefs) in the California state reading subsystem. Descriptive statistics point to three coalitions within the California subsystem glued together by beliefs concerning methods for reading instruction. I named these three coalitions as the California Phonics-Leaning, Dominant (CP) Coalition, the California Balanced-Leaning, Nondominant (CB) Coalition, and the California Whole Language-Leaning, Nondominant (CWL) Coalition. Even though analysis showed a statistically significant difference between the three coalitions concerning beliefs about reading testing and standards as well, descriptive statistics suggest that these are not the policy beliefs that hold the three coalitions together. Instead, it is likely that beliefs concerning reading standards and testing are better understood as secondary aspects to the policy subsystem. The ACF predicts that while coalitions are held together by similar policy beliefs, it also suggests that there will be less agreement concerning secondary aspects. Hence, if beliefs concerning reading standards and testing are seen as secondary aspects of the state reading policy subsystem, then the outcome of the data analyses is consistent with what the Advocacy Coalition Framework predicts.

RESULTS FOR THE TEXAS SUBSYSTEM

As described by Song (2003), the Texas policy network can also be subdivided into a core, or dominant, group of policy actors and a periphery, or nondominant, group of actors. Applying the ACF concept of dominant and nondominant coalitions, I grouped the Texas reading subsystem along similar lines, resulting in the coalitions in Table 6.

Grouping the policy actors who belonged to each of these policy organizations, I tested hypothesis 1 in the Texas reading subsystem using a two-tailed t-test of means differences. All together, three analyses of means differences were completed, comparing the following:

a. methods belief means of Texas dominant and nondominant coalitions,
b. standards belief means of Texas dominant and nondominant coalitions, and
c. testing belief means of Texas dominant and nondominant coalitions.

Table 7 shows the results of these t-tests. The results show no initial support for hypothesis 1 in the Texas reading subsystem. No statistical differences were found between the dominant coalition and the nondominant coalition within the Texas reading subsystem surrounding beliefs on reading methods standards and testing.

TABLE 6

Membership of the Texas Dominant and Nondominant Coalitions

Dominant Core	Nondominant Periphery
• Center for Academic and Reading Skills at University of Texas-Houston	• The Association of Texas Professional Educators
• Governor's Business Council	• Houston Chronicle
• Just For Kids	• National Urban Literacy Coalition-Houston READ Commission
• Texas Business and Education Coalition	• Southwest Educational Development Laboratories
• Texas Center for Reading and Language Arts at University of Texas-Austin	• Texas A & M University
• Texas Education Agency	• Texas Association of School Administrators
• Texas Elementary Principals and Supervisors Association	• Texas Association of School Boards
• Texas Federation of Teachers	• Texas Center for Educational Research
• Texas House Education Committee	• Texas Classroom Teachers Association
• Texas Office of the Governor	
• Texas Office of the Lieutenant Governor	• Texas Eagle Forum
	• Texas Public Policy Foundation
• Texas State Board of Education	• Texas Parent Teacher Association
• Texas Senate Education Committee	• Texas Reach Out and Read
	• Texas State Board for Educator Certification
	• Texas Senate Education Committee
	• Texas State Reading Association
	• Texas State Teacher's Association

TABLE 7

Difference in Belief Means of Dominant and Nondominant Coalitions in the Texas Reading Subsystem

	Reading Methods		Reading Standards		Reading Testing	
	Dominant	Non-dominant	Dominant	Non-dominant	Dominant	Non-dominant
Mean	2.50	2.70	4.41	4.53	4.33	4.05
Variance	.47	.43	1.40	0.93	1.53	1.50
Cells	20	20	22	19	21	19
df	38		39		38	
t	2.02		2.02		2.02	

Notes: *p<.05 ** p<.01 *** p<.001

Testing for Multiple Coalitions

Because there are more than two advocacy coalitions found in the California reading subsystem, it is logical to assume that there might be more than two coalitions in the Texas subsystem as well. Again, looking for ways to identify a boundary between two nondominant coalitions, I reexamined Song's (2003) data and found a small subgroup made up of the Texas Eagle Forum (TEF) and the Texas Public Policy Foundation (TPPF). While two organizations form a somewhat small coalition, this information supported the first part of Sabatier and Jenkins-Smith's (1999) definition of coalition boundary, i.e., those members of a coalition must have worked together in the policy subsystem. This would result in three Texas coalitions: the same dominant coalition as before, and two nondominant coalitions. Nondominant coalition #1 would have the same membership as previously listed, except now two members (the Texas Eagle Forum and the Texas Public Policy Foundation) would make up Nondominant coalition #2.

To reexamine the data for three coalitions, I performed a one-factor analysis of variance (ANOVA) on the Texas reading policy subsystem. The results from these analyses are presented in Table 8. They indicate statistically significant differences between the three coalitions only in the area of reading methods. No significant difference was found among the three coalitions in the areas of reading standards or reading testing. Descriptive statistics reveal the type of belief differences between coalitions. As shown in Table 9, the mean of beliefs in reading methods for the Dominant Coalition was 2.50, for the Nondominant Coalition #1 the mean was 2.90, and for the Nondominant Coalition #2 it was 1.

In sum, of the three possible reading beliefs presented in hypothesis 1, hypothesis 1a (reading instruction beliefs) is supported by the results of

TABLE 8
Results of the ANOVA on a Three-Coalition Texas Reading Policy Subsystem

Source	*Sum of Squares*		*Degrees of Freedom*		*Mean Square*		
	Between	*Within*	*Between*	*Within*	*Between*	*Within*	*F*
Methods	6.82	10.78	2	37	3.41	0.29	11.7***
Standards	5.35	40.85	2	38	2.67	1.07	3.2
Testing	3.26	55.14	2	37	1.63	1.50	3.3

Notes: *p < .05 ** p < .01 *** p < .001

TABLE 9

Descriptive Statistics of a Three-Coalition Texas Reading Policy Subsystem

	Reading Methods		
	Dom.	*ND#1*	*ND#2*
Mean	2.5	2.889	1
Min	1	2	1
Max	3	3	1
Range	2	1	0

the ANOVA in the Texas state reading subsystem. Descriptive statistics point to three coalitions within the Texas subsystem glued together by beliefs concerning methods of reading instruction. I am labeling these three coalitions as the Texas Phonics-Leaning Dominant (TP) Coalition, the Texas Balanced-Leaning, Nondominant (TB) Coalition and the Texas Pro-Phonics, Nondominant (TPP) Coalition. Unlike in California, the ANOVA results did not suggest statistically significant differences between the three coalitions concerning beliefs about reading testing and standards. However, these results can be interpreted in a manner similar to those in California. It is likely that beliefs concerning reading standards and testing are better understood as secondary aspects to the policy subsystem.

CONCLUSIONS AND IMPLICATIONS

The findings presented here provide support for hypothesis 1(a) regarding reading pedagogy. Sabatier and Jenkins-Smith (1999) suggested that proof of subsystem coalitions require evidence that policy actors had worked together to influence policy and shared similar beliefs concerning policy issues. Data for both the California and Texas reading subsystems clearly show that members who have worked together to influence reading policy, when divided into three coalitions, showed statistically significant differences in beliefs concerning reading methods. Therefore, hypothesis 1(a) is accepted. Hypotheses 1(b) and 1(c) are rejected. Beliefs about standards—hypothesis 1(b)—and testing—hypothesis 1(c)—are best interpreted as secondary aspects in state reading subsystems, which may vary to a much greater extent within coalitions than do beliefs concerning subsystem policy beliefs, such as reading methods.

A New Approach to Measuring Coalition Boundaries

The ultimate goal of this study was to determine whether a new, reliable method of measuring coalition boundaries could effectively be used within a subsystem. To do this, a two step procedure was used. An important first step was to determine whether active members of the subsystem have actually worked together in any fashion. In order to measure organizational interaction, I relied on prior research conducted by a colleague (Song, 2003) to initially group the subsystems into two coalitions. The data used by Song were based upon the same interviews that were used in this study. This type of prior research most likely will not be available to other ACF researchers. To duplicate the method used here, future research will need to gather organizational data and utilize a social network approach to initially group policy actors by coalition.

The second important aspect of coalition formation is that members of a coalition share common policy beliefs, though they may show less agreement on secondary beliefs. To test this aspect of coalitions, the extent levels of statements concerning relevant subsystem topics (in this case, reading methods, standards, and testing) were categorized by state (California and Texas) and coalition (dominant and nondominant). The measurement of beliefs is always a difficult series of decisions, each of which contain its own set of strengths and limitations. The method used to gather data from policy actors has its strength in the fact that the interview schedule specifically asked policy actors about their beliefs in three important areas (methods, standards and testing) and the scale used to measure beliefs was grounded in appropriate literature. However, the use of any Likert-type scale to pigeonhole beliefs has its limitations. By portraying beliefs in broad categories, researchers risk reducing important reading issues into simplistic terms and labels. This type of simplification was certainly not the intention of this study. The methods used to parse out policy actor beliefs suggest a thoughtful and complex process rather than an oversimplification of the issues.

It seemed logical to assume that those actors in the core of the policy domain make up the dominant coalition and those in the periphery make up the nondominant coalition in the subsystem. This initial assumption was only partially correct. Song's (2003) analyses were able to define the boundary between dominant and nondominant coalitions, but they initially were unable to define boundaries between nondominant coalitions. Using a social network approach for identifying the boundary between dominant and nondominant coalitions proved to be quite appropriate for a study using the ACF. However, using the core/periphery notion as the sole determinate for defining coalitions in a subsystem must be seen as only the first check of coalition boundaries as more than two coalitions can be found in subsystems.

Revising the New Approach for Use in Future Research

This new approach for identifying coalitions and the beliefs that glue them together proved appropriate for identifying coalition members in subsystems. This approach addressed both aspects important to identifying coalitions within subsystems—that members have worked together and that they share similar core beliefs but may differ on secondary beliefs— and thus added to the literature in an important way not previously fully attended to. However, in the case of state reading policy subsystems, the use of these two methods in combination, while conceptually appropriate, resulted in the creation of three coalitions in each state subsystem. In and of itself, this would not have been a problem, except that one coalition in each state ended up being quite small. Nonetheless, these small coalitions could have had an impact on the efficacy of the results. While the outcome of using such small coalitions is not completely unimpeachable, the fact that the coalition boundaries were associated with both interactivity (from the network analysis data) and common beliefs (from the belief, extent data) provides strong auxiliary evidence that these small coalitions are indeed important aspects of the subsystem. Future research will need to attend to this issue as small, extreme third coalitions may in fact be the core remnants of previous dominant coalitions and hence could exist in other policy realms as well.

Overall, this new approach to defining the boundaries of advocacy coalitions has a number of strengths, particularly in identifying the members of the dominant and nondominant coalitions. By using a two part process to gauge policy actor interaction and policy actor beliefs about events over time, as well as by checking for the possibility of multiple nondominant coalitions, future researchers should be able to effectively duplicate this new approach in virtually any subsystem. Similar data to that used in this study has already been collected concerning federal reading policy, suggesting that this type of data can be obtained at any governmental level. If scholars choose to use this new approach to measure advocacy coalition boundaries over an extended period of time, the results would provide the most powerful test to date of the Advocacy Coalition Framework and its ability to explain the complex processes of policymaking.

NOTES

1.   This research was conducted as part of the Center for the Improvement of Early Reading Achievement (CIERA), and supported under the Educational Research and Development Centers Program, PR/Award Number R305R70004 and the Field Initiated Studies Program, PR/Award Number R305T990369, U.S. Department of Education, and the Major Grants Program, Spencer Foundation.

However, the contents of the report do not necessarily represent the positions or policies of the funding agencies and you should not assume endorsement by them.

2.   To obtain a copy of the interview schedule as well as further coding examples, contact Cecil G. Miskel at the University of Michigan.

REFERENCES

Abrar, S., Lovenduski, J., & Margetts, H. (2000). Feminist ideas and domestic violence policy change. *Political Studies, 48*, 239–262.

Adams, M. J. (1998). *Beginning to read.* Cambridge, MA: MIT Press.

Ajzen, I., & Fishbein, M. (1980). *Understanding attitudes and predicting social behavior.* Englewood Cliffs, NJ: Prentice-Hall.

Alford, B. J. (2001). The Texas accountability system past, present and future through one educator's lens: A continuing journey toward system improvement. In R. A. Horn & J. L. Kincheloe (Eds.), *American standards: Quality education in a complex world* (Vol. 192, pp. 131–140). New York: Peter Lang.

Aukerman, R. C. (1971). *Approaches to beginning reading.* New York: Wiley.

Axelrod, R. (Ed.). (1976). *Structure of decision.* Princeton, NJ: Princeton University Press.

Balmuth, M. (1982). *The roots of phonics: A historical introduction.* New York: McGraw-Hill.

Bergeron, B. S. (1990). What does the term whole language mean? Constructing a definition from the literature. *Journal of Reading Behavior, 22*, 301–330.

Brooks, A. P. (1997, December 22). Bush's test-to-pass school plan called to blackboard. *Austin-American Statesman*, p. 4.

California Department of Education. (1995). *Every child a reader: Report of the California Reading Task Force.* Retrieved April 17, 2002, from http://www.cde.ca.gov/cilbranch/eltdiv/everychild1.htm

California Department of Education. (1998). *Chronology of state testing in California.* Retrieved September 3, 2002, from http://www.omsd.k12.ca.us/instruct/star/time.html

Carlos, L., & Kirst, M. (1997) *California curriculum policy in the 1990s: "We don't have to lead to be in front."* Paper presented at the Annual Meeting of The American Educational Research Association, Chicago.

Chall, J. S. (1996). *Learning to read* (3rd Ed.). New York: Harcourt Brace.

Charter School Development Center. (1999). *The state of the state standards and assessments.* Retrieved September 3, 2002, from http://www.csus.edu/ier/charter/news_1_15_99.html

Chen, P. J. (2000). *Australia's online censorship regime: The advocacy coalition framework and governance compared.* Unpublished dissertation, Australian National University, Canberra, Australia.

Coles, G. (2000). *Misreading reading: The bad science that hurts children.* Portsmouth, NH: Heinemann.

Denton, D. (1997). *The Texas Reading Initiative: Mobilizing resources for literacy.* Retrieved January 19, 2001, from http://test.sreb.org/programs/HHS/pubs/TexasReadingInitiative.asp

Edelsky, C. (1990). Whose agenda is this anyway? A response to McKenna, Robinson, and Miller. *Educational Researcher, 19*(8), 7–11.

Ellison, B. A. (1998). The advocacy coalition framework and implementation of the Endangered Species Act: A case study in western water politics. *Policy Studies Journal, 26*(1), 11–29.

Flesch, R. F. (1955). *Why Johnny can't read–and what you can do about it.* New York: Harper.

Garner, D. (2000). *An analysis of English/Language Arts/Reading as the foundation for public education in Texas.* Paper presented at a meeting of the Lone Star Foundation, Austin, TX.

Goodman, K. (1995, November 15). Forced choices in a non-crisis. *Education Week,* 1.

Goodman, K. S. (1986). *What's whole in whole language?* Richmond Hill, Ontario: Scholastic.

Goodman, K. S. (1993). *Phonics phacts.* Portsmouth, NH: Heinemann.

Goodman, K. S. (1998). Who's afraid of whole language? Politics, paradigms, pedagogy, and the press. In K. S. Goodman (Ed.), *In defense of good teaching* (pp. 3–38). New York: Stenhouse.

Heintz, H. T. (1988). Advocacy coalitions and the OCS leasing debate: A case study in policy evolution. *Policy Sciences, 21,* 213–238.

Heinz, J. P., Laumann, E. O., Nelson, R. L., & Salisbury, R. H. (1993). *The hollow core: Private interests in national policy making.* Cambridge: Harvard University Press.

Horn, R. A. (2001). The question of complexity: Understanding the standards movement in Texas. In R. A. Horn & J. L. Kincheloe (Eds.), *American standards: Quality education in a complex world—the Texas case.* New York: Peter Lang.

Kingdon, J. W. (1995). *Agendas, alternatives, and public policies.* New York: Addison Wesley Longman.

Lakatos, I. (1971). History of science and its rational reconstruction. *Boston Studies in the Philosophy of Science, 8,* 42–134.

Lertzman, K., Rayner, J., & Wilson, J. (1996). Learning and change in the British Columbia forest policy sector: A consideration of Sabatier's advocacy framework. *Canadian Journal of Political Science, 29* (March), 111–133.

Lindsay, D. (1997, November 12). Double standards. *Education Week,* p. 1.

Lyon, G. R. (1997). *Statement of Dr G. Reid Lyon to the Committee on Labor and Human Resources.* Washington DC: National Institute of Child Health and Human Development.

Mawhinney, H. B. (1993). An advocacy coalition approach to change in Canadian education. In P. A. Sabatier & H. C. Jenkins-Smith (Eds.), *Policy change and learning: An advocacy coalition approach* (pp. 59–82). Boulder, CO: Westview.

March, J., & Simon, H. (1958). *Organizations.* New York: Wiley.

Mazmanian, D., & Sabatier, P. (1983). *Implementation and public policy.* Lanham, MD: Scott Foresman.

Microsoft Corporation. (1999). *Excel Version WIN 9.0.2720.* Troy, NY: Microsoft Software Development.

Mintrom, M., & Vergari, S. (1996). Advocacy coalitions, policy entrepreneurs, and policy change. *Policy Studies Journal, 24*(3), 420–434.

Moats, L. (2000). *Whole language lives on: The illusion of 'balanced' reading instruction*. Retrieved April 17, 2002, from http://www.edexcellence.net/library/whole-lang/moats.html

Moorman, G. B., Blanton, W. E., & McLaughlin, T. (1994). The rhetoric of whole language. *Reading Research Quarterly, 29,* 309–329.

Pressley, M. (1998). *Reading instruction that works: The case for balanced teaching*. New York: Guilford.

Ravitch, D. (2000). *Left back*. New York: Simon and Schuster.

Routman, R. (1996). *Literacy at the crossroads: Critical talk about reading, writing, and other teaching dilemmas*. Portsmouth, NH: Heinemann.

Sabatier, P. A. (1988). An advocacy coalition framework of policy change and the role of policy-oriented learning therein. *Policy Sciences, 21,* 129–168.

Sabatier, P. A., & Hunter, S. (1989). The incorporation of causal perceptions into models of elite belief systems. *Western Political Quarterly, 42*(September), 229–261.

Sabatier, P. A., & Jenkins-Smith, H. C. (1993). Policy change and learning: An advocacy coalition approach. Boulder, CO: Westview.

Sabatier, P. A., & Jenkins-Smith, H. C. (1999). The advocacy coalition framework: An assessment. In P. A. Sabatier (Ed.), *The theories of the policy process* (pp. 117–168). Boulder, CO: Westview.

Sabatier, P., & Zafonte, M. (1995). The views of bay/delta water policy activists on endangered species issues. *Hastings West-Northwest Journal of Environmental Law and Policy, 2*(Winter), 131–146.

Sato, H. (1999). The advocacy coalition framework and the policy process analysis: The case of smoking control in Japan. *Policy Studies Journal, 27*(1), 28–44.

Scientific Software Development. (2001). *ATLAS.ti: The knowledge workbench Version WIN 4.2* (Build 059). Berlin: Scientific Software Development.

Shepley, T. V (2002). *Texas reading policy: Problems, processes and participants*. (Final Report). Reading Policy Project, University of Michigan.

Shepley, T. V. (2003). *A tale of two cities: Coalitions, policy-oriented learning and major change in state reading subsystems*. Unpublished dissertation, University of Michigan, Ann Arbor, Michigan.

Smith, F. (1971). *Understanding reading*. Hillsdale, NJ: Heinemann.

Smith, N. B. (1934). *American reading instruction: Its development and its significance in gaining a perspective on current practices in reading*. New York: Silver, Burdett.

Song, M. (2003). *Influence in the reading policy domain: A cross case study*. Unpublished dissertation, University of Michigan, Ann Arbor, Michigan.

Stewart, J. (1991). Policy models and equal educational opportunity. *PS: Political Science & Politics, 26*(June), 167–172.

Taylor, D. (1998). *Beginning to read and the spin doctors of science*. Urbana, IL: National Council of Teachers of Education.

Weaver, C. (1994). *Understanding whole language: From principles to practice* (2nd ed.). Portsmouth, NH: Heinemann.

Wildavsky, A. (1962). The analysis of issue contexts in the study of decision-making. *Journal of Politics, 24,* 717–732.

Young, T. V (2002). *California reading policy: Problems, processes and participants*. (Final Report). Reading Policy Project, University of Michigan.

Zafonte, M., & Sabatier, P. (1998). Shared beliefs and imposed interdependencies as determinants of ally networks in overlapping subsystems. *Journal of theoretical politics, 10*(4), 473–505.

CHAPTER 9

SOCIAL CAPITAL IN EDUCATION

Taking Stock of Concept and Measure

Patrick B. Forsyth and Curt M. Adams

Authors review conceptual and operational definitions of social capital as found in the literature. They argue the importance of seeking definitional convergence across the social sciences and propose a definition consistent with much of the literature: Social capital is the social structure and cognitive dispositions that act as a resource for collective action. Based on this definition, a set of "theory-near" criteria are derived for adequate measurement of the cognitive and structural dimensions at the meso-level. Meso-level measurement, it is argued, is the appropriate level for school research. Three recently published social capital writings are examined against the criteria. Authors also present a demonstration study in which they attempt to generate operational measures that meet the criteria. Last, they reflect on the viability of theory-near operational measures of social capital and the specifics of what has been learned.

Educational Administration, Policy, and Reform: Research and Measurement
A Volume in: Research and Theory In Educational Administration, pages 251–278.
Copyright © 2004 by Information Age Publishing, Inc.
All rights of reproduction in any form reserved.
ISBN: 1-59311-000-0 (hardcover), 1-59311-000-0 (paperback)

INTRODUCTION

Although social capital as a concept has been around for some time and the literature on social capital is prolific, neither concept nor measure could be called convergent. The lack of convergence of term and measure, even within narrowly defined fields of inquiry like education, is problematic for a number of reasons, not the least of which are the lack of comparability of studies and erroneous comparison. Van der Gaag and Snijders (2002) comment that research progress in this field "has been limited because of the lack of standardized, reliable, and parsimonious theory-driven instruments for measuring social capital" (p. 1). It is not likely that these serious difficulties can be resolved in this chapter, but convergence may be promoted.

There have been previous efforts to sort out conceptual and operational complexities of social capital (Glaeser et al, 1999; Grootaert & van Bastelaer, 2001; Narayan & Cassidy, 2001; Paldam, 2000; Pope, 2002; Stone, 2001; Stone & Hughes, 2002; Van der Gaag & Snijders, 2002). This particular effort combines the interest of supporting conceptual convergence across the social sciences with promoting operational convergence in education related research. Bringing order to this field of inquiry would appear to be an insurmountable task. Findings drawn from work based on a variety of conceptual definitions and measures of a construct are often impossible to integrate. We are optimistic that the parameters of a general definition of social capital can be discerned and that a sample of education studies can be examined for consistency with that definition, while attending to the specific contextual conditions of school inquiry.

We start by reviewing social capital conceptual and operational definitions. A conceptual definition that incorporates what seem to be the essential elements is posed and then we derive a "theory-near" set of criteria for measurement appropriate for education applications. A sample of recent social capital studies from the education literature is examined, evaluating the conceptual and operational definitions against the proposed criteria. A demonstration study is attempted, paying close attention to the derived criteria for adequate measurement. Finally, we reflect on what has been learned and its utility for the future of social capital inquiry, especially in education.

DEFINING SOCIAL CAPITAL

At the very general level, social capital has been described as the glue that enables cooperative human action. That glue can be said to have both cognitive and structural dimensions (Grootaert & van Bastelaer, 2001).

Put differently, social capital requires operational channels of interaction and the dispositions to use them for some productive purpose. This concept is at least reminiscent of the general Hobesian question related to the emergence of social phenomena and the writing of Emile Durkheim (1966) and later economics influenced sociology, especially the exchange theories of George C. Homans (1961, 1974) and Peter Blau (1964). Only careful sorting out of the meaning and measure of social capital can determine if and how it is distinguished from these very elaborate theories of social action.

A brief encounter with social capital literature reveals the difficulty scholars have in sorting out social capital from its determinants and results (Edwards, 2002; Stone & Hughes, 2002). A main distinction can perhaps be drawn between those who define social capital as a set of resources and those who define it as a set of norms such as trust and reciprocity. An example of the former would be Pierre Bourdieu (1986) and the latter Robert Putnam (1993, 1995, 2000). But, when you examine this work closely, it becomes more difficult to say that Bourdieu defines social capital as a set of resources. For Bourdieu, it is social networks that give members access to group resources (Edwards, 2002). So, should social capital be defined by these networks or the resources that are made available through them? And, although Putnam (2000) appears to define social capital in terms of norms, he focuses largely on the networks created by memberships in voluntary organization.

Some of the confusion about which phase in the development of networks and norms should be defined as social capital can be overcome by conceptualizing the process as cyclical, rather than linear. Thus, a given amount of social capital is the outcome of a dynamic cycle of network and norm formation. There is some empirical evidence concerning a reciprocal relationship between interaction and trust (Powell, 1996; Tschannan-Moran, 2001). Moreover, contradictory causal directions found among other studies (Hoffman, Sabo, Bliss, & Hoy, 1994; Lewicki & Bunker 1996; Mattessich & Monsey, 1992; Mishra, 1996; Putnam 1993) suggest reciprocal causality.

In Table 1 below we have listed a sample of social capital definitions drawn from a variety of social science disciplines, including sociology and economics. What emerges from these definitions is a kind of conceptual convergence around the channels of interaction, what might be called networks or social structure, which appear essential to social capital. There is a similar convergence around shared trust, norms, values, and beliefs that some scholars have placed together in a category of cognitive elements (Grootaert, Chase & van Bastelaer, 2002). Finally, whether implicit or explicit, a third essential element emerges as potential or actual social action. If the structures and cognitive dispositions are not productive, it is difficult to think of the phenomenon as capital.

TABLE 1
A Sample of Social Capital Definitions

Putnam:	Those features of social organization, such as networks of individuals or households, and the associated norms and values, that create externalities for the community as a whole. (Grootaert & van Bastelaer, 2001, p. 4).
Coleman:	A variety of different entities [which] all consist of some aspect of social structure, and [which] facilitate certain actions of actors-whether personal or corporate actors-within the structure. (Grootaert & van Bastelaer, 2001, p. 4–5).
Edwards:	Social capital concerns the norms and values people hold that result in, and are the result of, collective and socially negotiated ties and relationships. (Edwards, 2002, p. 1).
Stone & Hughes:	Social capital can be understood as networks of social relations characterized by norms of trust and reciprocity, that can facilitate outcomes at varying social scales, from program and practice levels to the level of communities and nation states. (Stone & Hughes, 2002, p. 1).
Kawachi:	Social capital refers to those features of social relationships-such as interpersonal trust, norms of reciprocity, and membership of civic organizations-which act as resources for individuals and facilitate collective action for mutual benefit. (Kawachi, 1999).
Fukuyama:	Social capital is an instantiated informal norm that promotes cooperation between two or more individuals. (Fukuyama, 1999, p.1).

The theoretical relationships among these dimensions (structure, cognitive elements and collective action) are not clearly established in the literature. There is reason to argue that the three dimensions are dynamically related and not linear. Take, for example social trust, one of the primary dispositions almost universally included in social capital conceptualizations. The organizational trust literature suggests that interpersonal trust is formed as individuals perceive others as, for example, benevolent and reliable (Mishra, 1996). Thus, trust is shaped from the observed history of others' behaviors (Powell, 1996). Putnam (1992) has noted, trust not only lubricates cooperation, but cooperation also breeds trust. There is also evidence that, interactions made likely by organizational structures appear to increase trust (Lewicki & Bunker, 1996). Discerning cause and effect among these dimensions is difficult. Social capital, like trust as described by Powell (1996), "is neither chosen nor embedded but is instead learned and reinforced, hence a product of ongoing interaction and discussion" (p. 63). In view of empirically based causal uncertainty, the current state of social capital theory and research permit us to state a general definition that incorporates the constituent elements, but does not specify directional relationships among them. We offer a parsimonious definition of social capital: Those social structures and cognitive dispositions that act as a resource for collective action.

Paldam (2000) argues for defining social capital carefully so as to "have something against which it is potentially possible to assess the quality of different proxies" (p. 4). This, Paldam notes, is how it can be discerned that measurement is "theory-near." A review of the extant social capital research reveals great diversity with respect to theory-nearness. This is not surprising given that much social capital research has relied on existing data, data not collected or intended to be used in the examination of social capital (Driscoll & Kerchner, 1999). See especially Putnam (2000). Our definition is consistent with the general framework proposed by Grootaert and Bastelaer (2001). Their framework is built around two key dimensions of social capital: its scope (micro, meso, and macro) and its forms (cognitive and structural). We place the study of school community social capital at the meso level, suggesting that the relevant focal points for measurement would be networks (on the structure side) and trust (on the cognitive side), "meso" implying a focus on groupings extended beyond dyads and families, but not as extensive as those generally of interest to economists.

One way to think about the meso level of social capital related to school communities is found in the work of Bryk and Schneider (2002) who note that a "complex web of social exchanges conditions the basic operations of schools" (p. 20). They go on to elucidate the notion of relational trust, which:

> . . . views the social exchanges of schooling as organized around a distinct set of role relationships: teachers with students, teachers with other teachers, teachers with parents and with their school principal. Each party in a role relationship maintains an understanding of his or her role obligations and holds some expectations about the role obligations of the other. Maintenance (and growth) of relational trust in any given role set requires synchrony in these mutual expectations and obligations. . . . Schools work well as organizations when this synchrony is achieved within all of the major role sets that comprise a school community (Bryk & Schneider, 2002, pp. 20–21).

Just as at the micro level, social capital is based on individual-to-individual interaction and dispositions, at the meso level of social capital, the interest is appropriately on the synchrony among the critical role sets that make up the school community.

THEORY-NEAR CRITERIA FOR MEASUREMENT

What would ideal, meso-level, theory-near measurement of structural and cognitive dimensions of social capital look like? What follows is an analysis and construction of criteria that might be used to promote theory-near measures of cognitive and structural dimensions. Stone (2001) has addressed this task for family and community life scholars. But as Groot-aert and van Bastelaer (2001, p. 9) note, "The measurement challenge is to identify a contextually relevant indicator of social capital and to establish an empirical correlation with relevant benefit indicators." This has not been done for the context of public education in the United States.

The cognitive dimension of social capital refers to people's trust and attitudes toward others (Grootaert, Chase, & van Bastelaer, 2002). The approach frequently used to tap generalized trust is a single item measure of social capital: "Generally speaking, would you say that most people can be trusted or that you can't be too careful in dealing with people?" (Glaeser, 2001, p. 7). It is difficult to determine what this type of gross measure captures because its simplicity does not relate to more complex understandings of trust formation, nor is it empirically related to trusting behavior (Glaeser, 2001). Cognitive dimensions should be examined using trust measures that build on an extensive trust theory and that are context specific. Recent work by Hoy and colleagues and others has produced multi-item measures of teacher, parent, and student trust (Barnes, Forsyth, & Adams, 2002; Forsyth, Adams, & Barnes, 2002; Hoy & Tschannen-Moran, 1999; Tschannen-Moran & Hoy, 1998). This series of measures (when aggregated to school level variables) covers trust of one role group for another: teachers for colleagues, parents, students and the principal; parents for the school and the principal; and students for the principal. All of these measures assume that trust can only be measured indirectly. They are also based on the definition of trust drawn from a comprehensive review of literature defining trust as an individual's willingness to be vulnerable to another party based on the confidence that the latter party is benevolent, reliable, competent, honest, and open (Hoy & Tschannen-Moaran, 1999). To measure trust indirectly, these instruments ask respondents to report the degree to which they view others as benevolent, reliable, competent, honest, and open, all constructed to be context specific to schools and roles.

Not only should trust measurement be informed by contemporary trust theory and research, but to be "theory-near" at the meso level the ways trust data are used should reflect the need to describe the trust environment *in situ.* That is, to understand social capital as it operates in school communities it is important to examine the inter-group cognitive dispositions of the school's constituent groups (i.e. parents, teachers, students, administrators). Simple aggregation of individual trust scores to role group levels within a school ignores the importance of trust's reciprocity. Having reviewed the social capital measurement literature, we have given some thought to how this might be done adequately. First, instead of simply considering aggregate levels of trust, for example of teachers for parents, there should be a way to calculate the proximity of trust levels between role group pairs. For example, how proximate are the levels of parental trust of teachers (as reported by parents) and teacher trust of parents (as reported by teachers)? We will call proximate levels of high trust between paired school groups reciprocal trust. This approach approximates the function of the interpersonal trust measures used at the micro-level analyses of social capital. It also addresses the notion of synchrony in mutual expectation as discussed by Bryk and Schneider (2002).

Second, it is reasonable that the homogeneity or heterogeneity of trust perceptions within the schools' constituent role groups is relevant to the formation and outcomes of social capital. Again, simple aggregation of individual trust scores to role group levels within a school ignores the importance of role group synchrony. Aggregates alone provide no information about vital within-group distribution of scores. We call this proposed criterion cohesion. Lack of cohesion renders aggregate role-group trust scores difficult to interpret. A trust aggregate based on homogeneously high individual trust scores means something quite different than an aggregate based on a set of widely distributed individual scores. Two identical averages could have nearly opposite meanings for cohesion.

Third, in meso analyses trust measures need to be multi-directional in order to approximate the reciprocity examined at the micro-level. By establishing the multi-directional criterion, we call attention to the need to examine trust perceptions of all the primary role groups, not just teachers, as is often the case in the current education literature. If all the dyadic group pairings in the school community were examined by way of intergroup reciprocal trust measures, the need for multi-directional measurement would be addressed adequately and simultaneously. However, in the absence of inter-group reciprocal trust measures, the multi-directional measurement requirement can be addressed by separate trust measurement for and by each of the primary role groups. We argue that these three criteria enhance the likelihood of adequate measurement in educational applications, and that their use will ultimately provide a useful understanding of the formation, function and consequences of cognitive social capital.

It is equally important to understand the structural features among constituent role groups (i.e. parents, teachers, students, administrators). The structural dimension has been defined as that which "captures associational activity and the extent of networks within the community" (Grootaert, Chase, & van Bastelaer, 2002, p. 25). On one level, our social capital research target, the school community, already has its structural system (the network of role groups) in place. This is a very different situation from the usual social capital studies such as Putnam's, where the focus is on voluntary membership (Putnam, 2000). It remains to be seen if social capital research on school communities will require the same kind of complex measures that are emerging among economists and network sociologists. Lin (1999) for instance makes a distinction between access and use that seems useful here. An "access" approach to the study of networks in school communities simply describes the accessibility a role group has to other role groups and their members. However, a "use" approach requires descriptions or measurements of actual use, an approach that would clearly require labor intensive measurement techniques.

The social capital literature does provide direction for examining the structural dimension, however, measurement practice varies greatly by target population. Two extremes come to mind at the meso-level of network measurement. On the one hand there are gross measures like Putnam's (1992) that operationalize social capital as the density or number of voluntary organizational memberships in a given population. This approach has its critics. Paldam (2000) points to the differences in the number of contacts individuals have with an organization and suggests that a better network measure would weight membership by intensity (contacts). Lin (1999) suggests network links need to be weighted to account for status of individuals in the network, an idea that may vary in importance by culture. Putnam's approach, which appears to work reasonably well for examining macro level social capital, is probably less useful in school situations where primary structural features (role groups) exist by virtue of the school's conventional organization. On the other hand, Paldam (2000) reports highly complex approaches that map interaction networks and weights them by strength and importance. Theoretically important concepts necessary to include in structural measures can be borrowed from these approaches.

To capture contextually important variation among school communities in the structural dimension, we think some type of density indicator is a vital criterion of adequate measurement. Here density refers to the relative saturation of contact lines that can be drawn among potential interactors (Stone & Hughes, 2000). Total density would be the hypothetical case where there are contact lines among all individuals (as in micro analysis) and all role groups (as in schools). Whether or not meso analysis obviates the theoretical or practical need to include individual level density measurement is problematic. But, it is not clear how inter-group density could be calculated without aggregating some form of individual-to-individual exchanges. Stone (2001) discusses "density/integration" as the degree to which network members "are in each other's networks," potentially another way to operationalize density at the meso-level.

Equally important from a theoretical perspective, a similar measurement challenge arises with the intensity criterion, by which we refer not to relative saturation of possible contact lines but to their frequency of use. Paldam (2000) talks about this idea in terms of weak and strong links; Pope (2002) refers to "degree of engagement;" and Stone (2001) describes "strength of ties" in terms of intimacy, reciprocity, expectation of durability and availability and emotional intensity. Reflective measurement techniques, that is, asking respondents to report frequency of interactions per week, month, or year may be sufficiently sensitive for most school related uses.

Finally, a quality criterion having to do with the importance and relevance of interactions to the goals of the organization can be identified. It makes theoretical sense that interactions that are substantive and related to the ostensible purpose of the network would be important to social capital productivity. On the other hand, non-substantive interactions that simply reinforce perceptions of benevolence and trust clearly develop cognitive social capital as well. This is possibly a criterion uniquely important at the meso-level where organization is both purposive and personal. Precedent for consideration of this criterion can be found in the work of Paldam (2000) who discusses the "importance" of social connections or links and the Australian Bureau of Statistics (2000), which considers the "quality of relationships" as a network descriptor to be examined. Amato (1998) studied relationships in families primarily from the perspective of their "quality." Likewise, Stone (2001) argues for the importance of quality measures when examining family networks. There are self-report instruments that have been used to extract exchange-related data in network sociology and sociometry (Miller, 1975). These may prove useful for studying schools, since survey methods are routinely used to collect the proposed cognitive data as well.

In addition to the complex problems of measurement, there is the question of how the measures of social capital components can be combined to form some meaningful and interpretable conclusions. Grootaert, Chase and Bastelaer (2002) discuss the creation of social capital indices in which different variables "can be combined in an additive index with pre-selected weights, or combined in a multiplicative index" (p. 31). They add that social capital theory is not sufficiently advanced to suggest which approach is appropriate. Others like Svendsen (2000) and Narayan and Cassidy (2001) see factor analysis as a useful tool to weight components of indices of social capital.

To review, the problem of capturing meaningful data for the cognitive and structural dimensions of social capital as appropriately studied at the meso-level has been analyzed. We have argued that meso-cognitive measurement should tap inter-role-group trust (reciprocal trust), within role-group cohesion, and the trust perceptions of all role groups that make up the school (multidirectionality). Meso-structural measurement is more problematic. One approach would be to ignore structure in this research situation, assuming that the existing, formalized role-group structures of schools constitute the relevant structural dimension and to regard them as practically invariable. A second approach, one we think more likely to contribute to understanding social capital in this context, involves examining inter-role-group networks using criteria of density (comparison of actual and potential exchange partners), intensity (frequency of

TABLE 2
Criteria for Adequate Measurement of Social Capital

Cognitive Dimensions:	
1) Reciprocity	High, proximate trust levels between role-groups.
2) Cohesion	Within role-group trust agreement.
3) Multidirectionality	Including trust perceptions from all sectors.
Structural Dimensions:	
1) Intensity	Saturation of contact lines.
2) Density	Frequency of contact line use.
3) Quality	Relevance and importance of exchanges to purpose and goals.

exchange) and quality (importance of exchanges). How these data would be collected and combined to summarize the structural dimension at a meso level will require experimentation. As Stone (2001) has noted despite agreement about the importance of the structural dimension, thus far "studies of social capital rarely investigate social network characteristics explicitly (p. 24).

CONCEPTUAL AND OPERATIONAL ADEQUACY IN THE EDUCATION LITERATURE

Three recent and prominent empirical pieces that examine social capital will be tested against the general conceptual definition of social capital advanced earlier. Their measures will also be compared to the operational criteria for adequacy derived for theory-near, meso-measurement of the cognitive and structural dimensions of social capital. This exercise is not so much a critique of this work, as a demonstration of where our field of inquiry stands on the question of theory-near social capital measurement.

We turn first to "Social Capital and Dropping Out of High School: Benefits to At-Risk Students of Teachers' Support and Guidance," by Croninger and Lee (2001). Although Croninger and Lee offer no formal definition of social capital, it is clear that their focus is on the student-teacher network and their choice of measures further defines what they mean by social capital as including cognitive and structural elements surrounding that relationship. They used a sample of 11,000 individual students from the NELS:88 data. We argue that it is more appropriate to examine social capital using the school as the unit of analysis (meso level), rather than at the individual student level, since social capital is conceptually a human context variable. Individual level analysis takes the "social" out of the mix and focuses on individual access to capital.

Their approach to measuring the cognitive dimension of social capital does not consider reciprocal trust, cohesion, or multidirectional trust. Their design focuses on the social capital available to individual students, not school communities, as consisting of student trust of the teacher. They do not examine reciprocal trust of teachers for students. Since there is no aggregated role group of students, cohesion cannot be examined. They do not explore any other trust relations within schools, only student trust of teacher. Six items from the NELS data measure two dimensions of student trust of teacher, namely student perceptions of the teacher as benevolent and competent.

To measure the structural dimension of social capital Croninger and Lee (2001) used a single item asking teachers if individual students talked with them about schoolwork, academic decisions, or personal matters outside of class. Their design does not consider network density, intensity, or quality of exchanges. Since they examine random teacher-student dyads from a national sample to capture structure, it is impossible to consider network density. Moreover, the format of the item that produced the structural data did not allow the researchers to determine intensity (frequency of interactions) or quality.

Overall, our assessment of their approach to the measurement of social capital is that it is inadequate. The proxy used to measure structure is particularly weak. This study may be an argument for why social capital needs to be studied in school communities where the trust and network environments can be examined comprehensively. *Post hoc* constructions of social capital measures, typical of studies using large data sets, will of necessity be problematic until more theory-near measures are included in the data set.

Next, we turn to *Trust in Schools: A Core Resource for Improvement* by Bryk and Schneider (2002). Although not technically a book about social capital and schools, Bryk and Schneider do discuss social capital at length, and in fact, their conceptualization of relational trust emphasizes trust as a property of schools, an approach consistent with meso-level exploration of social capital in school communities. They cite and are inspired by Coleman's conceptualization of social capital "as a property of the relational ties among individuals within a social system" (p. 13). They note that Coleman sees two general causes of high levels of social capital, network closure and the easy articulation of mutual expectations and mutual assessment related to the meeting of obligations; the latter property is labeled trustworthiness by Coleman. The essential social capital elements are present in this approach: structural and cognitive dimensions that produce a cooperative resource.

Bryk and Schneider (2002) include extensive case analyses of three schools to test the adequacy of their relational trust theory. Their model is, or could be, an elaboration of social capital theory in the school context, incorporating cognitive and structural dimensions (both organizational and individual social exchanges) as they affect cooperative activity. However, in this research they did not use potential structural variables (i.e. peer collaboration, reflective dialogue, and outreach to parents) together with trust variables to create a social capital index. We are interested in the quantitative analyses contained in the book, particularly the conceptualization and measurement of trust as it represents an effort to operationalize social capital.

Bryk and Schneider's attention to the cognitive dimension of social capital is given to three trust measures: teacher-parent trust (13 items), teacher-principal trust (9 items), and teacher-teacher trust (6 items). These instruments are based on a definition of trust developed by Mishra (as is the Hoy-Tshannon Moran definition we referred to earlier) and overlap Mishra's criteria significantly (Bryk & Schneider, 2002). In their school level analyses, they averaged the three role-relational trust measures creating a composite. Examining the Bryk and Schneider approach from the perspective of the three criteria developed earlier (reciprocal trust, cohesion and multidirectionality), we find that they do indeed measure the trust of three different role groups. They fall short of true multidirectionality because all of these measures are taken from the teacher perspective. Consequently, reciprocal trust cannot be calculated among the role groups, and cohesion of trust perceptions within role groups is left unexamined. It is they who introduce the notion of inter-role group synchrony, but we see no effort here to operationalize that concept. Although this research makes significant contributions to conceptualizing the trust environment of schools, it does not advance a theory-near set of social capital measures. Their variables did include likely candidates for the analysis of the structural dimension of social capital (peer collaboration, reflective dialogue and outreach to parents), but these were treated as dependent variables and not incorporated with cognitive variables into an index of social capital.

Last, we turn to "Relational Networks, Social Trust, and Norms: A Social Capital Perspective on Students' Chances of Academic Success" by Roger Goddard (2003). Goddard relies on Coleman and Hoffer's (1987) theoretical components of structure and function to talk about social capital. His approach takes relational networks as the structural dimension and social trust and other norms as the functional dimension (Goddard, 2003). This cuts the concepts a bit differently than we do. Like Goddard, we see social networks as the structural element, but add a separate dimension (the cognitive) to cover trust and other norms. Moreover, we see collective action as function. No matter, Goddard clearly intends to include both dimensions that we call the structural and the cognitive in his operationalization of social capital.

Goddard (2003) measures social capital with an eleven item scale given to teachers and developed to tap both cognitive and structural dimensions, specifically trust/norms and networks. The data from this study were aggregated to the school level (n = 45) and factor analyzed using principal-axis extraction. By our count, three of the items tap network and the remaining eight items tap trust or norms supportive of academic achievement. It appears that there are six trust items equally divided between teacher trust of parents and teacher trust of students. The trust items seem to be aligned with three of the five trust dimensions included in our trust definition (benevolence, reliability, and competence).

Like the two previous studies, Goddard examines the cognitive dimension of social capital from the viewpoint of only one role category, teachers, a unidirectional approach obviating the possibility of calculating reciprocal trust. No effort is made to examine within group cohesion related to the two trust categories. With respect to the structural dimension, Goddard's measures tap both intensity (interaction frequency) and quality (interaction productivity). Perceptions about parent-teacher interaction frequency and quality are from the perspective of teachers only. Density (or what is sometimes called closure) is not examined.

Goddard's effort to measure social capital is more consistent with the criteria we evolved than either of the previous studies, at least with respect to the structural dimension. If, however, the structural dimension is to be measured by perceptions, like the cognitive dimension, it makes sense to make those perceptions multidirectional also, not just teacher perceptions. In addition, the items or techniques used to obtain data on intensity and quality can, in our view, be made more precise. The question as to whether the network variable should be measured in this straightforward way (simply asking respondents to comment on the frequency and quality of their exchanges), or whether some more indirect method of assessing the structure of a social group should be used has not been answered.

DEMONSTRATION STUDY

Examining new data, we attempt a demonstration study that is more theory-near than those we've reviewed earlier in the chapter. Our empirical exploration of meso-level social capital derives from the assertion that school community social capital should be operationalized according to both its cognitive dimension (measures capturing trust reciprocity, cohesion and multidirectionality), as well as its structural dimension (measures describing network density, intensity and quality). As previously illustrated, extant social capital studies often analyze at an inappropriate level (micro-rather than meso-), examine only one of the two constitutive dimensions, and/or ignore measurement criteria that would assure theory-nearness, such as those we've discussed. The purpose of this empirical demonstration is to explore the feasibility of operationalizing social capital according to both its cognitive and structural dimensions, while seeking to satisfy the adequacy criteria we established earlier.

Grootaert, Chase, & van Bastelaer (2002) note that in addition to measuring the structural and cognitive dimensions of social capital it is also important to measure social capital's output. Some education-related research examines social capital's effects on a measure of academic achievement (See: Croninger & Lee, 2001; Goddard, 2003; Israel, Beaulieu, & Hartless, 2001; Teachman & Paasch, 1996). Consistent with these precedents, we selected school performance as our output variable.

Data Sources

Data for this study were collected directly from schools and the state department of education database. A random sample of schools was drawn from the 847 public school population in one quadrant of a Midwestern state. These schools were affiliated with 101 school districts, of which 91 agreed to participate in the study. The final sample consisted of 79 schools: 22 elementary schools, 30 middle schools, and 27 high schools. Sampled school ethnicity and economic status were representative of the state's population. Fifteen parents, 10 teachers, and 15 students (5th, 7th, or 11th grade, depending on school level) were randomly selected from each school. The response rate was 56 percent (1,836 out of 3,239): 69 percent for teachers, 49 percent for parents, and 53 percent for students. The state department of education provided school socioeconomic status and prior school performance data.

Operational Measures

Reciprocal Trust

Reciprocal trust refers to proximate high trust levels of two role groups (i.e., parents and teachers). For example, when teacher trust for parents and parent trust for teachers are both high (proximate to each other), this condition constitutes reciprocal trust. Conversely, when parent trust of teachers is high but teacher trust of parents is low, parent trust is not reciprocated by teachers. Since the concept of reciprocal trust requires that two conditions be met (high levels of trust and proximity), low parent trust reciprocated by low teacher trust is not reciprocal trust. Low trust by both parties is reciprocated distrust. To test the utility of this construct, we operationalized reciprocal trust as the proximity of trust levels between parent and teacher role groups. The level of proximity was determined by 1) measuring parent trust of teachers and teacher trust of parents 2) classifying parent and teacher trust levels as high, medium, or low, and 3) comparing parent and teacher trust levels

The Parent Trust of School Scale (Forsyth, Adams, & Barnes, 2002) and the teacher trust of client items on the Trust Scale (Hoy & Tschannen-Moran, 1999) were used as the basis for calculating reciprocal trust. The Parent Trust of School Scale consists of 10 Likert items with an eight point response set ranging from "Strongly Disagree" to "Strongly Agree." Items were developed to reflect each of the five facets of trust: openness, honesty, benevolence, competency, and reliability (Hoy & Tschannen-Moran, 1999). Sample items include, " Kids at this school are well cared for," "This school is always ready to help," "I never worry about my child when he/she is there." An alpha of .97 calculated with data from this study confirmed strong internal item consistency as in previous studies.

Fifteen items on the Trust Scale (Hoy & Tschannen-Moran, 1999) measure teacher trust of clients. These items have a six point Likert response set ranging from "Strongly Agree" to "Strongly Disagree." Similar to the Parent Trust Scale, teacher trust of client items reflect the five facets of trust. Sample items include "Teachers in this school trust the parents," "Teachers think most of the parents do a good job," "Teachers can believe what parents tell them." An alpha of .91 calculated with data from this study confirms strong internal item consistency as in previous studies.

Next, a frequency distribution of the school level parent and teacher-client trust variables was calculated in order to classify school scores as high, medium, or low. Parent and teacher-client trust for each school were then juxtaposed in order to assign a reciprocal trust value for each school. The comparisons of parent and teacher-client trust levels for each school resulted in nine different combinations. Table 3 depicts the classification scheme.

TABLE 3
Reciprocal Trust Classifications

Parent Trust	Teacher-Client Trust		Reciprocal Trust
High	High	=	High
High	Medium	=	High
Medium	High	=	High
Medium	Medium	=	Medium
Medium	Low	=	Low
Low	Medium	=	Low
High	Low	=	Low
Low	High	=	Low
Low	Low	=	Low

Multidirectional Trust

We proposed that multidirectional trust, that is, measurement of perceived trust by all or most of the role groups within a school be used as a proxy for closure. Trust develops through the repeated exchanges between individuals and/or groups. Productive social capital implies high trust dispositions among all role groups for all other role groups. Adequate measurement of social capital then, requires tapping the trust perceptions of most or all of the role groups for the other role groups. While we do not exhaust all the possible trust relationships among role groups within a school, we tap enough of them to claim multidirectionality. Our multidirectional measurements of trust includes student trust of principal, parent trust of principal, teacher trust of teachers, teacher trust of principal, and the reciprocal trust between parents and teachers.

The Student Trust of Principal Scale (Barnes, Forsyth, & Adams, 2003) was used to measure student-principal trust. Twelve items with a four point Likert response set ranging from "Strongly Disagree" to "Strongly Agree" make up the scale. Sample items included "The principal at my school is helpful," The principal at my school is there for students when needed," and "The principal at my school treats all students with respect." An alpha of .96 calculated from data for this study indicates strong item consistency.

Parent trust of principal was operationalized with the Parent Trust of Principal Scale (Barnes, Forsyth, & Adams, 2002). The short form of the scale consists of 15 items with an eight point Likert response set ranging from "Strongly Disagree" to "Strongly Agree." Sample items include, "the principal at this school is well intentioned," "The principal at this school is always ready to help," and "The principal at this school keeps an open door." An alpha of .99 calculated from data for this study supports strong item consistency as found in previous studies.

The Trust Scale (Hoy & Tschannen-Moran, 1999) was used to measure teacher trust of teachers and teacher trust of principal. Eleven items on the scale pertain to teacher-teacher trust and eight to teacher-principal trust. All items have a six point Likert response set ranging from "Strongly Agree" to "Strongly Disagree." Alpha values calculated from these data were .93 and .94 respectively.

Cohesion

Social structures within organizations develop through the social interactions among the organization's agents. It is the combination of the individual agents' interaction patterns and relationships that cultivate organizational social capital. That is, social capital is a collective phenomenon formed through individual actions and attitudes aggregated to the meso-level. Aggregating data to the organizational level, however, may produce the unintended consequence of suppressing individual effects. For example, a school's parent trust level is determined by the aggregation of individual parents' trust of school scores. The dispersion of individual parent scores is lost in the aggregation process, yet the relative cohesion of parental scores clearly has importance for the accurate description of a group's trust. The concept of cohesion captures the relative homogeneity of a role-group's trust perceptions lost through aggregation. Cohesion was operationalized as the within school dispersion of scores on the teacher-client trust and parent-school trust variables. In this study, dispersion was measured by using the variances of these two variables.

Social Structure

Social structure refers to the network of relationships and social ties manifested within an organization. We believe that the meso-measurement of social structure dimension of social capital can be achieved with some precision by describing the density, intensity, and quality of associational activity among institutional agents. Ideally, to accomplish this, measures of structural social capital within schools should tap the contact lines among role groups, the frequency of use for these contact lines, and the importance of interactions among the role groups.

The Collaboration Survey (Tschannen-Moran, 2001) was used to operationalize school social structure. Three collaborative processes are measured with this scale: teacher collaboration with the principal on management decisions, teacher collaboration with teaching colleagues on instructional decisions, and parent collaboration on school level decisions. Items were developed to measure perceived teacher and parent influence on the aforementioned school decisions. Each collaboration item begins with a question followed by a decision type. Sample questions and decision types include: "To what extent do teachers have influence over these types of decisions? selecting personnel, determining how to allocate resources;" "To what extent do teacher committees have influence over decisions of this kind? determining professional development needs and goals, evaluating curriculum;" and "To what extent do parents have influence over the outcome of these types of decisions? determining areas in need of improvement, determining how to allocate resources." Alphas of .91, .91, and .96 calculated from data for this study indicates good item consistency.

School Performance

School performance was operationalized using the Academic Performance index (API) score for each school in the sample. The API scores ranges from 0–1500 with a state mean average of 1000. API scores are calculated by student performance on the state mandated criterion reference examinations (at least 80 per cent of the index), student attendance rates, and academic excellence rates.

Socioeconomic Status

The percentage of students within a school qualifying for the federal free or reduced lunch program was used as a proxy for socioeconomic status. Scores for this sample range from .07 to .97

Data Analysis

This empirical investigation was a priori; theory provided the rationale for exploring the importance of using "theory near" measures to study social capital within schools. Theories and empirical studies on the functionality of the cognitive and structural dimensions of social capital are sparse; therefore this study was exploratory. The objective was to analyze the relationships between the cognitive and structural sources of social capital and a measure of functionality, in this case school performance. These relationships were examined through two analytical techniques: bivariate correlations and hierarchical multiple regression. The aggregation of individual level data to school level data preceded the analyses.

Similar to other forms of multiple regression, hierarchical regression explains the variance in a criterion variable due to the set of predictor variables. Further, the standardized regression coefficients (ß) indicate the independent effect of each predictor variable on the criterion variable. Hierarchical regression has the additional advantage of partitioning variance in the criterion variable attributed to different predictor variables, or predictor variable sets. This feature allowed us to control for the effect of school socioeconomic status on school performance by partialing out the explained variance in school performance attributed to socioeconomic status. The order of entry for the variables in the model is crucial to the results. Pedhazur (1997) notes that the covariates (control variables) should be entered into the model first, followed by variables postulated to have larger effects on the dependent variable. For this study, school socioeconomic status was entered at model one, reciprocal trust and the other trust variables were entered at model two, and the structural variables of collaboration were entered at model three.

Results

The Pearson correlation coefficients are reported in Table 4. Reciprocal trust was positively related to school performance ($r = .58$, $p < .01$). Similarly, the dimensions of trust, parent trust of principal ($r = .43$, $p < .05$), teacher trust of teachers ($r = .54$, $p < .01$), teacher trust of principal ($r = .41$, $p < .01$) and student trust of principal ($r = .39$, $p < .01$), were positively related to school performance, suggesting that multidirectional trust perceptions are associated with higher school performance. Of the collaboration variables, teacher-principal (r = .33, p < .01) and teacher-teacher (r = .23, p < .05) collaboration were significantly related to school performance. The relationships between the cohesion variables (the variances) and school performance were not statistically significant. Analyzed as a whole, these results indicate that cognitive social capital dimensions of reciprocal trust and multi-directional trust as well as structural dimensions of teacher-principal and teacher-teacher collaboration are associated with school performance.

Table 5 displays the hierarchical regression results. As expected, socioeconomic status in step one (R = .71, p < .01) explained 50 percent of the variability in school performance. Results reported in step two (R Square Change = .15, p < .01) indicate that the cognitive dimensions of social capital predicted an additional 15 percent of the variability in school performance. In step three (R Square Change = .01, NS), the measures of the structural dimension (parent and teacher collaboration) added one percent to the final R Square (R Square = .66), but not a statistically significant improvement over step two in its predictive power of school performance. The ß values in step three indicate that only reciprocal trust and parent trust of principal independently accounted for a significant amount of the variability in school performance. Thus, these cognitive dimensions of reciprocal trust have functional attributes.

Performance of the reciprocal trust variable is of particular interest because it represents an experiment in school social capital measurement unique to this demonstration. As mentioned, its bivariate correlation with school performance was strong and significant (r = .58, p < .01). It is the only variable in the bivariate matrix significantly related to all of the other variables (and at the .01 level). Consistent with theoretical arguments, it was positively related to all trust and collaboration variables and negatively related to SES and the two variance variables. In the regression, reciprocal trust is the more powerful of only two social capital variables that predicted school performance (step 2, ß = .35, p < .01; model 3, ß = .30, p < .01). These results are encouraging with respect to the development of robust measures of social capital that incorporate the critical notion of reciprocity.

The two cohesion variables, parent-school variance and teacher-client variance, have bivariate correlations of −.21 and −.20 (both not significant but in the expected direction); however, their ßs, when regressed on school performance are low, but positive, indicating a likelihood that their effects are suppressed in step 3. This finding suggests that an alternative way to capture the importance of cohesion is needed, possibly by weighting the reciprocal trust value or the constituent means before combining them to form reciprocal trust rather than treating cohesion as a separate variable in the regression. At least two other variables, teacher-teacher trust and teacher-principal trust appear to have suppressed effects in step

TABLE 4
Correlation Matrix

	SP	RT	SES	PTP	STP	PC	TPC	TTC	VTCT	VPTS	TTP	TTT
SP	1.0	.58**	0.70**	.29**	.23*	.22	.33**	.23*	-.21	-.20	.19	.22
RT		1.0	-.41**	.43**	.38**	.46**	.43**	.52**	-.32**	-.32**	.41**	.54**
SES			1.0	-.10	-.01	-.12	-.23*	-.13	.16	.20	-.20	-.23*
PTP				1.0	.51**	.57**	.41**	.43**	-.26*	-.42**	.65**	.47**
STP					1.0	.32**	.24*	.21	-.21	-.12	.34**	.27*
PC						1.0	.30**	.37**	-.10	-.46**	.34**	.32**
TPC							1.0	.57**	-.21	-.22	.44**	.41**
TTC								1.0	-.35**	-.24*	.63**	.58**
VTCT									1.0	-.00	-.12	-.10
VPST										1.0	-.25*	-.26*
TPT											1.0	.74**
TTT												1.0

Notes: SP-School Performance; RT-Reciprocal Trust; SES-Socioeconomic Status; PTP-Parent Trust of Principal; STP-Student Trust of Principal; PC-Parent Collaboration; TPC-Teacher Principal Collaboration; TTC-Teacher to Teacher Collaboration; VTCT-Variance Teacher Client Trust; VPST-Variance Parent School Trust; TPT-Teacher Principal Trust; TTT-Teacher Teacher Trust.

TABLE 5
Hierarchical Regression Results

Model	ß	Significance
Step 1		
Socioeconomic Status	−.71	<.01 **
R = .71 **, R square = .50		
Step 2		
Socioeconomic Status	−.60	<.01 **
Reciprocal Trust	.35	<.01 **
Parent-Principal Trust	.28	<.01 **
Student-Principal Trust	.01	.95
Teacher-Principal Trust	−.10	.47
Teacher-Teacher Trust	−.15	.21
Parent-School Variance	.10	.26
Teacher-Client Variance	.03	.66
R = .80 **, R Square = .65		
R Square Change = .15**		
Step 3		
Socioeconomic Status	−.61	<.01 **
Reciprocal Trust	.30	.01 **
Parent-Principal Trust	.28	<.05 *
Student-Principal Trust	.01	.95
Teacher-Principal Trust	−.13	.34
Teacher-Teacher Trust	−.17	.16
Parent-School Variance	.11	.21
teacher-Client Variance	.05	.53
Parent collaboration	.03	.80
Teacher/Principal collaboration	.08	.37
Teacher/Teacher collaboration	.07	.57
R = .81 **, R Square = .66		
R Square Change = .01, NS		

Notes: * ≤ p .05; ** p ≤ .01

3. Their bivariate correlations with school performance are .22 and .19 respectively (not significant), but in Model 2 of the regression, their ßs are −.17 and −.13 respectively.

The results just reported consider a very narrow and relatively remote output measure for social capital, academic performance. These same social capital measures could prove more powerful when used with output measures that are more proximate to collective action, social capital's theoretically supported direct output.

LESSONS LEARNED ABOUT THE DEFINITION AND MESO-MEASUREMENT OF SOCIAL CAPITAL

Defining the concept as "those social structures and cognitive dispositions that act as a resource for collective action" did seem to function at the appropriate level of abstraction for all the tasks we addressed: Developing criteria for adequate measurement, reviewing existing research, and speculating and experimenting with possible approaches to measurement. Overall, the use of this straightforward definition can be productive for meso-level applications in education research.

Our meso-measurement of the cognitive dimension of social capital can be evaluated according to the criteria of reciprocal trust, cohesion and multi-dimensionality, just as the three previous studies were. The criterion of reciprocal trust, we think, is critical to formulating meaningful meso-measurement because conceptually it taps the level and proximity of trust between role-group dyads. We argue that readiness and potential for collective action would reside in reciprocated, high trust relationships between constituent role groups in schools. As explained in the previous section, we were able to construct a combined indicator of reciprocal trust between teachers and parents in our sample. The resultant ordinal level variable correlated highly and significantly with all of the trust and collaboration variables we considered. Moreover, it was the most important and significant variable in our model, which used social capital to predict academic performance.

Although this finding offers hope that meso-level reciprocal trust can be measured and that the construct is reasonably robust, we hope to find better ways to combine the two dimensions (trust strength and proximity) into a single reciprocal trust index. For example the average of the two group trust means weighted by the proximity of the two trust means might be effective and also retain more of the variance that had to be discarded in the categorical assignment method we used in our demonstration study. As an experiment, we averaged the Teacher Trust of Client and Parent Trust of School means for each school and then added a weight (1–10) to that average, based on the proximity of the two means, ten representing very high proximity. The weights were calculated by dividing the distribution of proximity scores (TTC subtracted from PTS) into categories each composed of 10 percent of the distribution. Resulting Reciprocal Trust scores were normally distributed and had relationships with the other variables in the regression equation very similar to our original reciprocal trust construction, including the dependent variable, school performance (R Square = .65 for step 3; Reciprocal Trust ß = .28, p < .03).

To capture the second cognitive criterion concept of cohesion (within group homogeneity of trust perceptions), we used the simple variances of the two constituent variables that make up our reciprocal trust variable (teacher-client trust and parent-school trust). We have argued that role group agreement on trust perception is a reasonable predictor of readiness for collective action. The larger the variance (indicating wide score dispersion on trust measures), the lower the cohesion. In the table of bivariate correlations, both variances under consideration were negatively related to reciprocal trust, as expected. Or, stated differently, cohesion is positively related to reciprocal trust. When entered into the general regression equation predicting academic performance, our two cohesion measures (Parent-School Trust Variance and Teacher-Client Trust Variance) were not significant predictors. Despite the disappointing performance of the cohesion operationalization, we are reluctant to discard it given its theoretical reasonableness. We wonder if the independent measures of cohesion within the two groups could be added as weightings to the reciprocal trust index?

To achieve multidirectionality, the third criterion of cognitive measurement of trust, we included measures of teacher trust of parent, student, other teachers and principal; parent trust of principal and school; and student trust of principal. Our analytical method, multiple regression, worked against us here. As expected, many of these trust measures were highly correlated. Thus, after accounting for the always powerful effects of SES and one or two of the strongest trust variables in the regression analysis the effects of the remaining trust variables were suppressed. Finding that some of the trust variables do not make a unique contribution to the prediction of academic performance in this study does not advance an argument that these multidirectional trust variables are unimportant. It may be a specification problem (possibly an unspecified intervening variable) in addition to suppression. In our perfect world of operationalizing the cognitive dimension, all role-group pairs would be examined for reciprocity, simultaneously meeting the criterion of multidirectionality. Absent such utopian conditions, we are still persuaded that tapping the trust perceptions from multiple quarters of the organization will enhance the adequacy of social capital measures.

Our meso-measurement of the structural dimension of social capital can be evaluated according to the criteria of density, intensity and quality. Approaches to measuring structure, such as the "membership in voluntary organizations" proxy used by Putnam (2000), are possibly not sufficiently sensitive for meaningful application at the meso-level in school communities. Without adopting the complex approaches of network sociology, we evolved a set of criteria that should add precision to the characterization of networks in a specific context. Again, density refers to the proportion of possible interpersonal or inter-group links that are used (closed). Possible ways to tap density range from actually calculating a percentage based on reported exchange partners to examining the general reports of the "extent to which" these exchange channels exist. For this study we chose the latter approach, examining teacher collaboration with principal on management decisions, teacher collaboration with other teachers on instructional decisions, and parents collaboration with school staff on school level decisions.

The remaining two criteria of intensity (exchange frequency) and quality (importance and mission relevance) were tapped by our three collaboration measures. However, these measures can probably be best described as weak proxies for social capital's structural dimension. It was not entirely surprising then that none of the structural variables contributed significantly or uniquely to the explanation of academic performance even though the bivariate correlations between all three collaboration measures and reciprocal trust were reasonably strong and significant. It is not clear what role incorrect specification of the dependent variable and a failure to specify confounding variables may have played here. Nor is the meaning of the obvious suppression of effects of the collaboration variables clear.

Some conclusions are in order. First, the general conceptual definition of social capital offered early in this chapter seems both adequate and challenging. It requires that operational definitions of social capital address its formation by way of cognitive and structural dimensions and an outcome dimension by way of collective action. The conceptual definition appeared useful in organizing all phases of these analyses, including development of criteria of adequacy, critiquing extant research, and probing theory-nearness.

Our insistence that more attention be paid to meso-measurement as the appropriate standard for school research places additional challenges on scholars. Unless researchers address these challenges, social capital research will neither produce good theory nor practical knowledge for school improvement. Early modest success with crude social capital measures (significant findings) may have contributed to scholar complacence; however, these successes may have been more the consequence of the variable's power than the precision and validity of measures.

The cognitive dimension appears adequately operationalized as social trust. Yet, approaches taken by education researchers so far seem too limited in scope. Criteria for measurement adequacy (reciprocal trust, cohesion and multidimensionality) can help here. Although our success in demonstrating the utility of these criteria was limited, such criteria are useful in pressing for more precise meso-measurement.

The structural dimension poses an even greater challenge, partly because so little attention has been directed toward it in education research. What we have learned here can be framed as a series of questions:

1. Is it necessary to measure the structural dimension at the meso-level, when schools have mandatory role groups (parents, students, teachers, administrators) that constitute their structure?
2. How should the structural dimension be operationalized?
3. How should the structural dimension data be collected (self-reported perceptions, more objective observations)?
4. Are the appropriate measures aimed at reports of individual-to-individual exchanges, or perceptions of individuals about group-to-group interaction?
5. How should individual data be aggregated and combined into a single index of structural social capital?

In partial answer to these questions, we have proposed that the structural dimension does indeed need to be included in education study of social capital despite the existence of standard role groups in schools. Good theory development hinges on developing understandings of how the structural dimension develops, varies, responds to context, leadership, and combines with the cognitive dimension to effect readiness for collective action. Having reviewed much of the current social capital literature, we believe the structural dimension is best examined as the social network of the school community, with particular attention paid to the networks surrounding and constituting the primary role groups. Three criteria (network density, intensity and quality) can be used to shape adequate indicators. Our opportunistic measure of the structural dimension in the demonstration study proved inadequate, falling short on all three criteria.

Finally, there is the problem of a general, meso-level social capital index, somehow computed from information about both cognitive and structural dimensions of the school community. As mentioned earlier, social capital scholars outside of education are unsure about the appropriate ways to do this as well (Grootaert, Chase, & Bastelaer, 2002).

One suggestion would be to use Structural Equation Modeling (SEM) to test the theory underlying our conceptualization of social capital as well as

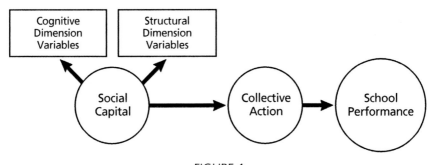

FIGURE 1
Theoretical Social Capital Model

the relationship between social capital and other meso-level constructs. Using SEM, social capital would be treated as a latent variable and the structural and cognitive dimensions would be the measures, or indicators, of social capital. A plausible model is illustrated in Figure 1. Testing such a model is contingent on the development of valid and reasonably precise and practical measures of the structural dimension appropriate for the school context.

REFERENCES

Amato, P. (1998). More than money? Men's contribution to their children's lives. In A. Booth & A. Creuter (Eds.), *Men in families: When do they get involved? What difference does it make?* New Jersey: Erlbaum.

Australian Bureau of Statistics. (2000). *Measuring social capital: Current collections and future directions.* Retrieved August 18, 2003, from www.abs.gov.au

Barnes, L. B., Forsyth, P. B., & Adams, C. M. (2003). *Student trust of principal: Scale development.* Working Paper: Oklahoma State University

Barnes, L. B., Forsyth, P. B., & Adams, C. M. (2002, April). *Parental trust of principal: Scale development.* Paper presented at the annual meeting of the American Educational Research Association, New Orleans.

Blau, P. M. (1964). *Exchange and power in social life.* New York: Wiley.

Bourdieu, P. (1986) The forms of capital. In J. E. Richardson (Ed.), *Handbook of theory for research in the sociology of education.* Westport, CT: Greenwood.

Bryk, A. S., & Schneider, B. (2002). *Trust in schools: A core resource for improvement.* New York: Russell Sage Foundation.

Coleman, J. S., & Hoffer, T. B. (1987). *Public and private high schools: The impact of communities.* New York: Basic Books.

Croninger, R. G., & Lee, V. E. (2001). Social capital and dropping out of high school: Benefits to at-risk students of teachers' support and guidance. *Teachers College Record, 103*(4): 548–581.

Driscoll, M. E., & Kerchner, C. T. (1999). The implications of social capital for schools, communities, and cities: Educational administration as if a sense of place mattered. In J. Murphy & K. Louis (Eds.), *Handbook of Research on Educational Administration* (2nd Ed., pp. 385–404). San Francisco: Jossey-Bass.

Durkheim, E. (1966). *The rules of sociological method.* 8th ed. Translated by John A. Spaulding & G. Simpson. G. Simpson (Ed.), New York: Free Press.

Edwards, R. (2002). *Social capital: Basic concepts and definitions.* In The Sloan Work and Family Encyclopedia. Retrieved August 18, 2003, from http://www.bc.edu/bc_org/avp/wfnetwork/rft/wfpedia

Forsyth, P. B., Adams, C. M., & Barnes, L. B. (2002). *Parental Trust: Scale development.* Paper presented at the annual meeting of the American Educational Research Association, New Orleans.

Fukuyama, F. (1999). *Social capital and civil society.* Paper presented at the IMF Conference on Second Generation Reforms, George Mason University.

Glaeser, E. L. (2001). *The formation of social capital.* Retrieved August 18, 2003, from www.isuma.net/v02n01/glaeser/glaeser_e.shtml

Glaeser, E. L., Laibson, D., Scheinkman, J. A., & Soutter, C. (1999). *What is social capital? The determinants of trust and trustworthiness.* National Bureau of Economic Research. Retrieved August 28 from www.nber.org/papers/w7216

Goddard, R. D. (2003). Relational networks, social trust, and norms: A social capital perspective on students' chances of academic success. *Educational Evaluation and Policy Analysis, 25*(1), 59–74.

Grootaert C., & van Bastelaer, T. (2001). *Understanding and measuring social capital: A synthesis of findings and recommendations from the social capital initiative.* Retrieved August 15, 2003, from www.worldbank.org/socialdevelopment

Grootaert C., Chase, R., & van Bastelaer, T. (2002). *The social capital assessment tool: Instruction manual #3: Analysis.* Retrieved August 15, 2003, from www.worldbank.org/socialdevelopment

Hoffman, J., Sabo, D., Bliss, J., & Hoy, W. K. (1994). Building a culture of trust. *Journal of School Leadership, 4,* 484–501.

Hoy, W. K., & Tschannen-Moran, M. (1999). Five faces of trust: An empirical confirmation in urban elementary schools. *Journal of School Leadership, 9*(4), 184–208.

Homans, G. C. (1961). *Social behavior: Its elementary forms.* New York: Harcourt Brace Jovanovich.

Homans, G. C. (1974). *Social behavior: Its elementary forms* (2nd ed.). New York: Harcourt Brace Jovanovich.

Israel, G., Beaulieu, L., & Heartless, G. (2001). The influence of family and community social capital on educational achievement. *Rural Sociology, 66*(1), 43–69.

Kawachi, I. (1999). Social capital and community effects on population and individual health. *Annals of NY Academy of Sciences. 896,* 120–130.

Lewicki, R. J., & Bunker B. B. (1996). Developing and maintaining trust in work relationships. In R. M. Kramer & T. R. Tyler (Eds.), *Trust in organizations: Frontiers of theory and research* (pp. 114–139). Thousand Oaks, CA: Sage.

Lin, N. (1999). Building a network theory of social capital. *Connections, 22,* 28–51.

Mattessich, P. W., & Monsey, B. R. (1992). *Collaboration: What makes it work?* St Paul, MN: Amherst H. Wilder Foundation.

Miller, J. (1975). Isolation in organizations: Alienation from authority, control, and expressive relations. *Administrative Science Quarterly, 20,* 260–270.

Mishra, A. K. (1996). Organizational responses to crisis: The centrality of trust. In R. M. Kramer & Tom R. Tyler (Eds.), *Trust in organizations: Frontiers of theory and research* (pp. 261–287). Thousand Oaks, CA: Sage.

Narayan, D. & Cassidy, M. F. (2001). A dimensional approach to measuring social capital: Development and validation of a social capital inventory. *Current Sociology, 49*(2), 59–102.

Paldam, M. (2000, June). Social capital: One or many?: Definition and Measurement. Paper presented at the IMAD Conference, Portoroz, Slovenia.

Pedhazur, E. (1997). *Multiple regression in behavioral research: Explanation and prediction.* (3rd ed.). Fort Worth, TX: Harcourt Brace.

Pope, J. (2002). *Social capital and social capital indicators: A reading list.* Retrieved August 130, 2003, www.publichealth.gov.au

Powell, W. W. (1996). Trust-Based forms of governance. In R. M. Kramer & Tom R. Tyler (Eds.), *Trust in organizations: Frontiers of theory and research* (pp. 51–67). Thousand Oaks, CA: Sage.

Putnam, R. D. (2000). *Bowling alone: The collapse and revival of American community.* New York: Siman & Schuster.

Putnam, R. D. (1995). Bowling alone: America's declining social capital. *Journal of Democracy, 6,* 65–78.

Putnam, R. D. (1993). The prosperous community: Social capital and public life. *The American Prospect, 4,* 11–18.

Putnam, R. D. (1992). *Making democracy work.* Princeton, NJ: Princeton University Press.

Stone, W. (2001). *Measuring social capital: Towards a theoretically informed measurement framework for researching social capital in family and community life.* Research Paper No. 24. Retrieved August 28, 2003, from www.aifs.org.au

Stone, W., & Hughes, J. (2002). *Measuring social capital: Towards a standardized approach.* Paper presented at the Australasian Evaluation Society International Conference, Wollongong, Australia.

Svendsen, G. T. (2000). *Social capital: A standard method of measurement.* Retrieved August 18, 2003, www.hha.d/eok/nat/staff/gts_form.htm

Teachman, J., & Paasch, K. (1996). Social capital and dropping out of school early. *Journal of Marriage & Family, 58*(3), 773–784.

Tschannen-Moran, M. (2001). Collaboration and the need for trust. *Journal of Educational Administration, 39*(4), 308–331.

Tschannen-Moran, M., & Hoy, W. K. (1998). A conceptual and empirical analysis of trust in schools. *Journal of Educational Administration, 36,* 334–52.

Van der Gaag, M., & Snijders, T. (2002). *An approach to the measurement of individual social capital.* Paper presented at the SCALE Conference on Social Capital, Amsterdam, Netherlands.

CHAPTER 10

AN EXPLORATORY ANALYSIS OF FACULTY TRUST IN HIGHER EDUCATION

Alan R. Shoho and Page A. Smith

This study involved the development of an instrument to measure faculty trust in higher education. First, after an extensive review of the literature, a set of items to operationalize faculty perceptions of trust in colleagues, students, and the dean was developed. Second, the instrument was field-tested and refined using a representative sample of university faculty. Third, factor analysis was used to identify three primary factors of faculty trust. Cronbach alphas were calculated for each factor. Finally, this study found no significant trust differences between female and male professors, although there were significant differences found between professors of varying academic ranks (i.e., adjunct, assistant, associate, and full professor) The findings are discussed within a context of implications for future research involving the higher education trust instrument.

INTRODUCTION

In recent years, developments in the organizational sciences have prompted scholars to focus their interests on the salience of trust. We rely

Educational Administration, Policy, and Reform: Research and Measurement
A Volume in: Research and Theory In Educational Administration, pages 279–303.
Copyright © 2004 by Information Age Publishing, Inc.
All rights of reproduction in any form reserved.
ISBN: 1-59311-000-0 (hardcover), 1-59311-000-0 (paperback)

on others to protect us from domestic and international harm; we share the highways with those who we expect to abide by established traffic regulations; we trust businesses to provide us with quality food and adequate shelter; we count on our government to ensure the rights and privileges of all citizens. In essence, we depend on others to act in accordance with our expectations. Hence, we place our trust in people and social institutions to forward our very existence. As a subtle commodity, trust serves to moderate uncertainty and derail anxiety in a complex world (Luhmann, 1979; Solomon & Flores, 2001). Indeed, trust serves as a fragile covenant between participants orchestrating individual behavior and group order in social endeavors. In short, trust is critical to social functioning. It abets human survival in an intricate world.

Although much recent media attention has been directed toward public distrust of businesses and politicians, a burgeoning body of research is emerging that supports trust as a key element in formulating and maintaining interpersonal communication and organizational effectiveness (Axelrod, 1984; Gambetta, 1988; Good, 1988; Mayer, Davis, & Schoorman, 1995; McAllister, 1995; Solomon & Flores, 2001). Throughout the 1980s and 1990s, economists, organizational theorists, psychologists, and sociologists have pursued the concept of trust and how trust is cultivated and utilized in organizational settings. Research has also indicated that trust represents a critical element in the development of healthy and purposefully directed school environments (Hoy, Hoffman, Sabo, & Bliss, 1996; Hoy, Tarter, & Witkoskie, 1992; Tarter, Bliss, & Hoy, 1989; Tarter, Sabo, & Hoy, 1995). Moreover, studies of trust and climate reveal that certain administrator behaviors (Henderson & Hoy, 1983; Hoy & Henderson, 1983; Hoy & Kupersmith, 1985) and collegial interactions (Hoy, Tarter, & Witkoskie, 1992; Tarter, Bliss, & Hoy, 1989; Tarter, Hoy, & Bliss, 1989 Tarter, Sabo, & Hoy, 1995) do indeed buttress the case that trust is critical in healthy and open learning environments.

Faculty trust represents a critical component of educational organizations, one that may well affect student academic performance, faculty efficacy, and institutional health. However, there exists little research on faculty trust in higher education. Hence, the purpose of this study was twofold: 1) to identify a working definition of trust based on a review of the extant literature; and 2) to develop a reliable and valid measure of higher education faculty trust at the organizational level.

DEFINITION OF TRUST

Although scholars across many disciplines have widely acknowledged that trust can precipitate cooperative and healthy behavior in human endeavor, there appears to be an equally pervasive lack of agreement on a commonly accepted definition of the concept. Conceptually, trust is a complex social construct and a plethora of definitions of trust exists.

The empirical study of trust emerged from the Cold War era as the world community sought ways of moderating the suspicion prompted by an escalating and ominous arms race. Deutsch (1958) defined trust as an expectation by an individual in the occurrence of an event whereby that expectation leads to behavior that the individual perceived would have greater negative consequences if the expectation was not confirmed than positive consequences if it was confirmed. The study of trust was further embraced in the mid-1960s in response to the skepticism and disillusionment of the nation's youth toward institutional authority. Rotter (1967), pursuing an interpersonal description of trust, postulated that trust is an expectancy held by an individual or a group that the word, promise, verbal or written statement of another individual or group could be relied upon. Following the shifting social dynamics of the 1960s, trust researchers targeted the American family and the literature assumed an interpersonal focus in the 1970s and 1980s (Johnson-George & Swap, 1982; Rempel, Holmes, & Zanna, 1985). Accordingly, Zand (1971) identified trusting behavior as consisting of actions that increase one's vulnerability to another whose behavior is not under one's control in a situation in which the penalty (disutility) one suffers if the other abuses that vulnerability is greater than the benefit (utility) one gains if the other does not abuse that vulnerability. And in response to the ethical redesign of the corporate landscape, trust research in the 1990s and beyond has focused on issues of social and economic justice as they relate to subordinate-management relationships (Fukuyama, 1995; Kramer & Tyler, 1996; Schoorman, Mayer, & Davis, 1996; Warren, 1999; Solomon & Flores, 2001). Hence, Mayer, Davis, and Schoorman (1995) assert that trust is "a willingness of a party to be vulnerable to the actions of another party based on the expectation that the other will perform a particular action important to the trustor, irrespective of the ability to monitor or control the party" (p. 712).

After an extensive review of the literature, Hoy and Tschannen-Moran's definition of trust was employed for this study. Hoy and Tschannen-Moran (2003, 1999) defined trust as: "an individual's or group's willingness to be vulnerable to another party based on the confidence that the latter party is benevolent, reliable, competent, honest, and open." Hence, the latter definition was targeted because it captures the key elements of contemporary analyses of trust and has been applied to the study of organizational trust in educational settings.

Benevolence

One of the most enduring facets of trust is a sense of benevolence, "the confidence that one's well-being or something that one cares about will be protected by the trusted party or group" (Hoy & Tschannen-Moran, 1999, p. 187). Unmitigated goodwill in a relationship between actors assists in developing an assurance that the vulnerability of one party will not be exploited by the other. Thereby, benevolent behavior on behalf of stakeholders in a relationship may serve as a catalyst in the development and growth of trust.

Reliability

Knowing that a person, group, or organization with which they are interacting is reliable can buoy an individual's sense of trust. Reliability represents the degree to which one person or party in a relationship can depend on the other to provide that which is needed. Although to a limited degree trust is predicated on predictability, the prospect of simply knowing how an individual will consistently react to a given situation is insufficient in terms of fully understanding trust. To be meaningful, trust must proceed beyond predictability (Deutsch, 1958) We can trust a person to be angry or upset with certain events. Likewise, we can count on someone to exhibit distracting, coercive, and authoritarian behaviors in order to achieve their goals. It is however, when these predictable actions are perceived to be detrimental to our own personal well-being that trust ebbs. Reliability extends beyond mere predictability by amalgamating predictability with benevolence. In an interdependent environment, reliability insures that when something is required from another person, that individual can be depended on to accommodate the expectation.

Competence

Past research on organizational trust suggests that competence is a key developmental element (Butler, 1991; Butler & Cantrell, 1984; Cook & Wall, 1980; Kee & Knox, 1970; Lieberman, 1981; Mishra, 1996; Solomon & Flores, 2001). Without the belief that one party in a relationship possesses the competence to successfully fulfill his or her expected role, the other party is unlikely to generate trust in that person. Competence forms a conceptual foundation that increases the likelihood that one person will react to trustworthy behavior on the part of the other. For example, a faculty member may well believe that a dean has the best interests of a college and its faculty members at heart, but persistent evidence of managerial ineptitude is unlikely to develop trust in the dean on the part of the faculty member. To forward subordinate trust, the dean must demonstrate a significant degree of institutional prowess. Moreover, the increased use of self-managed work teams in organizations emphasizes the salience of competence in the nurturing of trust and productive cooperation. Indeed, many organizational ventures in today's workplace are predicated on trust that has been conceived by organizational members demonstrating competence in a specific task domain.

Honesty

Researchers and scholars consistently recognize honesty as a salient aspect of trust (Butler & Cantrell, 1984; Cummings & Bromley, 1996; Hoy & Tschannen-Moran, 1999). Honesty conveys straightforwardness of conduct, integrity, and probity to actors in a relationship. Straightforwardness serves to lessen the need for and costs of negotiating trust when interacting with others. Reliable information that represents the factual "bottom line" aids interpersonal actors in understanding those issues that can contribute or detract from organizational productivity. Integrity belies untrustworthiness. Organizational participants who stress integrity in their interactions with others are hard-pressed to knowingly violate a trust, pledge, or responsibility. They can be counted on to exhibit consistent behavior even under conditions of organizational turbulence and change (Vitell & Davis, 1990). Probity describes a protracted history of honesty and integrity on the part of an individual. Organizational stakeholders evidence probity by making and honoring commitments.

Openness

An atmosphere of openness contributes to trust by forwarding a realistic assessment of interpersonal and organizational achievements and problems. "Openness does not mean hostility, nor does it mean sweetness and light" (Ouchi, 1981, p. 100). When people engage in the process of openness they voluntarily share personal information with others and thereby accept a mantle of vulnerability to others (Butler & Cantrell, 1984; Mishra, 1996). Open communication initiates a relational reciprocity between partners in that the exchange of personal information by one party aids the other party in feeling confident to do the same. Hence, both actors enjoy a confidence that neither party will be exploited and consequently the possibility of trust development is enhanced. In organizational settings where openness is present, participants freely exchange thoughts and ideas and perceptions of trust are intensified.

RATIONALE FOR THE STUDY

The review of the literature shows that most of the research on organizational trust has been conducted in the K–12 public schools and in the business sector, yet the problem is an increasingly important one for American institutions of higher education. The prospects of continued fiscal constraints and expanding organizational responsibilities highlight the need for stakeholder trust in colleges and universities. There is, however, a paucity of research on both individual and organizational trust characteristics as they relate to higher education. This research is an attempt to fill that void.

Past research in K–12 public schools has found that different aspects of faculty trust exists among colleagues, clients, and administrators (Hoy, Smith, & Sweetland, 2002; Smith, Hoy, & Sweetland, 2001) Trust has also been conceptualized as an important element of effective leadership styles (Bass, 1985). Furthermore, trust in organizational leaders has been found to influence job satisfaction, organizational commitment and citizenship behavior, and lower turnover intentions (Bycio, Hackett, & Allen, 1995; Howell & Avolio, 1993). But what about trust in higher education? Does faculty trust in deans, colleagues and students serve to abet the effort of colleges to achieve their goals? Are there differences in the level of faculty trust in salient university groups? Given the work environment of higher education institutions where individual autonomy is interfaced with organizational interdependence, we believe faculty trust merits serious exploration. Thus, we theorize that university faculty members have different levels of trust in students, their colleagues, and the dean. In order to probe faculty trust in higher education, a valid and reliable instrument needs to be conceptualized and tested. Therefore, the purpose of this research was twofold. First, we conceptualized and field-tested an instrument to gauge perceptions of faculty trust in students, colleagues, and the dean. Second, this study sought to address any differences in faculty trust across gender and academic rank. To be sure, the current study is exploratory in that we have to first develop some measures of organizational trust in higher education institutions.

Our primary interest in this investigation is to test the utility of the higher education trust instrument we have developed by examining the degree of trust in and among different types of faculty members. First, we raise the simple but important question as to whether females and males have different perceptions of trust in higher education. Next, because our sample included university professors, we were intrigued with the question of whether there were significant differences in the level of trust among the four academic ranks (i.e., adjunct, assistant, associate, and full professor). In brief, three general research questions guided this study:

1. What are the dimensions of faculty trust in higher education and how can they be measured?
2. Are there statistically significant differences between female and male faculty members in the level of faculty trust in an institution of higher education?
3. Are there statistically significant differences in the degree of faculty trust between adjunct, assistant, associate, and full professors in an institution of higher education?

DEVELOPMENT OF A MEASURE

The study began with an exploration of the current trust literature in an attempt to locate any empirical indicators of faculty trust in higher education. However, after canvassing the literature on trust, we failed to discover any higher education measures that targeted the five faces of trust conceptualized in our definition. Hence, our search led us to the school climate literature where we unearthed several measures designed by Hoy and his colleagues (1999, 1998, 1991, 1985) to gauge faculty trust in public K–12 schools. Their efforts represented a beginning for this study. Subsequently, we contacted the authors and were granted permission to employ the conceptual design of the Trust Scale[1] (Hoy & Tschannen-Moran, 2003, 1999) in our research. We then set about formulating items that would map higher education trust. First, we generated a list of items we both agreed would tap the concept. Each item was discussed in terms of what it was measuring and only those items for which we could get complete agree-

TABLE 1
Sample Items for Each Aspect of Faculty Trust

Trust Dimension	*Sample Items*
Faculty Trust in Colleague	• Faculty in this college is open with each other.
	• Faculty in this college is suspicious of each other. *
Faculty Trust in Dean	• The Dean in this college keeps his or her word.
	• The Dean doesn't tell faculty what is really going on. *
Faculty Trust in Students	• Students in this college are reliable.
	• Students in this college are caring toward one another.

Notes:　*This item is reversed scored.

ment were retained (see Appendix A). We insured all five facets of trust (benevolence, reliability, competence, honesty and openness) were represented in each trust referent (colleagues, students, and the dean). The items were formulated for university faculty to describe the extent of trust that existed among colleagues, between faculty and students, and faculty and the dean. Examples of items included the following: "Faculty in this college trust each other;" "Students in this college can be counted on to do their work;" and "The dean in this college is competent in doing his or her job." Sample items for each trust scale are given in Table 1.

AN EXPLORATION

To get an empirical check on this set of items, we did two things. First, higher education colleagues from our university examined the items for face validity. Second, we asked two professors at other universities to examine, critique, and talk with their colleagues about the items. At this stage of the investigation, we were simply searching for ways to get at the nature of trust in higher education. The initial list of 34 items (see Appendix A) quickly became one of 30 items. Our two outside colleagues recommended that four items be dropped from the initial item list due to redundancy and confusing verbiage. The data were also subjected to an exploratory factor analysis to see what items clustered together and those that did not. In addition to insuring that each trust referent contained items targeting all five facets of trust, items with initial factor loadings in the exploratory analysis of at least .40 were retained (Kerlinger, 1973). Items were discarded if their factor loadings fell below 40. Examples of items eliminated in the exploratory factor analysis included: "The students in this college have to be closely supervised," and "The students in this college talk freely about their lives outside."

A REFINEMENT

A pilot study was initiated to map the domain of the construct and refine the measure and meaning of faculty trust through factor analytic techniques. In piloting the instrument, a sample of faculty was taken from 35 departments across the University of Texas at San Antonio (UTSA). In this study of faculty trust, the individual constituted the unit of analysis. Given the exploratory nature of the investigation, we were concerned with obtaining individual perceptions of faculty trust across one university. Various academic disciplines were represented ranging from education to engineering to liberal arts. Each respective department was contacted by

TABLE 2
Demographic Representation of the Sample (n = 217)

Academic Rank (n = 206)	*Gender (n = 208)*	
	Male	*Female*
Full Professor	36	5
Associate Professor	43	16
Assistant Professor	48	23
Adjunct Professor	19	13

Notes: Some participants did not report either their gender or academic rank.

the investigators for participation in the study. Out of the 35 departments in the university, 32 departments agreed to participate in this study.

Initially, researchers were going to administer the ten-minute survey at pre-arranged departmental meetings. However, 16 out of the 32 departments that agreed to participate in the study requested that the survey be administered through e-mail attachment or campus mail. For the rest of the departments, the survey was administered at departmental meetings during the fall of 2002. The final sample consisted of 217 professors of varying academic ranks across the university. In sum, the sample represented 53% of the total tenure and tenure-track faculty at the University of Texas at San Antonio. Despite some logistical challenges, the sample was representative of the faculty composition within the university across all demographic variables collected.

Each faculty member responded to the instrument containing the 30 surviving items from the original 34-item instrument. In addition, demographic information of the participants was collected based on their academic rank and gender (see Table 2).

ANALYSIS

The first task was to refine the trust measure. To that end, a principal component analysis with varimax rotation was used to examine the 30-item measure. Using a screen test with eigenvalues greater than one, three strong factors of faculty trust were identified. The first factor was called collegial trust and described the general degree of trust among faculty colleagues. Collegial trust was measured using items such as "Faculty in this college trust each other," and "Faculty in this college are suspicious of each other (score reversed)." The second factor, student trust, denoted the faculty's trust in students and was tapped by such items as "Students in this college are reliable," and "Students in this college are caring toward one another." The third factor, trust in the dean, described faculty perceptions of their trust towards the dean of their respective college. Items used to assess this factor included: "Faculty in this college trust their dean" and "The dean in this college is unresponsive to faculty's concerns" (score reversed). The factor analysis produced loadings as shown in Appendix B. Due to weak factor loadings, two of the items were eliminated. The remaining 28-items measured the three aspects of faculty trust and explained over 63% of the variance.

RESULTS

The analysis produced three distinct clusters of items: faculty perceptions of trust among colleagues; faculty perceptions of trust in students; and faculty perceptions of trust in the dean. The items all loaded as expected and the Cronbach Alpha reliability coefficients were good: .93 for collegial trust; .84 for student trust; and .96 for trust in the dean. Not surprisingly, these three dimensions were positively correlated (see Table 3) and formed a consistent archetype of trust for each referent cluster- dean, colleagues and students. Since great care was taken to generate items in each subset describing the five facets of trust, it was predictable that strong to moderate correlations among the respective referents would emerge. Hence, collegial trust was significantly related to faculty trust in students and trust in the dean. In addition, faculty trust in the students was significantly related to trust in the dean, albeit, to a lesser degree.

We identified and subjected to factor analysis thirty items, which we predicted would define three aspects of higher education trust. Twenty-eight of the thirty items loaded as predicted. Two items did not cluster as anticipated and thus were dropped from the instrument. The factor analysis provided strong support for the construct validity of the measure of faculty trust in universities. Moreover, the faculty-dean relationship of trust proved to be the strongest of the three dimensions followed by collegial trust. Stu-

TABLE 3
Correlations among Trust Dimensions

Trust Dimension	Collegial	Student	Dean
Collegial	1.000	.515* (.265)	.501* (.251)
Student		1.000	.354* (.125)
Dean			1.000

Notes: *Correlation is statistically significant at .01 level (2 tailed). Effect sizes are in parentheses.

dent trust was shown to have the lowest albeit still acceptable measure of internal reliability.

In brief, the results of the analysis demonstrate that the Higher Education Faculty Trust Inventory (HEFTI) is a parsimonious, reliable, and valid measure. The HEFTI taps three critical aspects of trust in higher education. Hence, the Higher Education Faculty Trust Inventory is composed of three subtests: a 9-item scale to measure trust in colleagues, an 8-item scale to measure trust in students, and an 11-item scale to measure trust in the dean. Next, we explored some relationships between the three factors of faculty trust and personal characteristics.

Trustd, Gender, and Academic Rank

The personal characteristics examined in this study were gender and academic rank. These features were targeted based on the stature and status accorded them in institutions of higher education. We were intrigued by the prospects of how faculty trust might shadow gender and academic rank.

First, are there statistically significant differences between female and male faculty members in the degree of faculty trust in an institution of higher education? To answer this research question, the mean scores on the three subscales of the organizational trust inventory were compared. The results revealed no significant differences between female (n = 59) and male (n = 149) faculty members on the three measures of organizational trust (note: the N's differ because not all participants identified their gender). For collegial trust, women had a mean of 25.74 and men had a mean of 27.05 (F (1, 198) = 1.638, p = .202); for trust in students, women had a mean of 17.10 and men had a mean of 17.56 (F (1, 197) = .963, p = .328); and for trust in the dean, women had a mean of 35.92 and men had a mean of 35.13 (F (1, 200) = .239, p = .625) (see Table 4).

TABLE 4
Mean and Standard Deviations for Female and
Male Faculty on Trust Subscales

Group	Collegial Trust		Trust in Students		Trust in Dean	
	M	*SD*	*M*	*SD*	*M*	*SD*
Female (N=59)	25.74	7.79	17.10	3.67	35.92	10.89
Male (N=149)	27.05	6.03	17.56	2.65	35.13	10.23
ANOVA F-score	1.638		.963		.239	
p-value	.202		.328		.625	

TABLE 5
Mean and Standard Deviations among
Academic Ranks on Trust Subscales

Group	Collegial Trust		Trust in Students		Trust in Dean	
	M	SD	M	SD	M	SD
Adjunct Professor (N=32)	29.50	6.65	18.06	3.61	38.47	9.26
Assistant Professor (N=71)	27.19	5.32	17.31	2.47	38.47	7.09
Associate Professor (N=62)	26.19	6.55	17.47	3.00	33.73	10.66
Full Professor (N=41)	25.20	7.28	17.20	3.15	30.50	12.54

Second, are there statistically significant differences in the level of faculty trust between adjunct, assistant, associate, and full professors in an institution of higher education? To address this research question, a multivariate analysis of variance (MANOVA) was performed. Because a significant F was found for the MANOVA (Wilk's lambda = .915, F = 18.931, df = 3; 612, p = .0001), this demonstrated that there was a significant difference between academic ranks on the three measures of higher education trust. Subsequent analyses of variances (ANOVA) were performed on each subscale (see Table 5). For collegial trust, there were statistically significant differences among academic ranks with adjunct and assistant professors demonstrating higher degrees of collegial trust than tenured associate and full professors (F (3, 194) = 3.03, p = .031). This result may be indicative of the higher education culture where individual autonomy and academic freedom are highly valued. In contrast, there were no significant differences found when examining trust in students (F (3, 193) = .580, p = .629). This finding illustrates that academic rank does not produce differing levels of trust towards students. Finally, similar to collegial trust, untenured faculty ranks had much higher levels of trust in the dean than tenured faculty ranks (F (3, 196) = 7.077, p = .0001). This finding has widespread implications and is further probed in the discussion section

DISCUSSION

Our factor analysis of the items relating to higher education faculty trust defined three relatively distinct factors. The first factor, collegial trust, gauged the extent to which faculty members trusted their colleagues; the second factor, trust in students, measured the degree to which faculty members trusted their students; and the third factor, trust in the dean, measured the degree to which faculty members trust the dean of their college. The relationship between these three concepts was found to be statistically significant, yet moderate to weak in their effect size. We were struck, however, by the inverse relationship between trust and academic rank. In other words, the data suggest that the level of trust tends to diminish with ascending academic rank. We found it interesting that tenured faculty members were less likely to demonstrate levels of trust than their junior colleagues. Perhaps, assistant professors, who are relatively new to the university and striving for tenure, align themselves with greater levels of trust in the dean due to what Kramer (1999) refers to as role-based trust. Role-based trust is extended to an individual who occupies a particular role in an organization rather than being based on specific information about the person's motives, intentions, and capabilities. Certainly, in any employer-employee relationship, early subordinate trust is predicated on the initial rapport developed with the person who hires them. Obviously, there are a number of possibilities why trust appears to erode as faculty members ascend the academic ladder. The prospects of high turnover rates in the deanship, the socialization process to university politics in general, and an academic culture that nurtures autonomy and independence may arrest the development of trust. These issues involving trust pose intriguing propositions for future research.

In examining faculty perceptions of trust, some might think that women would be more trusting than men. That was not the case in our sample; there was no significant difference between men and women as they described the extent of faculty trust in higher education. Further, men were no more or less trusting than women in higher education. When it comes to levels of trust in higher education involving colleagues, students, and the dean, gender was not an issue. This finding appears to contradict the popular notion that men are from Mars and women are from Venus (Gray, 1993).

Is there a statistically significant difference in the degree of faculty trust between adjunct, assistant, associate, and full professors in higher education? There were significant differences in perceived levels of trust among academic ranks. This finding is disturbing in that it suggests that as faculty members ascend through the academic ranks they are more likely to become less trusting of their colleagues and the dean. This has serious implications for those stakeholders who are concerned with developing an open and healthy higher education culture. Professors who have achieved tenure and higher academic rank are apparently confronting issues that retard further trust development and stymie previous trust experience. But what issues? Are there factors of tenure and academic rank in higher education cultures that preclude the growth of trust? What organizational factors support or detract from the continued development and maintenance of higher education trust? Indeed, this issue provides fertile ground for further study. Continued trust research may well assist in unearthing reasons why higher education cultures are difficult to change and why they are not readily akin to becoming learning organizations.

CONCLUSION

Although this research was exploratory, it underscores some important issues. First, a general index was developed to assess the degree of faculty trust in higher education and to measure the extent to which faculty trust their colleagues, students, and the dean. The index is reliable and stable. Second, the higher education trust measure is composed of three subtests: a student trust scale to measure faculty trust in students, a subset of items to measure faculty trust in the dean, and a collegial trust scale to measure faculty trust in colleagues. Finally, although no gender differences were evident when it came to faculty trust, an intriguing finding did surface in the area of academic rank. Our foray into higher education trust produced the rather unanticipated discovery that as professors ascend academic rank, trust ebbs. That is, as professors are promoted to higher ranks and attain more institutional clout they tend to exhibit less stakeholder trust. The prospect of less trust among key players in higher education does not bode well for colleges and universities that purport organizational openness and institutional health. Prima facie, this revelation hastens concern and indeed merits further consideration.

Administrators and faculty confronted with trust-based organizational dilemmas may well need to assess these situations to better ascertain how to improve their learning and working environments. This study is a modest first step toward designing an instrument capable of operationalizing trust in colleges and universities and examining three salient referents of higher education trust. However, identifying trust is only half the issue; in fact, the other and perhaps more important half is the cultivating and nurturing of trust-based organizational behaviors that will develop open and productive exchanges in learning and working environments. As colleges and universities continue to reflect the promise of greater stakeholder involvement, the saliency of trust in higher education will need to be further probed and examined. Trust may well prove to be a key element in facilitating and developing strategies to buttress participant excellence at the university level.

LIMITATIONS AND FUTURE RESEARCH

The Higher Education Faculty Trust Inventory (HEFTI) represents an attempt to measure faculty perceptions of trust in three specific referent areas found in higher education environments. As in any exploratory research, this study was garrisoned by a number of limitations. First, the unit of analysis employed in this research was the individual and not the organization. Due to the limitations of the sample, which was one university population, we targeted individual responses across the university for our pilot study. Future administrations of the HEFTI should target the collective perceptions of members of their respective colleges; that is, the unit of analysis should be the organization. Second, since the unit of analysis employed in the study was the individual, the population of respondents from college to college varied widely. Despite the high level of departmental approval to participate in the study, the actual sample collected did not produce a similar level of individual participation. Certain colleges within the university were overrepresented while the respondent numbers from other colleges were underrepresented. Subsequent studies of higher education trust using the HEFTI at the organizational level should remedy this dilemma. Another limitation of this study was that the research was confined to one university. In future studies involving the HEFTI, investigators should seriously consider sampling a wider array of higher education institutions.

This study constitutes a modest attempt to identify and measure three salient referents of higher education trust. It is a beginning and not an end. There are a host of other research questions that need to be addressed. For example, there is ample evidence that certain aspects of organizational health are critical to the maintenance and evolution of trust in public schools (Hoffman, Sabo, & Hoy, 1994; Hoy, 2002; Hoy, Tarter, & Kottkamp, 1991; Hoy & Tschannen-Moran, 2003; Solomon & Flores, 2001; Tschannen-Moran, 2001), but what about higher education? A number of questions for future research remain:

1. To what extent are organizational health factors related to trust development in higher education environments?
2. Do perceptions of faculty trust in the dean, students and colleagues differ between community colleges and four-year institutions? Between research universities and teacher colleges? Between public and private universities?
3. To what extent does age of the respondent affect faculty trust in the three referent groups?
4. To what extent is faculty trust in the dean related to professors' propensities to innovate and take risks?
5. To what extent does faculty trust influence departmental culture or climate? How does faculty trust in the department chair differ from faculty trust in colleagues, students, or the dean?
6. To what extent does faculty trust in colleagues relate to aspects of collaboration and cooperation? In other words, how does faculty

trust influence the creation of learning communities in higher education?

7. Is faculty trust in colleagues salient to the development of professionalism?

8. Is there a relationship between faculty trust in students and the promotion of a more humanistic pupil control orientation?

PRACTICAL IMPLICATIONS

For deans and other university leaders interested in the practical consequences of this study, we make a case that the HEFTI provides a reliable and valid diagnostic tool. The HEFTI is user-friendly—a short descriptive instrument that is simple to administer and only takes faculty members a few minutes to complete. Our experience suggests that while some faculty members enjoy the opportunity to describe anonymously the interpersonal relations in their college, others are reluctant to provide data despite their reliance on data collection for their own research. This is an interesting quandary for researchers of higher education and in particular those investigating faculty and organizational issues.

Deans and university leaders can use the HEFTI to map personal trust perceptions of them as perceived by their respective faculty members, the interpersonal interactions among faculty colleagues, and between faculty and students. A trust profile of the college or university can be drawn from the faculty responses to the HEFTI. Then deans, university leaders, and faculty can decide if the general trust level of the college or university is in need of attention. However, many university administrators are hesitant to broach the topic of faculty trust for fear of what the results may reveal. Conversely, administrators willing to undertake an examination of faculty trust are often surprised to see that their perceptions of organizational trust are quite different from those of their faculty (Hoy & Tarter, 1997). In fact, it is common for deans and university leaders to describe trust in their colleges or universities more favorably than their faculty. The question then is not who is correct, but rather why the differences in perceptions. If faculty perceive the dean or university leadership as untrustworthy or suspicious, then it is important for the leadership to come to know why that is the case, and then take appropriate action. The HEFTI provides a snapshot of organizational trust; it does not provide an explanation or reason for the result. Hence, the HEFTI can be used as a diagnostic tool to identify symptoms of interpersonal and organizational trust issues in universities.

One useful method for improving faculty trust is organizational development. Such a perspective addresses both personal and organizational needs; it is a planned effort to make people and organizations more productive (Hanson & Lubin, 1995). Both faculty and university leadership must recognize problems and be willing to change. The HEFTI can be employed to identify trust discrepancies in perceptions between the dean and faculty, but that is only the first step in changing things. Next, a problem-solving team must be established, one that typically is composed of faculty. The team must take on the problem, diagnose its causes, develop an action plan, implement the plan, and assess its usefulness.

Labeling a problem is not the same as solving it. Only the faculty members and Deans themselves can solve trust issues; there are no quick or one size fits all fixes. The HEFTI is a tool; it cannot solve the problems. It can, however, underscore important features of the college or university in need of change. Armed with such knowledge, both faculty members and university leaders are in a position to engage in a positive strategy of generative learning and change. Faculty members want to work in organizations characterized with trust and positive interpersonal relationships. The current research represents a beginning to understanding more about the dynamic interrelationships between students, faculty, and university leaders. Where this beginning leads depends on the willingness of university stakeholders to be open and receptive to what the HEFTI yields.

NOTE

1. We would like to thank Wayne K. Hoy of The Ohio State University and Megan Tschannen-Moran of the College of William and Mary for allowing us to employ their conceptual framework in the design of the Higher Education Faculty Trust Inventory and for providing technical feedback on earlier drafts of this chapter.

REFERENCES

Axelrod, R. (1984). *The evolution of cooperation*. New York: Basic Books.

Bass, B. M. (1985). *Leadership and performance beyond expectations*. New York: Free Press.

Butler, J. K. (1991). Towards understanding and measuring conditions of trust: Evolution of a condition of trust inventory. *Journal of Management, 17,* 643–663.

Butler, J. K., & Cantrell, R. S. (1984). A behavioral decision theory approach to modeling dyadic trust in superiors and subordinates. *Psychological Reports, 55,* 19–28.

Bycio, P., Hackett, R. D., & Allen, J. S. (1995). Further assessments of Bass's (1985) conceptualization of transactional and transformational leadership. *Journal of Applied Psychology, 80,* 468–478.

Cook, J., & Wall, T. (1980). New work attitude measures of trust, organizational commitment, and personal need non-fulfillment. *Journal of Occupational Psychology, 53,* 39–52.

Cummings, L. L., & Bromily, P. (1996). The organizational trust inventory (OTI): Development and validation. In R. Kramer & T. Tyler (Eds.), *Trust in Organizations*. Thousand Oaks: Sage Publications.

Deutsch, M. (1958). Trust and suspicion. *Journal of Conflict Resolution, 2*, 265–279.

Fukuyama, F. (1995). *Trust: The social virtues and the creation of prosperity*. New York: Free Press.

Gambetta, D. (1988). Can we trust? In D. Gambetta (Ed.), *Trust: Making and breaking cooperative relations* (pp. 213–238). Cambridge, MA: Basil Blackwell.

Good, D. (1988). Individuals, interpersonal relations, and trust. In D. Gambetta (Ed.), *Trust: Making and breaking cooperative relations* (pp. 31–48). New York: Basil Blackwell.

Gray, J. (1993). *Men are from Mars, women are from Venus: A practical guide for improving communication and getting what you want in your relationships*. New York: Harper-Collins.

Hanson, P. G., & Lubin, B. (1995). *Answers to questions most frequently asked about organization development*. Thousand Oaks, CA: Sage.

Henderson, J. E., & Hoy, W. K. (1983). Leader authenticity: The development and test of an operational measure. *Educational and Psychological Research, 3*(2), 63–75.

Hoffman, J., Sabo, D., & Hoy, W. K. (1994). Building a culture of trust. *Journal of School Leadership, 4*, 484–581.

Howell, J. M., & Avolio, B. J. (1993). Transformational leadership, transactional leadership, locus of control, and support for innovation: Key predictors of consolidated-business-unit performance. *Journal of Applied Psychology, 78*, 891–902.

Hoy, W. K. (2002). Faculty trust: A key to student achievement. *Journal of School Public Relations, 23*, 88–103.

Hoy, W. K., & Henderson, J. E. (1983). Principal authenticity, school climate, and pupil control orientation. *Alberta Journal of Educational Research, 2*, 123–130.

Hoy, W. K., Hoffman, J., Sabo, D., & Bliss, J. R. (1996). The organizational climate of middle schools: The development and test of the OCDQ-RM. *Journal of Educational Administration, 34*, 41–59.

Hoy, W. K., & Kupersmith, W. J. (1985). The meaning and measure of faculty trust. *Educational and Psychological Research, 5*, 1–10.

Hoy, W. K., & Sabo, D. J. (1998). *Quality middle schools: Open and healthy*. Thousand Oaks, CA: Corwin.

Hoy, W. K., Smith, P. A., & Sweetland, S. R. (2002). The development of the organizational climate index for high schools: It's measure and relationship to faculty trust. *The High School Journal, 86*(2), 38–49.

Hoy, W. K., & Tarter, C. J. (1997). *Road to open and health schools: A handbook for change*. Thousand Oaks, CA: Corwin.

Hoy, W. K., Tarter, C. J., & Kottkamp, R. B. (1991). *Open schools, healthy schools: Measuring organizational climate*. Newbury Park, CA: Sage.

Hoy, W. K., Tarter, C. J., & Witkoskie, L. (1992). Faculty trust in colleagues: Linking the principal with school effectiveness. *Journal of Research and Development in Education, 26*(1), 40–47.

Hoy, W. K., & Tschannen-Moran, M. (2003). The conceptualization and measurement of faculty trust in schools: The omnibus T-scale. In W. Hoy & C. Miskel (Eds.), *Studies in leading and organizing schools* (pp. 181–208). Greenwich, CT: Information Age.

Hoy, W. K., & Tschannen-Moran, M. (1999). Five faces of trust: An empirical confirmation in urban elementary schools. *Journal of School Leadership, 9*(3), 184–208.

Johnson-George, C.E., & Swap, W.C. (1982). Measurement of specific interpersonal trust: Construction and validation of a scale to assess trust in a specific other. *Journal of Personality and Social Psychology, 43,* 1306–1317.

Kee, H.W., & Knox, R.E. (1970). Conceptual and methodological considerations in the study of trust and suspicion. *Journal of Conflict Resolution,* 14, 357–365.

Kerlinger, F. N. (1973). *Foundations of behavioral research* (2nd ed.). New York: Holt, Rinehart, and Winston.

Kramer, R. M. (1999). Trust and distrust in organizations: Emerging perspectives, enduring questions. *Annual Reviews: Psychology, 50,* 569–598.

Kramer, R. M., & Tyler, T. R. (1996). *Trust in organizations: Frontiers of theory and research.* Thousand Oaks, CA: Sage.

Lieberman, J.K. (1981). *The litigious society.* New York: Basic Books.

Luhmann, N. (1979). *Trust and power.* Chichester, England: Wiley.

Mayer, R. C., Davis, J. H., & Schoorman, F. D. (1995). An integrative model of organizational trust. *Academy of Management Review, 20,* 709–734.

McAllister, D. J. (1995). Affect- and cognition-based trust as foundations for interpersonal cooperation in organizations. *Academy of Management Journal, 38*(1), 24–59.

Mishra, A. K. (1996). Organizational responses to crisis: The centrality of trust. In R. Kramer & T. Tyler (Eds.), *Trust in organizations* (pp. 261–287). Thousand Oaks, CA: Sage Publications.

Ouchi, W. (1981). *Theory Z.* Reading, MA: Addison-Wesley.

Rempel, J. K., Holmes, J. G., & Zanna, M. D. (1985). Trust in close relationships. *Journal of Personality and Social Psychology, 49,* 95–112.

Rotter, J. B. (1967). A new scale for the measurement of interpersonal trust. *Journal of Personality, 35,* 651–665.

Schoorman, F. D., Mayer, R. C., & Davis, J. H. (1996). Organizational trust: Philosophical perspectives and conceptual definitions. *Academy of Management Journal, 38*(1), 24–59.

Smith, P. A., Hoy, W. K., & Sweetland, S. R. (2001). Organizational health of high schools and dimensions of faculty trust. *Journal of School Leadership, 11,* 135–150.

Solomon, R. C., & Flores, F. (2001). *Building trust in business, politics, relationships, and life.* New York: Oxford University Press.

Tarter, C. J., Bliss, J. R., & Hoy, W. K. (1989). School characteristics and faculty trust in secondary schools. *Educational Administration Quarterly, 25*(3), 294–308.

Tarter, C. J., Hoy, W. K., & Bliss, J. R. (1989). Principal leadership and organizational commitment: The principal must deliver. *Planning and Changing, 20,* 129–140.

Tarter, C. J., Sabo, D., & Hoy, W. K. (1995). Middle school climate, faculty trust, and effectiveness: A path analysis. *Journal of Research and Development in Education, 29,* 41–49.

Tschannen-Moran, M. (2001). Collaboration and the need for trust. *Journal of Educational Administration, 36,* 334–352.

Vitell, S. J., & Davis, D. L. (1990). The relationship between ethics and job satisfaction: An empirical investigation. *Journal of Business Ethics, 9,* 489–494.

Warren, M. (1999). *Democracy and trust.* Cambridge, UK: Cambridge University Press.

Zand, D. E. (1971). Trust and managerial problem solving. *Administrative Science Quarterly, 17,* 229–239.

APPENDIX A:
LIST OF THE ORIGINAL 34 ORGANIZATIONAL
TRUST INVENTORY ITEMS

Trust in the Dean

15.

The Dean in this college is unresponsive to faculty's concerns.

3.

The Dean of this college does not show concern for the faculty.

30.

The faculty in this college has faith in the integrity of the Dean.

17.

The Dean in this college typically acts with the best interests of the faculty in mind.

20.

The Dean in this college keeps his or her word.

16.

The Dean in this college is competent in doing his or her job.

5.

Faculty in this college trusts their Dean.

28.

Faculty in this college can rely on the Dean.

22.

The Dean doesn't tell faculty what is really going on.

14.

The faculty in this college is suspicious of most of the Dean's actions.

26.

The Dean openly shares personal information with faculty.

31.

The Dean in this college is forthright in his/her interactions with the faculty.

Trust in Colleagues

7.

Faculty in this college trusts each other.

19.

Faculty in this college is suspicious of each other.

1.

Faculty in this college has faith in the integrity of their colleagues.

9.

Faculty in this college typically looks out for each other.

4.

Faculty in this college is open with each other.

18.

Faculty in this college believes in each other.

23.

Even in difficult situations, faculty in this college can depend on each other.

24.

When faculty in this college tells you something you can believe it.

11.

Faculty in this college is not competent in their teaching responsibilities.

33.

Faculty in this college are trusting.

Trust in Students

29.

Students in this college can be counted on to do their work.

6.

Students in this college are reliable.

21.

Faculty in this college believes what students say.

10.

Students in this college are caring toward one another.

8.

Faculty in this college believes students are competent learners.

25.

Students in this college are secretive.

2.

The students in this college talk freely about their lives outside of college.

12.

Faculty in this college trusts their students.

13.

Students in this college cheat if they have the chance.

27.

The students in this college have to be closely supervised.

32.

Students in this college are high flyers.

34.

Students in this college are deceptive.

Note: Items in italics were deleted.

APPENDIX B:
FACTOR ANALYSIS OF THE 30 ORGANIZATIONAL TRUST INVENTORY ITEMS

Items By Factor	Factor	I	II	III
I. Trust in the Dean				
17.	The Dean in this college typically acts with the best interests of the faculty in mind.	.89		
28.	Faculty in this college can rely on the Dean.	.88		
30.	The faculty in this college has faith in the integrity of the Dean.	.86		
16.	The Dean in this college is competent in doing his or her job.	.85		
15.	The Dean in this college is unresponsive to faculty's concerns.	-.84		
20.	The Dean in this college keeps his or her word.	.84		
3.	The Dean of this college does not show concern for the faculty.	-.84		
22.	The Dean doesn't tell faculty what is really going on.	-.81		
5.	Faculty in this college are reliable.	.80		
14.	The faculty in this college is suspicious of most of the Dean's actions.	-.74		
26.	The Dean openly shares personal information with faculty.	.46		
II. Trust in Colleagues				
7.	Faculty in this college trusts each other.		.88	
18.	Faculty in this college believes in each other.		.84	
4.	Faculty in this college is open with each other.		.82	
1.	Faculty in this college has faith in the integrity of their colleagues.		.82	
19.	Faculty in this college is suspicious of each other.		-.80	
9.	Faculty in this college typically looks out for each other.		.74	
23.	Even in difficult situations, faculty in this college can depend on each other.		.70	
24.	When faculty in this college tells you something you can believe it.		.66	
11.	Faculty in this college is not competent in their teaching responsibilities.		-.41	
III. Trust in Students				
12.	Faculty in this college trusts their students.			.75

Items By Factor	Factor	I	II	III
29.	Students in this college can be counted on to do their work.			.74
8.	Faculty in this college believes students are competent learners.			.70
10.	Students in this college are caring toward one another.			.69
6.	Students in this college are reliable.			.64
21.	Faculty in this college believes what students say.			.61
13.	Students in this college cheat if they have the chance.			.50
25.	Students in this college are secretive..49			.49
27.	The students in this college have to be closely supervised.			-.31
2.	The students in this college talk freely about their lives outside of college.			.25
Eigenvalues		11.77	3.90	2.25
Cumulative % of Variance		39.23	52.23	59.71

Notes: Items in italics were deleted.

APPENDIX C
FACTOR ANALYSIS OF THE 28 ORGANIZATIONAL TRUST
INVENTORY ITEMS

Items By Factor	Factor	I	II	III
I. Trust in the Dean				
17.	The Dean in this college typically acts with the best interests of the faculty in mind.	.89		
28.	Faculty in this college can rely on the Dean.	.88		
30.	The faculty in this college has faith in the integrity of the Dean.	.86		
16.	The Dean in this college is competent in doing his or her job.	.85		
15.	The Dean in this college is unresponsive to faculty's concerns.	.84		
20.	The Dean in this college keeps his or her word.	.84		
3.	The Dean of this college does not show concern for the faculty.	-.84		
22.	The Dean doesn't tell faculty what is really going on.	-.81		
5.	Faculty in this college trusts their Dean.	.80		
14.	The faculty in this college is suspicious of most of the Dean's actions.	-.74		
26.	The Dean openly shares personal information with faculty.	.46		
II. Trust in Colleagues				
7.	Faculty in this college trusts each other.		.87	
18.	Faculty in this college believes in each other.		.83	
1.	Faculty in this college has faith in the integrity of their colleagues.		.83	
4.	Faculty in this college is open with each other.		.82	
19.	Faculty in this college is suspicious of each other.		-.80	
9.	Faculty in this college typically looks out for each other.		.73	
23.	Even in difficult situations, faculty in this college can depend on each other.		.68	
24.	When faculty in this college tells you something you can believe it.		.63	

Items By Factor	Factor	I	II	III
11.	Faculty in this college is not competent in their teaching responsibilities.		-.40	

III. Trust in Students

		I	II	III
12.	Faculty in this college trusts their students.			.76
29.	Students in this college can be counted on to do their work.			.75
8.	Faculty in this college believes students are competent learners.			.71
10.	Students in this college are caring toward one another.			.71
6.	Students in this college are reliable.			.63
21.	Faculty in this college believes what students say.			.63
25.	Students in this college are secretive.			.51
13.	Students in this college cheat if they have the chance.			.50
Eigenvalues		11.69	3.88	2.20
Cumulative % of Variance		41.73	55.56	63.40

Notes: Items in italics were deleted.

CHAPTER 11

THEORETICAL AND EMPIRICAL FOUNDATIONS OF MINDFUL SCHOOLS

Wayne K. Hoy, Charles Quincey Gage, III, and C. John Tarter

Mindfulness is more than being alert; in fact, it is a complex concept with scholarly roots in social psychology. This chapter develops the construct of school mindfulness as a collective property. After reviewing the conceptual and empirical underpinnings of both individual and organization mindfulness, a theoretical framework for the study of school mindfulness is proposed and then operationalized using factor analytic techniques. Mindfulness is focused on the faculty, the principal, and the school and their respective measures are short, reliable, and valid. Finally, a research agenda is sketched to demonstrate the heuristic nature of the construct.

INTRODUCTION

The art of life, it seems to me, is more that of the wrestler than of the dancer with respect to this: One must be prepared for onslaughts sudden and unexpected. *Marcus Aurelius*

Educational Administration, Policy, and Reform: Research and Measurement
A Volume in: Research and Theory In Educational Administration, pages 305–335.
Copyright © 2004 by Information Age Publishing, Inc.
All rights of reproduction in any form reserved.
ISBN: 1-59311-000-0 (hardcover), 1-59311-000-0 (paperback)

It is easy to become seduced by automatic and mindless behavior; in fact, a central premise of this analysis is that mindful organizations and mindful behaviors are much more difficult to attain than most people realize or are willing to admit. Organizations and people have to work at being mindful; to do otherwise is to court mindlessness. Our ultimate goal is to help make mindfulness a habit of mind. But this particular inquiry has two more attainable and specific purposes: a theoretical one—to conceptualize mindfulness and an empirical one—to operationalize it. To those ends, we draw and build upon earlier work on mindfulness (Hoy, 2003; Langer, 1989; Weick & Sutcliffe, 2001).

CONCEPTUALIZING MINDFULNESS

The construct of mindfulness can be examined on two levels, the individual and the collective. We begin with individual mindfulness and its theoretical underpinnings because it informs the construct of organizational mindfulness, which is the primary focus of this inquiry.

Mindfulness: An Individual Characteristic[1]

Too often educators take in information and act without much reflection because they have been successful in similar situations. Success sows the seeds of its own destruction. This tendency to act on initial mindsets is what psychologist call *premature cognitive commitment*, that is, individuals tend to seize on standard classifications, use routine rules and procedures, and then proceed to be seduced by their habits. Even when the routine ways don't work, they simply do more of the same in the belief that more is the key to fixing the problem. They fall victim to and are trapped by absolute categories and their routines, and find it difficult to break set and respond to a dynamic world in novel ways.

There is in all of us a "habit of mind" to adopt routine categories that make sense out of complexity, which is one reason individuals find formal rules and regulations so appealing. Ideologies of all kinds rationalize and justify behavior; they provide us with identities, rules of action, and standard interpretations (Trungpa, 1973). Once formed, such mindsets are difficult to break. Yet, it is the very creation of new categories and novel perspectives that characterizes mindfulness; rigid reliance on old categories and distinctions reinforces mindlessness. When teachers and administrators comply with senseless rules and orders, they are mindless; when they substitute their judgments for routine responses, they turn mindful.

Mindlessness evolves from repetition; people get used to doing things the same way; their responses become routine, automatic, and secure. Organizational members do things a certain way because "that is the way it is done here." Rules and routines bring stability, efficiency, predictability, and a general comfort to employees that things are being done "correctly."

The single-minded pursuit of objectives hinders mindfulness, whereas an emphasis on process facilitates it. For example, teachers and administrators often emphasize goals and objectives at the expense of process; they ask, "Can I do it?" rather than "How can I do it?" The latter question focuses on process by defining steps to achieve goals and is guided by the positive general principle: "There are no failures, only ineffective solutions" (Langer, 1989, p. 34). In contrast, an outcome approach typically presents facts as absolutes rather than conditionals, a tact that further discourages novel options and interpretations. To break the tyranny of unreflective behavior, *facts* are better viewed as conditional statements that are *true only in some situations*. Such a stance promotes thoughtful inquiry, searches for appropriate as well as inappropriate conditions, and encourages playfulness with ideas.

Context is another powerful force that produces mindless behavior because it controls our interpretations and makes one susceptible to what Langer calls "context confusion." People confuse the context regulating the behavior of another with context determining their own behavior. They assume that others' motives and intentions are the same as their own, which often is not the case. The consequence is narrowness, rigidity, and little examination of behavior from different perspectives. Contextual confusion reinforces viewing action from a single viewpoint. In sum, basic causes of mindlessness that influence our daily behavior are repetition, premature cognitive commitment, an emphasis on outcomes, and context confusion.

Mindfulness depends on the creation of new categories whereas mindlessness relies on rigid old ones. Mindfulness requires openness to new information, multiple perspectives, and a playful approach to ideas. Most events have multiple interpretations; mindful individuals search for novel, varied, and subtle meanings. For example, behavior can usually be cast in positive or negative terms, that is, strange can be creative, indecisive can be flexible, and weak can be sensitive. Mindfulness calls for a positive, playful, and nimble mind.

Mindfulness gives individuals more control over their contexts by helping them create different and useful perspectives. Langer (1989) gives the example of the Birdman of Alcatraz who was sentenced to life in prison with no hope of parole. One day he found a crippled bird that had flown into his cell window. He nursed the bird back to health and by noticing more and more cultivated an interest that led him to become an authority on bird diseases. Langer explains:

> Instead of living a dull, stale existence in a cell for forty odd years, the Bird-man of Alcatraz found that boredom can be just another construct of the mind, no more certain than freedom. There is always something new to notice. And he turned what might have been absolute hell into, at the least, a fascinating, mindful purgatory. (p. 74)

The point is that mindful individuals need not be trapped in narrow contexts; there is always something new to notice. The trick is see the unusual and avoid the anesthetic of routine.

Mindfulness also requires that expectations be tested rather than simply accepted. Too often individuals make assumptions and then verify them by accepting confirming and overlooking disconfirming information. Thus, they see more and more confirmation based on less and less data and their beliefs become more and more certain. The trouble begins when individuals fail to notice that they only see what is consistent with their beliefs and is only acerbated by the belief that "seeing is believing." That is wrong. Weick and Sutcliffe (2001) put it this way:

> Believing is seeing. You see what you expect to see. You see what you have the labels to see. You see what you have the skills to manage. Everything else is a blur. And in that "everything else" lies (sic) the developing unexpected event that can bite you and undermine your best intentions. (Weick & Roberts, 1993, p. 46)

In brief, mindfulness redirects attention from the expected to the unexpected, from the confirming to the disconfirming, from the comfortable to the uncomfortable, from the explicit to the implicit, from the manifest to the latent, from the factual to the probable, and from the simple to the complex (Weick & Sutcliffe, 2001). Mindfulness is a paradox: problems are viewed as opportunities, and successes are seen as problematic; mindfulness is both optimistic and skeptical. *Mindfulness is ongoing scrutiny of existing expectations, continuous refinement of those expectations based on new experiences, appreciation of the subtleties of context, and identification of novel aspects of context that can improve foresight and functioning.*[2] Mindfulness is hard work because it requires attention, flexibility, vigilance, openness, and the ability to break set.

Organizational Mindfulness: A Collective Property[3]

Mindful organizations have mindful leaders and participants, but organizational mindfulness is an organization property—a description of the collective and not of individuals per se. Weick and Sutcliffe (2001) use the theoretical underpinnings of individual mindfulness to examine and apply that thinking to organizations. Consider the following:

Imagine it's a busy day, and you shrink San Francisco airport to only one short runway and one ramp and one gate. Make planes take off and land at the same time, at half the present time interval, rock the runway from side to side, and require that everyone who leaves in the morning returns the same day. Make sure the equipment is so close to the envelope that it's fragile. Then turn off the radar to avoid detection, impose strict controls on the radios, fuel the aircraft in place with their engines running, put an enemy in the air, and scatter live bombs and rockets around. Now wet the whole thing down with seawater and oil, and man it with twenty-year-olds, half of whom have never seen an airplane close-up. Oh, and by the way, try not to kill anyone (Weick & Roberts, 1993, p. 357).

It is difficult to think of an environment that is so full of the unexpected and requires mindful decision making just to survive. Most organizations are not as precarious as this depiction of a working aircraft carrier. But Weick and Sutcliffe use the aircraft carrier as a prototype of highly reliable organization; that is, a mindful organization. They argue that five processes promote mindfulness in organizations: *preoccupation with failure, reluctance to simplify interpretations, sensitivity to operations, commitment to resilience, and deference to expertise.* We propose to use this framework to conceptualize and then operationalize mindful school structures.

Preoccupied with Failure

To focus on failure at first blush seems wrong and counterproductive, yet a preoccupation with failure is functional for the organization because it promotes continuous scanning for problems, large and small, but mostly small. The key is to identify small problems before they become large ones or crises. Mindful leaders and organizations avoid preoccupation with their successes, in part, because success breeds complacence and even arrogance, which ultimately leads to vulnerability. To the contrary, organizational mindfulness requires paying attention to small mistakes and seeking to eliminate them. For example, if new data show high achievement levels for *most* students in their schools, then mindful organizations examine the results with an eye to finding reasons for why the few failed. An old Vedic proverb captures mindfulness, "Advert the danger not yet arisen." The word is "advert" not avert. To call attention and catch the early warning of trouble, organizations must be continuously open and alert to new information and subtle changes (Langer, 1989). Mindful school structures are sensitive to all mistakes, but especially small ones.

Reluctance to Simplify Interpretations

Mindful school structures and their leaders are also reluctant to accept simplifications because of the need to understand the subtleties of the situation. Most of us want to simplify things to reinforce the belief that we are in control and understand things. A basic goal of mindfulness, however, is to simplify less and see more. Knowing that schools are complex and unpredictable, principals and teachers of mindful schools position themselves to see as much as possible, and then try to reconcile different interpretations without destroying the nuances of diversity and complexity. For example, differences in the perceptions between African Americans and whites or between males and females toward school activities need explanation and interpretation. Rival explanations should be developed and tested. Subtleties in the situation are important; in fact, the more complex the situation, the more important the nuances.

Sensitivity to Operations

Mindful organizations are sensitive to the unexpected. Surprises are inevitable and leaders know it. With the unexpected in mind, principals try to see the "big picture." They try to detect problems early, make continuous adjustments, and prevent them from enlarging. Mindful principals need to be unremitting in their scan for possible trouble; hence, they try to stay close to teaching and learning so that they understand what is happening and why. There should be a close tie between sensitivity to school operations and sensitivity to interpersonal relationships. When teachers refuse to speak freely, they enact a system that knows less than it needs to know to remain effective. School principals need to stay on top of teaching and learning because the real-time information limits time lag in information processing.

Commitment to Resilience

Mindful school structures are committed to resilience. Because no organization or system is perfect, mindful principals know better than most that they must develop a capacity to detect and recover from mistakes. No amount of anticipation and readiness is going to prevent mistakes and surprises. Schools must learn not only deal with the unexpected by anticipation but also *by resilience* (Wildavsky, 1991), that is, schools and their principals have to be sufficiently strong and flexible to cope with unpleasant surprises. Mindful school structures are not paralyzed by failure; instead, they detect, contain, and rebound from mistakes; principals and teachers are resilient.

Deference to Expertise

Finally, mindful school organizations are not administrative structures with rigid policies, rules, and procedures. Instead they are fluid decision-making systems that *defer to expertise* and not to status or rank. Rigid structures are replaced by enabling procedures in which consulting and listening to those with expertise are paramount (Hoy, 2003). Authority is situational and anchored in expertise. Mindful school structures defer to expertise regardless of rank or status.

THEORETICAL FRAMEWORK FOR MINDFUL SCHOOL STRUCTURE

In brief, organizations that are mindful anticipate the unexpected by developing a state of organizational readiness in which scanning, anticipating, containing, removing, and rebounding from the unexpected are ever present. Hence, we theorize that a mindful school structure has a well-developed organizational capability for mindfulness with five hallmarks:

- Focus on failure: Mindfulness catches trouble and the unexpected early. Mindful schools should constantly scan for potential failures that could evolve into much more serious issues. Teachers in such organizations need to identify and report problems early and be rewarded for so doing.
- Reluctance to simplify: Mindfulness comprehends the potential importance of issues despite their small size. The school world is complex, unstable, and often unpredictable. There is an inherent tendency to move toward simplification, but to simplify is often to erase parts of the problem. Mindful organizations simplify less and see more by embracing nuance and complexity.
- Sensitivity to technical operations: Mindfulness is sensitive to teaching and learning. The school's focus should be on its core technology—teaching and learning. Frequent assessing of teaching and learning prevents latent failures in the system from creating larger and serious problems.
- Resilience: Mindfulness removes, contains, or rebounds from the effects of the unexpected. The mindful school develops and refines the capacity within teachers and administrators to detect, contain, and overcome inevitable mistakes.
- Deference to expertise: Mindfulness embraces a structure and process that require decisions to migrate to expertise. Flexible systems encourage individuals with the most relevant knowledge about a specific problem to be involved in its solution, regardless of their status or position.

OPERATIONALIZING MINDFUL SCHOOL STRUCTURE

Using the theoretical formulation of mindful school structure developed above, items were written by the researchers to capture the elements of organizational mindfulness. The format was a 6-point, Likert-response set from strongly disagree to strongly agree. Teachers were asked to indicate the extent to which they agreed with the statements. Sample items for each of the five elements included the following:

- Mistakes are seen as important sources of information. (Focus on failure)
- Teachers are encouraged to have a difference of opinion. (Reluctance to simplify)
- My principal is involved in instructional decisions. (Sensitivity to technical operations)
- When things go badly, the teachers bounce back quickly. (Resilience)
- Teachers in this school value expertise more than authority. (Expertise)

Items were formulated that tapped each proposed facet of school mindfulness. The development of the instrument went through a number of phases:

1. The researchers created a pool of items.
2. A panel of experts reacted to the items.
3. A preliminary version was field tested with teachers.
4. Two pilot studies were performed to identify and refine the factor structure.
5. Finally, reliability and validity of the instrument were assessed.

Developing Items

A pool of items that described each of the five elements of collective mindfulness was constructed. More specifically, brief descriptors of each of the behaviors were written. One hundred eleven items were created by the researchers, about 20 to 25 for each of the aspects of mindfulness. The items were concise, accurate descriptions of teacher attitudes and behavior.

Panel of Experts

To check the content validity of the items, all statements were submitted to a panel of experts, professors of the College of Education at The Ohio State University. The panel was asked to vet the questions as to how well the items tapped each element of the theoretical framework. Only items for which there was complete agreement were selected for the pilot form; 67

items survived the panel of experts, with a minimum of 11 items for each element of collective mindfulness (See Appendix A).

Field Test

Before the survey instrument was formally tested, an informal field test was conducted to check the clarity of the directions of the survey and the appropriateness of the items. A small group of experienced teachers was asked to examine the questionnaire with an eye toward the ease of responding to the measure. Feedback was generally positive. The teachers agreed that the items were simple, direct, and easily understood. A few minor editing changes were made, but the pilot instrument remained intact.

PILOT STUDY 1

Following the panel review, field test, and revisions, the 67-item questionnaire (see Appendix A) was piloted to explore the factor structure of the measure.

Sample

A convenience sample of 101 teachers, representing more than 90 schools, in central Ohio and North Carolina was asked to respond to the questionnaire.

Results

The data were analyzed using principal components analysis with a varimax rotation. The initial loadings were grouped into five components in an attempt to match the elements of the conceptual framework that generated the items. The component structure did not make conceptual sense because virtually each of the five components had items from multiple aspects of mindfulness. Thus, in order to simplify the analysis, a series of five exploratory principal components analyses were run using the following guidelines:

- First, unless there was a compelling conceptual reason to maintain the item in subsequent analysis, all items were deleted that loaded highly (above .40) on two or more factors.
- Second, each item had to load at a minimum of .50 on one of the components to remain.
- Third, the ultimate goal was simple structure, that is, high loadings on one dimension and low loadings on all the others.

As we proceeded through the iterations of principal components analysis, it became clear that there were two dominant components; the five elements of the conceptual framework were not independent aspects of mindfulness. The two components explained 48% of the variance and 34 items remained and loaded on one or the other of the components.

What was conceptually intriguing about the two components is that all the elements in the first component explained mindfulness of the principal, whereas, those in the second explained mindfulness of the faculty. Moreover, a close examination of the items revealed that most of the aspects of mindfulness were represented in each group. Alpha coefficients of reliabilities for the two sets of items were .95 and .84 respectively.

PILOT STUDY 2

Before conducting the next pilot study to refine the mindfulness instrument, new items were added to insure that all five aspects of mindfulness were represented in both the mindfulness of the principal and of the faculty. In addition, to balance the instrument, each of the elements had at least two items that were negatively stated and two items that were positively stated. Some of the redundant items were eliminated leaving 20 items for principal and 20 for faculty mindfulness, or a total of 40 items on this version of the questionnaire.

Items

The items on the revised questionnaire were as follows:

Sensitivity to Teaching and Learning (Principal)

- My principal often provides feedback about teaching and learning.
- My principal is an expert on teaching and learning.

- My principal does not really know what is happening in most classrooms.
- My principal is removed from classroom activities.

Commitment to Resilience (Principal)
- When things go badly, the principal bounces back quickly.
- Administrator burnout is a problem in this school.
- When a crisis occurs the principal effectively deals with it, so we can get back to teaching.
- In times of crisis, my principal takes too much time to deal with the situation.

Reluctance to Simplify (Principal)
- My principal negotiates differences among faculty without destroying the diversity of opinions.
- My principal often jumps to conclusions.
- Teachers in my building are encouraged to share information.
- The principal of this school does not value the opinions of the teachers.

Expertise (Principal)
- The principal welcomes challenges from the teachers.
- The principal in this building defers to the knowledge of the teachers.
- Teachers in my building are encouraged to share information.
- The principal of this school does not value the opinions of the teachers.

Focus on Failure and Mistakes (Principal)
- In this school teachers communicate their mistakes freely with the principal.
- Teachers do not trust the principal enough to admit their mistakes.
- Mistakes are seen as important sources of information.
- In my building we focus on problem solving no matter who is to blame.

Sensitivity to Teaching and Learning (Faculty)
- Teachers in my building waste a lot of time.
- In this school teachers with teaching problems can usually find someone to help resolve them.
- Most teachers in this building are reluctant to change.
- In this school teachers welcome feedback about ways to improve.

Commitment to Resilience (Faculty)
- When things go badly, the teachers bounce back quickly.
- Too many teachers in my building give up when things go bad.
- This school has difficulty rebounding from mistakes.
- People in this school can rely on each other even when things are tense.

Reluctance to Simplify (Faculty)
- Diversity of ideas is celebrated in my building.
- Teachers negotiate differences among each other without destroying the diversity of opinions.
- Teachers in this school often jump to conclusions.
- Teachers don't tolerate differences of opinion in this school.

Expertise (Faculty)
- Teachers in this school value expertise more than authority.
- In our school the people who are most qualified to make a decision, make it.
- People in this school respect power more than knowledge.
- In our school, many decisions are made by those not qualified to make them.

Focus on Failure and Mistakes (Faculty)
- Teachers in my building learn from their mistakes and change things so they do not happen again.
- Mistakes are seen as opportunities to improve rather than signs of weakness.
- In my building teachers hide mistakes.
- Teachers in my building are hesitant to admit personal failure for fear of retribution.

The revised mindfulness measure was now ready for further testing. Principal components analysis was a useful tool for reducing and culling the initial set of items. In the second pilot, we relied upon principal factor analysis with varimax rotation to further refine the instrument. In addition, we decided to do a preliminary check of the predictive validity of the measure. To that end, we incorporated two measures that were predicted to be related to mindful organizational structures: enabling bureaucracy and collective efficacy both were hypothesized to be positively correlated with mindfulness.

Sample

The sample of this study was more diverse and larger than the first. The teachers came from 103 schools in central Ohio, Oklahoma, North Carolina, Michigan, New York, Texas, and Virginia. Professors from Ohio State, St. John's University, University of Michigan, Oklahoma State University, North Carolina State University, University of Texas at San Antonio, and the College of William and Mary were instrumental in helping us collect these data.

Instrument

In addition to the 40-item instrument to measure school mindfulness, teachers were asked to respond to an enabling bureaucracy scale and a collective efficacy scale (see Appendix B). These additional scales were used as a predictive validity check. The validity and reliability of the scales are found in Hoy and Sweetland (2001); Goddard, Hoy, and Woolfolk Hoy, (2000); Hoy and Hoy (2003).

Data Collection

Data were collected from 103 different schools in 7 states. Our colleagues administered the scales to teachers in their classes and from randomly selected individuals in nearby schools. Specific attention was given to soliciting only one teacher from each school so that the respondents represented one school each.

Results

First, we factor analyzed the forty mindfulness items using principal axis technique with varimax rotation. Based on the results of the first pilot study, a two-factor solution was specified and found. Factor 1 was identified as principal mindfulness and all the principal items loaded most strongly on that factor. Likewise, the second factor was defined by only those items that measured mindfulness of the faculty. There were no exceptions; all items loaded most heavily on the theoretically expected factor.

Six of the 40 items, however, had substantial dual loadings and were, therefore, eliminated. And, the 34 remaining items were refactored using a two-factor solution. The results of this second analysis provided an even cleaner picture of the two factors of school mindfulness—principal mindfulness and faculty mindfulness.

TABLE 1
Factor Structure for of the School Mindfulness Scale for the Pilot Study

Mindfulness of Principal (MP)	*MP*	*MF*
The principal welcomes challenges from teachers.	.79	
When a crisis occurs the principal deals with it so we can get back to teaching.	.77	
My principal negotiates faculty differences without destroying the diversity of opinions.	.77	
The principal of this school does not value the opinions of the teachers.	−.73	
My principal is an expert on teaching and learning.	.72	
My principal often jumps to conclusions.	−.71	
Teachers do not trust the principal enough to admit their mistakes.	−.69	
Mistakes are seen as important sources of information.	.68	
In times of crisis it takes my principal too much time to effectively deal with the situation.	−.68	
My principal does not really know what is happening in most classrooms.	−.58	
Cumulative Variance	28.39	
Alpha Coefficient	.92	
Mindfulness of the Faculty (MF)		
When things go badly teachers bounce back quickly.		.74
Teachers in my building learn from their mistakes and change so they do not happen again.		.69
In this school teachers welcome feedback about ways to improve.		.66
Teachers negotiate differences among each other without destroying the diversity of opinions.	.33	.63
Too many teachers in my building give up when things go bad.		−.58
Teachers in this school value expertise more than authority.		.54
Most teachers in this building are reluctant to change.		−.53
Teachers in this school often jump to conclusions.		−.49
People in this school respect power more than knowledge.	−.32	−.47
In my building teachers hide mistakes.	−.38	−.45
Cumulative Variance		48.03
Alpha Coefficient		.85

The final exploratory factor analysis of these pilot data was performed with the aim of simplifying and reducing the length of the scale. Three goals guided the factor analysis:

- First, simple structure—items should load high on one factor and low on the other.
- Second, the 20 best items would be selected such that for each element of mindfulness there was one positive and one negative statement.
- Third, all items had to make conceptual sense by loading on the anticipated factor.

The results of the factor analysis are reported in Table 1. All the items loaded on the appropriate factor, which supported the construct validity of school mindfulness. Although simple structure was approached, three items had a loading on the second factor above .3 (see Table 1). Both factors had strong reliabilities—.92 and .85 respectively.

SOME VALIDITY EVIDENCE

Next, we did a preliminary check of the predictive validity of the school mindfulness scales (Appendix C) by correlating them with enabling bureaucracy and collective efficacy. Let's examine each of these concepts separately.

School Structure and School Mindfulness

There are clear conceptual similarities between mindful schools and school structures that enable teaching and learning. Both require trust, openness, flexibility, cooperation, and organizational learning. Similarly, both are concerned with problem solving, collaboration, and anticipating the unexpected. There are some differences, however. Mindfulness directs attention to a preoccupation with failure, an attribute not typically associated with enabling structures (Hoy, 2003). Further, success can be a problem in enabling organizations because it sows the seeds of its own destruction. For example, principals often attribute a school's success to themselves, or, at least, to their teachers rather than to fortuitous circumstances. Therefore, as the school grows more confident, the school may begin to focus on its successes rather than to be alert to its shortcomings. Nonetheless, there is more compatibility between school mindfulness and enabling structure. Thus, we predicted that enabling school structure is related to both dimensions of school mindfulness. Enabling school structure, as predicted, has a significant correlation of .56 (p < .01) with faculty mindfulness, .87 (p < .01) with principal mindfulness, and .83 (p < .01) with the overall index of school mindfulness.

Collective Efficacy and School Mindfulness

Collective efficacy is the shared beliefs of teachers that the faculty as a whole has a positive effect on student learning. The consequences of high collective efficacy are the acceptance of challenging goals, strong organizational effort, persistence, and resilience to the task at hand (Goddard, Hoy, & Hoy Woolfolk, 2000), which are all characteristics that seem highly compatible with mindful principal and teacher behavior. Similarly, high collective efficacy is associated with low conflict, teacher sense of control over their own work, and a general trust in their colleagues (Goddard, Hoy, & Woolfolk Hoy, 2000). Hence, we hypothesized that collective efficacy would be correlated with all dimensions of school mindfulness. Indeed, that was the case. Collective efficacy was positively correlated with teacher mindfulness (r = .65, p < .01), principal mindfulness (r = .47, p < .01), and with the overall index of school mindfulness (r = .62, p < .01). In spite of the efforts to make principal mindfulness and faculty mindfulness independent (orthogonal factor analysis was used), it probably is not surprising that the two are moderately correlated (r = .54, p < .01). The results are summarized in Table 2.

The confirmation of the hypotheses linking mindful school structure, enabling school structure, and collective efficacy support the validity of school mindfulness as conceptualized in this study.

TABLE 2
Some Validity Evidence: Pilot Sample Correlations of
Mindfulness with Criterion Variables

Variables		FM	PM	SM	ES	CE
Faculty Mindfulness	(FM)	(.85)				
Principal Mindfulness	(PM)	.54**	(.92)			
School Mindfulness	(SM)	.84**	.91**	(.92)		
Enabling Structure	(ES)	.56**	.87**	.83**	(.93)	
Collective Efficacy	(CE)	.65**	.47**	.62**	.58**	(.89)

Notes: **p<.01

Alpha coefficients of reliability are one the diagonal

Short Forms

At this stage, the analyses have produced three reliable measures of mindfulness—the mindfulness of the principal (10 items), mindfulness of the faculty (10 items), and mindfulness of the school structure (20 items), each with validity support. Although the results were gratifying, we wondered if a yet more parsimonious measure of each property lay hidden in the existing scales. In other words, could the scales be shortened without losing their psychometric properties?

To answer this question, we examined the factor loadings for each scale; we selected those items with the strongest loadings while making sure that all five elements of mindfulness were included and that about half were positive and half were negative statements. Seven items for each dimension of mindfulness were identified as follows:

Short Scale for Principal Mindfulness
- The principal welcomes challenges from teachers.
- When a crisis occurs the principal deals with it so we can get back to teaching.
- My principal negotiates faculty differences without destroying the diversity of opinions.
- The principal of this school does not value the opinions of the teachers.
- My principal is an expert on teaching and learning.
- My principal often jumps to conclusions.
- Teachers do not trust the principal enough to admit their mistakes.

Short Scale for Faculty Mindfulness
- When things go badly teachers bounce back quickly.
- Teachers in my building learn from their mistakes and change so they do not happen again.
- In this school teachers welcome feedback about ways to improve.
- Teachers negotiate differences among each other without destroying diversity of opinions.
- Too many teachers in my building give up when things go bad.
- Most teachers in this building are reluctant to change.
- People in this school respect power more than knowledge.

The short scale (Appendix D) for the overall index of school mindfulness is simply a composite of the above fourteen items. The psychometric properties of the short scales were impressive and using the shorter measures loses little. No reliability coefficient loses more than .02. Moreover,

TABLE 3
Comparison of Reliabilities and Correlations of the Long and Short Forms
in Pilot Sample

Form	Reliability	Short Form	Reliability	Correlation
Principal Mindfulness (10 items)	.92	Principal Mindfulness (7 items)	.91	.98
Faculty Mindfulness (10 items)	.85	Faculty Mindfulness (7 items)	.83	.98
School Mindfulness Index (20 items)	.92	School Mindfulness Index (14 items)	.90	.99

the correlation between the forms is near 1.00. Table 3 compares the alpha coefficients of reliability for the long and short scales and their correlations.

A COMPREHENSIVE TEST OF THE MINDFULNESS SCALES

Having developed three measures of mindfulness in the field and pilot studies, the next step was to evaluate the scales using a more comprehensive sample of schools with a much larger number of teacher respondents. Our goals were to confirm and demonstrate the stability of the factor structures and to evaluate the utility and psychometric properties of the variables. To that end we collected data from a cross-sectional sample of middle schools in Ohio.

Sample

Survey data from 75 middle schools in the state of Ohio were collected. These schools were distributed in eleven counties. Although the sample selected was not random, care was taken to insure participation of urban, suburban, and rural schools. Currently, the distribution of middle schools in Ohio is 39% rural, 34% urban, and 27% suburban. Correspondingly, the study's schools are distributed across 19% rural, 41% urban, and 40% suburban settings. Of the 612 school districts in the state, 43 participated in the study. Staff completed a total of approximately 2,600 usable surveys. The sample was also similar to the population of middle schools in Ohio in terms of student enrollment, average teacher salary, average teacher experience, and the size of the faculty. In brief, the sample of schools was fairly typical of middle schools in Ohio.

Data Collection

Data were collected from the middle schools at regularly scheduled faculty meetings. A member of the research team explained the general purpose of the study, assured the confidentiality of all responses, and asked teachers complete the questionnaires. Because this project was part of a larger study of organizational properties and because the unit of analysis was the school, two random groups of teachers responded to different surveys. One set of teachers responded to the mindfulness items along with other questions, and the second group of teachers described other school properties, including enabling structure. No attempt was made to gather data from faculty who were not present at the meeting, but virtually all teachers returned usable questionnaires.

Factor Analysis and Reliability of the Mindfulness Scales

A series of factor analyses was conducted to check the factor structure of school mindfulness and to assess its construct validity. Principal axis factoring was the extraction method used in a varimax orthogonal rotation with Kaiser normalization applied to all 20 items. First, we factor analyzed the 20-item scale. Items were expected to load on the two hypothesized dimensions of school mindfulness—mindfulness of the principal and mindfulness of the faculty.

The results supported the construct validity of the scale and demonstrated the stability of the factor structure. That is, the two hypothesized dimensions of school mindfulness were confirmed and explained more than 66% of the variance. The structure of the 20-item scale was the same for this comprehensive sample as it was for the pilot. Moreover, alpha coefficients were .96 for principal mindfulness, .93 for faculty mindfulness, and .95 for the overall measure. A comparison of the factor structures for the pilot study and the current comprehensive sample is reported in Table 4.

Next, we checked the factor structure of short 14-item mindfulness scale. Again we hypothesized two dimensions of school mindfulness—mindfulness of the principal and mindfulness of the faculty. As anticipated the two factors were confirmed, which together explained nearly 72% of the variance. Alpha coefficients were .96, .91, and .94 for principal mindfulness, faculty mindfulness, and overall school mindfulness respectively. The results of the factor analysis are reported in Table 5.

TABLE 4
Comparative Factor Analyses of 20-item Mindfulness Scale in Two Studies

Item	Pilot	Comprehensive
Mindfulness of Principal		
The principal welcomes challenges from teachers.	.79	.88
When a crisis occurs the principal deals with it so we can get back to teaching.	.77	.81
My principal negotiates faculty differences without destroying the diversity of opinions.	.77	.83
The principal of this school does not value the opinions of the teachers.	−.73	−.92
My principal is an expert on teaching and learning.	.72	.87
My principal often jumps to conclusions.	−.71	−.75
Teachers do not trust the principal enough to admit their mistakes.	−.69	−.87
Mistakes are seen as important sources of information.	.68	.56
In times of crisis it takes my principal too much time to effectively deal with the situation.	−.68	−.58
My principal does not really know what is happening in most classrooms.	−.58	−.76
Cumulative Variance	28.39	52.61
Alpha Coefficient	.92	.96
Mindfulness of the Faculty		
When things go badly teachers bounce back quickly.	.74	.77
Teachers in my building learn from their mistakes and change so they do not happen again.	.69	.91
In this school teachers welcome feedback about ways to improve.	.66	.78
Teachers negotiate differences among each other without destroying the diversity of opinions.	.63	.74
Too many teachers in my building give up when things go bad.	−.58	−.80
Teachers in this school value expertise more than authority.	.54	.62
Most teachers in this building are reluctant to change.	−.53	−.55
Teachers in this school often jump to conclusions.	−.49	−.55
People in this school respect power more than knowledge.	−.47	−.64
In my building teachers hide mistakes.	−.45	−.67
Cumulative Variance	48.03	66.16
Alpha Coefficient	.85	.93

TABLE 5
Factor Analysis of the 14-item Mindfulness Scale (Short Form)
from the Comprehensive Sample

Item	*MP*	*MF*
Mindfulness of Principal (MP)		
The principal of this school does not value the opinions of the teachers.	−.93	
The principal welcomes challenges from teachers.	.91	
Teachers do not trust the principal enough to admit their mistakes.	−.87	
My principal negotiates faculty differences without destroying the diversity of opinions.	.86	
My principal is an expert on teaching and learning.	.84	
My principal often jumps to conclusions.	−.80	
When a crisis occurs the principal deals with it so we can get back to teaching.	.75	
Cumulative Variance	56.2	
Alpha Coefficient	.96	
Mindfulness of the Faculty (MF)		
Teachers in my building learn from their mistakes and change so they do not happen again.		.91
Too many teachers in my building give up when things go bad.		−.82
When things go badly teachers bounce back quickly.		.79
In this school teachers welcome feedback about ways to improve.		.79
Teachers negotiate differences among each other without destroying the diversity of opinions.		.75
People in this school respect power more than knowledge.		−.60
Most teachers in this building are reluctant to change.		−.55
MF Variance	15.5	
Cumulative Variance		71.73
Alpha Coefficient		.91

SOME FURTHER VALIDITY EVIDENCE

We now examine the predicted correlations of the mindfulness scales with the same criterion variables that we used in the pilot study. The theoretical reasoning and predictions are the same; that is, both enabling structure and collective efficacy are positively related to all aspects of mindful organi-

TABLE 6
Validity Evidence for Comprehensive Sample: Correlations of Mindfulness
with Criterion Variables

	Principal Mindfulness	Faculty Mindfulness	School Mindfulness
Enabling Structure	.64 (.66)a	.51 (.50)	.66 (.67)
Collective Efficacy	.50 (.49)	.80 (.79)	.69 (.69)

Notes: *The short form is in the parentheses; all correlations are significant beyond the
.01 level.

zation. A look at the results in Table 6 show that the hypotheses are supported for both the long (20-item) and short (14-item) forms. All the predictions are confirmed; both collective efficacy and enabling school structure are significantly related to all aspects of the mindfulness variable. Moreover, the correlations are virtually the same regardless of whether the short or long form is used to measure the variables (see Table 6).

SUMMARY AND CONCLUSIONS

The notion of mindfulness has been of interest to social psychologist for some time (Langer, 1989; Langer, 1997; Weick & Sutcliffe, 2001). Ellen Langer pioneered the development of the construct of mindfulness more than a decade ago, but only recently has attention turned to collective and organizational mindfulness (Hoy, 2003; Weick & Sutcliffe, 2001). We began our analysis by tracing the roots and emergence of the study of mindfulness in individuals and then considered the use of the concept to explain high reliability organizations. Using the elements of mindful organizations suggested by Weick and Sutcliffe (2001), we developed a theoretical framework for the analysis of mindfulness in school settings in terms of five elements:

- Focus on mistakes
- Reluctance to simplify
- Sensitivity to teaching and learning
- Commitment to resilience
- Deference to expertise to solve problems

Clearly, mindful organization is a complex concept that is *not simply being alert*, rather it describes a set of behaviors and beliefs that enables the organization to cope with the unexpected by constantly scanning, anticipating, containing, removing, and rebounding from surprises and mistakes.

Based on the theoretical framework, we turned to the problem of the empirical nature of mindfulness in schools. How can these aspects of mindfulness be deciphered and measured? Our strategy for describing mindfulness is to capture it empirically by representing its elements as simple forms of common faculty and principal behavior and beliefs in schools. Now, to that end we joined forces and together with our colleagues developed more than 100 examples of what mindfulness might be. We subjected those behaviors to a critical analysis by both ourselves and a panel of expert professors. Then, we tested this bank of items with a small group of experienced teachers in the field by soliciting their suggestions.

Drawing on their feedback, we refined the items and then submitted them to a diverse sample of teachers in 90 schools in Central Ohio and North Carolina. Using principal components analysis, we identified two dominant aspects of mindfulness, principal and faculty, each of which included all five elements of our theory.

Next, we piloted the refined and revised measure of mindfulness in a more diverse and larger sample than the first—103 schools in Ohio, Oklahoma, New Jersey, North Carolina, New York, Texas, and Virginia. With the help of principal axis factoring, we were able to reduce the number of items in our measure to 20, 10 to measure principal mindfulness and 10 to measure faculty mindfulness. The factor analytic results supported the construct validity, and a series of theoretically derived hypotheses were used to test its predictive validity. The results proved encouraging.

Finally, a third test of the construct and its measure was performed using about 2600 teachers from 75 schools in Ohio. The results supported the construct validity, confirmed the factor stability of the measure, underscored the two related aspects of mindfulness in schools, and provided highly reliable measures for each. In brief, we have developed two sets of reliable and valid measures for school mindfulness. A long form contains 20 items and a shorter form has 14 (see Appendix C). The parsimonious 14-item measure works as well as the slightly longer measure and has the same strong psychometric properties in terms of both reliability and validity.

The under girding theory of mindfulness argues persuasively that mindful schools should be learning organizations, that is, information pertinent to their operation should flow across the school quickly and allow the school to anticipate problems and respond to surprises in a robust fashion. Beyond organizational learning and responsiveness, it seems reasonable to suggest that mindful schools will have cultures imbued with trust, efficacy, and humanism (Hoy & Miskel, in press). Similarly, school mindfulness should be related in positive ways to motivation, structure, and politics. Further, the processes of organization—decision making, leadership, and communication—should be improved by mindful organization or, to the reverse, seriously hampered by organization mindlessness. The research questions, hypotheses, and challenges are manifold. Ultimately, the generated hypotheses must be strained through the sieve of adequate empirical test before they can be considered accurate representations of reality (Merton, 1957). We have provided a modest first step in this endeavor with the theoretical development of the construct of school mindfulness and its reliable and valid measurement.

NOTES

1.   This theoretical analysis builds upon Langer's pioneering work (1989) on mindfulness and the earlier conceptual work of Hoy (2003).
2.   This definition of mindfulness is adapted from Langer (1989) and Weick and Sutcliffe (2001).
3.   This section draws heavily from Weick and Sutcliffe (2001) and Hoy (2003).

REFERENCES

Goddard, R. D., Hoy, W. K., & Woolfolk Hoy, A. (2000). Collective teacher efficacy: Its meaning, measure, and impact on student achievement. *American Educational Research Journal, 37*, 479–508.

Hoy, W. K. (2003). An analysis of enabling and mindful school structures: Some theoretical, research, and practical consideration. *Journal of Educational Administration, 41*, 87–108.

Hoy, W. K., & Miskel, C. G. (in press). *Educational administration: Theory, research, and practice* (7th Ed.). New York, NY: McGraw Hill.

Hoy, A. W., & Hoy, W. K. (2003). *Instructional leadership: A learning-centered guide.* Boston, MA: Allyn & Bacon.

Hoy, W. K., & Sweetland, S. R. (2001). Designing better schools: The meaning and nature of enabling school structure. *Educational Administration Quarterly, 37*, 296–321.

Langer, E. J. (1989). *Mindfulness.* Cambridge, MA: Perseus Books.

Langer, E. J. (1997). *The power of mindful learning.* Cambridge, MA: Perseus Books.

Merton, R. K. (1957). *Social theory and social structure.* New York, NY: The Free Press.

Trungpa, C. (1973). *Cutting through spiritual materialism.* Boulder and London: Shambhala.

Weick, K. W., & Roberts, K. L. (1993). Collective mind in organizations: Heedful interrelating on flight decks. *Administrative Science Quarterly, 28*, 357–381.

Weick, K. W., & Sutcliffe, K. M. (2001). *Managing the unexpected.* San Francisco: Jossey-Bass.

Widlavsky, A. (1991). *Searching for safety.* New Brunswick, NJ: Transaction.

APPENDIX A:
PILOT FORM I

DIRECTIONS: The following are statements about your school. Please indicate the extent to which you agree with each statement along a scale from strongly disagree (1) to strongly agree (6). There are no correct or incorrect answers so please give us your candid and anonymous judgments.

1. In my school there is little tolerance for error.
2. Diversity of ideas is celebrated by staff in my building.
3. Criticism of any kind is not welcome by teachers in my building.
4. When things go badly, the principal bounces back quickly.
5. It is generally easy for teachers to obtain expert advice when they need it.
6. The faculty in this school believes in the premise that "if it is not broken, don't fix it."
7. Teachers are encouraged to have a difference of opinion
8. My principal does not really know what is happening in most classrooms.
9. This school has difficulty rebounding from mistakes.
10. Problems in this school are solved by those with the knowledge regardless of their experience or position.
11. Skeptics and curmudgeons are welcome in this school.
12. In this school, small problems are usually caught before they become big ones.
13. In this school problems have a way of persisting.
14. Teachers in my building are encouraged to share information.
15. My principal is an expert on teaching and learning.
16. Mistakes are seen as important sources of information.
17. My principal is good at negotiating differences among faculty without destroying the diversity of opinions.
18. The principal goes by the book.
19. Teacher burnout is a problem in this school.
20. Teachers in my building are hesitant to admit personal failure for fear of retribution.
21. There is a healthy skepticism among the faculty in this school.
22. Teachers in my building waste a lot of classroom time.
23. Many teachers in my building give up when things go bad.
24. People in this school respect power more than knowledge.
25. In this school problems with teachers and parents are "nipped in the bud."
26. The principal expects no deviation from the rules.
27. Teachers take responsibility for their mistakes.
28. My principal is removed from classroom activities.

29. In this school major problems immobilize the principal.
30. Teachers and principals in this school are continually scanning for problems and mistakes.
31. In this school teachers generally do not know what is happening in each other's classrooms.
32. Teachers with a difference of opinion keep it to themselves.
33. Most teachers in this building are reluctant to change.
34. The principal welcomes challenges from teachers.
35. In this school teachers with teaching problems can usually find someone to help resolve them.
36. Rules in this school are flexible guidelines, rather that fixed procedures.
37. In my building we focus on problem solving no matter who is to blame.
38. My principal often jumps to conclusions.
39. My principal is involved in instructional decisions.
40. When things go badly, the teachers bounce back quickly.
41. In our school the people who are most qualified to make a decision make it.
42. Teachers in my building learn from their mistakes and change things so they do not happen again.
43. In this school, there is one right way to do things.
44. When things go wrong, nothing happens to fix them.
45. In this school teachers welcome feedback about ways to improve.
46. Teachers in this building defer to the authority of the principal.
47. My principal comes into my class regularly.
48. People in this school can rely on each other even when things are tense.
49. In my building teachers hide mistakes.
50. Questioning the status quo is encouraged in this school.
51. In this school, when things get tough, we get going.
52. There is little question that the principal of this school is the boss.
53. My principal often provides feedback about teaching and learning.
54. Teachers are encouraged to spot mistakes and report them.
55. Most teachers in my building believe that teaching and learning are simple, direct processes.
56. Mistakes are seen as opportunities to improve rather than signs of weakness.
57. The problems in this school overwhelm teachers.
58. Teachers in this school value expertise more than authority.
59. There is a sense of urgency to improve teaching practices in my building.
60. Teachers do not trust the principal enough to admit their mistakes.
61. If we are having problems in my building, there is usually a simple reason why.

62. The principal in this building defers to the knowledge of the teachers.
63. When something goes wrong, teachers spontaneously look for ways to fix the problem.
64. Many problems in this school are solved informally.
65. In this school, teachers communicate their mistakes freely with the principal.
66. Skepticism is not welcome in my building.
67. Teachers in this school see problems as opportunities.

APPENDIX B:
PILOT FORM II

DIRECTIONS: The following are statements about your school. Please indicate the extent to which you agree with each statement along a scale from strongly disagree (1) to strongly agree (6). There are no correct or incorrect answers so please give us your candid and anonymous judgments.

1. Diversity of ideas is celebrated by staff in my building.
2. When things go badly, the principal bounces back quickly.
3. Teachers are encouraged to have a difference of opinion.
4. My principal does not really know what is happening in most classrooms.
5. Home life provides so many advantages that students here are bound to learn.
6. This school has difficulty rebounding from mistakes.
7. In this school, the authority of the principal is used to undermine teachers.
8. The principal keeps a close check on sign-in times.
9. Teachers in my building are encouraged to share information.
10. My principal is an expert on teaching and learning.
11. Mistakes are seen as important sources of information.
12. Students here just aren't motivated to learn.
13. My principal negotiates faculty differences without destroying the diversity of opinions.
14. The administrators in this school use their authority to enable teachers to do their job.
15. The principal of this school does not value the opinions of the teachers.
16. Teachers in my building are hesitant to admit personal failure for fear of retribution.
17. Teachers in my building waste a lot of classroom time.
18. Too many teachers in my building give up when things go bad.

19. People in this school respect power more than knowledge.
20. In our school many decisions are made by those not qualified to make them.
21. The administrative hierarchy in this school enables teachers to do their job.
22. Teachers in this school often jump to conclusions.
23. Teachers in this school do not have the skills to deal with student disciplinary problem.
24. My principal is removed from classroom activities.
25. The principal corrects teachers' mistakes.
26. Teachers in this school are able to get through to the most difficulty students.
27. Most teachers in this building are reluctant to change.
28. The principal welcomes challenges from teachers.
29. The administrative hierarchy obstructs student achievement.
30. In this school, teachers with teaching problems can usually find someone to help resolve them.
31. Teachers here are confident they will be able to motivate their students
32. If a child doesn't want to learn, teachers here give up.
33. In my building we focus on problem solving no matter who is to blame.
34. My principal often jumps to conclusions.
35. The opportunities in this community help ensure that students will learn.
36. The principal closely checks teacher activities.
37. Teachers negotiate differences among each other without destroying the diversity of opinions.
38. The principal supervises teachers closely.
39. When things go badly, the teachers bounce back quickly.
40. Teachers in my building learn from their mistakes and change so they do not happen again.
41. Administrative rules help rather than hinder.
42. When a crisis occurs the principal effectively deals with it so we can get back to teaching.
43. Even when things go wrong,, the principal forges ahead.
44. Teachers here don't have the skills needed to produce meaningful learning.
45. Administrative rules in this school are used to punish teachers.
46. Learning is more difficult at this school because students are worried about their safety.
47. In this school teachers welcome feedback about ways to improve.
48. Administrator burnout is a problem in this school.
49. People in this school can rely on each other even when things are tense.

50. In my building teachers hide mistakes.
51. Administrative rules in this school are substituted for professional judgment
52. Questioning the status quo is encouraged in this school.
53. In this school red tape is a problem.
54. Teachers in this school believe that every child can learn.
55. My principal often provides feedback about teaching and learning.
56. Mistakes are seen as opportunities to improve rather than signs of weakness.
57. The principal monitors everything teachers do.
58. The administrative hierarchy of this school obstructs innovation.
59. Teachers don't tolerate differences of opinion in this school.
60. Drug and alcohol abuse in the community make learning difficult for students here.
61. Teachers in this school value expertise more than authority.
62. Teachers do not trust the principal enough to admit their mistakes.
63. The principal in this building defers to the knowledge of the teachers.
64. These students come to school ready to learn.
65. Administrative rules in this school are guides to solutions rather than rigid procedures.
66. The principal rules with an iron fist.
67. Rules in this school enable authentic communication between teachers and administrators.
68. In times of crisis, it takes my principal too much time to deal effectively with the situation.
69. The administrative hierarchy of this school facilitates the mission of this school.
70. In this school teachers communicate their mistakes freely with the principal.
71. In our school the people who are most qualified to make a decision make it.

APPENDIX C:
SCHOOL MINDFULNESS SCALE©

DIRECTIONS: The following are statements about your school. Please indicate the extent to which you agree with each statement along a scale from strongly disagree (1) to strongly agree (6). There are no correct or incorrect answers so please give us your candid and anonymous judgments.

1. Teachers negotiate differences among each other without destroying the diversity of opinions.

2. The principal welcomes challenges from the teachers.
3. Mistakes are seen as important sources of information.
4. In times of crisis my principal takes too much time to deal with the situation.
5. In this school, teachers welcome feedback about ways to improve.
6. Too many teachers in my building give up when things go bad.
7. My principal negotiates differences among faculty without destroying the diversity of opinions.
8. My principal is an expert on teaching and learning.
9. Most teachers in this building are reluctant to change.
10. My principal does not really know what is happening in most classes.
11. When things go badly, the teachers bounce back quickly.
12. Teachers in my building learn from their mistakes and change so they do not happen again.
13. Teachers do not trust the principal enough to admit their mistakes.
14. The principal of this school does not value the opinions of the teachers.
15. Teachers in this school value expertise more than authority.
16. When a crisis occurs, the principal effectively deals with it so we can get back to teaching.
17. My principal often jumps to conclusions.
18. People in this school respect power more than knowledge.
19. Teachers in this school often jump to conclusions.
20. In my school building, teachers hide mistakes.

© Hoy & Gage, 2003

APPENDIX D
SCHOOL MINDFULNESS SCALE (SHORT FORM)©

DIRECTIONS: The following are statements about your school. Please indicate the extent to which you agree with each statement along a scale from strongly disagree (1) to strongly agree (6). There are no correct or incorrect answers so please give us your candid and anonymous judgments.

1. Teachers negotiate differences among each other without destroying the diversity of opinions.
2. The principal welcomes challenges from the teachers.
3. In this school, teachers welcome feedback about ways to improve.
4. Too many teachers in my building give up when things go bad.
5. My principal negotiates differences among faculty without destroying the diversity of opinions.
6. My principal is an expert on teaching and learning.
7. Most teachers in this building are reluctant to change.

8. When things go badly, the teachers bounce back quickly.
9. Teachers in my building learn from their mistakes and change so they do not happen again.
10. Teachers do not trust the principal enough to admit their mistakes.
11. The principal of this school does not value the opinions of the teachers.
12. When a crisis occurs, the principal effectively deals with it so we can get back to teaching.
13. My principal often jumps to conclusions.
14. People in this school respect power more than knowledge.

© Hoy & Gage, 2003

CHAPTER 12

THE OUTSIDER-WITHIN

Toward a Socially Critical Theory of Leadership

Khaula Murtadha and Colleen L. Larson

This paper examines how African American women make sense of their roles as leaders within poor and marginalized school communities. Strong African American women have provided leadership for formal educational systems serving poverty populations since the dismantling of slavery. However, this alternative image of leadership has been largely overlooked within the profession. By examining and juxtaposing the historical and contemporary narratives of inspirational leaders, this study reveals that the theories and practices of the African American women portrayed in this paper do not neatly align with masculine or feminist images of school leadership. Four dominant themes emerged in the leadership of these women: critical institutionalism, rational resistance, an ethic of risk and urgency, and deep spirituality. These themes exemplify and illuminate the outsider-within standpoint of African-American women leaders who have historically had to fight against the educational systems in which they worked to better serve the children and families of their communities.

Educational Administration, Policy, and Reform: Research and Measurement
A Volume in: Research and Theory In Educational Administration, pages 337–370.
Copyright © 2004 by Information Age Publishing, Inc.
All rights of reproduction in any form reserved.
ISBN: 1-59311-000-0 (hardcover), 1-59311-000-0 (paperback)

INTRODUCTION

> Somewhere, on the edge of consciousness, there is what I call a mythic norm, which each one of us within our heart knows "that it is not me." In America, this norm is usually defined as white, thin, male, young, heterosexual, Christian, financially secure. It is with this mythical norm that the trappings of power reside within this society. . . . There is a pretense to a homogeneity of experience . . . that does not in fact exist. Audre Lorde

For over five hundred years, the dominant conceptual imagination in the United States has overlooked the material reality of racism and cultural annihilation in its theoretical formulations. Audre Lorde points out that American society is flooded with constructions and theories that are normed on and reflective of the perspectives and realities of white, middle class, men only. These formulations have been infused in society as well as in its institutions. Both organization and leadership theory are almost entirely derived from white male perspectives. The roots of administrative theory raise critical questions about the efficacy of organization and leadership theory for people who are not white, male, or middle class.

Although research on the leadership of women has increased over the past twenty years, the absence of critical inquiry into the epistemological and methodological significance of race in theories of leadership has limited the power of inquiry in the field. Many critical theorists have shown how hegemonic systems replicate and sustain patriarchal and class structures; however, dominant Euro centric lenses have led to research and reform initiatives in leadership theory and practice that neglect issues of race in schools entirely. Gloria Anzaldua (1987) argues that black men and women have been all but obliterated through dominant theoretical discourse:

> . . . because we are often disqualified and excluded from it, because what passes for theory these days is forbidden territory for us, it is vital that we occupy theorizing space, that we not allow white men and women solely to occupy it. By bringing in our own approaches and methodologies, we transform that theorizing space (p. xxv).

PURPOSES

This paper examines how African American women make sense of their roles as leaders within poor and marginalized school communities. Theoretical perspectives informed by women of color are sparse in the educational leadership literature (Capper, 1993; Marshall, 1993). Blount (1998) points out that very little is known about African American women leaders constructions of leadership. Further, we know too little about how leadership for minority and poverty populations might differ from leadership that is needed in middle class, mainstream schools.

In this paper, we examine the enduring themes of leadership depicted in African American women's experiences in leading school communities. Strong African American women have provided leadership for formal educational systems serving poverty populations since the dismantling of slavery. How did these women envision leadership for a marginalized population? What did they believe they needed to do to create greater educational equity and opportunity for children who were historically excluded from formal educational systems? And how do these early images of leadership for education in marginalized communities endure in the contemporary narratives of African American women today?

By examining and juxtaposing the historical and contemporary narratives of inspirational leaders, we find that the African American women portrayed in this study do not neatly align with masculine or feminist images of school leadership. Orthodox leadership theory and practice has historically been rooted in notions of maintaining institutional stability, enacting rational decision-making, and establishing organizational hierarchy. Feminist scholars have rooted their theories of leadership in images of care, connection, and nonhierarchical relations. However, feminist constructions of leadership, too, are largely rooted in Euro centric experience. Neither masculine nor feminist approaches to leadership capture the dominant, enduring, themes in the historical and contemporary narratives of African American women working in marginalized school communities. As outsiders within majority white systems and institutions, this study reveals that African American women have historically struggled and continue to struggle against the educational systems in which they work. Collectively, these narratives counter mainstream conceptions of leadership and articulate what we call a socially critical construction of leadership theory and practice.

The historical-contemporary biographies of the African American women portrayed in this paper reveal that many of the concerns fueling the leadership of women long ago, persist in the practices of African American women leading school communities today. Using the progressive-regressive methodology for analyzing historical and contemporary narrative (Siddle Walker, 1996), this study reveals four enduring themes in the leadership narratives of African American women: critical institutionalism, rational resistance, an ethic of risk and urgency, and deep spirituality. These themes exemplify and illuminate the outsider-within standpoint of African-American women leaders who must often fight against the very systems in which they work to better serve the children and families of their communities.

The findings of this study reveal that black women leaders have throughout history been committed to educating the black community as well as to fighting inequity and injustice in the racist and divided schools and communities in which they worked. To these women, both historical and contemporary, education and equity are not separate pursuits. The marginalization and oppression of the African-American community in the United States was a hard and deeply institutionalized reality that effective black women leaders fought against. This enduring purpose and focus of leadership remains in the contemporary narratives of black women leading schools today. Fighting against institutionalized norms of racial marginalization and inequity, then, is central to a socially critical, womanist construction of leadership.

CONCEPTUAL AND METHODOLOGICAL FRAMEWORK

A socially critical theory holds established societal and institutional norms and systems up for scrutiny. A womanist theory is grounded in the collective experiences and life world of African American women. According to Alice Walker (1983), a womanist is:

> 1. . . . a black feminist, or feminist of color. From the black folk expression of mothers to female children, "you acting womanish," i.e., like a woman. Usually referring to outrageous, audacious, courageous, or willful behavior. Wanting to know more and in greater depth than is considered "good" for one. ... 2. . . . Committed to survival and wholeness of entire people, male and female. 3. . . . Loves the spirit. . . . Loves struggle. 4. Womanist is to feminist as purple is to lavender (p. xi).

A socially critical, womanist, stance shares many of the same concerns of feminist research; however, it differs in that it is rooted in the historical, societal, and cultural, realities of the African-American community in the United States. These differences in cultural and economic positioning are crucial to understanding the unique perspectives of black women leading schools today.

Research on women in leadership has shown how gendered expectations as well as masculine myths about "the one right way to lead" have prevented women from being hired for administrative positions in schools. In the past twenty-five years, prevailing masculine assumptions about the nature of leadership have been challenged through feminist critique. This growing body of research illuminates the weaknesses inherent in the assumptions of masculine, Euro centric leadership, and reveals the power and effectiveness of leadership informed by feminine and feminist perspectives (Dunlap & Schmuck, 1995; Martin, 1986; Noddings, 1984). However, theorists' efforts to portray how women differ from men have produced a "universal" image of female leadership: Men lead this way, women lead that way. This distinct bifurcation of the sexes prevents researchers from seeing how and why women's images of leadership may differ based on their positions within society as well as within formal educational systems.

Beverly Gordan (1995) suggests that "African American women ... are outsiders who participate, but do not hold full membership in the black male community, the white male community, or the white feminist community." Patricia Hill-Collins (1998) argues that any changes in this marginal status requires us to reclaim the black feminist intellectual tradition by discovering, reinterpreting, and analyzing the literary and intellectual works and societal deeds of black women from a womanist standpoint. Because women of color are typically outsiders on administrative teams that are overwhelmingly white and/or male, they often work at the marginalized edges of large, bureaucratic, school systems. Further, they typically lead schools that are under supported and economically depleted, and they are expected to establish and carry out educational agendas that often clash with what they and their communities see as vital to the education of black children.

Methodological Framework

Similar to feminist theory, the womanist perspective makes lived experience central to inquiry, and uses dialogue as a means of accessing knowledge and making meaning of lived experience. Womanist theory departs from feminist theory in that it is underpinned by an enduring ethic of care for and recognition of the African-American community within a dominant white society. Feminist research as well as more orthodox literature in leadership theory lacks a womanist concern for and understanding of issues unique to the black community.

Our concern for capturing the enduring themes of strong African American women working on behalf of their school communities suggests a need to examine historical as well as contemporary narratives of leaders. Nested in the historical-contemporary methodology of Vanessa Siddle-Walker (1996), this study examines the enduring images of leadership found in the narratives of African American women. This inquiry into the lives of women leaders began with a comprehensive review of narrative literature on African American women leaders in education. Through this literature, we examined the primary themes emerging in the stories of leadership across these narratives and then selected three women from this body of literature whose biographies exemplified these themes and were robust enough to reveal the images of leadership guiding the practices of early black leaders in education. We then turned to the contemporary narratives of four practicing administrators. The contemporary women selected for this study were identified by Midwestern superintendents as outstanding urban school leaders in their districts. A historical/contemporary progressive-regressive comparison of these narratives reveal that the concerns of early African American women remain deeply nested in the beliefs and practices of African American women leading schools today. The contemporary Black women leaders depicted in this study, like their foremothers, are struggling to enact leadership practices that makes America a better place for African American children and families. Like their foremothers, their leadership is nested in a strong commitment to social justice. In fact, this study reveals that a focus on and concern for leadership for social justice has endured in the narratives of black women for almost 150 years. In the next section, we examine the narratives of three foremothers of African American education in the United States.

AFRICAN AMERICAN LEADERSHIP: FOUNDING MOTHERS OF EDUCATION

Anna Julia Cooper, Mary McLeod Bethune, and Nannie Helen Burroughs are but a few of the African American women who have established schools and distinguished themselves as political activists as well. Their resistance to interlocking systems of race, gender, and class oppression was strengthened with a spirit of conviction, and a conviction of spirit. They possessed a powerful ethic of risk and they were driven by a strong sense of urgency. Each woman was propelled by a desire to push the community forward and to pull their children into a new and more beautiful world of freedom, hope, education, and opportunity.

Black women through individual efforts, community galvanization, church alliances, sisterhood, and fraternal associations, have sought the 'means' to live in rather than abandon hope within US society. Throughout history, education has been an integral component of that hope. To many African American women, education was a path to equity and greater power in an inherently inequitable racial order. To the African American community, education provided entry into voter registration and political decision-making; it was a means to greater freedom and opportunity for African American people.

Black educational leaders have historically set a national agenda of uplifting their race from a legacy of white supremacy, slavery and segregation. According to Hill-Collins (1998), such determined activism on the part of women is rooted in a very personal and visceral response to seeing their fathers and sons lynched, their children lost to guns and drugs, and their brothers thrown in jail. The historical narratives examined below remind us that the difficult realities that many African American communities face today are remnants of a long, sordid, and racist history of oppression in U.S. society. Through these narratives, we surface the logic of leadership these women used to educate a newly freed African American community.

Anna Julia Cooper: Finding One's Life Purpose

Anna Julia Cooper was born before slavery ended. She grew up in a time when newly freed African American people believed that their road to opportunity would be found in education. According to some sources, Cooper began her teaching career, when she was just ten years old, a bright, eager tutor for older, uneducated community members. She continued teaching until she was well into her eighties.

Cooper believed that a person's work must be sustained by the knowledge of one's sense of purpose in life. This knowledge came through a deeply spiritual connection to something beyond oneself. Cooper's belief in the power of spirit came from her own understanding of the sustenance and guidance she had attained through her own spiritual journey. She believed that one needed to occasionally stand aside from the engrossing pursuit of human interests in order to listen to the passion of an inner voice. This voice provided insight into one's path.

To Cooper, education was critical to the advancement of the African American community. She believed that a good education for black children required training the mind and empowering the spirit. She condemned those schools that ignored the spirit:

> What is the [educational] need today? Is it not the power to think, the power to will, the power to appreciate true relation, which have been enumerated as the universal aim of education? The old education made him a "hand," solely and simply. It deliberately sought to suppress or ignore the soul. We must, whatever else we do, insist on those studies which by the consensus of educators are calculated to train our people to think, which will give them the power of appreciation and make them righteous. (Lemert & Bhan, 1998, p. 251)

To Cooper, schools that focused solely on educating the "hand" or teaching technical skills were miseducating black youth. She objected to only "manual" training because it failed to teach children how to think. Therefore, she insisted on strengthening the curriculum for African American students in classical subjects. In doing so, she dramatically increased the number of students who were accepted to prestigious colleges. To her, a real education instilled the "power to think, the power to appreciate, and the power to will the right and make it prevail. . ." (p. 251). However, Cooper knew that "willing the right action" and "making it prevail" could not be attained by individual endeavor alone; rather, it required a coalescing and empowering life force that sustained the black community as a whole as it struggled to make its way against a racist and oppressive society. Therefore, to Cooper, schools that were neglecting the child's inner being, their connection to this vital and sustaining communal force, were stripping children of the powers that could nourish them.

> Religion must be a life made true. . . One needs occasionally to stand aside from the hum and rush of human interests and passions to hear the voices of God. And it not infrequently happens that the all-loving gives a great push to certain souls to thrust them out, as it were, from the distracting current for awhile to promote their discipline and growth, or to enrich them by communion and reflection (p. 64).

Amidst the rush and distracting currents of a racist and sexist nation, Cooper exerted her voice as a feminist and, in her own words, as a race woman, an activist against racism. She was a self-assured woman, prolific in her writing, reserved, yet, socially open to the community members who needed her.

A contemporary of Mary Church Terrell, Ida B. Wells-Barnett, Booker T. Washington and W. E. B. Du Bois, Cooper along with other early activists believed that their efforts in education were inextricably linked to the struggle for social justice. These early activists believed that equity and justice were essential for reform and progress, and that this "moral standing was a steady rock upon which the race could lean" (Giddings, 1984, p. 81). All black institutions were focused on this coalescing goal.

As the turn of the 20th century neared, Cooper courageously documented the sentiments of black people fighting for social justice in, *A Voice from the South by a Black Woman of the South.* She asserted that black people had been forsaken by the Federal government. This put the black community in the uncomfortable position of having to fight against continuing oppression and discrimination in the society in which they lived. They were being subjected to intensifying violence, and they were suffering from too little political power. Cooper was an outspoken leader of social programs and causes for the poor in the District of Columbia, and she was a regular contributor of critical letters and columns to newspapers.

A substantial part of her time was also spent as a popular public speaker. In 1886, as a recent graduate of Oberlin College she spoke to a meeting of the exclusively male, clergy of the Protestant Episcopal Church. This talk was titled, "Womanhood: A Vital Element in the Regeneration and Progress of a Race." This highly controversial speech proclaimed her disgust for institutions and individuals who did little to improve the lot of the black population:

> Only the black women can say when and where I enter, in the quiet, undisputed dignity of my womanhood, without violence and without suing or spe-

cial patronage, then and there the whole Negro race enters with me (Giddings, 1984, p. 63).

Cooper believed in speaking her truth to people holding positions of power in established institutions.

Like other women of her time, Cooper's unrelenting work on behalf of her community coincided with rearing seven children. When she was young, she took in two foster children, and later in life adopted five orphans. True to her nature, Cooper was always ready to bring others into her home. There were few distinctions between her home life and her work life, work and home were woven into a seamless web of purpose.

In her seventies, Cooper took over the presidency of Frelinghuysen University, a school providing educational opportunities to the working poor in Washington, D.C. When facility costs threatened the financial stability of the struggling school, Cooper opened the doors of her home to the school.

> I may say honestly and truthfully that my one aim is and has always been . . . to hold a torch for the children of a group too long exploited and too frequently disparaged in its struggling for the light. I have not made capital of my race, have paid my own way and have never asked a concession or claimed a gratuity. Nor on the other hand have I ever denied identification in every handicap and every limitation that the checkered history of our native land imposes. In the simple words of the Master, spoken for another nameless one, my humble career may be summed up to date-She hath done what she could (Giddings, 1984 p. 340).

To be a black leader, according to Cooper, was to act with responsibility and obligation, to do what ever was necessary to resist racism and patriarchy and to protect and provide a haven for children who are too often ill protected in a racist society. Anna Julia Cooper's quiet, self-assured, moral courage was a role model for and teacher of future educators and activists—including the women discussed below, Mary McLeod Bethune and Nannie Burroughs.

Mary McLeod Bethune: Advancing the Dreams of Her People

When asked about her work, Mary McLeod Bethune explained that it was her "sacred duty to interpret the dreams and the hopes and the problems of my long-suffering people" (Giddings, 1984, p. 227). In 1904, with little more than a dollar and fifty cents, she opened the Daytona Educational and Industrial School for Negro Girls on an old dumping ground after her first five pupils, girls aged 8 to 12, helped her clear away the debris. From the inception of the institution, Bethune was dedicated to: "training of the heart as well as the head and hand" (Daniel, 1970, p. 96).

Born in South Carolina in 1875, Mary McLeod, was one of seventeen children of Samuel and Patsy McLeod, former slaves. For primary schooling she walked five miles to school and later was chosen to receive a scholarship to attend Scotia Seminary in Concord, N.C. A second scholarship supported her attendance at Moody Bible Institute in Chicago where she was the only African American student. While in Chicago she began planning to do missionary work in Africa. However, those plans did not work out and she went on to several teaching positions in Augusta, Georgia, Sumter, South Carolina, where she met and married her husband, and then on to a mission school in Palatka, Florida.

In 1904, a strong desire to develop her own school drove her to Daytona, Florida. From the beginning, her school was tightly linked to the community she served. Bethune worked to not only meet the needs of her young students, but to embrace those of a suffering and largely uneducated community struggling against a closed and racist society as well. Therefore, like Cooper, Bethune believed that a proper education required more than educating the mind or training the hand; it had to develop inner strength. In 1930, she expressed this view in her annual report to the board of trustees:

> The administration and faculty have had due regard for the prime purpose of educational programs—the development of character and personality do not fall second even to intellectual attainment. The endeavor has been to foster an atmosphere that will develop the finest and best in the mind and soul of every young man and woman (Daniel, 1970, p. 96).

To support the soul's development as well as to provide leadership and resources for a needy community, Bethune believed in getting the children actively engaged in their communities. In the school, she worked to create a culture of community engagement tied to religious commitment:

> The students, aside from the high atmosphere that has been made possible on the campus, have applied their Christian training by active participation in the religious life of the community, by making visits to the sick and needy, and by the periodic distribution of alms to the poor. (Daniel, 1970, p. 98)

Because racial segregation remained firmly in place throughout Bethune's time, she recognized and responded to the unique challenges of providing effective leadership for a struggling African American community. The needs of an oppressed population that had to cope with the lingering social, psychological, and economic effects of slavery were great. Therefore, Bethune knew that she had to define education and its purposes broadly. For example, community services like health and education were woven together in Bethune's school. Because there was no provision for health care for the African American community along a two hundred-mile stretch of the Atlantic coast, the school designated a room with a bed for medical services. "That small provision filled a real need of the Negroes of the East Coast and grew into a full-fledged institution, the Mcleod Hospital and Training School for Nurses" (Daniel, 1970, p. 101). Various civic and racial organizations established their headquarters on school grounds. The school auditorium served as a rallying point for community meetings. The school library was the only one opened to blacks in the county. The school also served as a demonstration and conference site that offered forums on "health, thrift, home-ownership, property improvement, local beautification, home craft, and the profitable management, of gardens, poultry flocks, and dairy herds" (p. 102). An "Evening Opportunity School" offered adult education. Thus, Bethune based the educational agenda of the community by the needs of the people within it.

In the 1930s, Bethune was invited by President Hoover to the General Session of the White House Conference and Child Health Protection, and was later asked by Roosevelt to serve on the National Youth Administration as the director of the Negro Division. This was considered an obscure position until Bethune charted the:

> tasks that faced the NYA and started mobilizing all available resources to accomplish those objectives . . . Within months of her appointment, both the press and the Braintrusters [people appointed to administrative government positions during the Roosevelt administration] had come around to recognize her as a formidable presence (Giddings, 1984, p. 221).

Many of Bethune's speeches drew attention to the efforts and struggles of every day women and linked them with the spirit of religion. At a Chicago Women's Federation meeting in 1933, she spoke of the invaluable historic contributions made to the development of religion in US society. She pointed out,

> In no field of modern social relationship has the hand of service and the influence of the Negro woman been felt more distinctively than in the Negro orthodox church. . .It may be safely said that the chief sustaining force in support of the pulpit and the various phases of missionary enterprise has been the feminine element of the membership.. .Throughout its growth, the untiring effort, the unflagging enthusiasm, the sacrificial contribution of time, effort and cash of the black woman has been the most significant factors, without which the modern Negro church would have no history worth the writing (Williams, 1993, p. 252).

The preeminence of African American women in the unofficial leadership and followership roles of the church taught Bethune that institutional position and the authority of hierarchy was no match for the power of a spirited sisterhood. Propelled by the force of spiritual connection, these resilient women discovered all they could achieve when they banned together. One of those challenges was fighting the hierarchical authority of a decidedly male religious institution. The black church was a truly black institution. Nevertheless, Bethune and other women of her time often found that women were barred from the established decision making processes of the church. Therefore, just as they had to fight segregation and exclusion from white institutions, black women also had to fight the sexism of the only institution that existed to serve them.

By banning together, Bethune and other women of her community found the sustenance and camaraderie of spirit that empowered women to cope with the formidable challenges they faced as a community. The transformational spirit nurtured in the church enabled these women to confront the inequities of established institutions, and to risk personal and collective acts of liberation.

Bethune was unequivocal in her advocacy for women as exemplified in her struggle to develop the National Council for Negro Women (NCNW). She was, according to Giddings (1984), adamant about the unheralded achievements of women, always believing "in women's possibilities", always encouraging them to "go to the front and take our rightful place; fight our battles and claim our victories. . . Next to God we are indebted to women, first for life itself and then for making it worth living" (p. 228).

Nannie Helen Burroughs: Following A Spiritual Mandate

Educator, civil rights advocate, and religious leader, Nannie Helen Burroughs, was only twenty-one years old when she became a national leader. Her sudden rise to notoriety was an outgrowth of a presentation she made at the annual conference of the National Baptist Convention in Richmond, VA, "How the Sisters are Hindered from Helping." According to Hine (1993) Burroughs' outspoken eloquence powerfully expressed the "righteous discontent" of women in the Baptist church who were once enslaved by white men and were now suppressed by their own black brothers in the established church of the black community. Burroughs' speech served as a catalyst for the formation of the Women's Convention Auxiliary, the largest women's organization in America. Burroughs proclaimed:

> We're a race ready for crusade, for we've recognized that we're a race on this continent that can work out its own salvation. A race must build for nobility of character, for a conquest not on things, but on spirit. (Lerner, 1972, p. 553)

Burroughs was born in Orange, Virginia in 1879. She moved with her mother to Washington, D.C. in 1883, and was educated through the high school level at the Colored High School. This is where Burroughs met Anna Julia Cooper, one of her inspirational teachers. Upon graduation, Burroughs was employed in Louisville, Kentucky where she organized a women's industrial club and conducted domestic science and secretarial courses for young black women. And although she was frequently sought after to speak at various kinds of religious gatherings, Burroughs, thought little of talk without action.

> What's the sense of talk if you don't do something? You talk, and people get stirred up and think they'd like to do something, and that makes them feel good; and they go off happy and satisfied, feeling as though they're some account in the world because they've felt like doing something and they haven't done one thing to help one soul come alive (Daniel, 1970, p. 114).

To Burroughs, effective leaders were doers. They recognized their obligation to improve the life chances of those around them, and from the beginning, that is what Burroughs set out to do.

Burroughs' childhood dream of establishing an industrial school for girls came true when she mobilized the energies of the Woman's Convention to build her school. On Oct. 19, 1909, the National Training School for Women and Girls opened at the corner of fiftieth and Grant in the far northeast area of Washington, D.C. At the close of Burroughs' first year as President, the school had enrolled thirty-one students. Twenty-five years later the school educated more than two thousand young women at the high school and junior college level. These girls came from all over the United States, Africa, and the Caribbean.

Like Cooper and Bethune, Burroughs emphasized the importance of spiritual character as well as technical skills. To her, racial advancement in American society required training in "the 3 B's the Bible, bath, and broom." Underpinning these values was Burroughs' belief that the African American people needed to take responsibility for themselves and for others within the community. Children needed to learn to keep their homes and their bodies clean, to not bring shame to themselves or their families, and to dress with dignity.

Burroughs' staunch advocacy for African American working women was expressed through her participation in the National Association of Colored Women during the early decades of the twentieth century. She also founded the National Association of Wage-Earners. As president, Burroughs worked along side other well known clubwomen like Mary McLeod Bethune who was the vice president of the association. These women used educational forums to draw public attention to the plight of female domestic and factory workers who were paid far less than their work was worth, faced gender-based wage discrimination and often labored under the worst conditions.

As a member of the Association for the Study of Negro Life and History, Burroughs presented a paper at the association's 12th annual meeting held in Pittsburgh in 1927. Burroughs' (1949) paper, titled, "The Social Value of Negro History (Jan. 1, 1928) contained a forceful message emphasizing "the duty the Negro owes to himself to learn his own story and the duty the white man owes to himself to learn of the spiritual strivings of a despised but not an inferior people." Burroughs, along with other club women worked zealously through writings and public lectures to counter sanctioned racism, segregation, and inequity. Driven by a strong spiritual force, Burroughs felt that her work for racial equality was a mandate from heaven.

Burroughs flatly denounced institutionalized segregation and pushed her people toward racial self-help and self-reliance. She had little faith that the African American population would be given equity. In a 1934 *Afro-American* news article, Nannie Burroughs is quoted as saying: hound dogs are kicked but not bulldogs." With lines like these, this woman inspired men and women to get tough and to use "ballots and dollars" to fight racism instead of "wasting time begging the white race for mercy." To Nannie Burroughs, the established system needed to be challenged. After a "human revolt" by frustrated black men and women in Harlem, Burroughs' message revealed her sense of impatience and urgency. She said:

> The colored man has reached the endurance limit—the point where the Declaration of Independence says, it is time to revolt when the "invasion on the rights of the people seem most likely to effect their safety and happiness and obstruct the administration of justice." Yes, a long train of abuses caused the Harlem uprising. . . Day after day, year after year, decade after decade, black people have been robbed of their inalienable rights (Daniel, 1970, p. 133).

Burroughs' appeal rested in her commitment to overcoming what appeared to many people of her time as wholly unattainable. However, she believed that anything was possible through the collective power and spirit of people. She knew that instilling a resiliency of spirit and a belief that the impossible is always possible was critical to the survival of the African population in the United States and it remained critical to creating indomitable individuals and to empowering communities within a racist and sexist society. Burroughs nurtured this spirit through the founding assumptions she advanced within the school:

> We make our girls believe in themselves and in the power to do anything that anybody else can do, be it ever so difficult. On one of the walls in the chapel is written- 'We specialize in the wholly impossible.' This is the spirit of the National Training School, and everyday in every way we teach that lesson. It gets into our minds, our souls, our blood, our hands, and our feet. The very building up of the institution itself is symbolic of that spirit. (Daniel, 1970, p. 134).

THE LINGERING SPIRIT OF SOCIALLY CRITICAL, WOMANIST LEADERSHIP: CONTEMPORARY NARRATIVES

The leadership of Cooper, Bethune, and Burroughs was fueled by a deep concern for African American children and their families. This concern prompted them to challenge institutional norms, energized them to resist inequity, and increased their sense of risk and urgency to improve the life world and life chances of the black community. How do these concerns inform the image/s of leadership held by African American women today? In this section, we turn our attention to the lives of four contemporary administrators in schools. In these narratives, we find the enduring commitments of their black foremothers. Collectively, these narratives provide a useful lens for understanding the legacy of leadership remaining in the thinking and actions of African American women working in urban schools today.

Marilyn Smith: Creating Resiliency Through Spiritual Strength

Marilyn Smith has been the superintendent of an urban Midwestern school corporation for more than six years. Now, 50-something, Smith was the oldest of three girls, raised and educated in the elementary and secondary schools of the South. In her family, the importance of education was instilled early in life. After graduating from college, Smith taught in schools in Mississippi and Louisiana. Eventually she moved, obtained an advanced degree, and continued teaching in such varied places as Las Vegas, Nevada, New Mexico, and Texas. While in Texas, she attained a doctorate.

When Smith and her husband moved to the mid-west, she struggled against the institutional entrenchment of white patriarchy and ultimately became a school superintendent. Reflecting on her career, she named the challenges she faced as a highly educated black woman in a white, male dominated institution:

> I've been in the field for a long time. And I've basically worked with white males. Because in 1974 and 75—we weren't there. We weren't there even as assistant principals. It has been a predominantly male field, a predominantly white, male, field. It was a struggle to even get an assistant principal ship. [And to add to her frustration] ... the superintendent didn't even have a doctorate degree.

Even with an advanced degree, Smith faced the systemic racism and sexism of an institutionalized system dominated by white men. To Smith, the administrators in the district saw her as a threat. Despite her obvious competence, they refused to consider her for any administrative position. After months of applying and lobbying for a position, she was finally awarded an appointment as an assistant principal. But even then, she recalls that she was not given the same respect or responsibilities as other assistant principals in the system. The superintendent avoided giving her the authority and responsibilities that typically fell within the jurisdiction of an assistant principal. She remembers being routinely overlooked by the men above her in the system: "The principal was sick once, and the superintendent named the head counselor [in charge]." The superintendent's disregard and disrespect made Smith astutely aware of how powerfully "the system" was keeping her "in her place." Nevertheless, her resilience and indomitable spirit prevailed:

> It's kind of my philosophy. Don't let anyone cut your spirit. Once that spirit is cut it's doomed.

Smith asserts that a deep and abiding spirituality helped her to resist institutional practices that she believed were inequitable. To Smith, a deep abiding spiritual strength was critical to her own sustenance and survival as a school leader. She saw spiritual strength as being equally important for adults and children. She asserted that teachers could reach students through the force of spirit. She kept teachers ever mindful of the black child's vulnerability. To her, teachers had to safeguard the spirit of the children they educated. Through her own practice, she taught teachers to care for the emotional as well as the educational needs of children, or to do what Thompson (1998) calls, "othermothering." To Smith, othermothering was a critical component of effective leading and teaching:

> I would rather see a kid under a poor teacher who hasn't cut the spirit [of a child] and has the desire to do well, than with a competent teacher who is in need of no assistance in teaching math and reading and is a graduate of Harvard or Yale. Because you can easily cut that spirit.

When asked to describe what she meant by the spirit of a child, she responded:

> I'm talking about desires, dreams, hopes, wants and the courage to explore and learn—and the self-concept, to me that includes the spirit of a person. It's very powerful.

After serving as an assistant principal, Smith aspired to the principalship. Knowing that once again she would face obstacles within the system, she reasoned that the white, male superintendent and the school board of her district could not deny her a position if she had additional coursework. Over the years, she had observed that every administrator who had taken an educational sabbatical came back to a better position. So she took a full year off as assistant principal in order to pursue an internship that would better prepare her for her role as a school principal.

However, in Smith's case, neither her advanced experience in administration, nor the doctoral degree was enough to convince the Superintendent that she was ready for a principal ship. In fact, when Smith returned from her sabbatical, the school district refused to give her an administrative position. Fueled by the power of her own spirit and the courage to resist institutional inequity, she charged the district with discrimination.

Knowing that the system was on shaky legal ground because of Smith's proven competence and advanced education, the superintendent did an about face and offered Smith the principal ship she had earned. Nevertheless, the school system still controlled her school assignment. Predictably, she was placed in the toughest high school in the district. When she heard of her appointment, she recalled saying to herself: "Spirit, here we go!"

Smith spent two successful years at that school and was then reassigned to another failing school. This time, she was given an elementary school that had not come into desegregation compliance. It, too, was considered one of the worst schools in the district.

> The test scores were poor, and it was a school that was not attracting whites. 650 children living in the heart of the city attended the school. ... I got in there and the teachers knew I was assigned there to fail. I guess they felt sorry for me. [She laughs] They said, "Let's help this poor lady." Most of the staff was still white, despite the fact that 42 percent of the student population was African American.

Hill and Ragland (1995) have pointed out that African American women are often assigned difficult schools as "messiah's, scapegoats, and sacrificial lambs" (p. 20). Many of these women succeed at improving the academic standings of their schools, demonstrating not only competence at increasing test scores, but in advancing programs that respond to the needs of a resource and education poor community.

> We instituted a lot of programs: the first computer program for parents, an after school science program for kids. We won the Redbook award, and we were named a National Exemplary school. We got $100,000 [in awards]. We just did beautifully!

Smith beamed proudly as she talked about the many successes of the school and its broader community. But like her foremothers, she refused to take sole credit for the marked improvement in the school. To her, the school turned around because of the energized and collective spirit of the community:

> The school was wonderful because I was working with wonderful teachers and wonderful parents. We were all in it together and that's the way schools were supposed to be.

At staff meetings, Smith increasingly asked for help in decision making. She intentionally built the esteem and confidence of teachers, and consistently worked to instill the faith that the school was a good place. She believed, and she helped others to believe, that the teachers, parents, and children had the collective power to improve the school.

> It took me ten years to have people convinced that it was a safe environment. Ten years to convince parents that they could send their kids there. Ten years to convince a staff and community that they were second to none. Working with that spirit.

To Smith, success in the school was not attained by any specific curriculum innovation, strong hierarchical control, or more intense focus on standards, but by consistently and diligently working through and with the heart and spirit of the school community. Like Bethune, Smith believed that individually, black administrators, like black children, were easily destroyed by systems that that have long promoted racial hierarchy and white superiority. But collectively, the African American community could do anything.

As a curriculum supervisor, Smith ran the office without any budget. Even as she climbed the institutional ladder, she continued to build alliances and rely upon community strength to improve education for children. Doing the work of the community was central to her practice:

> My husband and I have always been givers back to the community. But if you understand the South—if someone was burned out you went there to help them out. If someone died we would take [the family] food. I'm from a culture of giving back in the community. If someone had a wedding and didn't have a wedding dress you said, 'Okay what can we contribute?'

Smith, like her foremothers in education, felt an obligation to others and a responsibility to work for the betterment of her people. She chose a path that departed from institutionalized traditions of institutional hierarchy and systems of control and in so doing used the power and the strength of a newly awakened community to inspire educational achievement.

Smith attributed her relentless energy and indomitable strength to the same deep cultural, communal, and spiritual forces that sustained her foremothers. These forces inured Smith to the often overwhelming opposition she faced within white educational institutions. The power of her conviction helped to inspire the strength, capacity, and commitment of teachers as well as of the greater community. Through a community rather than an institutional lens, Smith became a catalyst for improving the education and resiliency of children in her community.

Barbara Jones: Leading with Risk and Urgency

Over a period of more than twenty-five years, Jones worked with five different superintendents. Once a teacher, and a high school principal, she currently serves as an assistant superintendent of curriculum and instruction, Jones, a middle aged woman, learned a great deal about administration in urban schools. She was recognized throughout the corporation as a true leader.

Despite her subordinate position to the superintendent of the district, she was determined to use her own strength and talent as well as that of her colleagues to improve education for black children in the school district; however, she knew that the established structure often prevented that from happening. She stated:

> I haven't seen it work well when you've got a person on top of something—doing all the directing, all the everything. You get a bunch of robots who simply comply and I've come to learn in my old age that people have so much to give no matter who they are or what level of education, everybody is blessed with something to contribute and, if you can figure out how to maximize that and get it out of everybody you're going to get a better whatever it is you're trying to get.

Jones had little faith in institutional hierarchy. She rejected more conventional norms of delineating roles and responsibilities and, like others in this study, she insisted that significant improvement in education would come from the spirit and energy of people, all people. Hill and Ragland (1995) argue that emergent constructions of effective leadership reject top down and closed images of organizations. To Jones, leaders who maintained the "lone ranger, all knowing, iron-fisted approach to leadership within isolated kingdoms of bureaucratic, managerial, control" consistently did real damage to black communities (p. 46). Such approaches to leadership have historically kept black parents and their children at the marginalized edges of our schools (Larson & Ovando, 2001).

Jones believed that as a leader, she had to establish alliances, collaborations, and coalitions with the broader community. To her, these community initiatives were critical strategies for getting people meaningfully engaged in and committed to the education of children. Jones knew that if she worked with and through others, she could accomplish more. Through open school community engagement, she tapped into and fueled greater strength and confidence in the broader community. To Jones, it was not enough that she was confident and strong:

> Rarely do I do anything in isolation. Some would say it's lazy; some might say I don't know and don't have enough information; and maybe that's true; but I rarely do anything in isolation. So when I have a team of people we are truly a team, regardless of any title or who is subordinate to whom.

Jones's insistence on ignoring the hierarchy and doing what was needed to get the job done aligns with what Hurty (1995) found in a study of seventeen women principals. Hurty argued that these women were emotionally "committed to the education of the children in their care, competent in curriculum and instruction, energetic...and creative in their abilities to work with people toward needed change. She notes that "they agonized... they had dreams of what could be, while working with what is" (pp. 384–385). To Jones, collaboration and teamwork were not ploys for making people feel important, nor were they efforts to improve a deficient community, rather, for Jones, collaboration was crucial to keeping people focused on and soul connected to the purposes and importance of their collective project.

> I'll sit down with the instructional services team and become one of them as we work together because I've learned that when you're trying to create stuff—especially like curriculum, programs for children, difficult programs . . . .you have to have some commonality, some common ground. That's why I'm such a firm believer in having guiding principles about how you work. I'm a firm believer in being on the same page in terms of what our intent is. I believe in working with the people and getting the benefit of their ideas— and that works for me. I believe in working through the dignity and principles of people.

Jones's central concern for principle centered leadership mirrors that of respondents in studies conducted by Lunenburg and Ornstein (1991). These researchers found that initiation structures and consideration were critical to effective collaboration. *Initiation* processes included creative problem solving, developing a vision, and generating ideas. These processes generated needed dialogue and critique of underlying principles. *Consideration*, or what Jones sees as "working through the dignity of people" includes involving, motivating, and supporting others, as well as modeling integrity and being approachable. Jones sees her tendency to get people involved in soul centered projects as her greatest asset as a leader.

> I'm sort of at the center of the pack, rather than at the head of it. You ask the right questions, you're sincere, you're genuine. You focus on the other person instead of on yourself.

By breaking from institutionalized norms of hierarchy, and working toward establishing trust, and soliciting principle centered connections, Jones keeps educators focused on important issues for African American children in her community.

As previous narratives have shown, womanist leaders are fueled by a passion and determination to see all children learn, despite racism and poverty. But unlike many administrators, Jones sees racism and poverty, and she sees it kill the spirit of too many children and their families. Motivated by a fire in her belly, Jones acts from a very real and present sense of urgency. Because large numbers of black children find too little success in schools designed for 'other people's children,' many lose all interest in learning, and worse, they often lose faith in their ability to do so. Jones notes that the spirit of children is always damaged in classrooms where they do not succeed. Therefore, she was impatient with processes and hierarchical procedures that lethargically limp along as children sit in classrooms that harm their spirit and diminish their confidence in and their desire to learn, while still others are tragically lost to gangs and drugs.

> I've tried things the old way, trying to think every thing through-plan, plan, plan. You never get anything done. I'm more apt to say "Let's do it." Urgency, we're losing kids every year that goes past. I'd rather have something in hand. My urgency is fueled by what I know our kids don't know.

An important function of the leadership role, according to Jones, is to establish alliances, collaboratives, and coalitions that create survival strategies for black children in schools that often work against them. This explains why Jones wanted the new and badly needed curriculum to be developed in a thoughtful, but expedient way. Her sense of urgency made her anxious to get help to children who were being alienated from and harmed by the established Euro centric curriculum.

Because of Jones's strong spirit, sense of urgency, attentiveness to student support services and her strong belief in home visits, her staff affectionately called her "Mother Jones." Her conviction and sense of purpose penetrated all that she did. For example, in her task of redesigning curriculum, Jones had the opportunity to hire a new team of colleagues, and she was unequivocal in stating that she needed people who had strong and sacred spiritual centers.

> My professional life has been turned over to God. That is what I'm grounded in. I'm guided by some power other than self. I've come to look for people who are grounded in something spiritual and there is a difference in simply church -going and truly believing in something that guides your life purpose. Everyone [of the new appointees] brings a strength of character and they're grounded in a spiritual base, a divine guidance. If you are not guided by some power other than yourself, then you and I will probably not work well as a team.

Public schools are often not comfortable with "god-talk." Nor, are many researchers. But to Jones, as with many other women in this study, her purpose and focus were spiritual, not religious. People did not have to attend a particular church or ascribe to a specific religion; they only needed to be fueled by a force and a purpose greater than oneself.

To Jones, people on her team had to be driven by a deep vision of equity and a strong sense of professional purpose and commitment. But Jones's notion of vision was not the "vision thing" typically promoted in conventional planning in schools. Her talk of vision was tied to an understanding one's spiritual center. As the team planned curriculum change, she said:

> I know where we are headed. Our vision guides everything. If you have something in life that's guiding you, things will fall in place. This vision keeps me from being daunted by nay sayers, and I mean that seriously. It's part of my greatest strength.

In working with a community wide team, Jones mixed humor with seriousness. She urged the group to make decisions. However, when time was moving and the group was indecisive, Jones was not. She did not hesitate to remind the group of the importance of expeditiously doing the work necessary to better serve children and families. As an educational leader, she felt responsible for doing all that she could to improve the life chances of children, she felt compelled to do that through the energy and commitment of her community, and she consistently fought against bureaucratic systems that generated lethargy, rather than a sense of urgency.

Carole Collins: Reconnecting Schools to Communities of Color

A forty-five year old native of Little Rock Arkansas, Carole Collins attended school during the time that "the desegregation plan closed the one and only all-black high school in Little Rock." She praised the education she had received there:

> I had what I think was probably the best education possible in a predominantly African American setting. And I think it was for several reasons: I attended schools where teachers and administrators, everyone, understood and recognized the value of education as the vehicle to move out of your present plight or to improve the quality of life. That permeated elementary, middle and high school.

As Ladson-Billings (1998) points out, teachers who are attentive to and embrace the cultural and social differences of African American children have greater success in improving their academic achievement than those who ignore their backgrounds. For example, the black teachers at Collins' high school recognized the racist beliefs their students would eventually encounter in the colleges and universities they would enter. Collins explained how her teachers prepared her to survive in higher education:

> The teachers spent and inordinate amount of time that year preparing us for the change and saying to us: 'You have to be better than. You have to be. You can't go over to those schools embarrassing us. You need to go over there and you need to meet the challenge of those other students.' We spent a year like no other. We had to represent our high school—because it was not going to be a high school anymore. More than any other time, I think, that gave me a sense of what it meant to be an African American in a majority white population.

Collins attributes her success in college to the attentiveness of teachers who acted out of a sense of urgency and ensure that they would have both the academic and emotional support they would need to succeed in college. Collins graduated from college as a speech pathologist, worked in that field for three years and then furthered her education with a Master's degree in speech therapy and then worked in a large public school system. From there she became an elementary principal. When asked about her lack of classroom teaching experience and her atypical move into a principal's position she acknowledged that it was a controversial appointment.

> There are people who believe if you have not been a classroom teacher then you don't know what that's all about. I had the fortunate opportunity to work in the building of a woman principal who saw something in me that I didn't know I had—that led to me to enroll in a leadership course that the district offered. We were really challenged to demonstrate our leadership skills in that course. She encouraged me to do that, and as a result I was exposed to the deputy superintendent, the superintendent, and many of the central office staff who were looking for leaders. Shortly, thereafter, there was a job opening in the district—the only job open in the district—out of fifty some odd schools.

Collins obtained that position. When she was given her first assignment as a principal in a large, Midwestern, city school system, her initial concern was that the majority of the families in the school were white. She was not convinced that this school was ready for an African American principal.

> I won the respect of the teachers and the parents and the community, and it was an integrated school but it was in a predominantly white community. It was a good school, one of the higher achieving schools in the district. I had a good year and the test scores improved and everything was great, but it wasn't that challenging for me.

Collins was missing something central to her life's purpose by working in this relatively privileged school. She did not feel challenged and she was uneasy knowing that her skills were needed more elsewhere. Like other women in this study, Collins felt a special obligation to communities of color and the schools within them. This deeper spiritual conviction explains why she volunteered to transfer to one of the lowest achieving schools in her district. When she requested the transfer, she was called into central office. She was a popular principal and the community liked her. The superintendent was incredulous, "Why the change?"

> They could not fathom in their wildest dreams that someone would want to leave this high achieving school and go to a school that nobody wanted to work in, so they wanted to look me in my face and understand why I wanted to do it. So I told them. I said, "First of all it's my old elementary school. Some of my fondest memories have to do with having gone to that school. It was the best. I remember that we won all of the awards. We had the most beautiful school in the whole school district. Academically we were at the top. We won all the spell-bowls. Everything! I cannot imagine why a school with that kind of history is now the lowest achieving school in the district.

Collins was committed to enhancing education for children of color, children like herself.

> Because I'm from that neighborhood and because I know some of the same people live there, I have to figure out why. And I don't think that those people are that different from when I went to school there, and I know they are not that significantly different from me. So I want to go, I have an obligation to my community.

Carol was determined to find out why the school had performed so poorly and seemingly had so little support. She did not focus on the deficits of this community, but its lost potential. As an advocate for the school, she asked the superintendent difficult questions about equity, money and staff support, and she told him flat out that she would remove any teacher who was not committed to or capable of educating children of color.

> I said, "Let me tell you what I need. I need the ability to be able say to anybody that's working there: "If you don't want to be here, I will support your transfer. I will help you find a place to be. Secondly, I want an assistant principal, an assistant principal that I pick, who will help me to establish a clear focus for the instructional program. And I need for you to commit to me that I can come to you and request of you directly, the superintendent and the assistant superintendent, those things that I feel I must have. I'm not going to ask for any extravagant kinds of things, but the kind of things that I think that we need in that school, the things that will afford me the opportunity to do the same thing I did [at the previous school]. I want the same kind of money, the same resources, the whole nine yards. So they committed to doing that and they gave me the flexibility in the beginning. I was there for 2

years as a principal in an all black environment, a neighborhood school, and within 2 years the test scores began to improve.

In some schools, educators see the cultures and communities of people of color and people from low socioeconomic backgrounds as obstacles to be overcome or worked around. This belief often leads to the greater exclusion of minority populations from their schools. When administrators and teachers see communities in this manner, they rarely see how the school, its systems, its structures, and its processes actively support and perpetuate exclusion, discrimination, and inequality. However, Carol made the children and the community central to her concerns and focus as an educational leader. Because Collins knew this community and the people in it, she saw potential, whereas many before saw problems. The community hadn't changed; but the leadership of the school had.

Jane King: Challenging Institutionalized Biases and Prejudices

Jane King, an elementary school principal and former central office administrator is currently the leader of a school that serves primarily African American and white children who are poor. Three fourths of these students are bused because of court ordered desegregation. When asked why she was assigned to this particular building she explained:

> I don't really know why I was assigned here. The reason the superintendent gave was that when we return to unitary status [a reversal of the busing agreement that integrated African American students into white schools] we will have to have black administrators in those schools who are in predominantly African American neighborhoods.

However, soon after King assumed leadership within the school, she was disturbed by an established school culture that visibly lacked support for students and parents in the school community. She remembered walking into the building in those early days:

> I can walk into a building and tell if there is a good culture—there is strong spiritual force and folks understand that they are all working for the same thing. I didn't feel that when I walked in here. There was nothing that caused me to believe that there was that kind of unique connecting bond or culture to bring these people together. As they started bonding and connecting with me, and when they saw that I was open, and when I made it clear that there was going to be equity in the way people were being treated, and that I was going to try to provide and support particular needs that people had, people began to open up. So, now, all the kids are served equally.

King regularly communicated her image of the culture she wished to create through formal and informal meetings. Early after her arrival she met with her new staff and explained who she was and what she believed. She said:

> I believe that everyone can learn and that anything that can be learned can be taught. I believe that all people have inherent worth and value. That's one value I can't give up. I believe that students come to us with certain gifts and talents and that we have a responsibility to nurture and help develop those talents. To me, excellence is not a place. It is something that continually spirals but you never get there. I believe that people learn, but not from their experience alone. They learn by thinking about their experiences. In terms of achieving, people achieve when they have a clear vision as to where they are heading.

With more than thirty years of teaching and administrative experience, King names, without hesitation, the problems she sees as racism and bigotry in closed, institutionalized, systems of education. She consistently cautions the majority white teachers on her staff to resist the belief that they are saving the children of the inner city. She believes that this too easily ingrained image of black inferiority underpins the devastating effects of the low expectations that many teachers hold for African American children.

> They feel as if they are rescuing them. They are rescuing them from their pitiful selves. They were saying 'poor pitiful you.' They wouldn't dare stretch them and expect them to do anything well. They wouldn't dare expect them to come in and move quietly through the halls. They think that these kinds of kids can't do that. They wouldn't dare expect them to come to "back to school night" with their parents because these kinds of kids don't do that. Rescuing is a form of disrespect. Save me. We can't assume that we are the only people who will take care of these children.

King was vigilant in working with staff to move beyond deficit thinking about children. In breaking from patterns of leadership that depict the principal as the one who maintains stability, King recalls encouraging needed instability within the school. To her, the school and some of its problematic practices needed to be destabilized. She needed parents to stand up against deeply institutionalized norms that ill-served their children. So she taught parents how to support their children and how to navigate and challenge imposing bureaucratic systems and policies, especially those they did not understand. And when parents felt beaten down by teachers who failed to see the potential of their children, she instilled faith: "Your child is not a "D" child."

She encouraged parents to stand with their children and to support them within schools that systematically relegated them to the lowest rungs of the educational ladder. She recalls telling parents:

When school starts, introduce yourself to the teachers. Share with the teacher your child's maturity level, your child's abilities, strengths, and needs.

King was determined to let parents, teachers and students know that she cared about these children, and that she would do all that she could to further their education:

These are wonderful children. The staff sees me hugging them. I started hugging them on the first day. So now they come to get their hug black and white—it doesn't make any difference. I don't know if kids think I'm preaching or what, but I talk to them just like they're mine. I have to let kids know how important they are. I'll do whatever it takes to get them educated, provide additional resources; we do their laundry if we have to. Children have social and physical needs. I have children come and share their school work with me. I ask them, do you need me to help you? You can create a climate that impacts attendance and achievement if you care.

Just as King was determined to generate greater community-wide support for and a commitment to the children, she was also determined to increase their academic performance. But like others in this study, King rejected the institutional belief that her positional authority alone was enough to get people committed to critical reflection on persistent problem of bias, exclusion, white superiority, and racial hierarchy. To her, these issues underpinned many of the problems children encountered in schools. Therefore, she talked with her teachers all the time. She valued inquiry. She questioned their techniques, she challenged their methods, and she built teaching teams to talk about the operating assumptions of instruction.

I'm on my soapbox. I ask questions. How are the children reading? You have to monitor frequently and keep the routines open to dialogue and critique.

Attentive to professional development, King invited the school district's director of the office of multicultural education to assist the staff in designing lessons more appropriate for the children they served. She helped teachers to engage in critical conversations about their practice, and supported them in getting the professional development they needed to go beyond superficial understandings of race and multicultural issues.

King believed that the process of learning and knowing, even for teachers, required on-going dialogue. Therefore, she established a climate where discussions of student performance were not reduced to standards, labels, or test scores. Developing children for life in a real world, King's leadership was infused with an ideological analysis of pressing problems and a political project that was committed to eradicating oppressive practices of systemic racism in teaching and learning processes.

The experiences that African American women have with the intersecting systems of race, gender, and class oppression contribute to their ability to understand and negotiate issues of difference in diverse school communities. King was well aware of the unequal power relations between disparate racial, cultural, and ethnic groups and she recognized the impossibility of cultural neutrality among teachers, administrators, staff, parents, and students. This understanding separates King from the vast majority of administrators who typically claim to be color-blind in their treatment of children and of the communities they serve (Larson & Ovando, 2001). By focusing on glaring racial disparities in academic performance, King became a catalyst for purging the school of racist beliefs and assumptions. In so doing, she helped teachers, and parents to see the often overlooked potential of African American children.

TOWARD A SOCIALLY CRITICAL, WOMANIST THEORY OF LEADERSHIP: MAKING SOCIAL JUSTICE CENTRAL TO PRACTICE

In examining the narratives of these contemporary leaders of school communities as well as those of the foremothers of African American education, we begin to see several unifying themes that are notably missing from the leadership narratives of most white male and female administrators; these differences in perspective stem from life experiences unique to the African American community.

As much as large segments of white society would prefer to forget the history of its relationship to African American people, we see in this study that the constructions of leadership espoused by the African American women depicted in this paper were/are significantly shaped by this history. Black men, women, and children were brought to the US on slave ships. They endured the near annihilation of their culture and the violence of slavery, rape, and the decimation of their families. In the New World— against their will, they struggled to survive. Men and women who could not muster the will to live were physically and emotionally beaten down—spiritually broken. Millions died. Those who survived often clung to a rope of spiritual hope. Many of these men and women owed their lives to a deep spiritual force that sustained their energy, and steeled their will against the violence of racism and slavery. Abiding spirituality helped many African American people to stay with the struggle, to hang on, and to believe that the world could be a better place; if not for them, then for their children.

By reading the historical narratives of Anna Julia Cooper, Mary McLeod Bethune, and Nannie Helen Burroughs, we see this rich heritage of inner spiritual strength. Contemporary black women today continue to live in a society that is stratified by race, class, and language. Further, like their foremothers, these women regularly encounter conscious and unconscious racism in the schools in which they work. Unlike many of their white colleagues, the socially critical, womanist, leaders depicted in this study are not lulled into believing that the institutionalized norms in schools are fair or color-blind, and they refuse to participate in discourses or practices that pretend otherwise. As outsiders/within, these women stand apart from and often in opposition to established school system in ways that most white male and female administrators do not.

The synergy between the historical and contemporary narratives revealed in this paper help us to see that black women today have, not surprisingly, inherited many of the concerns of their foremothers. These women continue to fight institutions mired in conscious and unconscious, yet, broad-based discriminatory practices. They, too, stand in opposition to the very systems they are hired to lead. Because of deeply sedimented systems of segregation and tracking in schools and classrooms, these women entered schools that were immersed in an institutional logic that has historically sorted, labeled, and destroyed the spirit and confidence of too many African American children.

To the women in this study, resistance to the established racial order in schools was the only rational response. Each of these women took up the battle of their foremothers against a racist society. They were driven by a need to protect children who were not only being harmed by the exclusionary practices of their schools, but were dying in the street and losing their lives to gangs and drugs. This disturbing reality fueled a sense of urgency, an urgency that made the norms and traditions of large, lethargic, and ostensibly neutral systems of bureaucratic decision-making seem all the more irrational.

A socially critical, womanist leader, then, is one who is rationally resistant to systems and processes that ill serve people of color. To work against taken for granted systems and practices in schools, and to address deeply held biases and prejudices, administrators must have a good deal of personal courage, and a strong sense of moral conviction. The spirited sisters in this study all shared one important trait; they each possessed a good deal of self-knowledge and strong sense of purpose. They unapologetically connected the meaning of their work to their life purpose. For these women, spiritual grounding was critical to sustaining their resiliency and to succeeding as leaders of a black community living within an inherently inequitable society (Murtadha, 1999).

For many good reasons, the women in this study did not see education as being separate from spiritual connection. Rooted in the same spiritual forces that sustained their foremothers, these women effectively weaved education and spirituality into the fabric of their practice. Because schools, like most institutions in the United States, were never designed with the lives of marginalized populations in mind, the women in this study knew that many of the institutionalized norms of public schools would fail to address the needs of a struggling black community.

For example, the black church is the only truly African American institution established in the United States. This institution has historically provided a relatively small African American population with its strongest vehicle for building community within a dominant white society. To the women in this study, blurring of boundaries between the school and the church was natural and necessary; not for the purpose of indoctrinating children into any particular religion, but for tapping into the well spring of spiritual energy and resolve that the black church had always provided. To these women, finding ways of nurturing the spirit was necessary for sustaining a strong African American community and for developing the inner strength and moral conviction of black children and their families.

The words of these women offer inspiring portraits of leaders who saw beyond the economic limitations of the communities they served. They reached out to and built trust with the children and with communities that have historically had few reasons for trusting their schools. They knew that the silence of minority parents did not signal a disinterest in education or in their children. They understood that parental distrust of and resistance to schools is a rational response to a long and frustrating history of inequity, racism, and discrimination. Therefore, to these leaders, nurturing the trust and spirit of the community was just as important as nurturing the trust and spirit of children in schools.

Too often, teachers and administrators speak of the conditions of many minority children's lives as being intolerable and insurmountable. However, what was intolerable to these women had little to do with the school communities they served. These women were not shocked or deterred by the realities of their communities. In fact, they were more shocked and dismayed by what they found within the closed and unreceptive walls of bureaucratic schools. These schools were located in minority communities, but were not of them.

Unlike many administrators, these women soon learned that they could not really go "up" the hierarchy of the white institution to get the kind of support and help they needed to turn their schools around. Nor, could they bring about needed change by simply working through majority white faculties. Through an African American ethic of community, these women learned that combating institutionalized racism in a majority white society required the power and strength of a collective African American community. Therefore, these women knew that the help they needed did not reside "above them" in the institution, but rather in the enormous strength and potential of people within the broader community, a community they saw as the solution to many educational problems, not the cause of them.

The practices of these educational leaders were inspired by deep cultural and communal forces. Therefore, it is not surprising that their narratives consistently broke from the narrow role images of administrators working within an administrative hierarchy. They rarely spoke as building administrators filling bureaucratic roles. Rather, they saw themselves as mothers, political activists, mediators, ministers, neighbors, and counselors to a community and its children. To these women, the community was an integral part of the school. Unlike many administrators, they did not see the school as a self-contained institution that needed to be protected from a troubled community; rather, they saw the school as nothing less than a lighthouse to the community it served.

The critical-institutional stance of these women springs from their unqualified connection to and love for the children they served. This sense of oneness was visible in the relationships they extended to children and parents. Dillard (1995) reminds us that for African American women, nurturing and protecting children of the African American community hails from a long tradition of communal responsibility for African children. This tradition extends far beyond family and blood. These ties are communal, and they produce a community of 'othermothers.'

For these women, the normative practices of managing, teaching, and learning were all grounded in an African ethic of 'othermothering' (Thompson, 1998). Hence, they did not see the children in their schools as 'other people's children,' but as their own. This communal, African, ethic was not simply an adaptation to conditions in which birth mothers were not available, which was often the case when women were separated from their children during slavery; rather, it was a tradition of care rooted in African conceptions of community. This tradition of taking in children as if they were one's own enriches communal bonds as well as the lives of children, particularly in a broader society where African American children are often marginalized and despised. In schools serving black children, other mothering was an important means of strengthening African American ties, binding adult relationships, and providing care for children who were easily neglected in and rejected by 'objective' and 'color blind' systems of education.

The powerful and inspiring women depicted in this study knew what they had to do if they were to be effective leaders who made a difference in the lives and life opportunities of children. This resolve of purpose often pitted them against the established norms and accepted structures of schools. However, the stories of these women suggest a courage of conviction that was not intimidated by established institutional logics or prevailing systems of control. Collins asserts:

> One of the reasons that I have been able to do [this] is that I don't have any fear of failure, because there is really no failure. You may not be able to achieve as much as you had hoped to achieve, but generally you do make some inroads. I've already made them in the short time that I've been here. And it's my responsibility to keep making those inroads, and fueling a passion for equity is one of the most important components of that process.

She concludes:

One of the things that I have going for me personally is that you can see my sincerity. I'm here because I care about kids. You can put me in a hole, in the dark, in a corner, and just give me the critical things that I need to make a difference with kids—and I'm fine. There are so many people I'm told, that get into positions of authority and it changes their behavior. I am humbled by the responsibility of this job. And I cannot let this community down. I can't. I have to do everything I can to ensure that what they thought was going to happen with new leadership, is going to happen.

CONCLUDING REMARKS

A socially critical, womanist image of leadership diverges from conventional masculine and feminist images of leadership in several ways. First and foremost, it makes survival strategies for a marginalized and underserved African American community central to practice. The stories of these spirited African American women help us to see that leadership for a marginalized community requires educators who are capable of seeing and resisting rather than sustaining and enforcing deeply institutionalized systems of inequity.

In advancing a socially critical, womanist theory of leadership, we are not proposing, yet, one more, universalist theory of leadership—this time for African American women. The socially critical womanist theory of leadership is neither static not monolithic. There can be no unitary representation of African American women because they exist in diverse, sometimes contradictory, and often within multiple tensions of lived experience. We recognize that not all African American women wish to or are capable of enacting leadership in this way. We also believe that there are women and men of all races who are capable of being socially critical, leaders. To us, the stance these women have taken is not something that one enacts by virtue of being born an African American woman; but rather, it suggests a powerful and intentional way of challenging inequity by being in, struggling with, and understanding the purposes of ones' life as a leader in the world that one inherits.

The inspiring stories of these women, however, clearly demonstrate that the historical, sociological, political, and economic status of African American women in this country provide a distinguishing set of experiences that generates a distinctive way of seeing leadership for people of color and people of poverty. This separation from established leadership theory illuminates an image of leadership that is appropriately and atypically contextualized within the lived realities of African American communities in the United States.

The historical resiliency of the four themes, critical-institutionalism, rational resistance, an ethic of risk and urgency, and deep spirituality helps us to see the many limitations of "universal" theories of leadership grounded in the experiences and life positions of a privileged white, society. This alternative image of leadership also raises concerns about researchers' and practitioners' widespread speechlessness on issues of race, racial stance, and racial inequity in theories of leadership and administration. Through feigned 'color-blindness' and an enduring belief in a mythical norm that does not, in fact, exist—researchers and many school leaders continue to promote theories and solutions to educational problems that obfuscate and obliterate the lived realities and material world of people of color in this society.

This discussion provides a point of departure from universalist, white, male or female, middle class, constructions of leadership. The stories told in this paper surface the many ways in which universalist theories of leadership ignore the history as well as the systemic marginalization of diverse populations in institutions. In so doing, they push the very real concerns of these communities from consideration. Consequently, the universalist's claim to possess a neutral set of difference-blind theories and principles that are shared by all groups is not only misguided, but has been consistently harmful to diverse populations. As the stories in this study reveal, the universal stance operating in schools as well as in our theoretical formulations is not neutral, as its proponents claim, but rather reflects the concerns and privileges of a dominant culture and is complicit with a deeply institutionalized, albeit often unrecognized, racial order.

In portraying the enduring themes of leadership found in the historical and contemporary narratives of African American women, we hope to provoke a wider discussion on how race, gender and class changes what leaders must do if they are to provide effective leadership for the communities they serve. The findings of this study raise critical questions about the enduring pretensions of 'racelessness' in the theory and practice of leadership. They also illuminate the need for leaders in urban schools who are capable of critical-institutionalism, rational resistance, an ethic of risk and urgency, and deep spirituality. The socially, critical, womanist theory of leadership emanating from the findings of this study suggests a need for a vastly different approach to leading historically marginalized and underserved school communities.

REFERENCES

Anzaldua, G. (1987). *Borderlands/La Frontera*. San Francisco: Spinsters/Aunt Lute.

Blount, J. (1998). *Destined to rule the schools: Women and the superintendency, 1873–1995*. Albany: State University of New York Press.

Burroughs, N. (1949). *Words of light and life found here and there*. Washington D.C.: Nannie Burroughs Publications.

Capper, C. (1993). *Educational administration in a pluralistic society.* Albany: State University of New York Press.

Daniel, S. (1970). *Women builders.* Washington, DC: Associated Publishers.

Dillard, C. (1995). Leading with her life: An African American feminist (re)interpretation of leadership for an urban high school principal. *Educational Administration Quarterly, 31*(4), 539–563.

Dunlap, D., & Schmuck, P. (1995). *Women leading in education.* Albany: State University of New York Press.

Giddings, P. (1984). *When and where I enter.* NY: Morrow.

Gordon, B. (1995). The fringe dwellers: African-American women in the post modern era. In B. Kanpole & P. McClaren (Eds.), *Critical multiculturalism* (pp. 59–88). Westport, CT: Bergin and Garvey.

Hill-Collins, P. (1998). *Fighting words: Black women and the search for justice.* Minneapolis: University of Minnesota Press.

Hill, M., & Ragland, J. (1995). *Women as educational leaders.* Thousand Oaks, CA: Corwin Press.

Hine, D. (1993). *Black women in America.* Brooklyn, NY: Carlson.

Hurty, K. (1995). Women principals—Leading with power. In D. Dunlap, & Schmuck, P. (Eds.), *Women leading in education.* Albany, NY: SUNY

Ladson Billings, G. (1998). *The Dreamkeepers.* San Francisco: Jossey-Bass.

Larson, C. L., & Ovando, C. J. (2001). *The color of bureaucracy.* Belmont, CA: Wadsworth.

Lemert, C., & Bhan, E. (1998). *The voice of Anna Julia Cooper.* Lanham, MD: Rowman & Littlefield.

Lerner, G. (1972). *Black women in white America: A documentary history.* NY: Random House.

Lunenburgh, F. C., & Ornstein, A. (1991). *Educational administration.* Belmont, CA: Wadsworth.

Marshall, C. (1993). The politics of denial: Gender and race issues in administration. In C. Marshall (Ed.), *The new politics of race and gender* (pp. 168–174). London: Falmer.

Martin, J. R. (1986). *Reclaiming a conversation.* New Haven: Yale University Press.

Murtadha, K. (1999). Spirited sisters: Spirituality and the activism of African American women in educational leadership. In L. Fenwick (Ed.), *School leadership: Expanding horizons of the mind and spirit* (pp. 155–167). Proceedings of the National Council for Professors of Educational Administration. Lancaster, PA: Technomic.

Noddings, N. (1984). *Caring.* Berkeley: University of California Press.

Siddle Walker, V. (1996). *Their highest potential.* Chapel Hill: University of North Carolina Press.

Thompson, A. (1998). Not the color purple: Black feminist lessons for educational caring. *Harvard Educational Review, 68*(4), 522–554.

Walker, A. (1983). *In search of our mother's gardens.* San Diego: Harcourt Brace.

Williams, D. (1993). *Sisters in the wilderness.* Maryknoll, NY: Orbis.

ABOUT THE AUTHORS

Curt M. Adams is a research associate with Oklahoma State University, where he recently completed his doctorate in school administration, writing on *The Effects of School Structure and Trust on Collective Teacher Efficacy.* For the past three years, he has been project manager for "The Trust Project," an effort to examine the functions and consequences of interpersonal trust in the public schools of Oklahoma. His work on external trust measures (Parent Trust of School, Parent Trust of Principal, and Student Trust of Principal), has been the subject of recent AERA presentations.

Jane G. Coggshall is a doctoral candidate in the Program in Educational Administration and Policy at the University of Michigan. Her research interests include organizational theory, educational policymaking, and issues of social justice and urban education. Before entering graduate school, she worked as a middle school math teacher in New York City.

Patrick B. Forsyth is a professor of education at Oklahoma State University where he conducts research on school trust, academic performance and affective and structural dimensions of schools. His books include *Educational Administration: A Decade of Reform*, with Joe Murphy; *City Schools: Leading the Way*, with Marilyn Tallerico; and *Effective Supervision: Theory Into*

Educational Administration, Policy, and Reform: Research and Measurement
A Volume in: Research and Theory In Educational Administration, pages 371–374.
Copyright © 2004 by Information Age Publishing, Inc.
All rights of reproduction in any form reserved.
ISBN: 1-59311-000-0 (hardcover), 1-59311-000-0 (paperback)

Practice, with Wayne K. Hoy. Currently Division A Vice President of AERA, Forsyth has been Executive Director of UCEA and Corporate Secretary of The National Policy Board for Educational Administration.

Charles Quincey Gage, III is an assistant principal of Barrington Elementary school in Upper Arlington, Ohio. His main fields of interests are leadership,, motivation, and innovative school structures.

Ellen Goldring, Ph.D. is a professor of Education Policy and Leadership in the Department of Leadership, Policy and Organizations, Peabody College, Vanderbilt University. Her research focuses on school reform that connects families, communities, and schools. She also studies the changing roles of school leaders and their professional development. She is co-editor of *Educational Evaluation and Policy Analysis.*

Richard Halverson is an assistant professor in the Department of Educational Leadership and Policy Analysis at the University of Wisconsin-Madison. His interests include instructional leadership practice in schools, supportive software and instructional strategies to promote reflective inquiry about complex, discretionary practices among school leaders, classical accounts of the relation of theory to practice to current academic and professional conversations, and historical accounts of the how computing technologies will change American education.

Meredith I. Honig is an assistant professor of education policy and leadership at the University of Maryland, College Park. Her research and teaching focus includes policy design and implementation, organizational theory, urban social policy, public sector innovation, and school-community partnerships. Her related publications include "School-community connections: Strengthening opportunity to learn and opportunity to teach (with J. Kahne and M.W. McLaughlin) in the *Handbook of Research on Teaching* (American Educational Research Association, 2001) now in its fourth edition.

Wayne K. Hoy is the Novice Fawcett Chair in Educational Administration at The Ohio State University. His research interests include school properties that enhance teaching and student learning, especially organizational structure, culture, motivation, and leadership.

Sang-Jin Kang is a professor in the Department of Education, Yonsei University, Seoul, Korea. His research interests include methodological issues in multilevel modeling, school evaluation, and investigation of organizational effects. He also studies admission policy and evaluation of teaching in university settings.

Carolyn Kelley is an associate professor, Department of Educational Leadership and Policy Analysis at the University of Wisconsin-Madison. Her research and scholarly interests include educational politics and policy, organizational theory and behavior, teacher compensation, organizational leadership, and research methods.

Steven Kimball is an assistant researcher with the CPRE Teacher Compensation Project at the University of Wisconsin-Madison. He is currently conducting research on the impact of standards-based teacher evaluation and compensation systems.

Colleen L. Larson is an associate professor at New York University. Her work examines the politics of equity in institutionalized systems and policies. Recent publications include: *Leadership for social justice* (w/K. Murtadha) and *The color of bureaucracy (w/Carlos Ovando)*.

Helen M. Marks is associate professor in the School of Educational Policy and Leadership at The Ohio State University. Research interests focus on school organization and improvement, students' experience of school, education policy, and the social and political contexts of education. Her most recent publications include "Community Service in the Transition," co-authored with Susan Robb Jones, in the *Journal of Higher Education;* "Principal Leadership and School Performance: An Integration of Transformational and Instructional Leadership," co-authored with Susan M. Printy, in *Educational Administration Quarterly;* and "School Composition and Peer Effects in Distinctive Organizational Settings" in the *International Journal of Educational Research.*

Khaula Murtadha is an associate professor of Educational Leadership and Policy Studies at the Indiana University School of Education in Indianapolis. Her research interest is effective leadership in urban schools and she is currently writing about African American women in city school reform efforts. She has served as a consultant on multicultural curriculum policy, development, and implementation initiatives.

Susan M. Printy is an assistant professor in the Department of Educational Administration at Michigan State University. Her research and teaching interests relate to organizational theory, organizational learning, relationships among school members, and the use of data to promote school improvement. Her current work seeks to understand how principals use data to increase organizational capacity and internal accountability. She recently co-authored "Principal Leadership and School Performance: An Integration of Transformational and Instructional Leadership," in *Educational Administration Quarterly* with Helen M. Marks.

Stephen W. Raudenbush is a Professor, School of Education and by courtesy Professor, Department of Statistics and Professor, Department of Sociology; and Professor, Survey Research Center, at The University of Michigan. His research interests involve the development, testing, refinement, and application of methods for individual change and the effects of social settings such as schools, and neighborhoods on change.

Brian Rowan is a professor of education at the University of Michigan and a principal researcher in the Consortium for Policy Research in Education. His scholarly interests focus on the organizational analysis of schooling, paying special attention to the ways in which schools organize and manage instruction and affect student learning.

Thomas V. Shepley is a graduate of the University of Michigan's Ph.D. program in education administration and policy. He is currently working as an administrator in the Baltimore City Public School System, Maryland.

John W. Sipple is an assistant professor in the Department of Education at Cornell University. His research interests include organizational behavior, administration, and policy.

Alan R. Shoho is an associate professor of Educational Leadership and Policy Studies at The University of Texas at San Antonio. His research focuses on organizational cultures and how they affect the sense of alienation, trust, and ethical behavior of their stakeholders.

Page A. Smith is an assistant professor of Educational Leadership and Policy Studies at The University of Texas at San Antonio. His research agenda centers around concepts involving organizational trust, bullying, and school climate.

C. John Tarter is a professor of Educational Administration at St. John's University in New York. He teaches course in organizational theory, politics of education, and educational leadership. His research interests are organizational climate, decision making, and school leadership.

Nancy Vye, Ph.D., is Director of Education at American Healthways, Inc. Dr. Vye, formerly Senior Research Associate and Co-Director of Vanderbilt University's Learning Technology Center, is a learning scientist whose interests relate to problem-based learning and uses of technology for enhancing learning and teaching.

Printed in the United States
35319LVS00007B/16